SPEECH

Exploring Communication

Prentice-Hall, Inc., Englewood Cliffs, New Jersey

SPEECH
Exploring Communication

J. Regis O'Connor

Professor of Speech Communication
Department of Communication and Theatre
Western Kentucky University
Bowling Green, Kentucky

J. Regis O'Connor (Ph.D., Indiana University) is Professor of Speech Communication and former Chairman of the Department of Communication and Theatre at Western Kentucky University. Once a high-school teacher himself, Dr. O'Connor now supervises student teachers of speech, drama, and broadcasting. He has written numerous professional publications and holds memberships in the Speech Communication Association and in the Southern Speech Communication Association. Dr. O'Connor is listed in *Who's Who in Education,* in the *Directory of American Scholars,* and in the *Dictionary of International Biography.*

Staff Credits
Senior Editor: **Patricia B. Weiler**
Art Director: **L. Christopher Valente**
Design Coordination: **Shay J. Mayer**
Preparation Services Manager: **Martha E. Ballentine**
Buyer: **Roger Powers**

Outside Credits
Contributing Editor: **Lucy G. Mack**
Design Production: **George McLean**
Photo Research: **Rose Corbett Gordon**
Cover Design: **John Martucci/L. Christopher Valente**

Acknowledgments
Acknowledgments appear on pages 578–580.

The publisher would like to thank the following people for their contributions to this edition:

Linda Donnell
English Language Institute
Spring Branch Independent School District
Houston, Texas

Rita C. Harlien
Burges High School
El Paso, Texas

Jacquelyn Jarrett
Coronado High School
Lubbock, Texas

Barbara Smith
Miami High School
Miami, Oklahoma

The Publisher would also like to thank the following people for their contributions to previous editions of this book: Morgia Belcher (Washington), Mary Anne Ellis (Maryland), Carol W. Foster (Colorado), Joseph P. Haley (New Hampshire), Carol Haugeland (Arizona), Albert J. Higgins (Kansas), Jill Peterson Hoddick (Oregon), Frank Latimer, Jr. (Texas), Sister Maria Martin, IHM (Pennsylvania), Robert K. Mott (Illinois), Phyllis C. Nardy (Florida), Gregory Parker (Kansas), Charles Ringle (New Jersey), Sally W. Smisson (North Carolina), Eloise W. Smith (Indiana), Jared R. Towler (Connecticut), Kathryn Wagers (California), Larry James Winn (Kentucky), and Marc Zicari (New York).

SPEECH: Exploring Communication
Third Edition

ISBN: 0-13-827296-4
10 9 8 7 6 5

PRENTICE-HALL INTERNATIONAL, INC., London
PRENTICE-HALL OF AUSTRALIA, PTY. LTD., Sydney
PRENTICE-HALL CANADA INC., Toronto
PRENTICE-HALL OF INDIA PRIVATE LTD., New Delhi
PRENTICE-HALL OF JAPAN, INC., Tokyo
PRENTICE-HALL OF SOUTHEAST ASIA PTE. LTD., Singapore
EDITORA PRENTICE-HALL DO BRASIL LTDA., Rio de Janeiro

Supplementary Materials
A *Teacher's Resource Book (TRB)* is available for use with this text. The *TRB* includes the following:
Chapter-by-chapter teacher's guides
Chapter and unit tests
Audio-cassette tape of speeches and activities

Contents

unit **2** Interpersonal and
Group Communication   **81**

4   One-to-One Communication ——————— **82**

5   Group Discussion ———————————————— **110**

unit 3   Preparing for Public Speaking   147

Appendix of Speeches   540

Elements of Communication

unit 1

1 How Communication Affects Your Life

When you have completed this chapter you should be able to:

- Define the terms *communication* and *speech communication*.
- Identify some specific benefits of improving your speech communication.
- State the skills that make an effective speech communicator.
- Understand the importance of speech communication in your life.

Whether chatting with friends or addressing an assembled audience, you are sending and receiving messages—you are communicating.

Imagine yourself in a world without communication. You would be able to see and smell and taste and feel. But you would not be able to get your ideas across to others. You would also be unable to take in ideas that other people wished to express to you. In a very real sense, you would be isolated in a silence even more profound than that felt by a person who was deaf or mute.

Communication is a complex process, but one that is full of rewards. This chapter will begin with a few basic definitions and then move quickly to explore the rewards—the ways in which you can improve your own speech communication.

WHAT IS COMMUNICATION?

Communication is the process of sending and receiving messages to achieve understanding. You have undoubtedly heard the expression "Say what you mean and mean what you say." Saying what you mean is precisely what communication is all about. Anytime you speak a sentence, make a gesture, or merely grunt, you are "saying" you have some idea in your mind that you wish to transfer to another person. Words, body movements, facial expressions, and voice tones are all symbols you select in your attempts to transmit the meaning in your mind to the mind of your receiver.

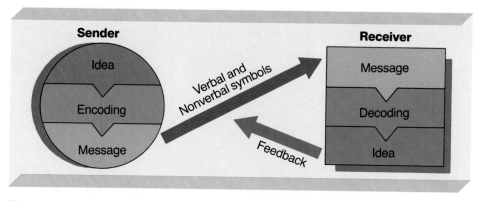

The communication process involves a sender transmitting a message to a receiver.

How Do People Communicate?

Human beings use various means of communication. You can show that you agree with someone just by nodding your head. You can walk in such a way as to indicate something about your personality or the way you feel. You can also communicate something about yourself to almost everyone you meet by what you wear. These are all examples of **nonverbal** communication.

Human beings, however, communicate best through speaking and writing. These are **verbal** forms of communication. By using words to stand for, or to symbolize, the ideas they have in their minds, people can transfer the meaning of those ideas to other people. That is what communication between people is all about—getting the meaning of thoughts one person has in his or her mind into the mind of another as clearly and accurately as possible. When people do this by transmitting words with their voices, it is called **speech communication.**

How Is Speech Communication
Used in Everyday Life?

You have probably heard and used the word *communication* many times, but have you ever thought about the many different ways people communicate through speech every day? Take time now to follow a typical high-school student through one day's activities.

6:45 a.m.   Awakes to a radio-alarm clock; listens to news, weather report, two commercials, and two musical recordings while getting ready for school.

7:15 a.m.	Eats breakfast; makes plans for baby-sitting that evening with younger sister while parents attend League of Women Voters' meeting to hear speeches by mayoral candidates.
7:30 a.m.	Leaves for school; meets new classmate on corner and describes school to him.
7:50 a.m.	Arrives at school; introduces friends to new classmate before directing him to his homeroom.
8:00 a.m.	School starts; listens to announcements over the public-address system; attends class where English teacher explains homonyms; watches a movie about the presidency of Theodore Roosevelt; takes a Spanish grammar test.
12:00 noon	Eats lunch in cafeteria with friends.
12:30 p.m.	Attends gym class and listens to instruction on the rules of volleyball; has conference with guidance counselor about next year's schedule; receives advice from art teacher on how to improve posters being made by class to advertise school play; conducts an experiment that demonstrates osmosis in science class.
3:00 p.m.	Attends school newspaper staff meeting to plan layout of next edition.
4:30 p.m.	Walks home with friend; stops to buy record heard on radio that morning.
5:30 p.m.	Arrives home; calls classmate to plan oral report on the causes of lead poisoning; calls family doctor to make appointment to interview her on number of cases of lead poisoning she has treated over the years.
6:00 p.m.	Walks dog, eats dinner, takes out trash.
7:30 p.m.	Listens to parents give instructions on when sister should be put to bed and where they can be reached in an emergency.
8:00 p.m.	Reads sister a story about astronauts before putting her to bed.
8:30 p.m.	Does homework.
9:30 p.m.	Watches television before getting ready for bed.

Communication played a large part in this student's day. Your life is also filled with communication situations. Actually, communication is so constant and widespread, you cannot escape its influence. Whenever you are awake and in the presence of others, you are communicating. Even though you may not be speaking to others, your appearance, eyes, and movements all represent communication.

Application

Daily Communication

Throughout this course, you will be keeping a speech notebook in which you will record ideas, thoughts, and feelings about how you communicate. Here is your first activity to begin your notebook.
Write down your own schedule for a typical day following the example above. Identify all your activities that involve communication. Estimate the number of hours per day that you spend using some form of communication.

WHAT TYPES OF SPEECH COMMUNICATION ARE THERE?

The events in the life of the typical student given in the last section are all examples of **interpersonal communication.** You also communicate when alone, through a kind of inward talking to yourself called **intra-personal communication.** This book is specifically about interpersonal communication—talk that takes place between two or more human beings. You will find that many different types of interpersonal communication exist.

One-To-One Communication

One-to-one communication involves talking with one other person. Included here are face-to-face conversations, telephone conversations, and interviews. Usually the sender and receiver switch roles often during one-to-one communication. The student whose day was described in the previous section was engaging in this type of communication when telling a new classmate about the school and when conferring with the guidance counselor. If you study the list of events, you will undoubtedly find many other examples of one-to-one communication in the student's day. Chapter 4 explores this very important type of communication in more detail.

Group Discussion

Group discussion is a second type of interpersonal communication. It involves three or more people with a common purpose. The purpose may be to solve a common problem, to make a decision, or to answer a

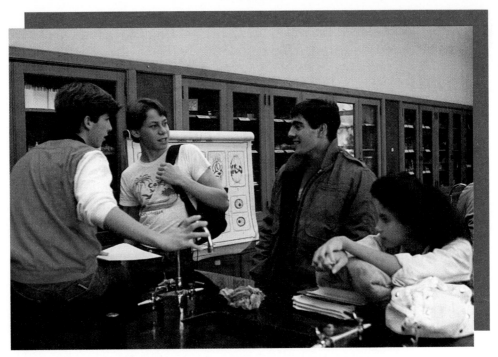

Group communication includes informal meetings to discuss common interests.

question that interests all the members of the group. Each member of a group generally has an opportunity to communicate.

Group communication includes such things as committee meetings, conferences, and workshops. Most group discussions take place in fairly small groups of fewer than fifteen members. The student you read about took part in a group discussion when plans were made for baby-sitting. A review of the student's day will uncover a number of other examples of group discussion. Group discussion is widely used because it offers one of the most effective ways of reaching decisions. Chapter 5 will explore this type of communication in depth. Later on, Chapters 13 and 14 will deal with *debate* and *parliamentary procedure.*

Public Communication

Public communication is a type of interpersonal communication in which one or more people communicate with an audience. A typical example of public communication is **public speaking.** At least since the time of Aristotle and Isocrates, public speakers have had a powerful influence on society. Teachers, attorneys, preachers, politicians, and many others have used this form of interpersonal communication to reach large numbers of people through the spoken word. Often those who have developed their skill at public speaking have found they have become better all-around communicators. Thus, this book devotes Chapters 6 through 11 to helping you acquire the ability to use this important form of public communication. In addition, models of various types of speeches are presented in the Appendix of Speeches, which appears at the end of the book.

Two other forms of public communication are **oral interpretation of literature** and **drama.** Oral interpretation of literature is a performing-art form in which literature is read aloud to an audience. Reading a story to a young child is perhaps the simplest example of oral interpretation of literature. Drama is a performing art that uses both language and action to present a picture of human life to an audience. The number of actors can vary from one to as many as the stage will hold. Chapters 16 and 17 will deal with these forms of public communication.

Mass Communication

In **mass communication** one person or perhaps several senders communicate with a large number of listeners. Usually these listeners are not physically present when the sending takes place. Newspapers and magazines are examples of mass communication. Because this book deals with speech communication, however, the types discussed here will be those of radio and television rather than written communication. Mass communication differs from the other types of communication because the receiver can "turn off" the sender at will, often by the simple flick of a switch. As you know, this is seldom possible in face-to-face communication. Chapter 15 will consider radio and television in depth.

Application

Classifying Your Communication

Bring your log of daily activities to class. Compile a report of your time distribution in the four types of communication. Then write a personal analysis, answering the following questions:

1. What percentage of my communication time is given to active participation? To passive participation?
2. What type of communication activity absorbs most of my time? The least amount of time?
3. Will my distribution of communication time likely change in the next ten years? If so, how?

In small groups, compare your results with other members. Discuss similarities and differences.

WHAT ARE THE BENEFITS OF SPEECH COMMUNICATION?

You've undoubtedly heard the expression "So-and-so just speaks to hear himself talk." Though there may be some tendency for everyone to do this at times, people usually use speech as a tool to gain very important benefits. What are some of these benefits?

You Learn by Communicating

One reason people use speech is to learn. Almost from the moment children learn to speak, they are asking questions. Teachers could not teach if they were not allowed to speak, and students could not learn if they were not allowed to listen and ask questions. If you give directions to someone about how to build a bookcase, that is teaching for you and learning for the other person. Both teaching and learning require speech-communication skills.

You Make Decisions by Communicating

Speech is important in helping people make decisions. Though many daily decisions may be labeled as "personal," arriving at a great number of them depends on speaking with others. You may make a "personal decision" to play basketball on the school team, but that decision might partly depend on a discussion with the coach. You may be trying to make up your own mind about whether to see a particular film but you might first wish to get advice from a friend. Many of your daily decisions demand tact and skill as a speaker.

Group decisions make even greater demands on a person's ability to use speech communication. Representatives of labor and management are called upon to display their finest skills in speaking around a bargaining table. Members of juries must often use speech to convince one another of the guilt or innocence of the accused. If you are asked to plan a school talent show or to work on the yearbook staff, your speaking skills and those of the rest of your group may largely determine the success or failure of that talent show or yearbook.

Decisions in government also involve communication. A city council, like Congress, holds debates and committee meetings on issues. The President has discussions with Cabinet members and other advisors to decide what policies to adopt. Officials of city, state, and national government make speeches to keep people informed. Citizens, informed about problems, then speak freely about them in order to affect the actions of their elected officials. The First Amendment of the Constitution of the United States guarantees such freedom of speech. With freedom, however, comes the responsibility to exercise it wisely. The freedom to say what you think does not give you the right to distort the truth or to harm others by your words. It does, however, give you the chance to try to persuade others to share your views and to reach the decisions you favor.

You Find Pleasure in Communicating

Another important use of speech is for pleasure. Human beings enjoy good conversation and the company of others. Psychological studies have shown that people need to interact with others to remain healthy and happy. The wider your experiences are and the better your skill at relating them, the more enjoyable you can be as a conversationalist. Whether face-to-face or over the telephone, good conversation can be one of life's most enjoyable pastimes.

Your Future Depends on Communicating

Speech communication skills are vital to your future. Learning is likely to continue throughout your life. Though you may not "learn something new every day," you probably will average that much during your lifetime. In learning, both in and out of school, communication is the key tool. Lee Iacocca, the dynamic chairman of Chrysler Corporation, has said: "The most important thing I learned in school was how to communicate. . . . You can have brilliant ideas, but if you can't get them across, your brains won't get you anywhere."

You are bound to spend a major portion of your adult working life communicating with others. You may not become involved in all forms of speech communication, but you will certainly be engaged in some of them. How well you succeed in communicating may have a great deal to do with how happy and successful you are in your future career.

Accurate directions, instructions, and information must often be communicated through the spoken word. Directions explaining how to perform a task or instructions about new methods and equipment require the giving and receiving of correct information by word of mouth.

In some jobs, speech communication is required to convince others. Salespeople must be persuasive in promoting their product or service. Managers must be capable of motivating their workers verbally. Elected officials must constantly convince the people they represent that they are adequately doing their job.

Studies conducted by the Menninger Clinic discovered that 70 percent of the workers who lose their jobs do so because they fail to communicate clearly, not because they do not have the technical knowledge to perform their work. In another study over a thousand people were asked to evaluate the importance of training in speech communication for themselves. Included in the group were accountants, homemakers, unskilled laborers, sales clerks, and professional people. Seventy-five percent of the group responded that skill in speaking was important or essential to their work. Ninety percent of the executives interviewed said speech training was particularly important to them.

Business and industry are realizing more every day the importance of having employees who are skilled communicators. Most professional people such as attorneys, clergy, doctors, and teachers must use speech extensively in their work. Unless you, too, develop skill in speaking, your success in life may be severely limited.

Careful listening is just as important to your future as is clear speaking. In a recent survey, California business leaders were asked what skills they looked for in college graduates seeking jobs. Almost 80 percent placed listening skills in their top five choices. A majority reported that listening was the most important skill for those seeking employment.

Good communication skills are vital in the medical professions. The ability to explain a procedure is as important as the ability to listen carefully. Both skills can save lives.

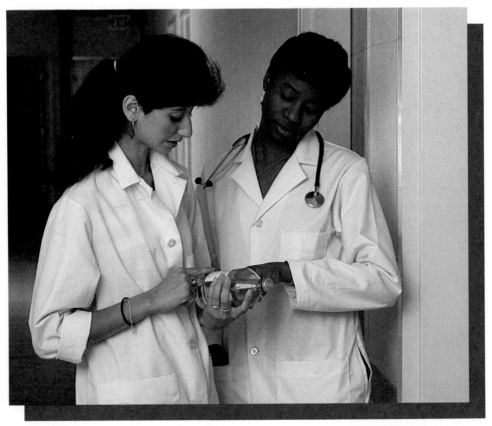

Careers

The following is a list of some of the careers for which communication skills are important.

Auctioneer	News reporter
Audiologist	Police officer
Children's librarian	Public information officer
City manager	Public relations representative
Clergy	Receptionist
Clinical psychologist	Salesperson
Commentator	Sales manager
County agricultural agent	Social worker
Director	Speech pathologist
Directory assistance operator	Speech writer
Disc jockey	Sports announcer
Drama teacher	Stage manager
Employment interviewer	Survey worker (Interviewer)
Fund raiser	Teacher
Hotel front-office clerk	Training representative
Interpreter	Travel guide
Labor relations manager	
Narrator	

In each chapter of this book you will find a Career Close-up. Notice, as you read them, the great number of careers that are connected by the common tool of speech communication.

Application

Speech and Careers

In small groups, each person should present his or her career goals to the other members of the group. Mention how speech communication is important in that career.

WHAT MAKES AN EFFECTIVE SPEECH COMMUNICATOR?

Throughout history the people who have had the greatest impact on other people's lives have been those skilled in speaking. In the United States, Thomas Jefferson, Abraham Lincoln, Susan B. Anthony, Franklin D. Roosevelt, Martin Luther King, Jr., and Margaret Mead were all effective communicators, able to speak with power and persuasiveness. As you have read, developing skill in speech communication is also important in your own life. What are the skills that make someone an effective communicator?

Sincerity   Effective speech communicators must be sincere. That is, they must themselves believe in what they say. Other people must believe they mean what they say in order for communication to be successful in the long run.

Knowledge   Effective speech communicators must speak knowledge-ably. Whether talking in a small group meeting, giving a public speech to a large crowd, or in one-to-one conversation, speakers should know enough about the subject to make it worthwhile for people to listen. At times this requires much research and preparation on a speaker's part. At other times, little advance preparation is needed. In any case, to be an effective speaker you must be able to speak with confidence and knowledge about your subject.

Organization   Effective speech communicators must be well organized. Some speakers are like the man who jumped on a horse and rode off first in one direction then in another. The rider wound up going nowhere and it definitely confused the horse! A clear message begins with a definite purpose and proceeds in a single direction to the end.

Listening   Effective speech communicators must know how and when to listen. At least half of the oral communication process involves listening. Occasionally you may talk to yourself, but most often you expect someone to be listening when you speak. Effective communicators know they may learn more during their listening time than when they are speaking. Good listening is often neglected, but a good speaker will remember this important "flip side" of the speaking process.

Confidence   Effective speech communicators must be confident. Building confidence as a speaker and controlling stage fright are not accomplished overnight. But a course in speech, and experience in

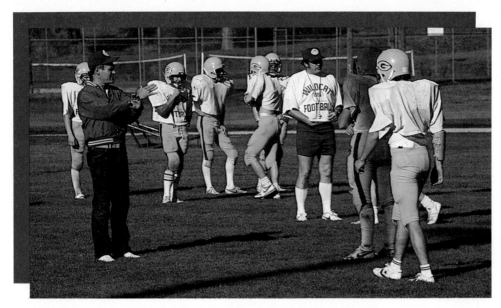

Football coaches need to be effective speech communicators. By using nonverbal communication, they help the whole team understand the play.

communicating with others are two of the best ways to achieve the needed confidence. Chapter 6 points out a number of ways in which you can control stage fright and build confidence for speaking.

Language   Effective speech communicators must use language carefully. A speaker's choice of words can make the difference in whether or not the message is received and understood as the speaker intends it to be. Learning to choose the best words to suit a particular audience and occasion is one of the most difficult tasks for a speaker. It is also what separates great speakers from the rest.

Nonverbal Communication   Effective speech communicators must make good use of nonverbal communication. Speakers "say" a great deal with the tone of their voice, their body movements, and their eyes. Even clothes and grooming communicate to others. Good communicators are aware of what they are communicating nonverbally as well as verbally.

Goal Setting   Effective speech communicators will generally be able to reach certain goals. When an effective speaker presents information about a topic, the receivers will almost always know more about the topic after listening than they did before. If a skilled speaker tries to convince an audience to accept his or her solution to a problem, the listeners will generally be partially or fully convinced.

Career Close-up

HIGH SCHOOL TEACHER

Communication skills are basic to the teaching profession. In addition to their expertise in particular subjects, teachers constantly communicate with their students both by speaking and by listening.

High school teachers have a bachelor's degree with courses concentrating in education and their subject area. Today most teachers continue their education by attaining a master's degree.

High school educators have an extensive knowledge of their subject. They also teach in a clear, well-organized way so that students will understand the subject's basic facts and concepts. Because excessive use of technical terms often confuses students, teachers explain the subject matter simply and in language the student will understand.

An ability to listen is another invaluable skill for teachers. By listening and being attentive to students' ideas, misunderstandings, and problems, teachers gain the information they need to design more effective teaching strategies. Instructors communicate new ideas well by being sensitive to students' needs and learning styles.

Teachers listen actively to student comments and respond enthusiastically to student concerns and questions. In this way student and teacher communicate to attain educational goals.

Teachers are also called on to communicate with groups outside the classroom. As spokespersons for other educators, as advocates for student concerns, and as advisors or experts in their subject area, teachers continually meet the challenge to renew ideas and information through communication.

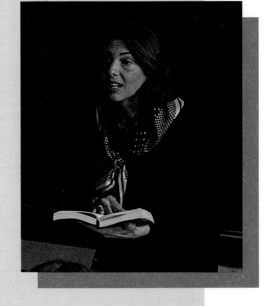

An attentive communicator, this teacher expresses interest in both her subject and her students.

At the end of each chapter you will find a checklist highlighting some important points for improving your speech communication. The checklist is a good way for you to review what you have learned in the chapter about being an effective communicator.

WHY STUDY SPEECH COMMUNICATION?

The benefits of good speech communication are clear. It can help you learn, make decisions, enjoy yourself, and succeed in your chosen career. The eight basic skills for becoming an effective communicator, as listed above, are also clear. With these factors in mind, you may ask why you should take a course to practice something you have been doing every day for years? Why not just continue speaking, keeping these eight factors in mind?

The answer is that speech communication is not that simple. Many people have problems communicating with others in various situations. Note the following questions, and answer them for yourself:

- Do you sometimes have trouble choosing the best words to express your ideas?
- Have you ever spoken without preparing your remarks carefully?
- Do you ever have difficulty paying attention when others speak?
- Do people ever ask you to repeat something because they could not hear or understand what you said the first time?
- Have you ever been asked to give a speech or be in a play and refused out of timidity?
- Have some of your in-class reports over the years fallen a bit flat because of the way you presented them?
- Do you sometimes feel that your friends do not listen to what you say?
- Can you argue effectively and logically with someone?
- Do you have difficulty remembering a speaker's main points several hours after hearing a speech?

If you answered "Yes" to any of the questions listed, a speech course can help you. Perhaps you can think of other reasons for studying speech communication, as well. Even if you are already an effective speaker, improvement is always possible.

This course will provide you with opportunities to practice oral communication in a variety of speaking situations. Some of them may be

Learning to communicate effectively means gaining a lifelong asset in your public and private life.

new to you. Interviewing, group discussion, public speaking, debating, oral interpretation of literature, and drama are among the types of situations included.

As you progress through the course, you will learn to identify your assets and your liabilities as a speech communicator. Listen carefully to your teacher's and classmates' comments. Do not assume your ways of speaking are necessarily the only ways or the best ways. Some of your methods may prove to be best. It will be reassuring to hear people say so. Other methods that you now use may not be best. This is where you can gain the most from a speech course. Make a determined effort to rid your speech of those habits that make you a less effective communicator. Being able to speak and being skilled at speaking are two very different things. This course can help you develop the skills you need to become a better speech communicator.

Application

Effective Speech Communication

In your speech notebook, write the eight "Effective Communicator Skill" key words from pages 13 and 14. Next to each word, write whether or not you need to make improvements in that skill. Keep this list for review periodically in this course to check your progress.

1 Chapter Review

■ Summary

Without communication people would truly be isolated, unable to give and receive ideas. Civilization itself would be impossible.

What is Communication? Communication is the process of sending and receiving messages to achieve understanding. When this process takes place orally, it is called speech communication. People may also communicate in writing and in nonverbal ways through gestures, movement, and dress. All aspects of your life are likely to involve communication of one form or another. Even "talking" silently to yourself is a form of communication, called intrapersonal communication.

What Types of Speech Communication Are There? Interpersonal communication (communication involving more than one person) can be divided into four different categories. One-to-one communication involves give and take between two people. Group discussion involves three or more people communicating and exchanging ideas. Public communication takes place when one or more speakers address a larger audience. Mass communication calls for one or more speakers and a very large audience, usually at a distance from the speaker. Television and radio fall into this last category. Though you will not be continually involved in all of these forms of communication, you are certain to be involved in some of them every day.

What Are the Benefits of Speech Communication? Communication is a very necessary part of learning and decision-making. It also adds enjoyment to people's lives and can play an important role in helping a person achieve success in almost any career.

What Makes an Effective Speech Communicator? Effective speech communicators must have several important skills. They must be sincere and thoroughly knowledgeable about what they are saying. They must be well organized, know how and when to listen, and be able to use language effectively. In addition, they must make good use of nonverbal communication and achieve the desired results from their audience.

Why Study Speech Communication?   A course in speech communication will give you a chance to practice the skills needed to become an effective speaker under the careful guidance of your teacher. A determined effort on your part will rid you of any poor speech habits you may have acquired and sharpen those positive ones you possess.

 Vocabulary

Define each term in a complete sentence.

communication
nonverbal
verbal
speech communication
intrapersonal communication
interpersonal communication
one-to-one communication

group discussion
public communication
public speaking
oral interpretation of literature
drama
mass communication

 Checklist

Effective Communicator Skills

1. Be sincere and say what you mean, both in words and in gestures.
2. Speak knowledgeably. Know your topic.
3. Have a clear speaking purpose.
4. Organize your thoughts.
5. Develop good listening skills.
6. Build your confidence and control stage fright.
7. Use language carefully by learning to choose the most appropriate words.
8. Use nonverbal language, such as tone of voice, body movement, and eye contact.
9. Set goals for communicating and reach them whenever it is possible.

Review Questions

1. Define communication.
2. Name several other forms of communication that people often use besides speech communication.
3. Name four general kinds of interpersonal communication.
4. Describe two major differences between public communication and mass communication.
5. Name four important goals that people can achieve through the use of speech communication.
6. Describe how speech communication relates to learning.
7. Give three reasons why speech communication is important in government and courts of law.
8. Name some ways in which people can make use of speech communication.
9. Name several careers in which skill in speaking is essential.
10. List several characteristics necessary to an effective speech communicator.

Discussion Questions

1. A well-known saying states, "You cannot NOT communicate." Have a class discussion focusing on the message of this saying. Think about these questions as you discuss: Do we reveal our feelings unintentionally? How does *not* talking to someone reveal our feelings? What impressions do we make on others by our personal appearance, our clothes, or our posture?
2. The Menninger Clinic study and the survey of California business leaders both point to the importance of speaking and listening skills on the job. As a class, cite five specific kinds of interaction that occur in business in which speaking skills are critical. Then cite five specific ways that listening skills are vital. Compile a list of ways in which you believe employees could lose their jobs because of poor communication skills.
3. Take part in a class discussion on the topic "How will this speech class be different from most of my other classes?" Give consideration to the role of your teacher as well as your own role in this class. Will each of you behave differently

than in most other classes? To what extent is it important to know the members of this class well? In what ways will you learn information about subjects other than speech communication theory?

4. There are a number of differences between conversation, group discussion, and public speaking, on the one hand, and oral interpretation and drama on the other. In a discussion with your classmates, identify these differences. Which have to do with the different characteristics of each type of communication? Which have to do mainly with people's attitudes toward them? Describe any elements that these types of communication have in common. In what ways are they alike?

5. As a class, discuss ways in which students can affect others through communication. Focus first on the immediate environment—the classroom. Then expand the discussion to include other people and situations, both in and out of school. Discuss the possible benefits to you and others that might result from improved communication skills.

▪ Critical Thinking

1. **Analysis** In small groups, review the skills of an effective communicator. Make certain that everyone in the group understands the exact definition of each of the criteria. Then answer the following questions: Which skill is most easily developed? Which skill is most difficult to develop? Which skill is easiest to observe? Which skill is most difficult to assess? Which skill should receive the most attention in this class? Why? As each group reports to the class, try to reach a consensus.

2. **Synthesis** History has been changed by great communicators. Discuss with your classmates various figures from American history who used effective communication skills to alter the course our country followed. Give specific names and events based on your knowledge of history. Discuss why communication skills were able to affect events.

Activities

In-Class

1. In pairs, role-play a conversation using as little nonverbal communication as possible. Then, as a class, discuss these questions: How difficult is it to omit gestures, facial expressions, etc.? How much of your message is lost to the receiver? Did you experience misunderstanding on the part of the receiver? How did the feedback differ from times when you used nonverbal signals?

2. In small groups, discuss what you think about public speaking. Have you heard a famous person speak? Have you done any public speaking? Would you like to be a public speaker? If so, what kind of public speaker interests you: a politician, a diplomat, a teacher, etc.? Take notes in your notebook on what you learn from your group.

3. Invite to class a popular radio disc jockey or local television personality. Ask him or her to share information about the speech training that is required for a career in mass communication.

4. Give a short speech in class in which you identify three careers that seem attractive to you at this time. Describe the speaking and listening skills that will be required in each career.

Out-of-Class

1. Attend a meeting of the forensics squad of your school. Observe their preparation, and talk with members to discover extracurricular contests that are available in public speaking, debate, oral interpretation, and drama. What differences exist in types of performance? What differences can you discern in type of preparation? Which activity appeals to you most? Why? What do you think these students will gain from competitive speech activities? What carry-over from these activities do you see in the adult world?

2. Attend a courtroom trial, a session of the U.S. Congress, a meeting of your state legislature, your city council, your local school committe, or any other governing body and report briefly to the class about your visit. What forms of speech communication were used? Which communicators did you think were most effective? Why? Present your findings to the class.

3. Make a list of as many types of nonverbal communication as you can think of. For one hour of the day, focus your attention on the many ways that you and others are using nonverbal signals. Take notes, jotting down your observations in your notebook.

4. Choose a career from the *Careers* list on page 12 or any other career that interests you. Interview someone in that career. Ask that person how important communication skills have been in that field, what kind of special training in communications is necessary or would have been helpful to him or her. Prepare a brief report for the class.

5. Observe closely one-to-one conversations both out of school and in school. Jot down notes in your notebook on how often the participants switch roles from sender to receiver.

6. Practice one-to-one communication by phoning a friend or by speaking face-to-face with a classmate or family member. Do you see room for improvement in your communication skills? Make an entry in your notebook about your experience and self-evaluation.

Chapter Project

Form four groups in class, as follows: (a) one-to-one communication, (b) group discussion, (c) public communication, and (d) mass communication. Each group should then clip pictures from magazines showing people engaging in the type of speech communication your group is responsible for. The group task will be to lay out and design an attractive poster collage depicting the assigned area of communication. Display these posters in the classroom.

2 The Process of Communication

When you have completed this chapter you should be able to:

- Explain the basic elements of the communication process.
- Describe the two functions of memory and the role of thinking in the communication process.
- State how the importance of shared interests relates to the communication process.
- Explain the nature of nonverbal communication and define the general categories of nonverbal symbols.

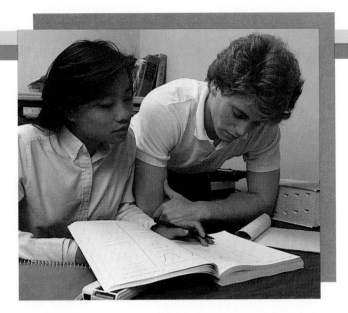

The way in which ideas are exchanged—the process of communication—will affect the outcome of a yearbook committee meeting as well as a study session with a friend.

Think for a moment about a recent conversation you have had with someone. It may have been with a classmate, a friend, a teacher, or one of your parents. No matter who the other person was, or what the topic, both of you talked automatically. You concentrated on the meanings being exchanged and probably never gave a thought to the process you were using. However, if you had some way of recalling how you felt when you first learned to talk at about age two, you would be much more aware of how difficult and complex the communication process really is. In fact, it is so complex, it's amazing that humans communicate with one another at all.

As you read this chapter you will explore the process of communication. You might ask, "Why should I analyze something I do so naturally? If I concentrate too hard on my speech, I might wind up not being able to speak at all!" There is not much danger of this happening, and a great deal can be gained from looking closely at the communication process. Even though you communicate naturally and automatically, examining each part of the process can help you see how your personal communication skills can be improved.

AN OVERVIEW OF THE COMMUNICATION PROCESS

Communication is the process we humans use to achieve understanding. When you want others to understand what is in your mind, you choose "words" to form your message, then "say" the message to your intended

Even during a game with friends, the communication process is taking place. For the game as a whole to be successful, each player must fulfill his dual role of sender and receiver of messages.

receiver. The receiver must "read" the message as it comes in if he or she is to understand the ideas you are trying to get across. Then the receiver reacts to your ideas. Often the whole process takes place in a few seconds, but a great deal happens in those few seconds! Let's take a step-by-step look at the process.

The process begins when you decide to communicate. Let's imagine you want to ask your dad for the use of the family car this evening. You have a purpose you want to achieve that requires you to talk with your dad. You will probably spend some time mentally rehearsing what you will say to your father in order to achieve your purpose of getting the car. When you actually begin speaking with him, you are changing the communication purpose in your mind into a message that your dad can see and hear. Your message consists of symbols, such as words, which stand for the ideas you wish to get across. Of course, the symbols are not the things they represent. Rather they are a code through which you can bring ideas such as "the family car" to your dad's mind as you talk with him. Words are by no means the only symbols we use to communicate either. As we shall see later in this chapter, nonverbal symbols often make up more of our message than words do.

While you are in the role of **sender,** your dad is the **receiver** of your message. If you ever hope to get your request to use the car across to him, he must also take an active part in the communication process. His first job is to interpret the symbols you are sending. This involves more than his simply hearing you. He must actively listen to your message and constantly turn your word-symbols into meaningful ideas in his mind. Then, once he understands your message, he must react to it in some way. His reaction is known as **feedback,** and is an important step in the communication process. Once he has decoded the message, he can't help but react—he is bound to provide you with some form of feedback. Even if he does not say a word in response and just sits there staring at you, that in itself is a reaction. Then it's up to you to interpret his reaction and decide whether you wish to start another cycle of communication in response.

If we put all this together, we might say that *communication is the process by which a sender encodes a message using symbols which a receiver then decodes to achieve understanding. The receiver then reacts using feedback to let the sender know how well the message has been received. The whole purpose of this process is to achieve greater understanding.*

Now, let's look at each step in the communication process in more detail. As you read through the rest of the chapter, remember that having a clear understanding of how you communicate can improve your personal skill as a communicator.

Feedback always occurs during the communication process.

DECIDING TO COMMUNICATE

Communication begins with an idea in your head which you decide you want to get into someone else's head. When you think of communication, you may first think of moving mouths, but that is only one step in the communication process. Before a person's mouth can move with meaning, the person's brain must have decided what ideas the mouth should express. You may have heard the expression "Be certain your brain is in gear before putting your mouth in motion." Actually humans *must* have their brains in gear before they can even begin to speak. Thus, the first step in communicating with another consists of having ideas in your head.

The Two Functions of Memory

Where do people get ideas? From infancy you begin collecting bits of information through your senses—sight, hearing, touch, smell, and taste. Human brains are like computers in many respects. As bits of information are received by the brain through the senses, they are put into the **memory,** which serves as the brain's storage bin, for later use in communicating.

But a person's memory differs from a computer's memory. For one thing, a computer can only store in its memory items that are intentionally put there. A human's memory will store items of information picked up both consciously and subconsciously. Have you ever done something or said something that later puzzled you? You could not figure out why or how you could have done or said that particular thing. Undoubtedly, at that moment, information or experience from your past, which had been stored in your memory, influenced what you did or said.

A second major difference between computer and human memories is that a computer can recall any information entered into its memory, no matter how much material has been entered or how long ago. A human, on the other hand, can often experience what is called "loss of memory."

Actually, what people experience is a loss of recall ability rather than a loss of memory. Have you ever *known* there was a joke you wanted to insert in a conversation but couldn't remember how it started or how the punch line went? That joke was stored in your memory, but you simply could not recall it at that moment. Later, when the pressure to recall the joke was gone, you probably remembered it with ease. Knowing that everyone experiences this difficulty at times can make you more tolerant of yourself and others who experience this problem during communication.

In addition to storing information and experiences, your brain also stores the words needed to express these ideas. Words are symbols that stand for ideas or experiences. Sometime during your early childhood, you adopted language as your primary means of thinking and communicating. Now, when you have an idea you wish to communicate, your brain scans its store of available words (your vocabulary) for the symbol that best identifies that idea. Although this process takes place in fractions of a second, it is quite complex. During this short period, you must decide on a word (a symbol) that best identifies your idea not only for yourself but for your receiver as well.

Reasoning

Your brain has another function besides storing ideas and the words that represent them in your memory. That function is **thinking,** or **reasoning.** Animals have memories, but humans have a highly developed ability to put two or more ideas together and produce a new idea. This ability to reason gives humans a tremendous advantage over other forms of life. Thus, you have two major advantages over other living beings. You can put ideas together by thinking, and you can label your ideas with words.

The process by which you obtain, store, reject, and combine ideas constitutes intrapersonal communication—a kind of subconscious talking you carry on continually within yourself. Having ideas is the start of interpersonal communication—communicating with others.

Needing to Communicate

Reasons for deciding to communicate with another vary greatly. For many people the mere presence of others is often sufficient reason to begin a conversation. People are social creatures by nature and feel a need for a certain amount of communication. If you are the type who starts a conversation with a stranger in a dentist's office, you may have a strong need to interact with others. People who have an above-average urge to communicate will strike up more conversations with strangers than persons without such a strong need. Sometimes people who seem to lack such a need to communicate may, instead, have a fear of being rejected by others. People having this fear seldom start a conversation with a stranger unless some other stronger need drives them to do so.

Research has indicated that the angle at which chairs are arranged can help people overcome fear of rejection and begin communicating. Seats which face one another on a 45-degree angle encourage conversation more than side-by-side seats, facing the same direction. Having some unusual object in the room, such as an abstract art print, can also make conversation between two strangers more likely, even if both are highly sensitive to rejection. The object appears to serve as an ice breaker, providing an excuse to talk about something impersonal.

Sharing Common Experiences and Interests

Have you ever tried to talk with someone who has never even heard about your topic before? For example, have you tried to explain to a younger brother or sister what a yo-yo is like and what fancy tricks can be done with one if he or she had never seen a yo-yo? People who do not share the same knowledge do not have the same **fields of experience.** Wilbur Schramm developed a model of communication which stresses how important shared fields of experience are to effective communication. The model shows that people communicate most easily about those topics with which both are already familiar.

Having common interests is one of the most frequent reasons for deciding to communicate. Did you ever notice how quickly the time slips by when you are having a phone conversation with one of your friends? Or what brief phone conversations you usually have with someone who doesn't share any of your interests?

A signal, or message, readily gets from one person to the other when it is about an experience both people share.

30

Sometimes your common interests with others can last a long time. Generally, family members and friends share common interests during their entire lifetimes. Even after long separations they find it easy to communicate with each other on many subjects.

With other people, however, you may find common interests for only a short period of time. You find it easy to talk with a classmate about a school play in which you are both performing. But when the play is over, you may decide that you do not have any other common interests. Carrying on a conversation with a salesperson is interesting to you both only until your business is completed. Then you may never have an occasion to communicate with that person again. Whether short-lived or enduring, common interests are an important reason for deciding to communicate.

Application

Memory

In small groups, discuss the frustrations of a memory lapse. Share experiences in which you have forgotten names or information for a test or even the punch line of a joke. Describe the circumstances and try to assess why you had the memory lapse.

CHOOSING SYMBOLS

Once you have decided to communicate with someone, the next step is to use symbols to **encode** your ideas. It might be nice if there were some method of simply pouring the ideas from your head into someone else's, but there isn't. You must transfer ideas into a symbol system, or **code,** known to both you and your receiver, and then hope that the receiver will **decode,** or translate, the symbols correctly. Of course, if the symbols are unknown to your receiver, you will fail to communicate. Imagine yourself conversing with someone who understands English but who knows nothing about roller coasters. If you suggest riding on a roller coaster, the person will have no idea what you are talking about and will be unable t o decode your message or respond to it.

You use symbols every day for a variety of purposes. A **symbol** can be a word, a gesture, eye contact, dress—anything that stands for an idea and is used to communicate. Since words are the symbols most often used, they will be explored in more detail first.

Language Symbols

Words are language symbols. They are also called **verbal symbols.** In certain respects language is like money. Language is a medium of exchange for ideas as money is a medium of exchange for goods and services. Putting a price on a new car is a way of making money represent that type of car. You've heard people make remarks such as "Oh, yes, she just bought a $20,000 sports car." In somewhat the same way, language represents, or symbolizes, the ideas people have in their minds. Notice that the phrase *$20,000 sports car* is not the same thing as the actual *sports car.* It is merely one way of representing a type of automobile. Words are not the ideas they represent. They are only a way of symbolizing those ideas.

People often think that a word will represent the identical idea in a receiver's mind that it represents in their own. Unfortunately, this seldom is the case. Have you ever found yourself talking to a friend about a person named Tom, only to discover that your receiver had a different Tom in mind during the first few moments of the conversation? Or consider the different images evoked by a word like *justice.* One person may picture the traditional symbol of a blindfolded woman holding a scale. Another may see a courtroom scene. A third might envision a criminal in prison. Some of these impressions are positive, others negative. Some are practical, others theoretical. Some are general, others specific. It is important to remember that words are symbols that can evoke different meanings in different minds. This realization will prevent much miscommunication.

Actually most words do have a basic meaning. This meaning is known as a **denotation.** The denotative meaning of the word *vacation,* for example, is a time of rest and freedom from work or study. Differences in meaning represented by the same word are largely because of connotation. **Connotation** refers to the meanings people attach to words that are beyond the dictionary meaning. They are meanings that come to different people because of their different past associations with an idea. Connotative meanings are emotionally charged. For example, when someone uses the word *vacation* in front of an audience, each member of the audience may attach his or her own meaning to that idea. For someone who doesn't like to leave work or study, the connotation may be quite negative. For someone who enjoys travel and change, the impression will be agreeable. Even though all the listeners share the same basic meaning, their strong associations with the word can often be more important than the basic meaning.

Thus, if you wish to communicate clearly, you must be careful in choosing the words to encode your ideas. You must remember that some of the people you speak to will not know the meaning of a word that

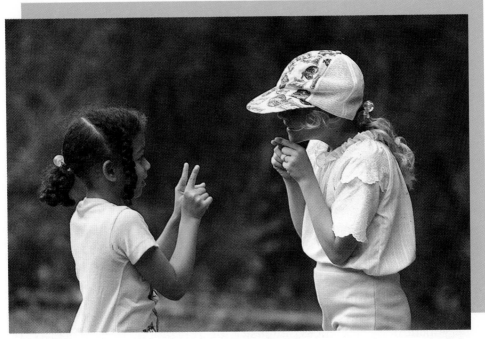

"How big was that bite you took out of my sandwich?" These girls are using nonverbal symbols to express a difference of opinion.

comes to your mind. Even if they do know the meaning of the word, they may attach a different connotative meaning to it. In most cases, however, your meaning will be clear if you use simple words, and adjust your vocabulary for the listener or listeners you are addressing on each occasion.

Nonverbal Symbols

Nonverbal symbols include all of the ways you encode your ideas without words. You may smile or nod to show you agree with someone. Tapping your foot may indicate that you are impatient. People who study nonverbal communication claim that well over half of the meaning exchanged in face-to-face communication comes from nonverbal symbols rather than from words.

Nonverbal symbols communicate a bit differently than verbal symbols. First, it is often more difficult to attach a definite meaning to a nonverbal symbol than to a word. Suppose you are talking with a friend, and your friend frowns at something you say. You will probably get a negative impression from the frown, but you may not be able to decide whether the frown means lack of understanding, disagreement, or something else. If your friend yawns while you are talking, it may mean boredom with what you are saying, or it may simply mean your friend is sleepy. Second, we receive feelings more than ideas from nonverbal symbols. If you ask a friend to go to the movies, and the friend responds with "I'd really like to go with you, but. . . ." while trying to avoid looking you straight in the eye, you will probably get the *feeling* that your friend really doesn't want to go to the movies with you. The words say the idea "I'd really like to go with you" but the eyes express the feeling "I don't want to go with you."

Kinesics   What are some of the most common nonverbal symbols? One category is body motions. The study of the use of body motions to communicate is called **kinesics.** Rolling one's eyes, frowning, staring, laughing, gesturing, crossing one's legs, or any similar body movements fall into this category. Unless you stop and think about it, you may not realize how much people depend on body motion to help them communicate. People in business often hold initial job interviews over the phone, but they will seldom decide to hire a person until that person has been interviewed face-to-face. They want to see how a job candidate "moves" as well as hear the person speak before making a decision. People express a great deal with their movements. They can communicate nervousness or calmness, intensity or relaxation, even sincerity or hypocrisy. In some cultures parents can often tell if little children are lying simply by whether or not the children are willing to look them in the eye. In other cultures children indicate respect for their elders by deliberately not looking directly into their eyes.

A highly specialized form of body motion communication is the sign language used by the deaf and those who communicate with them. Some people claim it is not an instance of nonverbal communication, since particular hand and finger movements simply stand for words. If you have ever seen it used by someone to whom it is second nature, however, you soon recognize it for the beautiful form of communication that it is—a painting of pictures in the air that can move and thrill you as it creates understanding.

Proxemics   A second category of nonverbal symbols involves the use of space to communicate. The study of spatial communication is called **proxemics.** People (usually without realizing it) arrange the distance between themselves and those with whom they are talking in such a way that the degree of closeness communicates in itself. When people are good friends, they usually express this by standing or sitting closer to each other than they would with strangers or new acquaintances. Closeness can also be a signal that a person wants to discuss personal matters. Greater distances indicate that the discussion is to be on an impersonal level. The table on page 35 shows approximate distances most Americans use for typical communication situations.

The way in which space is arranged in homes, offices, schools, and at other public places can communicate certain ideas. The Gateway Arch on the riverfront in St. Louis, Missouri, symbolizes the gateway to the West. The Astrodome in Houston, Texas, indicates the existence of big-time sports. The size and shape of your school's classrooms point out the present or past philosophy of education in your school system. The furnishings in your home give visitors an idea of your lifestyle.

Arrangements of furniture within a room, or space allotments within a building also communicate. Have you noticed that top executives generally have larger and more splendid offices than other employees? This is arranged to say to a visitor or a client: "This person has high status in this company. This person is important." People in their homes try to arrange their furniture to create the most inviting atmosphere for conversation and relaxation. Notice how space is used constantly to communicate in many different ways.

Paralanguage A third category of symbols that many researchers include as part of nonverbal communication is called paralanguage.

People use distance to signal the kind of communication they want or expect.

Distance	Typical Situation
touching to 18 inches (0 to 46 cm)	giving comfort or aid, whispering, conversing with close friends and family
18 inches to 4 feet (46 to 120 cm)	talking with friends or business associates, instructing in a sport
4 feet to 12 feet (1.2 to 3.6 meters)	discussing impersonal or business matters with someone in authority, taking part in a small group discussion
12 feet to 25 feet or more (3.6 to 7.6 meters or more)	public speaking, teaching a class, leading a pep rally

Paralanguage consists of the ways in which you say words. It includes volume, pitch, speaking rate, and voice quality. **Volume** indicates how loudly or softly you are speaking. **Pitch** is how high or low the sounds of your voice are. **Speaking rate** is how fast or slowly you are speaking. **Voice quality** is what makes people able to recognize you by your voice alone. Volume, pitch, and speaking rate change according to the particular speaking situation. Your voice quality, however, usually remains the same whatever the situation.

Volume and pitch work together to create **stress**—the amount of emphasis you place on different words in a sentence. By changing the words that are stressed in a sentence, you can change the meaning of the sentence. Consider the different ideas expressed in the following statements:

"*I* like him very much."

"I like *him* very much."

"I like him *very* much."

Using the same words, but changing the patterns of volume and pitch can make the words carry three quite different meanings.

Changes in the speaking rate can also change the meaning of your message. If you wished to be assured that a friend felt certain about a matter, which speaking rate would give you more confidence?

"I feel sure about that."

"I . . . feel . . . sure about . . . that."

The first sentence, spoken more rapidly, would cause most listeners to have greater confidence in their friend's "sureness."

In addition, paralanguage includes a number of specific sounds people make (coughing, grunting, saying "uh" or "er") as well as the silent pauses between words or sounds. Yawning, sighing, hissing, or snoring are also forms of paralanguage.

Unintentional Communication

Not all communication is intentional. At times you send a message (often through nonverbal means) that you do not mean to send, or that you are not even aware of sending. Edward T. Hall, a noted researcher in cross-cultural communication, tells the story of a United States diplomat in a foreign country who set up an appointment to meet with representatives of the local government. In the United States, the accepted method for keeping such an appointment is to arrive either slightly ahead of the stated time or no more than three or four minutes after it. Arriving any later than that demands an apology in our culture. The United States diplomat, however, was in a country where it was expected that a person might be as late as forty-five minutes without a word of apology or explanation. When the local residents arrived nearly an hour late and made no apology, the United States diplomat took it as an insult. But they had not intended to insult him or the United States and were probably not even aware that anything was wrong! This is an example of unintentional communication, using *time* as the channel of expression.

Similarly, mix-ups can occur if we use space, body movements, clothing, touching, eye contact, or language without full realization of the effect they may have on the receiver. In some parts of the world people stand very close and often touch one another when discussing business or other impersonal matters. Americans, however, usually do not do this. They generally consider touching or standing too close to be violations of their space.

The process of communication is complex. This model shows factors that typically affect every message and every sender and receiver of messages. A mix-up at any point can disrupt the whole process.

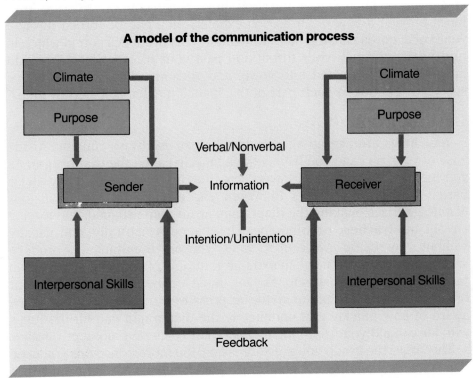

A model of the communication process

Climate

Purpose

Verbal/Nonverbal

Sender → Information ← Receiver

Intention/Unintention

Interpersonal Skills

Climate

Purpose

Interpersonal Skills

Feedback

Application

VOCALIZING

Once you have chosen the ideas you wish to communicate and the word symbols through which to express those ideas, it is time to set your vocal mechanism in action. Have you ever laid a wide blade of grass between your thumbs and blown against it to produce a shrill, vibrating sound? If you have, you know something about how speech sounds are made. Your lungs provide a flow of air as you exhale which can be forced through your vocal cords causing them to vibrate. This produces sound which in turn passes through your throat and past your tongue, lower jaw, and lips, where it is molded into vowel and consonant sounds to produce speech. Let's look at each part of the speech mechanism step by step.

Getting Enough Air

Your lungs are like an air compressor that is always running. At the base of your rib cage you have a thick muscle called the **diaphragm.** As you inhale, the diaphragm lowers, creating a larger chest cavity and a partial vacuum. Air rushes in. When you exhale, the center of your diaphragm rises, making the diaphragm again dome shaped, and forcing air out the **trachea,** or windpipe. This happens naturally, and usually without your being aware of it, when you are breathing. To produce speech, however, you need an extra large supply of air, particularly when you speak to a large group. So you must concentrate more on your breathing process to "pump up the air pressure" in your lungs. Becoming aware of how quickly and completely the diaphragm can fill the lungs with air can aid you in producing a forceful voice at a moment's notice.

The larger the group you are addressing, the more conscious you need to be of your breathing. When giving a public speech to a large audience without a microphone, you should remember two things about breathing.

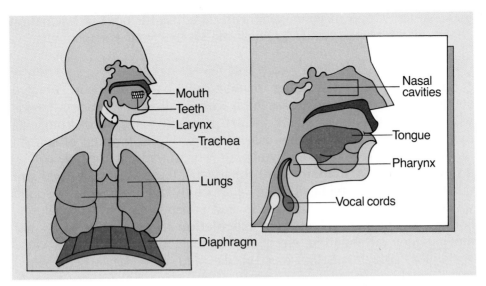

Vocalizing involves your respiratory system and your resonating chambers.

First, you should inhale through your nose rather than through your mouth, using your diaphragm to fill your lungs with air. Second, as you speak, pace your exhalation so that you will have enough air to complete longer thoughts without having to steal a breath at awkward moments.

Treating Your Vocal Cords with Care

Vocal cords vibrate to produce sound. As you begin to speak, these two folds of membrane located in your voice box, or **larynx,** tighten and move closer together, creating a narrow slit. When exhaled air is forced through this slit, the cords vibrate and produce sound, in much the same way that blowing air between your thumb and a blade of grass produces sound. Since women's vocal cords are usually a bit shorter and thinner than men's, women's voices produce a higher pitched sound. It is important not to strain your vocal cords by prolonged yelling or by constantly trying to make yourself heard above loud noises. Excessive coughing or clearing of your throat when it is clogged by a cold may also damage the vocal mechanism.

Making Use of Resonators

The sound produced by your vocal cords is weak and thin. Before the sound waves leave your mouth, however, they pass through several resonating chambers. These **resonators** are your **pharynx** (the back part of the throat), your **nasal cavities,** and your mouth. Each acts much as a hollow chamber does to amplify or increase sound. If you have ever spoken inside a stairwell or tunnel, you know how much a chamber can increase the sound of your voice. Fortunately, your built-in resonating chambers are always handy to boost the level of your vocal sounds.

Articulating Clearly

You are probably beginning to notice that the production of vocal sounds occurs in a kind of assembly-line fashion. The process begins with breath in the lungs and ends with the emergence of words from your mouth. The final step on this assembly line is the forming of sounds produced into recognizable symbols—words. This is the job of the articulators. The **articulators** are the tongue, teeth, lower jaw, and soft palate. By the movement of these organs into various positions, sound waves are molded into the vowels and consonants that form words. Sometimes speakers allow their **articulation** to become lazy. By not moving their articulators vigorously enough, they begin to produce "goin" for "going," "pacific" for "specific" and "wen" for "when." When they use their articulators correctly, however, speakers are able to produce clear, crisp sounds that are easily heard.

Once you begin to study it, you realize that the process of vocalizing —the producing of vocal sounds—is a very complicated one. Because it happens so rapidly in actual communication, you are rarely conscious of the individual steps. When you consider that vocalization is just one part of the total communication process, you realize how amazing human beings are. Look at the illustration on page 39 and notice how many different parts of the body are involved in vocalizing.

Now that you have looked at each part of the sending side of the communication process, let's put it all together in the form of a model. The one shown on page 41 is simply a way of picturing what occurs when a person begins to communicate.

Application

Proper Breathing Techniques

Practice breathing for public speaking. Stand up and place your hands at the base of your rib cage. Inhale deeply through your nose. You should feel your hands rise as you inhale, indicating that you are filling your lungs with air. Now say a loud, continuous "ooh" for as long as you can. Notice how your hands gradually sink in as you lose your supply of air. You may also be able to feel your diaphragm and rib muscles tightening near the end of your "ooh." For speaking you must be able to regulate the flow of outgoing air so you will not run out at an awkward moment.

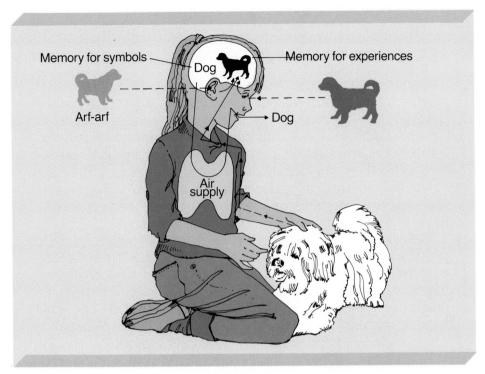

When the communication process is activated, both the mind and body respond.

RECEPTION

Perhaps when defining sound in your science class, your teacher asked you the question "If a tree falls in a remote forest and no person or animal is close enough to hear it, is there any sound?" The answer depends, of course, on how you define *sound*. But if you are talking about interpersonal communication and ask "If no one hears or sees a person sending symbols, is communication occurring?" the answer is "No!" Communication is a two-way process. When someone is sending, but no one is receiving, the only thing that is occurring is *sending,* not communication. Interpersonal communication is the process of using symbols to evoke a meaning in someone else's mind, similar to a meaning you have in your own.

So far this chapter has only dealt with the sending half of the communication process. **Reception** is a kind of mirror image of this first half. When senders select certain ideas from their memory bins and change them into sound or sights, the resulting messages go out across space to receivers' ears or eyes. The receivers then attempt to connect the symbols they receive with experiences in their own minds. This

PEACE CORPS VOLUNTEER

Peace Corps volunteers devote two years to working in developing nations, promoting world peace. The only essential prerequisite is a willingness to become totally involved in a foreign culture, to work hard despite difficult conditions, and to further understanding between cultures. Because people with every imaginable skill are needed (teachers, engineers, agricultural specialists, etc.), there are no absolute educational requirements. However, 96% of volunteers have attended college. Once accepted, a volunteer participates in a 13-week training program prior to foreign assignment.

The Peace Corps is based on the belief that communication is the key to achieving world peace and understanding. When volunteers have only thirteen weeks to learn the language of their community, they cannot rely on language alone to communicate. Volunteers are taught to supplement the use of language with such nonverbal symbols as nods, smiles, hand motions, and facial expressions to communicate their enthusiasm and willingness to help.

Peace Corps volunteers also become skilled in monitoring feedback during conversations in their communities. Volunteers study facial expressions and body language to determine whether they are being understood or whether they have unintentionally communicated something. In this way, misunderstandings can be corrected before any harm is done.

The discovery that communication is much more than the simple exchange of words is a truth that emerges from the Peace Corps experience. Through the skillful use of verbal and nonverbal communication, volunteers find there are a multitude of ways to express good will.

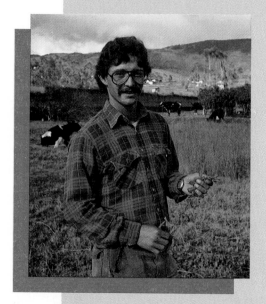

By word and deed, this volunteer promotes world peace.

process is called decoding. To the extent that the senders and receivers have similar backgrounds and experiences, they will probably achieve shared meanings. If the receivers have no experience of something the senders are describing or are not familiar with the symbols the senders use, communication will fail. If someone speaks to you in a language you do not understand, communication is difficult, at times impossible. The problem, of course, is primarily that you and the sender do not share enough verbal symbols for things. If you were looking at pictures, you might both understand the same basic idea—that of someone serving food, for example. But while you would use the English language symbol *waiter* to represent this concept, a person from France would use the symbol *garçon*. Unless you speak French, the word symbol used wouldn't mean anything to you.

Many people think that when communication fails it is always the fault of the sender. Actually, the receiver shares part of the responsibility for incomplete communication. Placing all the blame for poor communication on the sender is a bit like having a broken TV set and blaming your local channel because you can't see your favorite program. Besides an effective sender, communication involves a receiver who has sufficient knowledge, experience, and vocabulary to be able to tune in on different kinds of messages. It also involves good listening habits on the part of the receiver, a topic that will be considered in the next chapter.

These listeners are silent partners in the communication process. Unless the message is received and understood, the process is incomplete.

Feedback

The next time you have a casual conversation with a good friend, try this little experiment on her or him: Every time your friend talks, you stop reacting in any way. Do not say any words, or even utter any sounds. Do not nod or shake your head or move your hands, arms, or any part of your body. Do not even look into your friend's eyes, but stare off to the side of his or her left ear. If your friend is like most of us, he or she will soon ask what is wrong with you, or why you're not paying attention. As a matter of fact you may have been paying close attention, but you were not showing that you were! The signals that a receiver continuously gives to a sender indicating how well the message is being received are known as **feedback.** Feedback is terribly important for senders, since it allows them to discover such matters as whether they are speaking too fast, using words that are too complex, or even whether they are offending or angering their receivers.

Feedback can consist of words, nonverbal symbols, or both. Feedback makes it possible for speakers to judge how well they are communicating. Whenever anyone sends a message to another person, some sort of feedback takes place. Sometimes it is easy for the speaker to detect. For example, the listener is asleep. The audience begins to walk out during a public speech. The interviewer leans forward and says "Good, tell me more!"

At other times feedback is less obvious. TV news commentators, unable to see their listeners, must rely on mail or phone surveys to discover how the audience responds to their broadcasts. A person talking on the telephone must frequently rely on an occasional "uh-huh" to know the listener is still there. But no matter how difficult some feedback is to detect, it is always present whenever communication occurs. Short of leaving the presence of a sender, it is impossible for a receiver *not* to provide feedback. Even when a receiver sits perfectly still, says nothing, and keeps a deadpan expression on her or his face, the sender can read this as a lack of interest. The receiver has supplied feedback.

In face-to-face conversation, interviews, and small group discussion, a good balance of verbal and nonverbal feedback is possible. A good receiver will maintain a sufficient level of both forms of feedback to inform senders constantly about how effectively they are getting their ideas across.

When talking on the telephone, however, the sender cannot see the receiver, so the feedback is primarily verbal. The word *primarily* is necessary because nonverbal feedback, in the form of paralanguage, may be used at times as feedback over the phone. A change in the tone of voice or in the speaking rate, silence, and sounds that are not words are available to the listener as forms of feedback.

"Next time, have him ask for *verbal* feedback."

In public speaking, the usual form of feedback is nonverbal. This is because, if a large number of audience members began responding aloud, it would soon be impossible to hear the speaker. So most audiences confine their feedback to kinesic symbols—smiles, frowns, and nods of their heads. Some paralanguage, consisting of yawns, occasional boos or hisses, and clapping, may also be used as feedback.

Performers on radio or television sometimes receive feedback from a studio audience. Feedback from the audience at home will often be in the form of telephone calls or letters. This type of feedback usually reaches the sender after the performance. It cannot help the speaker adapt the message to the receivers during the performance.

Application

Reception and Feedback

Divide into teams of two. Practice giving feedback by role-playing with your partner. Ask this person to talk about something or someone he or she enjoys a great deal. This might be a favorite hobby, a favorite rock singer, or a particular sport. Be attentive while the person is speaking, giving positive feedback. Now role-play again, but this time give negative feedback. Reverse roles so that you are doing the talking and your partner is giving the feedback. Each team should then report the results to the class.

2 Chapter Review

■ Summary

People usually take the process of human communication for granted. However, a close look reveals its complexity and the reasons for communication breakdowns. Studying this process in detail can also uncover opportunities for people to sharpen their communication skills.

Communicating for Understanding   Communication is the process people use to understand one another. The sender transmits symbols —words and nonverbal signals—to the receiver. The receiver must decode the message and react to it by providing feedback to the sender.

Deciding to Communicate   Communication begins in your brain with an idea. Your brain stores information, including words, in your memory and enables you to reason. People communicate for different reasons, but sharing common interests is a major one.

Choosing Symbols   You must encode your ideas in order to exchange them. Code systems consist of verbal and nonverbal symbols. For communication to succeed, the symbols you choose must mean similar things to your receiver. Language is the symbol code used most frequently. However, nonverbal symbols, such as kinesics, proxemics, and paralanguage are frequently used together with language.

Vocalizing   Vocalizing begins with the diaphragm forcing air through the trachea during exhalation. As this air is forced between your vocal cords, the cords vibrate, producing sound waves. The pharynx, mouth, and nasal cavities act as resonating chambers, amplifying the sound. Finally, as the sound passes the lower palate, tongue, lower jaw, teeth, and lips it is formed into the vowels and consonants that make up words.

Reception   Reception is half of the communication process. Once the message leaves the sender, the receiver picks it up and decodes it into ideas. Unless the experiences and vocabulary of sender and receiver are similar, communication is difficult and sometimes impossible.

Feedback Communication is never complete without feedback. Feedback is the total of all receivers' responses that tells senders how they are "getting through." Feedback may be either verbal or nonverbal, or it may be a mixture of the two.

Vocabulary

Define each term in a complete sentence.

memory	nonverbal symbols	vocal cords
thinking	kinesics	larynx
reasoning	proxemics	resonators
fields of experience	paralanguage	pharynx
encode	volume	nasal cavities
code	pitch	articulators
decode	speaking rate	articulation
symbol	voice quality	reception
verbal symbols	stress	feedback
denotation	diaphragm	
connotation	trachea	

Checklist

Sender and Receiver Skills

1. Develop an understanding of the communication process to help your communication skills.
2. Remember that people have different needs to communicate.
3. Choose words carefully; they can evoke different meanings for each individual.
4. Recognize the importance of nonverbal symbols.
5. Adjust your volume, pitch, and speaking rate to the particular speaking situation.
6. Take care not to send the wrong message unintentionally.
7. Use appropriate breathing and crisp articulation.
8. Be a responsive listener. Provide both verbal and nonverbal feedback to the sender.

■ Review Questions

1. Explain where communication originates.
2. Name the functions of the brain that are most important to communication.
3. Explain what "loss of memory" means in everyday situations.
4. Name three factors that influence most people's decision to communicate.
5. Name the basic symbols of communication.
6. Define denotation.
7. Define connotation.
8. Name and give examples of three kinds of nonverbal communication that people use.
9. Name and give the functions of the parts of the body that are involved in the vocalization process.
10. Define feedback.

■ Discussion Questions

1. Ask some of your classmates to describe what they think of when you say the following words: "dog," "tree," "house." How many different responses do you get? What kind of dog, tree, or house do *you* picture? Discuss how past experiences create present images and thoughts. List ways you can be sure that the sender and the receiver are discussing the same ideas.
2. In small groups, discuss instances you have experienced in which conflict occurred because of nonverbal messages you either gave or received. Include tone of voice, and facial expressions. Discuss ways to clarify nonverbal messages.
3. Discuss with your classmates the importance of volume as a factor in communication. Does it offend you when a person speaks to you in a loud voice? Do you form an unfavorable opinion about someone who speaks in a very soft voice? If so, what sort of judgment do you make?
4. Territoriality is an aspect of proxemics that explains our attachment (even possessiveness) of our space. Discuss ways that you claim your territory. How do you feel if someone else sits at "your" desk in school? Do you have a particular chair at the dinner table? Is "your" room open territory for others in your home or do you

keep the door closed or locked? In what ways do we "mark" our territory if we have to leave our seat in an auditorium? Include in your discussion any circumstances under which you have willingly given up claim to "your" territory.

Critical Thinking

1. **Analysis** Analyze your need to communicate with others. Think about the following: Why do you need to communicate? With whom do you need to communicate? Are you nervous about communicating with certain people? Jot down your answers to these questions in your notebook. Then jot down possible resolutions of problems. Save your notes for reference later on.

2. **Evaluation** In small groups, discuss whether the clothes people wear make a difference in what others think of them. To what extent does choice of clothing reflect self image? To what extent are people stereotyped according to appearance? Be sure to give reasons for your opinions. Do you think it is correct to judge people by their clothing? At the end of the discussion each group will hand in two or three statements about the importance of appearance.

Activities

In-Class

1. Seated in a circle, each of you will tell the class your name and one bit of personal information. ("My name is Rosa, and I collect seashells.") The second person will repeat the information just given, then give new information about himself or herself. ("Her name is Rosa; she collects seashells. My name is Jeremy, and I play the guitar.") The third and all other participants will continue the process. Clearly, if you are a student near the end of the exercise you will have to recall as many as 30 names and personal facts. Your task

will be more difficult, but you will have the reinforcement of everyone before you.

2. Put three columns on the board: POSITIVE, NEGATIVE, and NEUTRAL. As a class, suggest words that are related to each other but that have different connotative factors for each category. Place each word in the proper column. See how many different words you can come up with.

3. Engage in a game of "charades" to discover the frustrations of total reliance on nonverbal symbols. Form two groups. Each group will write titles of books, movies, songs, and TV programs on small sheets of paper to be distributed to the opposing team. A maximum time limit should be set for each player, and a careful record kept of time for each team. No mouthing, pointing, or pantomiming of letters is allowed.

4. Try a "one-way/two-way" communication exercise. Working in pairs, one of you will be the *sender;* the other will be the *receiver.* The sender should think of a diagram of a geometric design and then explain to the receiver what to draw. The receiver will attempt to draw on his or her own paper what is being de-scribed. In the first phase of the exercise (one-way), the sender will describe the design as quickly and as accurately as possible; the receiver cannot ask questions or call for clarification. In the second phase of the exercise (two-way), the receiver should turn the paper over and begin a new drawing on the back. As many questions as necessary are allowed.

Each phase should be timed. When all teams have finished, have a class discussion about the activity. Identify the advantages and disadvantages of one-way and of two-way communication. Discuss the confidence and frustrations of both sender and receiver in each phase.

5. Invite to class a specialist proficient at sign language. Ask him or her to share with you the graphic movement of the language and to explain how it is taught to others. Learn to communicate using several of the basic signs.

Out-of-Class

1. Turn the sound off completely on your home television set, so that you pick up only the picture. Watch for three minutes, seeing how much you can understand. Then turn the sound up and close your eyes so that

you only hear the words. Can you understand more or less during this three-minute period? Which way gets more of the message to you as the audience? Make notes in your notebook on the types of verbal and nonverbal communication you missed when you only watched the picture, and what types of nonverbal communication you missed when only listening to the sound.

2. Say several different words aloud concentrating on how each part of the vocalization process works. Remember to practice good breathing habits. Can you feel your vocal cords vibrate? Which of the articulators are you using with a particular word? Block some of the resonators by holding your nose. How different is the quality of your voice?

3. Take photos of several people of various backgrounds, occupations, and ages. These people could be friends or family members, at home or at work. They can be young children playing in a playground, or classmates participating in sports. Using at least five of these photos, list the best ways to communicate with the people in them. Share your findings with a small group. Then participate in a class discussion on how communication might break down with each.

Chapter Project

In small groups compose a newspaper article entitled, "Twelk Sighted Near Campus." Give special attention to details of the physical characteristics and mannerisms of the "twelk." Design a lively plot that tells of the sighting and that provides the reader concrete information about who, when, and where. When finished, one group member should read the story aloud to the class.

As a class, compare the various stories. What can you learn about ways that we differ in interpreting word symbols. Discuss how this experience might be similar to times when people do not have a common understanding of a "real" English word.

3 Listening

**When you have completed this chapter
you should be able to:**

- Explain the difference between hearing and listening.
- State the barriers to effective listening and identify ways to overcome them.
- Describe several major responsibilities of an active listener.
- Identify several ways to improve your ability to analyze and interpret a message.

When you reach out with your mind and listen actively, you give yourself the chance to make new information—a song or a math theorem—your own.

If you are like most people, you probably think a good communicator is someone who can speak well. Speaking, however, is just part of the total process of communication. In order for speakers to get their messages across, someone must also be listening.

Listening is not an easy task. "Doesn't everyone know how to listen?" you might ask. The answer is "No." Effective listening involves more than just **hearing,** or the reception of sound. Hearing and listening are often confused. People think that if they can hear automatically, they can listen automatically. But this is simply not true. To be a good listener you must also understand and interpret sound in a meaningful way. A good deal of thinking must go on in effective listening.

When messages are misunderstood, it is easy to blame the speaker. The listener, however, must share the responsibility for effective communication. It takes a lot of concentration and effort to be a good listener. Statistics show, in fact, that most people are poor listeners. The average person misses about 75 percent of what he or she hears.

The encouraging fact is that no one has to remain a poor listener. Listening, like speaking, reading, or writing, is a skill that can be learned. Learning to listen, however, takes self-motivation and practice.

This chapter will give you information about the benefits of learning to listen effectively. It will also describe the most common barriers to good listening, and give you a few basic steps to follow in becoming a better or more active listener. You will also receive hints on how to remember what you hear, how to analyze the speaker's logic, and how to interpret nonverbal messages.

REASONS FOR LEARNING
EFFECTIVE LISTENING

Why learn to listen? There are many good reasons. As you read through the ones discussed here, think carefully about how each applies to you. The more reasons you can find to improve your listening behavior, the easier it will be to learn and practice good listening skills.

You Will Avoid Misunderstandings

Has one of your teachers ever asked for a homework assignment that you didn't realize was due? Have you ever been introduced to someone and then a few minutes later called the person by the wrong name? Misunderstandings such as these are easy to avoid when you become an active listener.

You will also be able to do things right the first time when you learn to listen effectively. If friends give you directions or tell you where and when to meet them, you won't have to ask for a recap or phone later with questions if you know how to listen well. You will be able, if you listen

These students weren't born understanding new and unfamiliar ideas. But, by listening attentively, they are taking a vital step toward understanding.

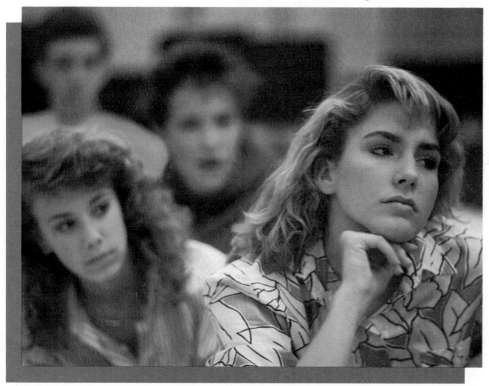

actively, to spend your energy on productive activities. You won't have to worry about how you are going to solve the problems created by poor listening.

In addition, practicing good listening skills may help you become more confident. You will know that you can understand and interpret correctly what other people say to you. People will learn to depend upon you.

You Will Get Along Better with Others

No one likes to talk to someone who doesn't listen. Think about the people you know. Which of them do you enjoy talking to? You probably most enjoy talking to those who seem honestly interested in what you have to say.

Listening attentively to your friends shows that you sincerely care about them, too. It is a very high compliment when you listen to another person. Just by listening you can give a speaker a feeling of confidence and self worth.

You Will Learn More About the World

You probably spend a lot more of your time speaking and listening than reading and writing. Therefore, most of what you know comes from what people tell you. Television and radio as well as conversations with friends, parents, and teachers, all contribute to your understanding of your immediate environment and the world in general. The more knowledge you gain, the more you will be able to enjoy and appreciate the things around you.

It is difficult to carry on a conversation with another person if your knowledge is limited. Active listening will help you acquire a storehouse of helpful and interesting information, and it will enable you to relate better to people with a variety of interests.

You Will Be More Successful in School and on the Job

Listening skills are very important in school. Grades and interest in school activities usually improve when students make an effort to develop their ability to listen.

Good listening skills can also favorably affect your future. Regardless of what your career plans are, you have a better chance of getting the job you want and being successful at it if you know how to listen. One salesperson analyzed a typical work day and discovered that one third of the salary received was for listening.

Think for a minute about all the jobs that require good listening skills. Telephone operators, nurses, auto mechanics, teachers, and lawyers must all be able to listen carefully in order to do a good job. What would

"I might as well be talking to a blank wall."

happen if a telephone operator kept giving callers the wrong number, or if a nurse didn't follow a doctor's instructions and wrote down the wrong medication? Consider a lawyer or judge who didn't pay attention to most of what went on in the courtroom. It is difficult to think of any job where good listening would not be an asset. In some jobs, it may even be a key ingredient in saving lives.

Application

Listening Effectively

Look again at the log of a typical day that you made in Chapter 1. Make a list of the activities during an average day that can be classified as listening. Jot down the number of hours per day that you normally spend listening (including time spent listening to the radio, TV, or tape player). Then, as a class, make a tally on the board to find out the *least*, the *average*, and the *most* number of hours per day for the class as a whole.

RECOGNIZING BARRIERS TO LISTENING

At one time or another, you have probably had the nerve-wracking experience of trying to carry on a conversation with someone in a noisy room. The sounds of traffic, machinery, or even a dance band can produce such a racket that it is often impossible to hear what the other person is saying. Or perhaps you have tried to call someone long distance on the telephone and could hardly hear them over the static on the line. Noises such as these can cut off communication entirely.

Noise, however, is only one possible barrier to communication. Anything that blocks or distorts the message that a speaker is trying to get across to a listener is a barrier to the communication process. Barriers can come from problems caused by the environment, the speaker, or the listener. Whatever the original source of the problem, a good listener should make every effort to overcome it.

Being able to recognize barriers is the first step toward overcoming them. In the next few pages, you will look at five different types of barriers as well as ideas for combating them.

Distractions

There are almost always **distractions** when people communicate. Some distractions are environmental. Perhaps there are people talking close by. A radio may be playing or a television may be on. Even the temperature of the room or the time of day may influence your ability to keep your mind on the speaker's message.

Another type of distraction can come from the speaker. Have you ever heard someone remark after listening to a public speech, "I'm not sure what was said, but the speaker spoke beautifully"? Actually, this is not a compliment. If the *way* the speaker delivered the message is all the receiver can remember, something is wrong.

Good listeners must learn to keep their minds on the basic message, not on the speaker's delivery. Whenever you find yourself concentrating on how relaxed a speaker looks, how smooth a speaker's gestures seem, or how pleasant someone's voice sounds, force your mind back to the content. Effective listening means concentrating on *what* the speaker says rather than on *how* it is said.

Whenever you feel yourself being distracted, whether it be by the conversations of other people, the temperature of the room, or the speaker, you should mentally remind yourself to listen. It helps if, as you enter the room for a meeting, speech, or play, you remind yourself that you aren't going to let anything distract your attention from the message you came to hear. Of course, this is easier to decide than to carry out.

With real determination, however, you will gradually become better at overcoming distractions of all types.

Daydreaming

Another very common barrier to listening is daydreaming. Daydreaming is really a form of internal distraction. Your mind wanders off and you miss much of what the speaker is saying. One of the reasons this happens is that people can think much more rapidly than they can speak.

The average public speaker articulates at the rate of about 150 words per minute. Research has shown, however, that listeners can understand the message just as well when the rate is as fast as 380 words per minute—more than double that of normal speech! Just think, if your teachers could learn to speak at the rate of 380 words per minute, you could learn about as much as you do now and be out of school before noon each day! Unfortunately, speakers cannot articulate at such a high rate of speed.

This big difference between comprehension speed and speaking rate makes it easy for people to acquire bad listening habits. Since listeners can often complete a sentence mentally before a speaker can complete it verbally, they may get bored and begin to think about something else. Instead of daydreaming, however, good listeners learn to use this extra time to concentrate on what they are hearing. Rather than letting yourself daydream about tomorrow's football game or the history exam you have

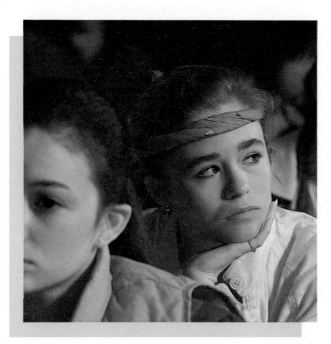

Daydreaming may not only distract you from the subject at hand, it can also rob you of opportunities to learn and grow.

next period, use your bonus time to summarize to yourself the main points the speaker is making. Think about the topic being discussed and ask yourself questions that will keep your mind on the subject.

Close-Mindedness

Try to recall some of the most recent arguments you have had. What were they about? Did you go into the discussions prepared to fight immediately to support your side, or did you really make an attempt to listen first to what the other person had to say? Were you prepared in any way to let the other person convince you that she or he was right?

When people disagree, they often become so involved with defending their own positions that they forget to listen to the facts that the other person presents. Responsible listeners, however, keep an open mind until they have heard all of the information. They listen to and weigh the merits of someone else's opinion, no matter how strong their own opinions may be.

People who refuse to expose themselves to ideas that are different from their own are basically **close-minded.** Such people may not even be willing to attend a speech by a candidate from another political party or to read a newspaper article that supports a position with which they disagree.

An **open-minded** person, on the other hand, does more listening than speaking. An open-minded person has the attitude, "I hold a certain opinion which I believe is true, but I am willing to listen carefully to the ideas and opinions of others before I make my final decision."

As a good listener, you should try to be open-minded and suspend judgment until you have heard all of the facts. Carefully consider all the information that is presented. Seek out situations in which you will hear views that are different from your own so that you will have a chance to practice careful listening. Certainly, when you get an opportunity to speak you will want the same kind of consideration and genuine listening from those who do not agree with you.

Overemphasizing the Source

If you heard a speech calling for more lenient treatment of juvenile offenders in our courts, would you be more convinced if it was presented by (1) a juvenile court judge, (2) a criminal, or (3) an ordinary citizen? When an experiment was conducted using this exact situation, the researchers found that those listeners who thought a judge was presenting the information were much more favorable in their attitude toward juvenile criminals than those who were told that the speech was being given by a criminal or an ordinary citizen. Those who thought the speaker was a criminal accepted the message least.

What does this experiment tell you about listening? For one thing, it tells you that people seem to accept a message more favorably from a person they respect than from a person whose reputation they question. However, it also points out the danger of paying too much attention to the source of a message and too little to the message itself.

Although you will naturally be influenced by your feelings about the speaker or your knowledge about the speaker's reputation, as a responsible listener you must be careful to evaluate what is being said apart from who is saying it. A message should not be judged entirely on the basis of how you feel about the speaker.

The next time you attend a public speaking event, you might take some time before the speech begins to analyze your feelings about the speaker as a message source. Do you like the speaker? Do you think the speaker is reliable? What do you know about the speaker's background? If the score is very low or high—if you have a most unfavorable or very high opinion of the speaker—you will know that you must be very careful in making judgments about what the speaker has to say.

Listening Only to What Is Easy to Understand

Another common barrier to good listening is listening only to what is easy to understand. If you become accustomed to "turning off" whenever you become confused, it won't be long before this behavior becomes a habit. If you avoid material that is difficult and only expose yourself to things that are already easy for you, you will never have the opportunity to improve your listening ability.

If you have studied a foreign language, you know that the first time you listen to someone speaking in that language it sounds very confusing. It is easy to become frustrated and give up because you get lost very quickly. As you practice and become more familiar with the foreign sounds, however, you soon begin to *enjoy* hearing that language.

The more often you challenge yourself by listening to difficult material, the better you will be at following and understanding what you hear.

Application

Classroom Distractions

As a class, sit quietly with your eyes closed and listen. Make a mental note of all the sounds you hear. After a few minutes help compile a list on the board. Which sounds were most distracting? Brainstorm with your classmates on how these distractions can be overcome.

The interest and attention shown by these listeners creates a climate of support and friendly challenge for the speaker.

BECOMING AN ACTIVE LISTENER

To become a good listener you should be ready to do some hard work. Remember that as a listener you have certain responsibilities both to yourself and to the speaker. Not only must you avoid the barriers to listening that were just discussed, but you must also actively do your part to insure that you get the most out of each listening experience.

Prepare to Listen

In order to hear and understand everything a speaker has to say, be ready to listen from the very beginning. This means arriving early enough to get a good seat at a play or getting to a meeting on time. If you go into a class after the teacher has already begun the day's work, you not only interrupt your classmates but you create a difficult situation for yourself. You then have to try to make sense out of what is being discussed without having heard the introductory remarks.

If you know that you will be doing a lot of listening, it is a good idea to get sufficient rest beforehand. If you are tired, hungry, or upset, it is much harder to focus on the message than if you listen when you are alert and rested.

Finding out as much as you can beforehand about a speaker's topic, the plot of a play, or the agenda of a meeting are other ways you can prepare yourself to listen. If you have thought in advance about some of the ideas you will be hearing, you can better understand what the speaker is talking about. You become like a runner who has used warm-up exercises before jogging. The runner can perform better because he or she has made a smooth transition from a relaxed to an active state. Sometimes, of course, it is not possible to discover information about a topic ahead of time. But do not overlook opportunities to prepare yourself to listen more effectively.

Expand Your Vocabulary

One aid that will help you to understand better and benefit more from what you hear is the development of a good vocabulary. Words are symbols that a speaker uses to convey ideas. In order for the ideas to reach their destination, however, the listener must also be familiar with the words the speaker has chosen. You can think of good listeners as being similar to good carpenters—the more tools they know how to use, the better the job they can do. The more words listeners have at their command, the more effective they can be. If your listening vocabulary is limited, so is your ability to learn new and useful things.

Can you define *epitome? regurgitate? calcify?* If you don't know the meaning of words such as these, you might consider spending some time each day expanding your vocabulary. Whenever you hear a word or phrase that is unfamiliar, find out its meaning right away. Then, search for opportunities to use the new word in your conversations during the next several days. Using the unfamiliar word yourself will implant it firmly in your memory so that its meaning will be easily recognized the next time you hear it used.

Apply the Message to Yourself

As an active listener, you must also apply the speaker's message to yourself as you listen. Search your mind for circumstances under which you could use the information you are hearing. Find something in what is being said that arouses your interest.

When you have freely chosen to get involved in some listening situation, you should have no difficulty in applying the message to yourself. If you like surfing, you should find it easy to relate to a speech on Big Sur. Many times, however, you will find yourself in a situation where the subject is not of great interest to you. Your tendency then, as an unwilling participant, may be to escape from listening.

Deciding not to listen in any situation is like betting the speaker will have nothing helpful to say to you. Either way you lose. Why spend your time and not get any personal benefits? Practice searching for ideas that can apply to you and your interests, regardless of the topic. You may be surprised at how many ways you will be able to relate what the speaker is saying to your own needs. Constantly ask yourself questions such as:

- Do I believe what this speaker is saying?
- How can I put this information to use?
- Do I feel differently about this subject than the speaker does?

Pick Out the Central Ideas

Many people, untrained in listening, become fascinated by stories, examples, and statistics and lose sight of the **central idea** a speaker is trying to communicate. Good listeners, on the other hand, who have learned to pick out the key ideas, have less difficulty in understanding what they hear because they know that they should not waste time trying to remember *all* the less important details.

Most well-organized public speeches contain very few main ideas, often no more than two or three. A play usually contains one main plot and perhaps a few subplots. The same is true of literary selections that are read aloud. Therefore, if you begin to look for these main ideas you will have a better understanding of the speaker's primary message. Other facts and details presented by the speaker, instead of confusing the issue, can be used to clarify these central points.

Learning to identify main ideas takes practice. A public speaker often mentions main ideas near the beginning and end of her or his remarks. Thus, when listening to a public speech, pay close attention to the speaker's introduction and conclusion, since there the speech's purpose and main points usually stand out in clear fashion. The rest of the speech may develop these central ideas by giving reasons for them. If you hear the same idea mentioned several times, you can be quite sure the speaker considers it an important point. Listen carefully for words and phrases such as "first," "second," "most important," "to summarize," and "remember." These verbal cues usually indicate an important point is coming next.

One good way to identify main ideas in formal speaking situations is to take notes in outline form. Most speakers organize their message in some way. If you make an effort, you are likely to become very good at recognizing different organizational styles and picking out main points. Outlining will also help you identify the relationships between ideas.

The organization of ideas in conversations tends to be somewhat less logical, mainly because ideas are generally not organized in advance.

Locating the speaker's main ideas in informal communication situations is therefore more difficult. But this problem can be offset by the increased opportunity you have to give feedback to the speaker and to participate in the communication.

When you listen to another person in an informal setting such as a one-to-one conversation, a group discussion, or a meeting, practice restating in your mind what you feel were the main ideas expressed. Then ask the speaker whether you are correct. This is particularly helpful when you are discussing a controversial topic with another person, since it is even more difficult to listen well to someone with whom you disagree. In one-to-one and small group situations it is important to use this opportunity to ask questions during the conversation to insure that you understand the main points being made.

Almost all speakers will appreciate a listener who focuses on the main message they are trying to present rather than on the small details used to illustrate their points. Learning to pick out a speaker's main ideas is one of the most useful listening skills you can acquire.

Provide Feedback

Good listeners encourage the speaker by providing feedback—by actively responding to what they hear. Signs of attention and interest help a speaker present the message in the most effective way possible. Most public speakers, for instance, even prefer frowns and the shaking of heads to blank stares or drowsy eyelids. At least the frowns let a public speaker know the listeners are following what is being said. If the audience makes no response, speakers have no way of judging whether they are speaking successfully.

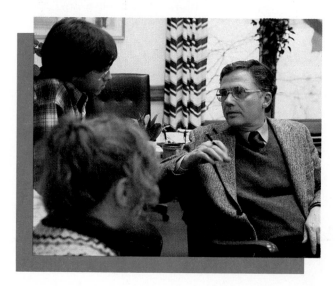

Facial expressions and other nonverbal signals leave no doubt about the attention and interest being generated between these students and their counselor.

It is just as important and much easier to give feedback when the communication situation is less formal. Feedback is extremely valuable in meetings, group discussions, or one-to-one conversations. Remember that when you ask a question, nod your head, or laugh, you are helping the speaker get the message across. Unless speakers know what your reaction is to their words, they cannot tell whether or not they are accomplishing their purposes.

Whenever you listen to any speaker, think about what types of feedback are appropriate. The following list suggests some of the more common ways in which listeners can let the speaker know that they are following the message.

- Look the speaker directly in the eyes much of the time.

- Nod your head slightly to indicate understanding or agreement.

- Frown or shake your head to show you disagree or don't understand.

- Smile or laugh at humorous remarks the speaker makes.

- In informal communications, occasionally interject a word of encouragement such as "Yes," or "I see."

- If seated, maintain an upright, alert posture. Don't slouch in your chair.

- In informal communications, lean forward to show interest in what the speaker is saying.

It is also important that your feedback be clear enough so that the speaker can easily interpret it. In many instances, the feedback you provide as a listener will be nonverbal. Nonverbal signs are very easy to misread. Thus, you must take extra care to insure that you are sending the message you intend through your facial expression, body posture, and eye contact.

Remember What You Hear

If one of the main reasons for learning to be a better listener is to acquire new information, it is important that you be able to remember what you hear.

You receive so many messages each day that you probably have a hard time sorting them out and deciding which ones should be remembered. Think for a moment about how many people spoke to you yesterday. Now, how many of their messages can you remember in detail? Unless you have an exceptional memory, you probably don't remember as many as you would like. It takes a conscious effort to remember what you hear, but it is worthwhile because that is the only way the information you receive will be useful to you.

One of the surest ways to remember something is to have a strong reason to remember it. The famous detective of fiction, Sherlock Holmes, once told his friend Watson that he knew nothing of the solar system. When Watson expressed astonishment that Holmes was unaware that the earth traveled around the sun, Holmes explained that he remembered only what was important to him: "What the deuce is it to me?" he interrupted impatiently. "You say that we go round the sun. If we went round the moon it would not make a pennyworth of difference to me or to my work." Though Holmes seemed a bit extreme in choosing what to forget, he was certainly motivated to remember what was important.

Did you ever notice how attentive everyone in a class becomes when a teacher says, "This will be on the exam"? Of course it's easier to listen closely when you are strongly motivated. When the conversation is boring or the meeting is dull, a good listener must rise to the challenge. There are many occasions when you have to *find* good reasons to remember.

Another way to remember something is to connect new information you are hearing with something you already know. This is called the **process of association.** An example of this process of association would be if a speaker claims that a certain part of the ocean is 15,000 feet (4600 meters) deep. You want to remember that number. If you already know that Mt. Whitney is approximately 15,000 feet (4600 meters) in altitude, you can associate the ocean depth with the height of the mountain. Later, you will likely remember the ocean depth by recalling, "Oh yes, that was about the same as the height of Mt. Whitney."

Application

Being an Active Listener

Five students should leave the room. A member of the class will then tell a story or incident that includes several important details. The students who left earlier will be called back into the classroom *one at a time.* The teacher will then select a student from the class to tell the story to the first one who returns. This student will tell what he or she heard to the next student who reenters the classroom, and so on, until all five have heard the story from the student preceding them into the room. The last student to return will tell the final version of the incident or story to the class.

Take notes in your notebook on how many errors have occurred since the original telling. Participate in a class discussion on how or why these errors in listening took place.

CRITICAL LISTENING AND THINKING

Although picking out main ideas, knowing the definitions of the words being used, and making good use of your memory are important, there is a great deal more you must do to be an effective listener. A good listener must also be able to interpret the sender's message. This can be done by considering factors such as motives, reasoning, and nonverbal communication. The active listener must be a critical listener. A **critical listener** is one who analyzes and interprets messages carefully. Your ability to analyze and interpret a message correctly depends upon how carefully you listen for what is "behind" the speaker's words.

You might remember that in *Alice in Wonderland* "things weren't always what they seemed." The same is often true in real life. It is up to you as a good listener to consider all factors involved in a particular message so that you are in a position to decide on the value and meaning of what you hear.

Listen for Faulty Reasoning

Part of your responsibility as a listener is to analyze what you hear. Listeners who believe everything they are told can get into a lot of trouble. Be especially alert when listening to messages that are meant to persuade you. Be prepared for the speaker who has not constructed an argument using sound reasoning but depends on misleading you.

Thus, in order to make intelligent decisions about the information that comes to you, you need to analyze the speaker's methods. Clever speakers will often seem to be giving you the facts when really they are misleading you with deceptive reasoning. It is important to be alert for false methods of reasoning, which are called **logical fallacies.** Descriptions of a few of the most common fallacies follow.

Name calling is the term used for the faulty reasoning involved when a speaker gives a person or idea a bad label without providing any evidence to prove what is said. When you hear a speaker call someone a criminal, a cheater, or a liar, don't be misled. Make sure the speaker gives good reasons for using such labels.

Card stacking is a method whereby the speaker, instead of presenting all of the important evidence, tells the audience only those facts that support the point she or he is trying to make. The speaker leaves out the bad aspects of the idea and neglects to point out the benefits any alternatives may have.

The **bandwagon technique** gets its name from the fact that the speaker asks the listeners to "jump on the bandwagon," to become part of a supposedly overwhelming group in favor of some person, product, or idea. The speaker tries to convince you that because everyone else is

MEDICAL SECRETARY

The medical secretary, an integral part of the physician's office, is usually the first person whom the patient contacts. The medical secretary acts as a receptionist, takes simple patient histories, transcribes medical records, manages insurance claims, and bills patients. Medical secretaries must be high-school graduates who have studied the secretarial sciences and English. One- and two-year associate degree programs are also available.

Good communications skills are an important part of the medical secretary's role. Despite many distractions, he or she listens carefully as patients relate symptoms or other problems. Active listening involves more than providing a receptive ear, however. The secretary needs to ask pertinent questions so that the nature and severity of a problem can be gauged. He or she also restates information back to the patient to make sure there is complete understanding. Since patients are sometimes frightened or in pain, a secretary needs to convey calm and capable assurance by speaking in even vocal tones and using reassuring nods and gestures. These techniques communicate to patients that their problems are receiving competent attention.

Developing good communications skills enables a genuine understanding of patients and their problems to a medical practice. Thus, physician and patient relationships improve. Medical secretaries who communicate effectively become invaluable members of the health care team by providing an all-important link between patient and doctor.

This medical secretary communicates a sense of caring and competence.

doing something—using a certain shampoo or voting for a particular candidate, for example—you should do it too or you will regret being left out. Television commercials use this approach often. Watch for it!

A **glittering generality** is a word or phrase that is so vague that everyone can agree on its value but no one is really sure exactly what it means. Politicians may say they are in favor of "freedom of speech" or "equal rights." Later, however, you may discover that what they meant by these terms is different from your own interpretation of the words.

A **testimonial** is the opinion of some well-known person on a particular subject. However, the person, although famous, may not be an expert on that subject. Is a movie star really more knowledgeable about dish detergent than anyone else? Whenever you hear a testimonial, make sure that you ask yourself, "Is this person really in a position to know the facts?"

In the fallacy called **begging the question,** speakers never really prove the points they are trying to make. They take it for granted (and sometimes may want you to, also) that their ideas are true without providing proof. Suppose a speaker says, "Juana is the best president our student council ever had. We should reelect her." If no reasons are given for believing Juana to be the best council president ever, the speaker is guilty of begging the question.

The term **non sequitur** is a Latin phrase meaning "It does not follow." A speaker guilty of a *non sequitur* may provide evidence to back up a statement, but if you examine the evidence you will find that it does not really prove the point. Suppose you were to campaign for class president by stating that you were the best candidate and then emphasizing how well you played tennis or how good you were at Chinese cooking; you would be guilty of this kind of faulty reasoning.

A **hasty generalization** occurs when the speaker does not really have enough evidence to support the broad conclusion drawn. Suppose during a recent visit to Denver, Colorado, friends of yours ate at three restaurants. When you ask them about the trip, they tell you Denver restaurants are terrible. Drawing the conclusion that all restaurants in Denver are bad just because the three they ate in were unsatisfactory is not good reasoning. Hasty generalizations are a very common type of faulty reasoning. You can often spot them by listening for telltale words such as "everyone," "always," "never," "all the time," and "nobody."

The fallacies of begging the question, *non sequitur,* and hasty generalization often occur not because speakers are attempting to deceive their audiences but because they have not given enough thought to their arguments. Good listeners, though, will insist on sound reasoning in the messages they hear. It is up to you, as a listener, to detect these common faults and logical fallacies.

Consider the Source

You have probably heard someone who disagreed with what another person had just said react by scowling, "Consider the source!" Such an attack on the speaker instead of his or her words is often unjustified, but the careful listener does need to pay close attention to the motives, biases, backgrounds, and viewpoints of the speakers he or she hears.

Consider, for example, a salesman trying to convince you to buy a new car. Though every feature he points out may be every bit as good as he says, listen for those features he fails to mention. He may be omitting them because he knows the competition is superior regarding those features. Ask him questions about areas where you feel his presentation was unclear. Make him provide you with solid evidence (facts, figures, examples from unbiased sources) that his cars are indeed safer, more economical, and more dependable than the competition's. Remember that, as a salesman, he is naturally going to be blind to certain defects in his own product, and biased against those of the competition. One of his primary motives is to sell cars. That is also his job, and he needs to be good at it. As the listener (customer) your job is to realize that the salesman has some purposes and motives that differ from your own. You need to listen "between the lines"!

Don't get stuck with a lemon. Before investing in a car or an idea, consider your sources of information about it.

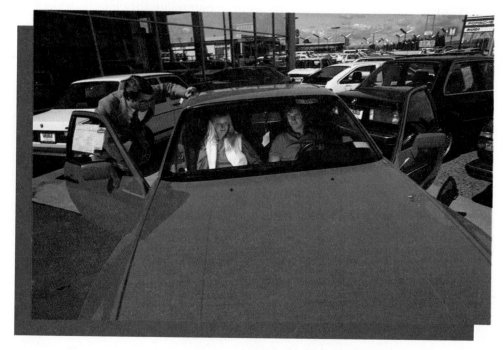

Part of "considering the source" means learning to distinguish between facts and opinions. A fact is that which the speaker proves to you with sound evidence—with examples, statistics, and testimony. An opinion, on the other hand, is just that—something the speaker *thinks* and *says* is a fact, but fails to prove with evidence. One of the chief characteristics of **propaganda** is the stating of opinions as though they were proven facts. Opinions sometimes turn out to be factual, but as a listener you are never in a position to know unless the speaker provides you with the evidence.

Finally, when "considering your sources," be wary of accepting the speaker's message because of his or her status, fame, or position. Well-known, famous, and highly intelligent people make mistakes just as the rest of us do. Judge each message on its own merits. When listening to someone you respect highly, try to separate the speaker from the message. Do the same when listening to someone whom you distrust or dislike. Valid, truthful, and helpful messages can come from those whom you may not hold in high regard.

Recognize Nonverbal Cues

In order to arrive at an accurate interpretation of a message, it is important to focus not only on a speaker's verbal message but also on the speaker's nonverbal communication. Analyzing nonverbal communication can give you important information about the speaker's attitude, emotional state, and motives. You will discover that the nonverbal portion of a message carries considerable impact in projecting the overall meaning.

A good speaker strives to use gestures, facial expressions, and a tone of voice that support and reinforce the verbal message. Sometimes, however, a speaker's verbal and nonverbal messages contradict. A good listener will recognize this and interpret the speaker's meaning by considering both the words and the nonverbal cues. Think for a moment of a parent scolding a small child. Along with a stern look and a serious voice, the child hears, "Johnny, we don't use crayons on the wall!" The words are important, but Johnny may cry as much because of the vocal tones and facial expressions as because of what is said.

Every communication situation combines nonverbal elements with verbal. Even a telephone conversation includes vocal tones, volume, speaking rate, pausing, laughing, and other forms of paralanguage. In Chapter 2 you learned that paralanguage is the *way* something is said rather than the words themselves. Thus it is considered a form of nonverbal communication. If you pay close attention while listening you will discover that the stress a person uses to say different words can make a big difference in the meaning you receive. Imagine having a

Words alone don't tell the whole story. This caller gets her full meaning across by also using pauses, tone of voice, and other forms of paralanguage.

telephone conversation with a classmate about your school's principal. Your friend makes the statement "I think Mrs. Jones is a fair person." If you had received these words in written form, you would not know whether your friend means that, in her opinion, Mrs. Jones is only an "average" person, or whether she means Mrs. Jones treats everyone equally. However, your friend's vocal stress on *fair* makes the meaning immediately obvious. Tone of voice is also important. Through tone a speaker can indicate sarcasm, disgust, anger, or other feelings that cannot be conveyed through words alone.

While paying close attention to the speaker's words, the careful listener must also be alert to the importance of all forms of nonverbal communication. The following list includes some of the elements you should take into account:

- movements
- gestures
- eye contact
- paralanguage (stress, voice tone, speaking rate, pauses, etc.)
- proxemics (how close the speaker is to the listener or listeners)
- body posture

By keeping all the senses tuned in, an active listener will pick up much more than those listeners who attend only to the speaker's words.

Use Feedback to Check Your Interpretation

Have you ever had a good friend ask you "What's the matter?" even though you had not said anything was wrong? Paying attention to nonverbal cues, as you know, is essential in order to understand fully a communicator's message. It is, however, very easy to misinterpret nonverbal communication. In the preceding example, your somber expression and slow movements, which your friend interpreted as an indication that you were unhappy, may have simply been the result of not getting enough sleep. Your friend, expecting to see your usual smiling face and fast walk, may easily have misread the nonverbal signs you were sending.

Although verbal messages create less of a problem, they too can be misinterpreted. If your teacher says, "The exam will be coming up soon," you may not worry because you assume you have another weekend in which to study. When your teacher announces later that day that the exam will be tomorrow, you may be upset. Such problems in communication happen all the time.

In order to avoid these breakdowns in communication it is important to check your understanding and interpretation of the messages you receive. Ask the speaker questions. Restate what you think the speaker has said so that you know whether or not your interpretation is correct. If your sister says, "I'll be back in a little while," you might ask, "Do you expect to be back before noon?" to be sure you understand what she means.

Many problems and misunderstandings can be avoided if you remember your responsibility as an active listener and do not expect the speaker to do all of the work. Remember that listening is an active process and requires that you do your part to improve the communication process.

Application

Identifying Logical Fallacies

Pretend you are trying to help a politician who is running for local office. Role-play a situation in class in which you try to persuade a classmate to vote for your candidate. Use one of the logical fallacies listed in this section of the book. When you have finished ask your classmates to comment on your technique. Are they able to tell which logical fallacy you used?

3 Chapter Review

■ Summary

Listening to speech involves much more than simply hearing. Listening is a learned process that requires a search for understanding and a careful interpretation of the speaker's words. People often fail to recognize the importance of listening, even though it is just as essential to communication as speaking.

Benefits of Learning to Listen Effectively Important benefits flow from improving your listening skills. A good listener avoids misunderstandings, learns many interesting and useful things, and attracts those who enjoy talking to someone who listens. People who work at listening are also more successful in their jobs because they can follow directions and relate easily to other people.

Recognizing Barriers to Listening Recognize barriers to listening, such as distractions and daydreaming, and learn to overcome them by concentrating on the speaker's ideas, suspending your judgments, and keeping an open mind until you have heard all of the facts. In addition, avoid overemphasizing a message's source and listening only to what is easy to understand.

Becoming an Active Listener An active listener does everything possible to bring about effective communication. Get into shape to listen. Research the subject beforehand, arrive on time, well-rested, and ready to listen, and expand your vocabulary in order to improve your listening comprehension. Pick out the speaker's main ideas, relate them to your interests, and provide feedback so that the speaker knows you are receiving the message. Then strive to understand and remember what you hear, so that the information will have value for you.

Interpreting the Message An active listener also listens critically and analyzes the speaker's verbal techniques and logic. The bandwagon technique, card stacking, and testimonials are just a few of the logical fallacies a clever speaker may use to persuade you of something. So a good listener must always "consider the source" of the messages, recognize speakers' motives and viewpoints, learn to distinguish fact from opinion, and judge the validity of messages separately from their sources. Just as a speaker's message is conveyed verbally and nonverbally, the effective listener provides verbal and nonverbal feedback to the speaker to make sure the message is interpreted correctly.

Vocabulary

Define each term in a complete sentence.

listening	process of association	glittering generality
hearing	critical listener	testimonial
distractions	logical fallacies	begging the question
close-minded	name calling	*non sequitur*
open-minded	card stacking	hasty generalization
central idea	bandwagon technique	propaganda

Checklist

Listening Skills

1. Communicate with the speaker by concentrating and making an effort to listen.
2. Give others confidence by showing that you are listening attentively.
3. Keep your mind on the basic message, not on distractions or the speaker's delivery.
4. Keep an open mind to the speaker until you've heard all the information. Remember the merits of other opinions.
5. Be prepared to learn difficult material; listen even when it is not easy to understand.
6. Prepare to listen by arriving early, well-rested, and informed about the topic.
7. Expand your vocabulary so that you will understand what is being discussed.
8. Train yourself to pick out the central ideas. Take notes if helpful.
9. Remember what you hear; use the process of association to improve your memory.
10. Check your understanding of the speaker's message by asking questions and restating ideas.

Review Questions

1. Define *hearing* and then define *listening.*
2. Name the elements that must be added to hearing in order to achieve active listening.
3. Name several things you can accomplish by means of active listening.
4. Name several barriers that may sometimes interfere with effective listening.
5. State what you can do to overcome the barriers you listed in question 4 above.
6. Name three techniques you can use to become a better listener.
7. Name three skills you can use to understand a speaker's message more easily.
8. Name four factors that you must consider in interpreting a speaker's message.
9. Name five logical fallacies used in deceptive reasoning.
10. Name the nonverbal elements that you should consider whenever interpreting a speaker's message.

Discussion Questions

1. As a class, discuss five different jobs that involve critical listening skills. Describe what kind of information would need to be transmitted in each type of job. Discuss the possible consequences of not listening attentively while doing each job.
2. As a class, discuss the types of nonverbal signals that you recognize when your listener: (a) agrees with the message, (b) disagrees with the message, (c) is not interested in the message, and (d) does not understand the message. Which type of feedback are we most likely to respond to? Which are we least likely to respond to? Which nonverbal signals are confusing? Why?
3. Discuss the ways in which you use the process of association to study for tests. How do you memorize information that must be retained for a test? Do you use special tactics to memorize items in sequence (such as the position of the planets or the lines and spaces on a music staff)? Jot down in your notebook any new and helpful ideas you gain from your classmates.

Critical Thinking

1. Analysis In small groups, discuss the types of nonverbal signals that you recognize when your listener: (a) agrees with the message, (b) disagrees with the message, (c) is not interested in the message, and (d) does not understand the message. Which type of feedback are we most likely to respond to? Least likely to respond to? Why? Report your opinions to the rest of the class.

2. Synthesis In small groups, discuss your favorite radio or TV commentator. Explain to your group why you enjoy listening to this person. If the commentator is on TV, explain whether it is also helpful to be able to see him or her. Gather together your group's ideas to share with the class.

Activities

In-Class

1. In small groups, role-play a conversation or personal argument in which each participant gives only one side of an issue and provides a series of reasons to support the position he or she favors. List the logical fallacies that are used by each. Discuss with your group which fallacies were easy to detect and which were difficult.

2. Three or four students will role-play a conversation in which one or more participants exhibit a severe case of close-mindedness. Analyze the communication/thinking patterns of each person. Note any person's failure to process or respond to information that could have opened up solutions or new viewpoints. Your teacher will list these on the board as they are discussed by the class.

3. Listen to a cassette or to a classmate giving an oral presentation on non-fiction material that is theoretical rather than narrative in style. Take notes on the material. Your teacher will give an open-note test on this the material. Did you note the information

that you needed to pass the test? Write a self-evaluation of your note-taking abilities.

4. Check your ability to pick out the main ideas in a message by outlining one of the next in-class speeches. Write down the speaker's main ideas in outline form as you listen. After the speech, compare your listening outline with the speaker's outline. How well did you pick out the main ideas?

Out-of-Class

1. Using old magazines, put together a collage on poster board that illustrates the numerous ways in which logical fallacies appear in advertisements. Share your project by giving an oral report.

2. The next time you have a discussion with relatives or friends, try this: Look them in the eye frequently, nod in understanding or agreement, maintain an alert posture and show a genuine interest in what they are saying. Do you notice any difference in their speaking when you provide positive feedback? If so, what changes can you identify? Make a notebook entry identifying ways to improve communication through the use of positive feedback.

3. Watch a television talk show. Evaluate the listening of each participant. Note nonverbal signals that indicate whether good listening is or is not occurring. Is there any misunderstanding that occurs in the conversation? Are there any obvious distractions? Does the host share time with the guests or dominate the conversation?

4. Listen on the radio to a number of disc jockeys from different types of programs: rock, country-western, easy listening, classical, etc. Analyze the different styles of communication that you hear. What image is each projecting? Write your findings as a notebook entry. Be prepared to discuss your analysis in class.

5. The next time you plan to attend a movie, a speech, a play, or watch a special television show, practice the following techniques for preparing to listen. Discover as much as you can about the speech topic, play script, or program in advance. Find out what you can about the speaker or actors. Arrive early and choose a good seat. Bring with you a strong determination to listen well. Observe the extent to which such preparation enhances your participation in the event.

6. Practice the following technique to remember the first names of the next five people to whom you are introduced. As you meet each one, concentrate on the person's name by repeating it to yourself immediately after hearing it. Several moments later, and again at the end of your conversation, intentionally use the name aloud in your conversation with the person. Does this technique help plant a person's name in your mind? Does using the person's name during conversation affect his or her response to you?

Chapter Project

Join one of four groups in your class. Each group will write and enact a 10-minute television segment that portrays the importance of listening skills. Each segment should include both a "feature" and commercials. Group I will use a "serial" format. Group II will use a talk-show format. Group III will use a children's-show format. Group IV will use a newscast format, including an editorial commentary.

Each group's project should reflect the major points emphasized in this chapter: benefits of effective listening, barriers to listening, strategies to promote active listening, ways to achieve better understanding through improved listening, methods of improving analysis and interpretation of messages.

At the end of each group's presentation, the class will analyze the content, evaluating the level of success of the production.

Interpersonal and Group Communication

unit 2

4 One-to-One Communication

5 Group Discussion

4 One-to-One Communication

**When you have completed this chapter
you should be able to:**

- Describe several factors involved in becoming an effective communicator.

- Identify and explain the important nonverbal aspects of one-to-one communication.

- Describe and practice effective use of the telephone in social and business situations.

- Identify at least three important factors to consider when you are being interviewed for a job.

Attentive and expressive communication is the key to every satisfying conversation, whether serious or humorous.

In Chapter 1 you were asked to list the various kinds of communication events in which you participated during a single day. Chances are good that your list was fairly lengthy and included many different kinds of communication situations. Which events from that list occupied most of your communication time? If you're like most people, the forms of one-to-one communication accounted for the majority of your time that day and most other days as well.

One-to-one communication plays a very important part in almost everyone's life. It occurs most often in face-to-face conversations, and in telephone calls and interviews. Speaking with just one other person demands speech skills that differ from those needed for other types of communication. These special skills are the subject of this chapter.

THE VERBAL ASPECTS OF CONVERSATION

Face-to-face conversation, as you have already discovered, is the most common form of one-to-one communication. **Conversation** consists of talk about various matters of common interest to both of the people involved. There is often no single goal or topic. Conversations, unlike many other types of communication, are usually not planned or rehearsed beforehand. But good conversation requires adherence to a few rules, which you should be aware of if you wish to be an interesting person to talk with.

A problem with a homework assignment can be resolved when both the student and teacher send and receive their messages accurately and courteously.

Send and Receive Messages Accurately

As in all types of communication, an important aspect of conversation is accuracy—the accurate sending and receiving of messages. Careful thought in advance about what you will say and how you will say it is not possible with unplanned conversations. But, on the other hand, having only one receiver makes it possible for you to adapt your words and topics to that particular person as you speak.

Choose words you are sure your receiver will understand. Your choices should largely depend on who your listener is. Your listener's age and experience must be considered, as well as the particular communication situation. You would not use technical words in describing automobile engines to someone not familiar with them, for example. Rather, you would explain what you mean in simple words, adding definitions for any technical terms you found necessary to include.

Close attention to the feedback you receive can help you make sure the listener understands you. If your listener looks puzzled, unhappy, or displeased, perhaps you will need to clarify your meaning.

You can rephrase an idea in a different way if your listener doesn't seem to understand what you mean. Giving an example or story as an illustration of what you mean is another way to clarify your message. Merely repeating what you have already said seldom helps to make your meaning clear.

Sometimes a speaker presents ideas too rapidly for another person to follow. Don't assume that your listener will understand your reasoning. Present your ideas in a logical, step-by-step way so that the other person will see how you reached your conclusions.

Listen carefully during conversation. Listening helps assure your understanding of the speaker's ideas. Concentrate on the ideas you are hearing and learn as much as you can. Remember that listening makes up one half of the communication process.

Nothing is more difficult for a speaker during a two-person conversation than having to speak to someone who does not seem to be listening. Provide supportive feedback while listening. Look interested in what the other person is saying. Smile, frown, or nod at appropriate times. Ask questions to clarify points of which you are not sure. It is by your feedback that you show your interest and understanding.

Be Courteous

Good conversation involves taking turns. Some of the most unsatisfactory conversations are those in which one party talks like a jackhammer and the other person simply sits there and takes a pounding. Of course, no one wants to have a conversation in which each person's speaking time is clocked with a stopwatch. But unless each speaker is willing to yield the floor regularly to the other, what starts out to be a conversation soon turns into a public speech with an audience of one. You have probably had conversations with people about whom you later thought: "Talking with him sure involves taking turns. He takes *all* the turns!"

Avoid interrupting to express an idea of your own while the other person is speaking. If what you have to say is valuable, it can wait until it is your turn to speak. Be careful, too, not to interrupt your listening to plan your next comment as long as the other person continues to speak. You may miss an important point he or she is making, and your inattention will eventually become apparent.

It is much easier for people to accept criticism about a situation than about themselves. When disagreeing with someone, avoid verbally attacking that person's character or motives. Unlike a letter that can be destroyed before it's mailed, words, once they have been spoken, cannot be unsaid. Try to explain how you feel about the issue calmly and logically without hurting the other person's feelings. Emotional outbursts of anger rarely lead to improved relationships between people.

Try to be open-minded. People often change their opinions after receiving new information. Even if you still disagree after hearing different ideas, show respect for the other person's point of view. That person, in turn, will then be more likely to give your ideas a fair hearing since he or she has already been shown the same courtesy.

Be Able to Speak on a Number of Topics

Conversation deals with topics of interest to both people involved. In order to carry on stimulating conversations you should try to develop a variety of interests. More people will seek your company if you can converse on a wide range of topics intelligently. Sports, music, politics, current events, fashion, communication, hobbies, school, and energy conservation are all possibilities. If, on the other hand, you are viewed as someone who only talks about your hobby or favorite sport, you will soon find yourself having fewer and fewer conversations.

When you change the subject during a conversation, use words or phrases to relate the new topic to the previous one. In this way your conversation will flow smoothly. Jumping from one unrelated topic to another without discussing any one of them thoroughly makes conversations less meaningful.

Of course, good conversation does not deal only with topics of interest to you. It deals with topics of interest to the other person as well. In conversations with friends, you should regularly attempt to bring up subjects you know the other person finds fascinating, even though these may not be your favorites. With new acquaintances, search for topics of common interest. When the other person brings up a subject that is new to you, listen carefully. Good conversation can be one of the most pleasant ways of learning about new ideas. No one likes conversationalists who constantly talk about *I* topics—topics that relate only to themselves and their interests. Neither do most people enjoy a steady flow of one-upmanship or put-downs. The person who constantly tries to "top" the other's remark, or who frequently makes mean remarks, even in fun, is not long appreciated.

Learn to Enjoy Conversation

Good conversation is an art you can develop. During periods when you are the speaker, speak dynamically and enthusiastically. No one likes to listen to someone who converses in a flat, dull monotone with a deadpan face and no gestures of any kind. To develop the art of conversation, let your enthusiasm for your topic show in your voice and body movements.

Try to make the conversation interesting and pleasant for everyone involved. Avoid talking too much about yourself. Using pet phrases and exclamations too often also makes conversation less interesting. Choose good standard language forms that will make your message clear and lively. Illustrate your ideas with stories your listeners will find relevant and fascinating.

Finally, learn to enjoy face-to-face conversation. You will find that it can provide one of life's most pleasant means of both teaching and learning. In addition, friendships can be established and deepened through good conversation. For those who take the trouble to develop it as an art, it can provide an enjoyable form of recreation and relaxation.

Application

Practicing Clarity in Conversation

The class should form into teams of two. One student should explain something that is of particular interest to him or her. This explanation might be about a hobby, a sport, a game, or the workings of a particular machine. Watch for feedback from your partner. Does he or she understand your explanation? Now reverse roles. You listen to your partner's explanation and then provide feedback. Do you both feel that you have learned something? Record in your notebook what you spoke about, what feedback you received, and what communication problems occurred, if any.

THE NONVERBAL ASPECTS OF CONVERSATION

Most forms of one-to-one communication rely heavily on the nonverbal means of communication. As you read in Chapter 2, researchers agree that in face-to-face communication over half of the meaning is carried by nonverbal signals. Even in telephone conversations, much of the message is transmitted through vocal tones, pauses, and sounds that are not words. Imagine how dull a face-to-face conversation with one of your friends would be if your friend stood at attention while speaking, looked straight ahead, never moved a muscle, and spoke in the monotone voice of a robot. Nonverbal communication—body movement, timing, eye contact, and vocal variety—add feeling and life to the words in a message.

Although nonverbal forms of communication account for a large proportion of meaning, they cannot convey as specific a message as words do. If someone smiles at you, you are likely to react in a generally positive way, but you may not be certain whether the smile means friendliness, agreement, understanding, or respect.

While nonverbal communication is not as specific in meaning as verbal communication, it often makes a deeper and longer-lasting impression. Review in your mind the last five times you were introduced to new acquaintances. Your first impressions were probably based largely

Amid the roar of jet engines, directing plane traffic on the ground would be an exercise in futility without nonverbal signals.

on such matters as the amount of enthusiasm shown, the facial expressions used, the ways in which the persons moved and gestured as they spoke, and the warmth of their smiles. If you are like most people, you have remembered those nonverbal signals better than what the people said.

Sometimes nonverbal communication acts as a substitute for language. This usually occurs in situations where words would be impractical or too time consuming. A jet pilot, for example, relies on the ground crew's hand signals to park a roaring plane.

More often, however, nonverbal communication occurs together with language as an aid to total communication. Nodding one's head while saying "Yes, I'll go with you" can strengthen that "Yes." The tone of your voice may deepen the impression that you're angry. Keeping these general principles about nonverbal communication in mind, look now at some specific types of nonverbal communication in one-to-one communication situations.

Using Body Motion (Kinesics)

If you have ever seen a good pantomimist perform, you know how much can be communicated through body motion, or kinesics. Marcel Marceau or Red Skelton can create a mood or tell a story simply through body movement, gesture, and facial expression. Most people similarly pantomime a bit in their everyday conversation.

What kinds of kinesic communication do people regularly use? One of the most powerful tools of nonverbal communication is found in the eyes. Strong messages about your feelings and attitudes are conveyed by how you look at another when speaking, how frequently you look, and how long you gaze into another's eyes. In the American culture, such people as employers and parents seem to expect great amounts of eye contact from a listener. They appear to want the other person in face-to-face communication to look them in the eyes regularly. However, when speaking, the person in authority often does not provide steady or regular eye contact to the listener. There is one predictable moment, though, when both parties are likely to establish eye contact. This is when either is about to finish speaking and yield the floor to the other. Eye contact at this point appears to serve as the major signal that the person is about to finish speaking.

When conversing with another—even someone in authority—it is important to avoid the extremes of too much or too little eye contact. Not looking at the speaker frequently enough may be taken as a sign of lack of interest. Looking too much at the other party may distract the person. Research has shown that in two-person conversations, speakers gaze at their listeners an average of 38 to 41 percent of the total conversation time. Listeners look at speakers about 62 to 75 percent of the total time.

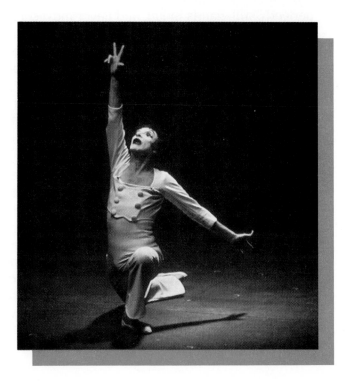

Using his body's "voice" alone, pantomimist Marcel Marceau communicates without a sound.

An unwillingness to look an interviewer in the eyes, for example, will probably leave a very negative impression, even though the interviewee's answers may be excellent.

Your eyes may be a most effective means of body-motion communication, but they have their greatest impact when viewed as part of a larger tool of nonverbal expression—the face. Your facial muscles can be arranged in an almost infinite variety of positions to express a wide range of emotions. They can also show the degree of interest you have in a conversation, and even give certain information about your personality. Though your face is capable of displaying a blend of different emotions, at any one time you are more likely to show single emotions such as anger, sadness, fear, surprise, happiness, or disgust with the greatest accuracy. It is important for you to be aware of your expressions and the messages they continually communicate to others.

Another widely used form of body-motion communication in two-person interaction consists of arm-hand movements. You can use your arms and hands to describe, locate, emphasize, and symbolize. Of course, some people "talk" more with their hands and arms than others. You probably have seen any number of persons making arm-hand gestures when talking on the phone. Holding some people's arms would make it nearly impossible for them to speak.

As with any form of communication, however, extremes in using arm-hand movements should be avoided. The interviewee who sits perfectly still, hands in lap, and never moves a muscle during a half-hour interview is likely to be seen as lacking in dynamism and drive. On the other hand, the conversationalist whose arms are continually waving about with the velocity of a windmill may distract the listener's attention from the basic verbal message. Arm and hand movements should grow out of a natural urge to complete the total communication process. They should never be forced, but instead reflect the real communication goals of the person using them.

Using Space (Proxemics)

In Chapter 2 you read about how much closer two friends will sit when talking than two strangers will. This is just one way in which people use space to communicate nonverbally. The study of spatial communication, or proxemics, can tell you a great deal about a level of communication that is often carried on subconsciously in two-person communication. It seems that all people leave an invisible territory around them that they consider their own private domain. Whom you allow to invade your territory, how closely, and for how long, says much about your feelings and reactions towards others.

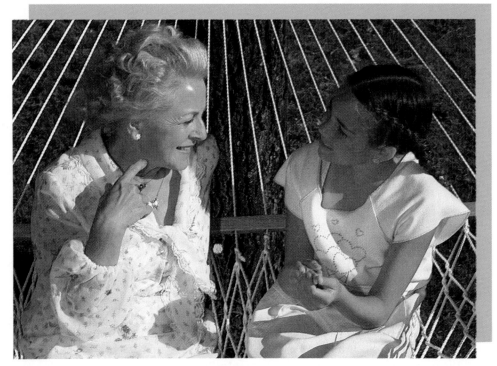

Emotional closeness is often expressed spatially, although spatial "comfort zones" vary according to custom and individual preference.

Family members or close friends generally allow close proximity when talking. Allowing another to sit close enough to touch you and being relaxed about it says to the other person "I like you, I trust you, I am willing to take you into my close confidence." On the other hand, sitting too close during a business interview or while talking with a new acquaintance may cause problems. Giving the other person too little breathing room may make that person feel uncomfortable. Americans like to reserve close distances for those they know well. Chapter 2 discussed basic distances, used in various communication situations.

You have probably met some people who regularly invade your space. A new acquaintance may stand so close while talking that your noses nearly touch. A student may take the seat right next to yours at the library study table when many other seats are available. These are usually unintentional instances of bothersome communication, but they can be annoying nevertheless. When such space invasion occurs, many people back away, turn their backs slightly to a seated invader, or lay their forearms on the table as a barrier to the intruder. While these signals may seem readily understandable to everyone—a kind of universal language—such is not the case.

Spatial miscommunication

Edward T. Hall, who has studied the different uses that people from various cultures make of space, reported many incidents in which diplomats from other countries repeatedly approached too close for the comfort of Americans. Every time a foreign diplomat got too close, the American backed up a step. The other, thinking the American was losing interest in their conversation, approached again. In a short time they often found themselves at the other end of the room. The foreigner had "chased" the American across the room without either being conscious of it. Since moving in too closely often causes embarrassment, it usually hinders communication. Watch your use of space so you don't make others uncomfortable. If others invade your space, realize that it is probably unintentional.

Using Time

Have you ever considered what an enormous impact time has on your life? You eat at certain times. You sleep for certain lengths of time. You often ask what time it is. You clock your life through birthdays and anniversaries. Time also has a great impact on communication.

Suppose one of your classmates says, "Did you hear? John just spent an hour and a half in the principal's office!" You know immediately John and the principal were not just chatting about the weather. The length of their conversation tells you their business must have been significant. Suppose one of your teachers announces "This test will only take five minutes." You can assume that the test you are about to take won't cover the entire book.

Executives frequently use time to tell visitors how highly they regard them and their visit. Those whose prestige is not great or whose business is not considered pressing may "cool their heels" in the outer office while the executive finishes up a few other matters. Allowing frequent interruptions such as telephone calls during a conversation may also make the other person feel less important.

Using Appearance

Appearance also acts as a nonverbal form of communication in two-person communication. One of the chief reasons businesspeople hold job interviews is their desire to see what kind of appearance a person makes before deciding to hire her or him. People are inclined to make snap judgments about others the first time they meet based largely on personal appearance. Hair style, clothing, height, weight, neatness — all communicate something about you, whether you like it or not. The visual image you present influences others' interpretation of your personality, your character, your intelligence, and your likeability. Sometimes these first impressions can be totally incorrect, but once made, they are very hard to erase.

You need not constantly go about looking as if you had just stepped out of a fashion magazine. Rather, the key ingredients for a favorable appearance are being neat and well-groomed. They are particularly essential for a good interview. If you are clean and carefully dressed, you will make a good first impression. At all times you will find these two things can have a marked influence on the opinions of others.

Using Paralanguage

Paralanguage refers to forms of communication connected with vocal sounds. It concerns how words are produced vocally, but does not include the words themselves. Suppose, for example, you scream at someone with whom you are angry "I've told you not to do that!" Your voice volume, the high pitch (tone) of your voice, and your rapid rate of speaking are all part of your paralanguage. These vocal characteristics communicate anger more clearly than do the words themselves. On the other hand, suppose you calmly answer a simple question. Your vocal cues are quite different. You use a lower volume, a lower pitch, and a slower rate. Again your calm attitude is conveyed less by what you say than by how you say it.

A common problem for many people during one-to-one communication is the habit of frequently inserting vocalized pauses into their speech. A **vocalized pause** consists of filling the spaces between words with non-meaningful sounds, such as "uh," "er," "like," or "you know." A certain number of vocalized pauses are acceptable, since they occur naturally in nearly everyone's speech. If they occur regularly and frequently, however, they are likely to make a negative impression on the listener. They can lead the listener to perceive the speaker as insecure, unsure of the information, possibly deceitful, or even stupid. Vocalized pausing is usually just a bad habit. Once a speaker is aware of it, such pausing can be cured with patience and concentration.

As you can see, paralanguage can be very important in one-to-one communication. It enables a listener to reach conclusions such as "He's tired," or "She's angry," or "She's kidding." Paying close attention to the type of information paralanguage conveys can make the difference between successful or unsuccessful communication.

Application

Discussing Aspects of Conversation

With a partner, role-play several face-to-face conversations. Vary the setting in which the conversation takes place. Settings might include a supermarket, a home, a bank, a classroom, or a bus. The situation might involve strangers, family members, friends, or teachers. After each role-play, the class will discuss the appropriateness and effectiveness of word choice, feedback, body movement, use of space, and other verbal and nonverbal techniques used in the conversation.

SPEAKING ON THE TELEPHONE

The telephone is a marvelous aid to human communication. Until such time as picturephones or some other new form of visual technology comes into widespread use, however, people must continue to rely totally on their voices when communicating over the phone. This means that telephone conversations are often more difficult than face-to-face conversations. Thus, a special effort is called for in order to make telephone conversation efficient, courteous, and pleasant.

Follow Conversational Rules for Social Calls

The telephone is very useful for extending invitations, deepening friendships, correcting misunderstandings, or simply enjoying good conversation. The telephone is especially valuable when distance makes face-to-face conversation impractical. For these purposes efficiency is

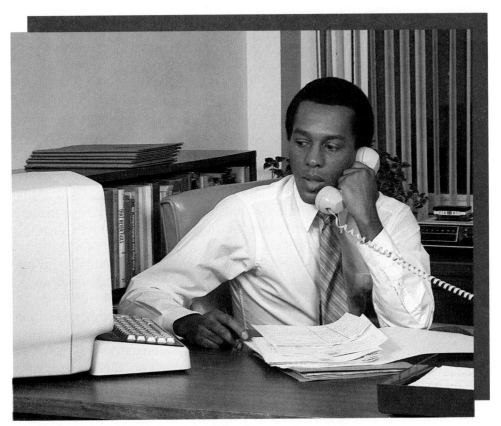

The etiquette for social calls is different from that of business calls. For both, however, ask if you are calling at a convenient time.

somewhat less important than courtesy and friendliness. Most of the rules for face-to-face conversations also apply to telephone conversations as well.

When you are the caller, you are disturbing the privacy of another person's home. Thus, you should make social calls at times when you are least likely to disturb the family or individual. Early in the morning, late at night, or at mealtimes are generally poor times to call.

Always identify yourself as soon as someone answers. Give your name first and then ask to speak to the person you are calling. When someone answers the phone, say, for example, "Hello. This is Joe Lincoln. May I please speak with Maria?"

When the person with whom you wish to talk reaches the phone, introduce yourself again. If the purpose of your call is to extend an invitation or correct a misunderstanding, you will want to make some brief opening comments before proceeding with your main purpose for calling. If you called simply to visit, use a more relaxed approach.

Avoid tying up the line for long periods of time. Others may be expecting a call or wish to make a call of their own. If you are the caller you are responsible for bringing the conversation to a close. Always be sensitive and avoid extending the conversation too long.

Follow More Formal Rules for Business Calls

Business calls are made for specific purposes. They may be made to give or receive information, to sell or buy a product or service, to make appointments, or to resolve problems. When making business calls, efficiency is of great importance. All businesses exist in order to make a profit. Wasting time on the telephone during business hours involves greater expense and less profit.

One way to increase efficiency is to be sure of the number you are calling. If you are not sure of the number, look it up. Another way to be efficient is to be prepared. Have any materials you intend to refer to or relay to your party at hand before placing your call. Also have writing materials ready to write down any information you may receive.

As soon as you reach the number, identify yourself, then ask for your party. Make a brief opening statement of courtesy, then relate your business immediately. Speak directly into the mouthpiece using a conversational volume. Don't forget that your vocal tones, rate, and articulation all play a part in conveying your message.

TAKING PART IN AN INTERVIEW

There are many different kinds of interviews. When interviews are mentioned, most people are likely to think first of the face-to-face communication held when someone is seeking employment—the job interview. But workers are interviewed periodically after they have been on the job for awhile. People with problems are interviewed by psychological counselors. Government officials are interviewed by news reporters seeking information. Couples are interviewed by members of the clergy before getting married. Students are interviewed by guidance counselors, teachers, and sometimes principals about their schedules, grades, or behavior. People applying for admission to a vocational school or college are usually interviewed before they are accepted. At some time in your life you will certainly take part in a face-to-face interview.

Unlike conversation, an **interview** is a more formal kind of communication event with a particular and definite goal in mind. An interview may last a few minutes or may continue for several days, but it is ordinarily planned in advance and directed toward a definite outcome.

Being Interviewed

Interviews are held with people seeking all kinds of jobs. These include positions in private industry, in government service, in schools, and in professional offices such as those of lawyers and doctors. Since many of the principles involved in job interviews are typical of other forms of interviewing, and since practically everyone engages in a job interview at least once in his or her life, emphasis here will be given to this type of interview.

Prepare Thoroughly   If you are seeking employment, you are the **interviewee.** A good job interview demands three things of the interviewee: thorough preparation, active participation, and good follow-up. Thorough preparation includes finding out all you can about the organization, the job, and the interviewer beforehand. It means preparing answers to the types of questions you can expect to be asked. It means readying questions of your own to ask the interviewer about aspects of the job and organization that interest you or may be unclear to you.

Some form of correspondence often takes place before a job interview. In this correspondence, ask for any brochures or other written information about the company. Read it carefully when it arrives. Educate yourself about the firm's history, its products or services, and its size. Try to discover who will conduct your interview and his or her name beforehand.

Though there are frequently unexpected questions during an interview, most job interviewers ask a number of similar questions. Here are some you should prepare answers to beforehand:

- Why do you want to work for this company?

- What experience have you had that prepares you for this position?

- What kind of grades did you receive in school? (Or what grades have you earned thus far in school?)

- What would you expect as a starting salary?

- If you are hired for this job, how long would you expect to stay with this company?

- What are your long-range career goals? (Or what do you expect to be doing five years from now?)

- What hobbies or outside interests do you have?

- How much do you know about this firm?

- What do you feel are your major strengths for this job?

Laws have been passed to insure equal treatment for all people applying for jobs. Because of these laws, you will probably not be asked any questions about your national origin, race, sex, religion, or marital status. Physical and mental handicaps usually are discussed only if they might relate to the performance or the duties of the job. Age can be discussed only if the interviewee is a minor or over seventy. If you should be asked questions you feel are improper, politely refuse to answer them.

A good interviewer will give you the opportunity to ask questions during an interview. Actually, your ability to ask intelligent questions will probably make a more positive impression on the interviewer than your answers to the interviewer's own questions. If it appears that the interviewer is about to close the interview without giving you such an opportunity, ask for it. Here are sample questions of the type you may wish to ask:

- What would my specific duties be?

- Can you tell me a little bit about the people with whom I would be working directly, including my immediate superior?

- What kinds of fringe benefits accompany this position?

- At what salary would I start? (Ask this late in the interview if it has not already come up.)

- What is the likelihood I would be asked to move to another town to keep my job or get a promotion? Would the company pay moving expenses?

Several of these questions apply mainly to an interview for a full-time position after graduation. However, even during brief interviews for summer employment, you will want to ask questions about duties, hours, fringe benefits, and wages. Don't be timid about such matters. You have a right to know about them before you accept a job, and your expectations will align more closely with the realities of the job.

Be an Active Participant   Your skill at verbal and nonverbal communication probably creates the single most important impression during an interview. The following suggestions will help to make that impression a favorable one.

Be on time for the interview. Several minutes early is perfectly acceptable. Five minutes late could spell disaster.

Be certain your appearance is neat, clean, and generally conservative. Good grooming applies to any job interview, even if the job itself requires work clothes and getting dirty. Sit in a relaxed manner, but do not slouch. You want to appear alert, but not overly tense. Do not fidget in your seat.

Answer the interviewer's questions completely, but do not ramble. Once you have answered a question fully, stop. At the other extreme, avoid single-word answers, such as "Yes" or "No." The interviewer wants to hear you talk. Do not try to bluff. If you do not understand a question, ask the interviewer to explain it. If you do not know the answer to a question, say so. If you are a "C" student, don't claim to be a "B" student.

Emphasize any of your past experiences that show you have been in a position of responsibility or leadership, no matter how insignificant they may seem. If you were class president in school, for example, mention it. If you have been a summer-camp counselor, mention that.

Speak in a voice that can be easily heard, but that is not too loud for the size of the room. Speak clearly. Show enthusiasm through your voice by varying volume, pitch, and rate of speaking.

Listen carefully to everything the interviewer says. Be sure to maintain regular eye contact with the interviewer as you listen. Keep a pleasant, interested expression on your face during the interview. You will make the best impression if you seem to be enjoying the interview and the challenge it provides.

An interviewee can make a positive impression by preparing answers ahead of time to questions that are likely to be asked.

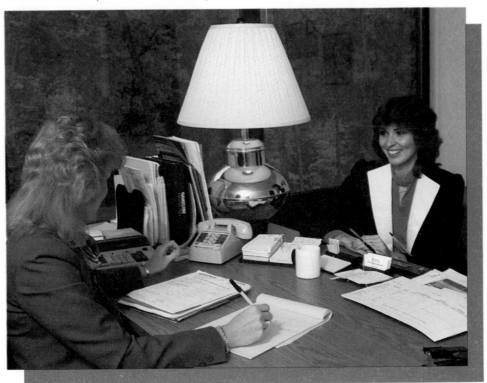

Career Close-up

TRAVEL AGENT

While travel agents need many complex abilities in order to unravel the maze of international travel for their clients, superior communication skills are their most valuable attribute. A high school diploma is the minimum requirement for employment, but most agencies prefer candidates who have had 2-4 years of college, including courses in foreign languages, English, and public speaking.

Travel agents will not survive in this competitive industry without the ability to relate well to clients. Since most of their business is conducted by telephone, agents must master this difficult form of one-to-one communication. As a result, they often need to rely on their voices alone to convey the helpful enthusiasm they want to project. With the skillful use of vocal tones, pauses, and other sounds to supplement their speech, telephone communication becomes more powerful.

Effective travel agents make a client feel special by listening carefully during conversations and responding to each concern. Because travel details are often complicated, agents strive to present information logically. They repeat information back to the client when necessary and listen for feedback that indicates understanding or a need for more information.

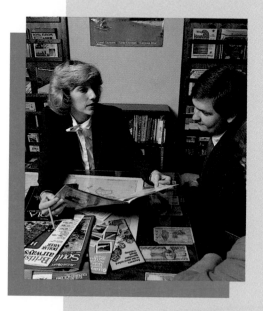

Successful travel agents develop a large clientele because they make the effort to practice skillfully the art of one-to-one communication. Although many agents try to be attentive, their clients will not perceive them as caring unless they dynamically communicate this attention through every telephone and personal contact.

Responsive communication is a hallmark of the travel agent.

Follow Up   If you are not offered a job at the close of the interview, correct follow-up may determine whether you will get it later. This generally consists of mailing a business letter to the interviewer the next day. In the letter, thank the person for the opportunity of being interviewed and enclose your résumé if you have not previously presented it. A **résumé** is a neatly typed summary giving your name, address, education, and previous work experience. Close the letter by offering to send any additional information the interviewer may want about you. Emphasize the fact that you hope to hear from the interviewer as soon as possible.

If you are offered the job during the interview, write a letter thanking the interviewer. Express your intention to do the job well.

Conducting an Interview

The interview is often a source of information. Businesspeople, government officials, and news reporters use interviews to gather material. Students conduct interviews when preparing material for reports or speeches. Suppose you need information about accidents involving bicycles for a report you plan on bicycle safety. Interviewing a local police officer about bicycle accidents would be a possible source of information for that topic. Experts in many fields are generally available in every community.

There is one main difference between being an interviewee and being an interviewer. The interviewer must manage the interview.

Prepare Thoroughly   After deciding what information you need, choose the person you wish to interview. Preferably, choose the best available expert on the subject. For example, if you need information about city government, and the mayor is unavailable because of a busy schedule, try contacting a member of the city council or someone working for a city agency who might be able to help you. A citizen involved in city affairs could also prove to be a good source of information.

Once you have located someone to consult, make an appointment for the interview. Be courteous. Tell the person why you wish an interview. Arrange a time and place convenient for the interviewee. Be sure to thank the person before concluding your conversation. Be polite even if the person refuses to grant you an interview.

Next you will need to study material available on your topic. An informed interviewer always does a better job. Also study any background information you can find about the person to be interviewed. Know all you can about the subject and the person with whom you will be speaking. Thorough research is the foundation of a good interview.

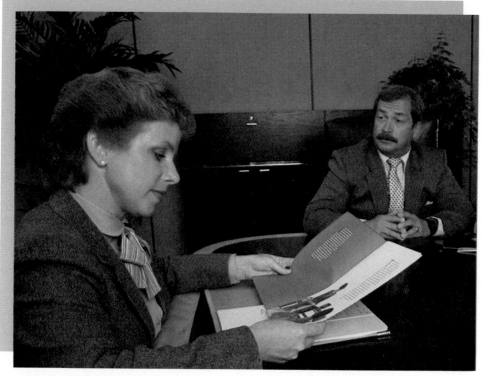

A successful interviewer must be alert to nonverbal messages and not get lost in pages of interview questions.

Finally, make a list of questions to ask during the interview. Remember that your interviewee's time is valuable. Do not plan to ask questions that could easily be answered by consulting books, public records, or other sources. Avoid questions that can be answered with only a yes or no.

Manage the Interview Carefully As the person conducting the interview, you are responsible for managing it well. Make sure your appearance will make a good impression. Arrive promptly. Greet your interviewee with a firm handshake and express your pleasure at being able to talk with him or her.

Start the interview by explaining its purpose. Try to make the interviewee relaxed and comfortable. People are more likely to speak freely if they feel at ease. Do not follow your list of questions too closely. Perhaps your interviewee will say something that will suggest questions you had not considered in advance. Go ahead and ask them. Without straying too far from the subject, encourage the interviewee to express his or her views fully. Perhaps the interviewee will want to ask you some questions. Constantly be aware of the nonverbal aspects of your interview. Maintain frequent eye contact. Smile frequently and show your interest. Give encouragement by nodding. Sit close enough to converse easily.

Using a tape recorder during the interview will assure that the information you gather will be accurate. Be sure, however, to ask permission of the interviewee before using a tape recorder. Once you have permission to use it, test the recorder to be sure it is working properly and place it so that the recording will be clear. If the interviewee refuses to allow you to use a tape recorder or is made uncomfortable by its presence, don't use it.

If you are unable to use a tape recorder, take notes of important points. Try to do this without interrupting the flow of conversation. You may wish to record several quotations to be included in your report. It would be a good idea to repeat these to the interviewee to be sure the quotation is exact.

End the interview when you have the information you need. If you notice that the other person is tired or anxious to get on with other matters, try to conclude quickly. Do not overstay your welcome. Conclude by expressing your thanks. Tell the interviewee how helpful he or she has been.

Follow Up   People like to know they have helped others. Follow up by sharing the outcome of your interview with the interviewee. You may send the person a copy of your report or speech. Include a letter thanking the interviewee again for the help you were given.

Write a letter even if a copy of the material using the interview is not available. Perhaps you can explain how you used the interview in your presentation. You may include favorable reactions from your readers or listeners. Remember to express your thanks before concluding.

Application

Discussing Interview Experiences

Ask an older person whom you know—a family member, a relative, a neighbor, or a friend—about any interviewing experiences he or she may have had. What was the purpose of the interview? How did the person prepare for the interview? Where did the interview take place? What were some of the questions that the interviewer asked? How did the person respond? Share your findings with your classmates in a small group discussion.

4 Chapter Review

■ Summary

One-to-one communication accounts for much of our daily communication. Most of us spend more time engaged in face-to-face conversation than in the other forms of speaking. While we take one-to-one conversation pretty much for granted, it involves certain special characteristics and rules.

The Verbal Aspects of Conversation Good conversation demands accuracy, courtesy, and a genuine interest in a range of topics. You should also learn to enjoy the art of conversation. The checklist can help you evaluate the effectiveness of your own conversational style.

The Nonverbal Aspects of Conversation Most forms of one-to-one communication rely heavily on the nonverbal channels. Sometimes nonverbal signals substitute for words. More often they occur together with spoken language to complement, emphasize, and sometimes contradict what is being said.

Body motion is very important in one-to-one communication. Eye contact can signal when a speaker is about to yield the floor to the listener. Too little eye contact can indicate a lack of interest. Too much can be distracting. People also use space during two-person conversations to signal greater or lesser degrees of intimacy. Being on time for meetings or interviews, giving sufficient time to conversations, and not allowing frequent interruptions during a discussion all speak clearly of your attitudes towards others. Neatness of appearance can often be a deciding factor in the outcome of a job interview. Finally, your speaking rate, voice pitch, volume, and vocalized pauses may sometimes make a greater impact than your words themselves.

Speaking on the Telephone Telephone conversation depends on the voice alone to convey the message. Whether using the telephone for social or business conversation, you must remember the importance of efficiency, courtesy, and friendliness.

Taking Part in an Interview Though there are many types of interviews, the job interview is the kind most commonly encountered. Being interviewed for a job demands careful preparation, active participation, and good follow-up. Conducting an interview also requires all of these things as well as careful management.

 ## Vocabulary

Define each term in a complete sentence.

one-to-one communication
conversation
vocalized pause

interview
interviewee
résumé

 ## Checklist

One-to-One Communication Skills

1. Choose words you are sure your receiver will understand.
2. Pay close attention to the feedback you receive in one-to-one communication.
3. Present your ideas in logical steps so that your receiver will be able to see clearly how you reached your conclusion.
4. Be a careful listener when you are conversing. Concentrate on what the other person is saying, and provide supportive feedback.
5. Be aware that good conversation involves taking turns. At the same time, show respect for the other person's point of view whether or not you agree with him or her.
6. Use body motion when conversing, but avoid making exaggerated gestures.
7. Be aware of the importance of space when conversing. Adapt yourself to the person to whom you are speaking by maintaining an appropriate distance.
8. Be punctual for appointments.
9. Be neat and well-groomed, especially when you participate in interviews.
10. Speak clearly and avoid vocalized pauses.

Review Questions

1. Name three common examples of one-to-one communication.
2. List three rules for having a good conversation.
3. Identify three ways to send messages accurately during conversation.
4. Name several nonverbal aspects of conversation.
5. State why telephone conversation is more difficult than face-to-face conversation.
6. List several speech elements that carry your message in a telephone conversation.
7. Describe several kinds of questions that you should be prepared to answer during a job interview.
8. Identify the kinds of questions you should be prepared to ask in a job interview.
9. Describe several factors that may influence the impression you make on the interviewer during a job interview.
10. Describe how you should follow up on a job interview.

Discussion Questions

1. Identify and discuss common problems that occur in one-to-one communication situations, such as interrupting, wandering attention, and not allowing the other person to speak. How can these problems be overcome if you are involved in a conversation with someone who allows these things to happen?
2. Study the following quotations.

   A single conversation across the table with a wise man is worth a month's study of books. (Chinese Proverb)

   Conversation is the laboratory and workshop of the student. (Ralph Waldo Emerson)

   Explain what each quotation means. Share with your classmates experiences you have had conversing with someone whom you consider to be "older and wiser." How did you feel about these conversations? Were you intimidated or made uncomfortable by the older person?
3. As a class, identify the various ways that individuals lay claim to space or their own territory at school and at home. Consider "your" desk in each class, "your" locker, "your" books, and "your" personal items at school. Consider "your" room, "your" place at the dining

table, "your" place in the family car, and "your" favorite chair. In your speech notebook, make a list of your personal spaces at home, at school, and wherever else you spend a great deal of time.

Critical Thinking

1. **Analysis:** Discuss the similarities and differences between a one-to-one conversation and an interview. How is the informal situation like the formal one? How do they differ?
2. **Evaluation:** Discuss what purpose a job interview serves for both the employer and the candidate for employment. Do you feel that it accomplishes more than the sending of a résumé? As an employer, how can it help you to evaluate a candidate? As a candidate, how can it help you evaluate the employer and the job?

Activities

In-Class

1. Join one of three groups in your class. Group I will focus on facial expressions by collecting magazine pictures, designing a collage, and writing word balloons over each face in the collage. Group II will follow the same procedure but will concentrate on pictures depicting various forms of body language: posture, kneeling, running, reaching, etc. The group will decide what specific messages are being sent with kinesics. Group III will also follow the same procedure but will gather and display pictures that show spacial relationships. Then the group will decide what messages are being sent by the figures' use of space.

   When the collages are complete, one member of each group will present an oral report, sharing the collage and explaining the ideas that were formulated in the group that designed it.
2. Form small groups. Each group should set up a display in the classroom that is made up of

various personal items. The class then visits each display. Each individual should visualize a "person" based on the items in the display. Each member of the class should then write a brief description of the "person." Discuss each "person" you have imagined with your classmates.

3. If videotape equipment is available, someone will videotape a class period during which members of the class are working in small groups. The tape will not include an audio recording. The class will view the tape and analyze the nonverbal signals communicated by the various members of the small groups. Which signals are sent without the person being aware of them? Which signals seem to be sent intentionally?

4. In small groups, develop one of the following three skits. Each skit will involve two speakers: a caller and a receiver of a telephone call. (a) Situation 1: Call someone you have just met to invite him or her to see a movie with you. (b) Situation 2: Call a dentist's office to make an appointment. (c) Situation 3: Call to announce that you are unable to honor a promise to babysit on a Saturday evening. The skits may be serious or humorous, but each should make an important point about telephone usage. Present each skit in class and discuss the lessons to be learned from each.

5. In small groups, design a Pre-interview Checklist. Include making arrangements for the interview, doing research, designing questions, and making plans to record the information. Lists from each group will be combined into a master list to be written on the chalkboard. You may then copy it in your speech notebook.

Out-of-Class

1. Have a conversation this week with someone outside your family or peer group. Choose an older person or young child with whom you do not normally communicate. Write an entry in your speech notebook about this experience. Include facts about both the conversation and your response to the conversation. Consider how easy or difficult it was to keep the conversation going. How do you think the other person felt about the experience?

2. In one of your classes that has no assigned seating, sit at a desk normally occupied by someone else. Observe how that student reacts to your

being in "his" or "her" space. How do you feel when someone violates "your" space? How does the other student react when you return to your "own" seat? Record the other student's reactions in your speech notebook.

3. Organize a Conversation Club that meets periodically to discuss certain topics of interest to members. Assign a specific topic for each meeting. You may want to encourage those people who share a common interest to become members. For example, there may be a number of people in your English class who enjoy reading. Your club could then devote each meeting to a particular type of literature.

4. Make a "nonverbal communication profile" of a television news commentator from one of the three major networks. Watch facial expressions, eye behavior, and appearance. Listen for vocal tones, speaking rate, volume, and voice quality. Keep lists of your positive and negative impressions of the commentator for a period of two weeks. Report your impressions to the class.

Chapter Project

Divide the class into two groups. One group will invent a company and assign jobs in the company to those who are members of the group. Each person with an assigned job will then write an advertisement for a new position that he or she would supervise. Post these ads on the class bulletin board or in some other suitable location.

Each member of the second group should then read the ads and select a job to apply for. Then, one at a time, the person applying for a job will role-play an interview with the person offering the job. (Before the interview, you may also wish to role-play a telephone call that obtains preliminary information about the job and sets up an interview.) Do all of this realistically by preparing a résumé, developing questions beforehand, and dressing appropriately.

When all interviews are completed, conduct a class discussion about the experience. Was it more difficult or was it easier than expected? Did practice help?

5 Group Discussion

When you have completed this chapter you should be able to:

■ Explain and give examples of the important role of group communication in life today.

■ Describe various types and forms of group discussion.

■ Describe several factors that affect group discussion.

■ Explain ways to prepare for group discussion.

■ Describe three aspects of group leadership.

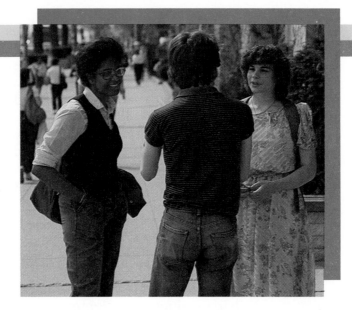

Informal socializing with friends, and a brief strategy session with the debate team, are both forms of group discussion. The success of each relies on cooperation among group members.

Group discussion is rapidly becoming one of the most widely used forms of interpersonal communication in modern society. In the world of business, managers may spend up to fifty percent of their time in meetings. Public meetings may be held to discuss the budget proposed by a school board or a city's new zoning laws. Students may be asked to carry out assignments in small groups.

People communicate in groups for several purposes. Sometimes three or more people come together in a group simply to enjoy social conversation. At other times groups meet in order to solve a problem or to reach a decision. Groups may also meet to share information. As in one-to-one conversation, there is often no single goal or topic and no planning of a group's social conversation beforehand. The rules for successful group conversation are similar to those presented for one-to-one conversation in Chapter 4. Therefore, in this chapter the focus will be on group discussion used to arrive at decisions and to share information, rather than on group conversation.

THE NATURE OF GROUP DISCUSSION

Group discussion occurs any time three or more people meet to solve a common problem, arrive at a decision, or answer a question of mutual interest.

The idea of *cooperation* is basic to discussion. It means that the members of the group must share a desire to achieve a common goal. They may not all wish to achieve that goal in exactly the same way. But they must be willing to devote their energies to reaching a group solution, rather than to promoting their own individual solutions or opinions. This does not mean that there won't be differences of opinion in group discussion. Rather, it means that each member must enter the group with an open mind, genuinely prepared to listen as well as to argue.

Discussion groups are generally formed for a definite purpose, to achieve a particular and sometimes urgent goal. Ordinarily, such a goal can be reached only when the members are *prepared*. If a member has prepared actively to participate and achieve the group's goal, she or he can not only help the group reach a decision but can also have considerable influence in forming the group's decision.

Types of Group Discussion

Discussion groups can be classified by their *purpose* and their *audience*. Groups classified by purpose usually meet for one of two reasons: **decision-making** or **enlightenment.** A board of directors of a corporation generally meets to decide upon action for the future. A group of TV commentators discussing unemployment on a news broadcast, on the other hand, generally has the enlightenment of the listeners as its primary purpose. Determining whether a discussion group exists for the purpose of decision-making or for enlightenment is one of the basic ways of classifying different types of groups.

In this closed-group discussion, a college representative talks about how his institution can help these students realize their academic goals.

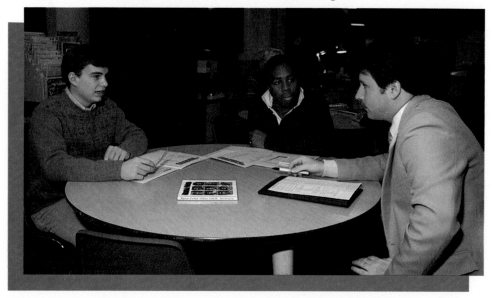

Groups can also be classified by their audience, that is whether they are engaged in closed-group or public discussion. If the members of the group are communicating only with each other, the discussion is a **closed-group discussion.** If they are also communicating with listeners outside the group, the discussion is a **public discussion.** It is a public discussion even if the audience is not physically present, as in the case of a TV or radio broadcast.

These types of discussion can, of course, occur in combination. When a group of students meets to study together before a big exam, it is a closed-group, enlightenment discussion. If those same students were gathered to plan a dance, the format would be a closed-group, decision-making one. When city council members discuss recreation facilities available in their city in front of an audience it is a public, enlightenment discussion. Suppose the council members were to discuss whether they should build a new city hall or repair the old one. If an audience was present, the discussion would be a public, decision-making one.

Forms of Discussion Groups

Probably the most common form for closed-group discussion is the committee. A **committee** is a small subgroup of a larger organization that has been given a specific task or set of tasks to perform. The committee is often used for decision making. Some committees have only the power to recommend action or policy to the larger body of which they are a part. Others can actually make a decision or carry out a task. A board of directors for a corporation is a special kind of elected committee. They have been given the authority to carry out decision-making tasks for the owners of the corporation.

Another common form of closed-group discussion is the **round-table discussion.** Perhaps you remember King Arthur's Round Table. It was, according to legend, a circular table around which King Arthur and his knights discussed their adventures. The purpose of the circular shape of the table was to prevent arguments about each knight's relative importance in the group. During a round-table discussion, a circular table is often used for the same reason. Although the term *round-table* is sometimes used to apply to almost any type of closed-group discussion, it most often means a closed-group session in which information-sharing or enlightenment of those taking part is the object. For example, a literary club would be using a round-table form if its members met to discuss the latest novel.

Public discussion often takes the form of a panel. A **panel** is a group that discusses a topic in front of an audience. The panel's purpose could be either enlightenment or decision-making. In either case they are discussing for the benefit of an audience as well as for themselves.

Experts give short speeches in this televised symposium.

A similar form of public discussion is the **symposium**. In a symposium, one group member gives a short, uninterrupted speech, which is followed by a speech from the next member, and so on until all members have spoken. A symposium, then, is really a series of short public speeches generally given by experts, and is thus not a true group discussion. In a symposium, the free interaction of ideas that is so important in group discussion does not exist.

Either the panel or the symposium can be opened up to questions or comments from the audience. When this is done, the form is called either a **panel-forum** or a **symposium-forum.** This arrangement can be quite effective with live or radio and television audiences where listeners or viewers can call in questions or reactions by telephone.

Application

Communicating in a Group Discussion

Participate in a group discussion in your class. Separate into groups of from five to seven. Imagine that your group is a committee that has been formed to discuss a problem that is facing your community or school. Decide upon the problem that your group will discuss. Choose a leader for your committee and discuss the problem that you have chosen. Try to come up with recommendations and solutions to the problem. After the discussion, your group leader will identify the problem and present your solutions to the entire class for discussion.

FACTORS AFFECTING GROUP DISCUSSION

Several factors affect whether or not a group discussion is successful. Two of these concern the formation of cliques within a group and the imposition of personal goals on a group. Four other factors deal with more concrete issues: group size, physical environment, seating arrangement, and the time when meetings are held.

Size of the Group

At least three people must be present in order to have a group discussion. Discussion groups seldom have more than fifteen members, however. Each member of a discussion group must have the opportunity to take part in the discussion. Too many members can cause verbal traffic jams, preventing the group from arriving at a decision. The group size that seems to work best for most situations is five or seven—not six! If a group has an even number of members, a vote on an issue would result in a tie, and the discussion would be deadlocked. If the group has an odd number, a tie could not occur.

Cliques Within a Group

When a clique develops within a group, it is almost certain to hamper the group's success. A **clique** consists of a few of the group members (often two or three) who become a separate group within the larger group. They may do so by talking among themselves much of the time, often about topics unrelated to the discussion. Or they may try to dominate the discussion, talking so much that other members have little chance to speak. Sometimes they will laugh and joke when the majority of the group is seriously trying to discuss the topic.

When a clique develops, someone outside it needs to exert leadership to halt its negative influence. Sometimes this can be done by encouraging everyone in the discussion group to participate. When the clique gets the group away from the subject, a leader needs to remind the members what the current topic is. In those cases where the clique is causing a constant, or major disruption, strong leadership must be exerted. This may mean calling on the members of the clique by name and asking them to stop the interference. In extreme cases, the other members of the group may need to expel the clique from the group.

Personal Goals of Members

People take part in groups to achieve some kind of common goal. The goal may be to make a joint decision, to solve a mutual problem, or to share information. In addition, each member of a group generally wishes to achieve certain personal goals. These may include a position of leadership, a feeling of comradeship, or a desire for security. Sometimes fulfilling personal goals helps to achieve group goals. At other times, personal goals may become barriers to group goals.

A personal goal involving leadership can have a strong effect on a group. Many people prefer to lead rather than follow. But it is difficult for several in a group to lead at the same time. In new groups, members sometimes spend so much of their discussion time in power plays for leadership that the group has no energy left to solve a problem or reach a decision. When a group forms, there is often a period of time during which the group must either elect leaders or wait for leaders to emerge naturally. This is normal. It is only when the group allows personal matters to overshadow group goals that jockeying for leadership positions must be controlled. The controlling of power plays is never easy. It requires a willingness on the part of those members seeking leadership to recognize the needs of the entire group and to place those needs ahead of a personal goal.

A member's need for acceptance by the group is another personal goal that can affect group discussion. Sometimes, the desire to be liked and accepted will cause a member to give way to majority influence. Research has shown that a person will go along with what he or she thinks is a majority opinion, even when it is directly opposite to his or her own view of the situation. Occasionally, two or three very persuasive members of a group can cause their opinion to seem like the majority opinion, when actually it is not. If other members of the group then "tag along," what is a minority view can become the group's decision or policy. To avoid this each member of a group should be sure that his or her opinion is heard and understood. No member should ever agree with another's opinion unless convinced it is the best solution the group can produce.

A third personal goal that involves a group's cohesiveness can also affect discussion. **Cohesiveness** is a kind of group spirit. The cohesiveness of the Three Musketeers, characters in the novel by Alexandre Dumas, was indicated by their motto, "All for one and one for all." When a group has cohesiveness, each member is dedicated to the unity of the group. The attainment of this personal goal of dedication allows a person to draw strength from being a member of a productive group. When cohesiveness is low, members generally put little effort into their discussions. Meetings may be carried on politely but are boring. They often end quickly. Important decisions are usually made hastily with practically no disagreement or weighing of evidence. With little cohesiveness, members do not really care about the group or its decisions, so they tend to make poor decisions. The only solution for this lack of cohesiveness is for members to become dedicated to the group and begin to be active and concerned about its goals. They must participate fully in the group's discussions and devote their energies to achieving quality solutions to group problems.

Physical Environment

The physical setting in which a group meets can affect its discussion. Members should try to avoid communication barriers caused by meeting in an unsuitable environment. For example, the temperature of the room should not be so high that members have trouble staying awake. On the other hand, the temperature should not be so low that people are uncomfortable.

Noise and visual distractions can prevent a successful discussion too. Doors or windows may have to be closed to keep outside noises or the activities of others from distracting group members. Conversations within the group which are not related to the discussion question should also be discouraged. The time for social conversation is before or after group discussion. A quiet, uncluttered room that offers privacy is the best environment for group discussion.

A cohesive group unites in the service of common goals.

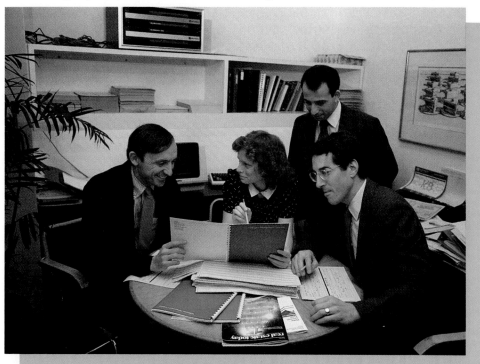

Seating Arrangement

As you read in Chapter 2, it is important to consider proxemics, or the use of space, when communicating with others. In discussion, comfortable seating arrangements can sometimes mean the difference between whether or not a group reaches its goal. Chairs should be placed close enough to make discussion easy. On the other hand, group members should not be made uncomfortable by being so close that they feel their personal space has been invaded.

Good seating arrangements will make it possible for each group member to maintain eye contact with every other member. Being able to look at each other helps to keep members actively engaged in the discussion process.

Time for Discussion

The best group discussions are held at times when members are most alert. Avoid scheduling a discussion just before lunch or at the end of a busy day. People who are hungry or tired are less able to reason well.

Groups should be sure there is enough time to share the information or to reach the decision called for by the discussion question. If the goal cannot be reached in one meeting, members should hold the next session as soon as possible. Members of the discussion group will remember better what was done at the first session if the second one follows shortly afterward. Summarizing what happened at the first meeting will also help members pick up where they left off.

If a discussion is expected to be lengthy, members may need a short break. After moving about and relaxing for a few minutes, a group is often able to resolve issues more successfully.

"Charlie's 10 P.M. meetings are always so restful."

Working with Groups

Your class will be divided into two halves. One half of the class will work on its own as individuals and the other half will work in groups of from five to seven members. Both the individuals and the groups will consider television commercials and will try to determine the characteristics that effective and memorable commercials have. Both the individuals and the groups will consider this topic for a period of time. The individuals will report their findings in class, and a leader chosen by each group will also report findings. As a class, discuss whether working together gave better results than working individually. Why or why not?

HOW GROUPS BEHAVE

You have probably noticed, as you have participated in discussion groups, that some group members behave very differently than others do. You may also have noticed that a particular student acts differently as a member of the debate squad than he or she does as a staff member on the school paper. You may even have recognized that *you* take different roles and behave quite differently depending on the particular group with which you are involved at a given time. Some groups succeed in accomplishing their goals, while others do not. Some seem to experience little controversy, while others appear to be constantly in turmoil. Just as it is important to recognize such differences in the behavior of groups and their members, it is also important to know why some groups succeed and others do not. To do so, you need to know about two aspects of group behavior—the relationship between the group task and group maintenance, and the life cycle of groups.

Task Versus Maintenance

Imagine you are behind a two-way mirror observing a group of your fellow students planning the upcoming senior prom. You can see and hear them, but they are unaware of your presence. Here's an excerpt of what you hear:

Jennifer: Can we get back to what we are going to do about the drinking and driving problem that was so bad last year?

Brad: Wait a minute! I don't think we've finished with the question about the music yet. Did we definitely decide on the band?

Roger:	Yes we did. About a half hour ago we finally took a vote, remember? You didn't vote for the Four Horsemen like most of us did, but it is settled. I agree with Jennifer. We need to talk about keeping people from driving while drunk.
Kimberly:	Well, I've heard that a lot of schools have started a kind of taxi service where several juniors drive home those who can't drive themselves. Maybe we could try something like that this year.
Susan:	Just how does that work, Kim? Do the juniors volunteer to do the driving? And who decides who is drunk enough to need a ride? It sounds like a good idea, but I'd like to know more about it.
Jennifer:	Brad, don't you have a cousin at Southern High where they tried something like that last year? Do you know what they did and how well it worked?

This little peek at a discussion group highlights the constant flipping back and forth between task and maintenance messages that the typical group engages in. **Task messages** are those primarily designed to help the group achieve its goals or complete its task. **Maintenance messages** are mainly for the purpose of keeping relationships among the group members harmonious so there is a positive climate in the group. In our prom-planning group, Jennifer began with a task message, that of refocusing the group's attention on the specific topic of handling drunk drivers. This type of task message has been labelled "initiating." When Brad attempted to sidetrack the group onto the topic of the band, Roger reminded him and the group as a whole that that matter had already been agreed upon by an earlier vote. Roger was using a maintenance message known as "standard setting"—pointing out standards of procedure that the group has already agreed upon, such as following majority opinion. Kimberly then used the task message known as "giving information or opinion" when she asked the group to consider the taxi service idea she had heard about. Susan responded with another task message, "seeking information or opinions," when she asked for more details about Kimberly's suggestion. Finally, Jennifer used the maintenance message called "gate keeping" by trying to draw Brad back to discussion of the drunk driving. "Gate keeping" messages are those designed to keep everyone in the group involved in the topic and to promote a sharing atmosphere. Notice that Jennifer's final remark to Brad was not only a maintenance message designed to draw Brad back into the discussion. It also served as a task message of "seeking information or opinions" to further the group's progress towards a decision about how to handle drunk drivers.

Task Messages

Initiating — messages that propose a general group task or goal; suggestions for how the group should proceed; ideas for solving a problem

Seeking Information or Opinions — messages that ask for information or facts; requests for ideas, estimates, or suggestions

Giving Information or Opinion — messages that offer facts or information; statements of opinion, belief, or suggestion

Clarifying and Elaborating — statements that help clear up confusion or define terms; messages that indicate alternatives and issues before the group

Summarizing — messages that pull together ideas shared by group members; restating group problems, suggestions, and conclusions

Consensus Testing — messages that ask whether the group is approaching agreement or nearing a decision

Maintenance Messages

Harmonizing — messages designed to reduce group tension, to reconcile disagreements, or to get members to explore differences

Gate Keeping — messages to encourage the participation of other group members, help keep channels of communication open, and promote sharing

Encouraging — messages to show friendliness to other group members; facial expressions or remarks that show acceptance, warmth and responsiveness

Compromising — remarks that show a willingness to admit errors, give in, or modify one's position

Standard Setting and Testing — remarks made to determine whether the group is satisfied with its procedures; pointing out rules or norms the group may wish to adopt or has already adopted

Task and maintenance messages help groups work smoothly toward goals.

Once you realize that not all messages spoken in group meetings are directly related to the content of the discussion, but that some are designed to accomplish very necessary maintenance functions, you will understand better why groups behave as they do. Here are two lists describing several of the most common types of task and maintenence messages encountered in groups. The next time you find yourself involved in a group discussion, watch and listen for them.

The Life Cycle of Groups

Discussion groups seem to experience life cycles just as individuals do. As each of us develops and matures from infancy through adolescence into adulthood, so groups go through similar stages of progress. One writer has identified and labelled four stages in the life cycle of discussion groups: **Forming, Storming, Norming,** and **Performing.** During each stage, group members must attend to four aspects of the group's life if the group is to reach its goals and achieve its task. They must, of course attend to the task itself; they must monitor the relationships among the individual members of the group; they must pay attention to behavior patterns of the group as a whole; and they must attend to the leadership of the group. Let's see what typically happens during each stage of group life.

Forming   This stage is like infancy. When members of a new group first come together, each person listens to the others as they state their reasons for being a part of the group, and what they hope the group's goals and accomplishments will be. Individual members are anxious as they try to discover whether they will feel comfortable in this group and will be accepted. Everyone is polite. No one emphasizes differences of opinion during the forming stage. Rather, everyone is searching for as much similarity of views and goals as possible. Members are also looking for leadership and guidance during this first stage, much as the infant is dependent on parents for guidance. If no designated leadership already exists, members will quickly move to establish it. The forming stage may be smooth and pleasant for a group when members find they have compatible goals and interpersonal styles. It can also produce much tension and anxiety if members find little similarity and compatibility.

Storming   Once a group discovers sufficient similarity of goals and personalities in the first stage, it is ready to move into the storming stage, that is, the adolescent stage that is usually the most difficult stage in the life of a group. Here, individual members challenge differences of goals and approaches as part of an effort to express their individuality and to wield power and influence over the group. Often the designated leader-

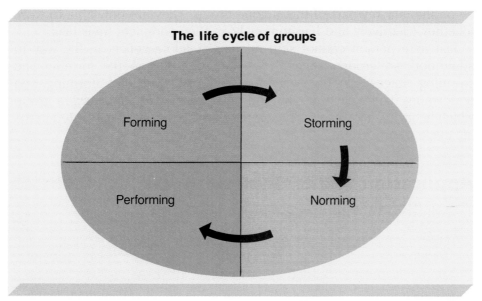

The life cycle of groups

Forming   Storming

Performing   Norming

A life cycle of forming, storming, norming, and performing is the group equivalent of childhood, adolescence, and adulthood.

ship is challenged while members struggle with wanting to have sufficient control over the direction of the group. It is also during this storming stage that the group is trying to create order and establish the operating rules for its decision making. This stage is a time of maximum struggle for the group as members wrestle with both the demands of their task and issues of power and influence within the group. This stage can be frustrating, but will help the group learn to confront and resolve conflict.

Norming Once the group begins to resolve the conflicts over who is to exert influence and what procedures it will use to accomplish its goals, it moves into the calmer stage called norming. Here the group becomes a cohesive unit, ready to tackle its task. Members are now learning to function effectively as a group, trusting each other as they negotiate the best ways of working out the group's goals. They are beginning to share leadership functions as they allow members with special insights and knowledge to lead at appropriate places in the discussion. They are learning to trust one another as the group as a whole begins to experience success.

Performing In this final stage, trust and even affection among members blossom. As the group efficiently works out the details of its task, members feel a strong bond of unity, that is, each member feels that he or she is a key part of this unique group. They are now able to work together effectively and harmoniously as they complete their task.

Just as a person cannot skip infancy or adolescence on the way to adulthood, so groups appear to be unable to skip the forming and storming stages on their way to the adult stages of norming and performing. The next time you find yourself part of a discussion group which is having a "stormy" time, recall that this is a necessary step in the life cycle of any group.

Application

Task and Maintenance Messages

Choose someone to write all of the different categories of task and maintenance messages on the chalkboard. Then as a class, brainstorm statements that a leader or group member might make for each kind of message. Keep a record of the best statements in your notebook for future reference.

PREPARING TO PARTICIPATE IN A GROUP

Many opportunities for discussion in groups exist in school situations. Members of student government, clubs, and teams use discussion groups to share information and to solve problems. A classroom group discussing a bill pending in the state legislature may report its recommendation in a persuasive letter to lawmakers.

A successful discussion should be planned in advance. Sometimes a leader of the group or several of the group's members will make plans for the discussion. Another very good way to plan is for all members of the group to hold a prediscussion meeting. During the planning stage, members of the group can choose the topic they want to talk about. They can decide on the type of question they want to discuss and take time to word the question carefully. Finally, they can write an outline or list of questions about the topic. This outline or list can then serve as a guide during the discussion.

If all members are not present during the planning meeting, those who did not attend should be notified of the question to be discussed. They should also be given the outline to guide them in doing research on the topic.

Choose a Topic

The first step in making a discussion a success is to choose a suitable topic. A topic for group discussion should be interesting, significant, and manageable.

A well-chosen topic must be of interest to at least several persons. The members of the group themselves will participate best when the topic is of interest to the group as a whole as well as to each individual member. If the discussion is to be a public one, the subject should already be of interest to the audience or be one about which they can become interested.

It is not enough, though, that the topic be interesting. It should also be significant. The topic should affect the lives of the group members and of the audience, if one is present at the time of the discussion. For example, it might be interesting, but not very significant, for a high school group to discuss the question "How can sales managers develop better on-the-job relationships with their sales representatives?" Such a topic would lack a sense of immediacy for most or all of the students involved.

Finally, a well-chosen topic must be manageable. Discussion is a slow process at best. A group should not attempt, for example, to solve the world's economic problems in a one-hour discussion. Groups should choose a topic that can be discussed thoroughly in the time allotted.

Decide What Type of Question to Discuss

After an interesting, significant, and manageable topic has been chosen, it should be worded in the form of a question. Groups usually discuss one of three types of questions. These are questions of fact, questions of value, or questions of policy. **Questions of fact** deal with whether a situation exists, under what circumstances it exists, or how it may be defined. "Is the United States' use of nuclear power on the decline?" is basically a question of fact.

Questions of value go a step beyond those of fact. While questions of fact deal with the existence of something, **questions of value** revolve around the worth of the object, person, or situation. A question of value emphasizes whether a thing is good or bad, desirable or undesirable, promising or hopeless. If a question requires judgments of worth, it is usually called a question of value. "Is the two-party system the best political system for the United States?" would be a question of value.

Questions of policy are usually the most complex type of discussion questions. Questions of policy are also those most commonly discussed. **Questions of policy** are questions that are directed toward a course of physical or mental action. Questions such as "How much and what kind of support should our school give to its drama program?" and "What role should the federal government assume in the fight against industrial pollution of our waterways?" are questions of policy. These often include the word *should.* A group does not necessarily need to have the power to put its decision into action in order to discuss such a question. Many groups that can only recommend action may nevertheless have great influence on policy decisions.

Word the Question Carefully

As soon as a question is chosen, someone needs to narrow it down by wording it in clear, concise, and unbiased language. Many discussions become cloudy, and many more fail to achieve productive results, because no one has taken the time to state the question in a careful way.

In wording a discussion question, the most important thing to remember is that it should *be worded as a question,* not as a statement. Furthermore, it should usually be worded so that it has three or more possible answers. A question such as "Should taxes be cut?" allows only a "Yes" or "No" answer. This tends to turn the discussion into a debate, with two group factions, each arguing for its own opinion. A better way to phrase this question would be: "How should our government revamp the tax system?" With the question phrased in this manner, the question of taxes becomes just one of several possible solutions to be considered.

A well-worded question should also *be clear.* Avoid unclear questions such as "What about our school system?" This is not a question of fact, value, or policy. A group would not get very far if they tried to discuss such a vague question. The words within a discussion question must also be clear. Group members should agree on definitions for all the words used in each question. Suppose your group is to discuss the question "What action should our representatives in Congress take regarding international terrorism?" The phrase *international terrorism* should be defined before the discussion in started.

Conciseness is also important in a properly worded discussion question. Extremely long and involved wording can confuse, rather than clarify, a group session. Picture yourself trying to discuss the following question: "What kinds of required subjects, such as Math, English, and History, and what kinds of electives, such as Band, Debate, and Typing should high-school students be made to take or be allowed to take at various grade levels?" This exaggerated example could be discussed better with the wording: "Which subjects should be required and which should be elective in grades nine through twelve?"

Finally, if you are given the responsibility for wording a discussion question, be sure that your wording is not one-sided or **biased.** Suppose you were opposed to raising money for a class trip by having a bake sale.

Career Close-up

SYSTEMS ANALYST

Systems analysts design and maintain information (computer) systems for businesses, government agencies, and other organizations using a variety of computers and data processing tools. To complete any task, analysts must be able to work effectively with groups of people. They meet with programmers, managers, and other employees to create information systems and find solutions to problems. Educational requirements for this profession include a bachelor's degree in computer sciences, electrical engineering, or business administration.

Because analysts realize they must have everyone's cooperation to achieve their goals, they cultivate group discussion before a meeting takes place by sending employees detailed information about a meeting's agenda, requesting their suggestions, and contacting them personally to let them know their contribution is needed.

During group discussions, the analyst actively encourages group members to speak openly. He or she listens carefully and responds to employees' and managers' proposals and opinions. Brainstorming, another important technique analysts use, focuses a group on producing creative ideas instead of evaluating them, thus generating many more potential solutions.

As technology becomes increasingly complex, one person cannot solve every computer problem. The analyst's use of group discussion to utilize each employee's expertise toward the solution of problems is precisely what makes these specialists so valuable to businesses.

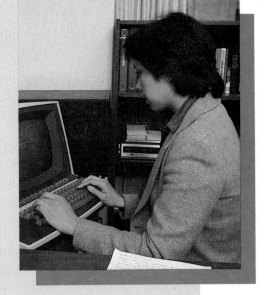

The systems analyst uses group discussion to solve complex problems.

You would display your bias if you used wording such as "How can we earn money for the trip without selling anything?" On the other hand, "How can we earn money for the trip?" would be asking an unbiased question.

Prepare the Outline

If you were driving from New York to California for the first time, you would probably use a road map. You would plot the best route beforehand, and decide about how far you would drive each day. If you were planning a leisurely vacation, however, you might not adhere to a strict schedule. Whenever an interesting side trip presented itself, you might depart from your planned route. A discussion outline serves much the same purpose as a road map does on a vacation. It provides the necessary guidance to keep the group moving toward its goal. But it should never be followed so rigidly that it stifles creative thinking among the members. Just as leisurely vacation travelers readjust their plans, so a discussion group should feel free to depart slightly from its outline because of changing conditions.

Since questions of policy are most common, the emphasis here will be on preparing an outline for such a question. A policy question generally demands an outline with three main divisions or phases:

1. Analysis of the background and causes of the problem or situation.

2. Consideration, evaluation, and comparison of alternatives or various possible solutions.

3. Agreement and disagreement about the best solution or action to take.

Most policy discussions will include each of these phases, usually outlined in the above order. The actual discussion, however, might sometimes move briefly into one of the latter phases before an earlier one is completed.

The discussion outline could easily be drawn up by the entire group in a prediscussion meeting. Outlines are general in nature. Questions rather than statements are used in main heads and subheads. Before the actual discussion, a leader may want to draw up a more specific outline consisting of questions within each phase which will be used to stimulate group members' thinking during the discussion. It is probably best if the leader's detailed outline is not distributed to the members in advance. Answers will then occur freely and naturally during the discussion. However, in some forms of public discussion, such as radio or television programs, it may be necessary to give the members of the group a preview of the kinds of questions that they will be asked to deal with.

Research the Topic

All members of a group should prepare for discussion by doing research on the topic. The first step in doing research is to think carefully about the topic and the prepared basic outline. Search your memory for any experience or knowledge you may already have that relates to the question to be discussed.

If you are discussing a question of fact, you will need information on the background and causes of the problem. Use newspapers, magazines, books, or interviews to gather the information you need.

When discussing a question of value, you will need to do more than collect information. You will have to analyze that information in order to compare and judge various possible solutions.

Discussing a policy question also requires the gathering of information and then the consideration of all alternatives, as well as ideas, before choosing a solution or course of action. You probably will have decided upon a solution you favor before taking part in the actual discussion. Be prepared to support your opinions with facts and sound reasoning. Remember to keep an open mind when listening to the opinions of others.

Application

Preparing for a Group Discussion

Form into groups of from five to seven members. Choose a topic for a future group discussion. Consider only those topics that every member of the group is interested in. It may be school-related, a topic of local interest, or a topic that is international in nature. Decide upon the wording of the discussion question and upon the kind of research that is needed to gather information about the question. Each person in the group should then do individual research on the topic. Save your research information in your notebook for the next application.

LEADING A GROUP

In most groups, certain members exercise greater degrees of influence than do others. Such influence is referred to as group leadership. Researchers used to feel that leadership ability was something that certain people had and others did not. If you had it, you turned out to be a group leader. If you didn't, you would only be a follower in practically any group in which you found yourself.

The more recent view is not quite so simple. It holds that a given group possesses a kind of group personality, called **syntality.** Syntality is like an individual's personality. Whenever any group member says or does something that has a major influence upon group syntality, that person is exercising leadership in the group. A member's influence or leadership of the group can vary from day to day.

Different Forms of Leadership

In some discussion groups all the leadership tasks are handled by a single group member. Jean may already be president of a club, so all the leadership functions of that group naturally fall to her. Mark may be elected by group members to serve as leader of a different group. Ricardo may be named leader of a committee by the principal. If all the leadership duties fall to a single individual, that person is called an **appointed leader.** An appointed leader is usually a very busy person during the discussion.

Some discussion experts suggest dividing the functions of the leader among several, or even among all, of the group members. One may begin the discussion. Another may keep participation balanced and the discussion moving toward its goal. A third may tone down arguments that arise. Another may watch the time limit and conclude the discussion with a summary. Whenever this shared form of leadership is arranged beforehand, it is also a form of *appointed leadership.*

Still other researchers have found it is best not to appoint or assign any particular duties to anyone. Ideally, all the group participants should understand what leadership functions are necessary. If they do, some group member will handle each function of leadership as the need for it arises during the discussion. This natural form of leadership is known as **emergent leadership.**

Leadership Roles

A discussion has three basic parts—a beginning, a middle, and an end. Whenever any group member fulfills one of the functions of beginning the discussion, regulating communication, or concluding it, he or she will be acting as a leader at that particular moment.

Beginning the Discussion   The introduction of group members to each other and to the audience, if the discussion is public, is of primary concern at the beginning of a discussion. Effective leadership and group cohesiveness depend on members being acquainted with each other. Any time two or more people you know come together, the question should pop into your mind "Do these people know each other?" If the answer is "No," your immediate task is one of making introductions.

The rules for properly introducing people taking part in group discussion are the same as those used on social occasions. They are based first on age, then sex, and then status. When introducing persons of different ages, begin by mentioning the older person's name first. "Mr. O'Rourke, I'd like you to meet Janice Schmidt, a reporter on our school newspaper." When introducing persons of opposite sex, mention the woman's or girl's name first. "Mimi Rivera, may I introduce my teammate, Greg Chiang." If there is a difference in the status of the two individuals, begin with the person of higher rank. "President Franklin, allow me to introduce Jesse Stoner, our newest member." Introduce members of a group to an audience in order from left to right so the audience can locate each person as he or she is introduced.

The second task when you begin a group discussion is to introduce the topic. The group will have already worded the topic for discussion as a question. The question should be repeated to the group and, if the discussion is public, introduced to the audience. Stating the question at the start of the discussion will prevent uncertainty about the subject to be discussed.

Finally, enough background information about the question should be given to show why the group has assembled to discuss it. Assume seven members of your class are about to begin an in-class panel discussion. The topic is "Energy." If you were chosen as leader, you could begin the discussion briefly and effectively by opening the discussion like this:

"For the remainder of the period today, our panel is going to discuss the question 'What sources of energy should the people of this country use during the rest of this century?' As you know, we are all concerned about the suitability of nuclear power and the diminishing resources of oil and gas as sources of energy for our nation. Today we will compare these sources with other energy sources such as the sun, wind, and coal to find the best possible combination to use for the next twenty years."

Regulating Communication   Several leadership tasks must be attended to during the central part of any discussion. All members should feel free to speak their minds fully and frankly. This means that the leader must not only invite but also encourage members to contribute to the discussion. The leader should promote the idea that each individual's ideas are valuable and need to be aired. Encouraging such participation is frequently done by means of a general statement early in the discussion. Then, if the need arises, the leader may use more specific urging at necessary points along the way.

Keeping participation balanced during discussion is another leadership task. In any group some members are going to talk more than others. This is all right as long as no one monopolizes the discussion, and no one sits back and says nothing. The leader must exercise tact when suppressing those who talk too much. An appropriate comment might be "Sam, that's a very interesting point you just made. I wonder what some of the rest of us think about that. Sarah, what is your opinion?" But the leader must be careful not to embarrass or put a quiet member on the spot by suddenly asking "Mike, what do you think?" A better approach might be "This seems to be a critical point we are discussing. Why don't we get everyone's opinion on this?" Then, by starting with other people, the leader gives the quiet member time to plan ideas and words.

A leader must also be prepared to step in when two or more members of the group begin to argue. Progress cannot be made in a discussion that becomes an argument. This is especially true if those who are arguing freeze everyone else out or begin to deal in personal attacks. Group morale and productivity will quickly decline. When this occurs, the leader must step in with a comment such as "David, Maureen, I think each of your positions is pretty clear to all of us. Perhaps we need to hear some other opinions on this matter. Leon, do you have an opinion about this you'd like to share with us?" By taking the floor away from those arguing, you can often stop an argument.

Leaders are expected to keep the discussion on the track. This means recognizing a major detour from the prepared outline as it develops and gently reminding the group that it is getting off onto a side issue. An excellent way for a leader to keep the discussion moving towards its goal is by inserting brief summaries for the group after they finish discussing each major part of the outline.

Sometimes a few group members may have excellent ideas, but they aren't very successful in expressing them clearly to the group. When this happens, it becomes the leader's job to save each worthwhile idea. A leader may say something like "I think that's a fine idea, Maxine! If I understand you correctly, you're saying. . . ." If you restate the idea in clearer terms, others will be able to understand it.

Finally, leaders are responsible for watching the time limit. This can be an especially important leadership function in public discussions, such as those produced for radio or television.

Concluding the Discussion   There are two major concluding functions of leadership. First, when leaders feel the group has adequately covered the discussion question or a preset time limit has almost been reached, leaders should summarize the major ideas and outcomes of the discussion. At the same time they must be careful not to overload the summary with their own ideas. Second, leaders should save enough time for group members to disagree with the summary or to insert a minority opinion if they wish.

Conducting a Group Discussion

Using the topic that you researched in the previous Application, conduct a group discussion. Choose a leader who must be able to use the knowledge of task and maintenance messages presented earlier in this chapter. At the end of the discussion, the participants should be prepared to provide useful feedback about the techniques of the group leader, their own participation in the discussion, and the reaction of the audience. Summarize your reactions to your own participation in your speech notebook.

HANDLING CONFLICT IN GROUPS

Ideally groups make decisions by members' sharing ideas through calm and reasoned communication. We all recognize, however, that in the real worlds of business, government, industry, and even the family, meetings frequently involve much conflict, and communication that is often neither calm nor reasoned. Though it is natural for members of decision-making groups to come to a meeting with some conflicting goals and problems, how they go about handling their conflicts can determine whether they all win or all lose by the time they part company. Consider the example of a couple who wishes to sell their car. They are asking $1,000 for it. Another couple becomes interested in buying the car, but say they can offer only $800 for it. The two couples share an interest in completing the sale. The first couple has already bought a new car and wants to sell the old car quickly to help pay for the new one. The second couple sees the car as their dream car. But the two parties also have a major area of conflict to deal with—the sale price. If they handle the conflict successfully, they will both win a great deal of what they want. If they cannot come to agreement on some sale price, they will both lose in important ways.

When such conflict arises, as it does regularly in many areas of life, skill in group communication provides one of the major keys to success. When nations are threatening war against one another, experienced diplomats are asked to try to settle the matter through negotiation. When labor and management cannot agree on a contract, they use bargaining and mediation in the hope of avoiding strikes and layoffs which mean lost income and wages for both sides. Within the family, meetings may be held in attempts to reduce conflict among parents and children. When conflict arises, as it frequently does in groups, success in handling it depends largely on how well you can apply several communication skills.

Identify the Warrants of the Opposition   When two viewpoints develop in a group, or members seem to be locking into conflict over an issue, the first communication skill you need to call into action is that of careful listening. This is because it will be difficult, if not impossible, to manage the conflict until you understand its causes. Too many times, unfortunately, once people realize they have a conflict with another person or group, they immediately begin stating only their *position* on the question, and avoid telling their reasons, or **warrants,** for holding that position. Here is an example:

> Jim, the manager of his school's baseball team, needed additional storage space for uniforms. Therefore, he went to the school secretary and requested the key to a storage room next to the gymnasium. The secretary told Jim that another student, Kyle, had already requested use of the storage room. Jim was furious. Coach Martin had promised Jim use of that room. Jim went to Kyle and demanded the key. Kyle refused, and a loud argument followed. Hearing the noise, Coach Martin rushed into the room. "Okay," said the coach. "Suppose you tell me what the problem is."
>
> "Beats me," said Kyle. "I just went to the secretary and got the storage room key, as you told me to do. Now Jim here wants to take the key away from me."
>
> "And, Kyle, do you remember why I asked you to get the key?" said the coach. He smiled knowingly.
>
> "Sure, " said Kyle. "You said you needed it for somebody who wanted to store some uniforms."
>
> "Oh," said Jim with embarrassment. "Sorry."

Had the two boys shared with one another their reasons for wanting the key, they would have avoided an unnecessary disagreement. When you find yourself on one side of a question, first listen for the other side's interest in taking their position. Listen for their "why." When you think you understand the other side's point of view, tell them what you think their reasons are for taking their position. When you do that, they get the feeling they are not wasting their time talking to you. Careful listening builds trust between the two sides.

Explain the Warrants of Your Position   Of course you also need to communicate the warrants, or grounds, on which your position is based. Just as you may not know precisely the warrants of your opponents' position, they can only guess at the warrants of your position unless you explain these warrants carefully. Since your interests are driving you to take your position, you should not be timid about sharing these interests. Explain them in specific, concrete terms with the sense of urgency in your voice that you feel inside.

Many times, once people understand that you too have legitimate reasons for your viewpoint, they become more willing to give you a more open-minded hearing. This is especially true if you can also show them that both of you share certain interests in common, as was the case in the example of the boys and the storage room. In that example, the interests of both sides corresponded perfectly.

Respect Your Opponents' Interests   While it is entirely appropriate to attack a *problem* vigorously, you should carefully avoid attacking the *people* on the other side, as Jim did in the example. Actually, it is not enough to avoid attacking others. You also need to show clearly that you personally support them. Let your opponents know that you respect them. Be courteous, and show your appreciation for their time and effort in trying to work with you towards the best solution.

Work for a Reasonable Solution   Push hard and continuously for decisions based on reason. Work to convince the other side that everyone will benefit more in the long run by an agreement worked out by following fair procedures and fair standards. Perhaps you have heard the age-old method for dividing a pie fairly between two children. You allow one child to cut the pie, and the other to choose the first piece. Though not all complex discussion problems lend themselves to such

To avoid conflicts, participants in a group discussion should address themselves to issues rather than to the personalities and motivations of other group members.

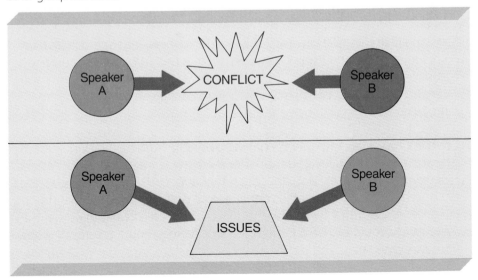

clearcut solutions, there is much to be gained by a constant search for solutions that meet the important needs of both parties. At the same time that you are insisting that the other side listen to reason, you must constantly be willing to accept their statements that strike you as reasonable. When both parties are willing to use objective, factual bases for arriving at solutions, the chances of both winning are markedly increased.

Maintain Dialogue As elementary as this sounds, you would probably be amazed to know how often people clam up as soon as they realize there is a conflict. Since we feel uncomfortable with disagreement, we often simply give up searching for an acceptable solution in our effort to relieve the discomfort. When that happens, everyone loses. If the couples who couldn't agree on price when trying to negotiate the sale of a car simply parted company as soon as they learned they were $200 apart, the sellers would lose an opportunity to make an early sale, and the buyers a chance to get their dream car. All too often when a division develops within a discussion group, people on each side spend most of their time talking among themselves about "the unreasonable position of those other people" rather than communicating with the other side. Holding such mutual agreement parties makes people feel good, but does nothing to solve the conflict. Actually, it frequently serves to deepen the disagreement when the two sides *do* get back together. Only by facing the disagreement with the other side can you ever hope to arrive at an equitable solution.

Application

Handling Conflict

In small groups of from five to seven members, analyze the conflict presented below. Discuss ways in which the two parties could go about resolving the conflict. You do not need to develop a solution. You need only identify the ways in which the parties might approach the problem.

Your town has two parcels of land available for development. One is near a major highway and the other is on the outskirts of town. A land developer wants to put an office building on the parcel near the highway. A group of local residents would prefer to see the building on the other parcel of land. They argue that an office building near the highway would increase traffic dramatically and would create a serious safety problem.

OUTCOMES OF DISCUSSION

If a group meets in an enlightenment discussion (see page 112), it is considered successful when members have learned new information about the topic from each other. It is also successful if members have learned new ways of looking at a situation because of the ideas they have exchanged. In concluding an enlightenment discussion, it is often useful for each member to give a brief summary of the new ideas they have learned during the discussion.

A decision-making group, on the other hand, is successful when its problem is solved or a decision is reached. A group can do this in one of three ways. All of the members can agree on a solution or decision. This is called **consensus.** A decision can also be reached when the members agree to **compromise.** That is, each member or group of members gives up part of the solution or decision they want. In exchange they retain another part of the solution they favor. A **majority vote** is the third way of reaching a decision. The solution or decision favored by over half of the members becomes the solution or decision for the entire group.

Consensus is the most desirable of the three possible outcomes. When everyone genuinely agrees on a single solution, everyone is happier and more committed to helping carry out the group's decision. Unfortunately, consensus is not the most common outcome of group discussion. Compromise and majority votes are frequently necessary. However, compromise and majority votes, when they arise out of honest differences of opinion, are better than false consensus. **False consensus** occurs when several group members keep serious disagreement to themselves and "go along just to make it unanimous." False consensus is an outcome that usually does the group more harm than good.

Application

Reaching a Consensus

Separate into groups of from five to seven. Prepare a statement about your school that will be presented at a student council meeting. The statement should be no longer than 100 words and can be on any subject that the group chooses. The statement will be given to the student council to take whatever action that it thinks is appropriate. It should be signed by all members of the group to show that a consensus has been reached. If an agreement cannot be reached, no statement will be issued, and a member of the group will explain the lack of a consensus to the class.

Participants in a brainstorming session generate creative ideas quickly—with no fear of criticism—by means of free association.

ALTERNATIVES TO GROUP DISCUSSION

This chapter has dealt primarily with the form of group communication called group discussion. Group discussion is one of the most widely used forms of group communication in everyday life. However, group discussion can be a rather slow and difficult process, especially when the group is large. Let's look briefly at two alternative forms of group communication—brainstorming and the nominal technique. Each has certain advantages over group discussion in certain situations.

Brainstorming

Brainstorming is a technique sometimes used in business when it is desirable to produce a large number of creative ideas in a short period of time. Like group discussion, **brainstorming** usually involves three or more people who meet to solve a problem or to share information. A brainstorming session, however, consists of rapidly throwing ideas out on the table, without taking time to evaluate each idea as it is spoken. Since the purpose is only to generate ideas, criticism of any ideas presented is not allowed during a brainstorming session. Group members are encouraged to mention any idea about the topic that occurs to them, even if it seems unusual. The purpose is for each member's idea to spark additional ideas in other members. Brainstorming is only a first step in solving a problem or reaching a decision, however. The ideas are recorded, but not evaluated during the brainstorming session. Evaluating and sorting through the ideas occurs during a later group-discussion session. Sometimes the group discussion of ideas is conducted by the same members who participated in the brainstorming session. Sometimes a different group takes part.

The Nominal Technique

The nominal technique is an alternative form of group communication designed to reduce two problems that often arise in group discussion. One of these problems is the amount of time group discussion takes. The second is the fact that a few members may try to dominate a group discussion. Others may not get a word in edgewise.

A group using the **nominal technique** begins by asking each member to write down a list of possible solutions to the group's problem. There should be no more than seven to nine members in the group, and this first step should take only about 10 to 15 minutes. Each member is then asked to state one idea from her or his list. Each idea stated is listed so that all may see the entire list. The group may ask for a second or third idea from each member. The list may be public, depending on the size of the group and the number of ideas desired. The third step consists of a brief discussion of the ideas on the board. This discussion is primarily to clarify, but may also involve some evaluation of the ideas. Next a secret vote is conducted with each member ranking the ideas in order of personal preference. Finally the rankings are tabulated, and the solution with the highest ranking becomes the group's solution.

The nominal techniques may reduce the amount of time needed to reach a decision and may prevent a few members from dominating the whole group. However, the nominal technique does not permit an in-depth discussion of a problem. Such a discussion usually produces the wisest decision.

Application

Communicating by Brainstorming

Form a brainstorming group with from four to six of your classmates. The purpose of your brainstorming session will be to find a new name for your town or city, your school, a local street, or for some other place that each member of your group is familiar with. Everyone in the group must participate. Appoint one member to record all suggestions. Which are appropriate? Which are inappropriate? Why?

5 Chapter Review

■ Summary

Group discussion is rapidly becoming one of the most widely used forms of interpersonal communication. This chapter has focused on group discussion used to arrive at decisions and to share information.

The Nature of Group Discussion   In group discussion, three or more people meet to solve a common problem, reach a decision, or answer a question of mutual interest. It may be closed, or it may be public if members interact with an audience.

Factors Affecting Group Discussion   Group size, physical environment, seating arrangement, and time of day all affect discussion. A clique can hinder group success, as can the personal goals of members.

How Groups Behave   Behavior patterns can determine a group's success or failure. Leaders must constantly communicate both task and maintenance messages in order to progress toward group goals and must keep harmony among members. The life cycle of groups—forming, storming, norming, and performing—also affects their behavior.

Preparing to Participate in a Group   The topic must be interesting, manageable, and phrased as a clear, unbiased question of fact, value, or policy. A detailed outline must be prepared to keep the group on track.

Leading a Group   Leadership affects a group's overall personality. Leadership activities include introducing group members and the topic; encouraging full participation, suppressing arguments, keeping the discussion on track, and clarifying ideas; and watching the time limit, summarizing the discussion, and eliciting opinions.

Handling Conflict in Groups   Handling group conflict involves listening to the other side; expressing your interests; attacking problems, not people; using reason and being open to reason; and talking the conflict through to resolution.

Outcomes of Discussion For enlightenment groups, success means knowing more about the topic after discussion than before. For decision-making groups, it means reaching a decision by consensus, compromise, or majority vote.

Alternatives to Group Discussion For decision making, group discussion may be too slow or else dominated by a few members. Two alternatives, *brainstorming* and the *nominal technique*, can often help.

 # Vocabulary

Define each term in a complete sentence.

group discussion	clique	biased
decision-making group	cohesiveness	syntality
enlightenment group	task messages	appointed leader
closed-group discussion	maintenance messages	emergent leadership
public discussion	forming	consensus
committee	storming	compromise
round-table discussion	norming	majority vote
panel	performing	false consensus
symposium	question of fact	brainstorming
panel-forum	question of value	nominal technique
symposium-forum	question of policy	warrant

 # Checklist

Group-Discussion Skills

1. Understand the purposes for communicating in groups.
2. Be prepared to participate actively in group discussions.
3. Avoid forming cliques or personal goals that hinder group success.
4. Know how to bring the group back to the subject.
5. Be aware of task and maintenance messages within a group.
6. Take group life cycles into account during discussions.
7. Research the topic beforehand.
8. Practice ways to handle and resolve group conflict.

Review Questions

1. Describe the main purposes of any group discussion.
2. Name the two types of closed-group discussion.
3. State the size limitations that are recommended for effective group discussion.
4. Name some personal goals that may interfere with a productive group discussion.
5. Describe the three main types of discussion questions.
6. State why discussion questions answerable by yes or no should be avoided.
7. Identify the kinds of activities a leader should always perform at the beginning of a group discussion.
8. State under what circumstances a group leader should intervene.
9. Identify the responsibilities of a leader when concluding a group discussion.
10. Name three possible methods by which a group may arrive at a decision.

Discussion Questions

1. As a class, identify ten topics for class discussions and write them on the chalkboard. Discuss each topic to be sure it is of interest to a large number of students in your class. If few students are interested in the topic, eliminate it. Check the wording of each remaining topic to be sure it meets the topic guidelines presented in this chapter. Copy the final list in your speech notebook. The list can be used in future class discussions.
2. What constitutes leadership? What qualities are most important in the student leader? As a class, determine whether you prefer appointed or emergent leadership. Why? Then design a critique sheet that can be used to evaluate a group discussion leader.
3. Discuss with your class the three methods that can be used to reach agreement in a group: consensus, compromise, and majority vote. What are the advantages and disadvantages of each method? Which method does your class prefer? Under what conditions might one method work better than any of the other methods? Why?

Critical Thinking

1. **Analysis:** Discuss the life cycle of groups. Apply the theory to groups that you belonged to. Explain what happened at each stage of the cycle that you have witnessed. Is the theory accurate? Are there any other stages that you would add?

2. **Evaluation:** Do you believe that leadership is a talent that one is born with, or is it an ability that can be acquired and developed? In answering this question, think of all of the aspects of group behavior that you have learned about.

Activities

In-Class

1. Form into small groups of from five to seven people. Imagine that you live in a coastal community that is threatened by an approaching storm. Residents must be evacuated inland to safer ground. You and the other members of your group belong to a committee that is charged with the responsibility of organizing the evacuation. You have the resources of the community at your disposal, but people in the area live in houses that are spread over a wide area. You have only thirty minutes to come up with an appropriate plan.

   After your group has discussed the problem and come up with a solution, discuss the following: Who became the group leader? How did that come about? Did everyone participate in the discussion? Did the group move through the normal stages of growth? Which stage was the most difficult? Compare your results with the other groups in the class.

2. When your class begins to give public speeches in class, the problem of scheduling is sure to arise. Form into groups of from five to seven people and attempt to solve the problem before it arises. Each group should discuss the following questions: What is the best method for determining speaking order? What should be done to keep the class on schedule if assigned speakers are absent? What is an appro-

priate penalty for failing to be prepared to give a speech on an assigned day?

Your group will report its scheduling recommendations to the rest of the class in the form of an oral statement. The class as a whole will then decide by consensus, compromise, or majority vote on all three issues. This decision could be applied to the scheduling of future public speaking assignments.

3. Ask several students in class to be a part of a group discussion on a topic of their choice. The rest of the class can watch the discussion, taking notes on the task and maintenance messages used during the discussion. As a class, review and analyze the discussion.

Out-of-Class

1. Observe a panel discussion by either attending a meeting of your local school board or city or town council or by watching a panel on television. Take careful notes, especially in terms of task/maintenance messages. Afterwards, analyze the dynamics of the communication experience, giving special attention to the task/maintenance factors. Based on these criteria, which participants were most effective as group members? Place your analysis in your speech notebook. Share your findings with your classmates.

2. Interview an adult who is in a job or a career that you find interesting. Ask the interviewee about group discussions that occur in that occupation. Find out about how the processes and outcomes of group discussions are affected by such factors as goal setting, type of leadership, and life cycle stages. Be certain that you gather information on informal discussions, as well as formal ones. Write your findings in your notebook.

3. Compile a list of ten topics that interest you and that you would like to discuss in class. Make your list as diverse as possible. Include topics that cover a wide area of interest. File the list in your notebook for quick reference when discussion topics are being considered in class.

4. Look through a local newspaper for accounts of discussions of various current issues. Clip the articles and label them "value" or "policy" questions. Bring the articles to class and share them with your fellow classmates.

■ Chapter Project

Plan a symposium-forum for a special audience. Complete this project in the following ten steps.

1. Form a committee to choose five topics that are of interest to particular audiences. For example, a symposium on "Contemporary U.S. Poets" would interest an American literature class; a symposium on "U.S./Franco Relations, Now and in the Past" would appeal to a government class. If you prefer to develop a program for an audience outside the classroom, consider a program that might interest your parents, such as "Speech Training: Not *a* Basic—*the* Basic" or a program that might appeal to incoming students at your school, such as "Life at _____ High School."
2. As a class, choose the "best" topic by one of the three methods of group decision-making. (Make certain the topic is well-worded and in the form of a question.)
3. Select from five to seven participants for the symposium.
4. Decide who will lead the symposium, using one of the two methods described in your text.
5. As a class, develop an outline for the discussion and assign subtopics to the participants.
6. Have each participant research his or her specific area of the topic.
7. The participants will then meet to discuss their research and to make minor adjustments, if necessary, in the outline.
8. The participants practice the symposium in class. Those not directly involved in the presentation must keep a written critique of the presentation. These will be submitted to the participants.
9. Publicize the event if it is to be a public performance. Invite an audience if it is to be a special-interest program.
10. Present the symposium before your audience.

Preparing for Public Speaking

unit 3

6 Building Confidence

**When you have completed this chapter
you should be able to:**

- Define the term *stage fright* and state its causes.
- Explain how to control stage fright to help you become an effective speaker.
- Describe some specific methods for gaining confidence.
- Understand the importance of humor and body movements in gaining confidence for speaking.
- Understand the importance of speech critiques in becoming a more confident speaker.

The ease you feel in a group may evaporate when you face an audience alone. It's natural to feel stage fright, and as you learn to control it, your self-confidence will grow.

"The human brain is a wonderful thing. It starts working the moment you are born and never stops until you stand up to speak in public." This quote from well-known entertainer George Jessel illustrates what is probably the most common problem faced by those who give public speeches—the problem of **stage fright.**

Until now you have been learning about and participating in the "calmer" forms of speaking. As you begin your study of *public speaking* you probably feel less calm about standing alone in front of the class than you did about doing an interview or taking part in a small group meeting. That age-old scourge of public speakers, stage fright, may begin to bother you even before your teacher assigns your first speech.

Stage fright is a significant problem for most beginning speakers—an obstacle that can make the difference between success or failure in accomplishing your speech purpose. In this chapter you will face stage fright squarely. You will explore its causes, see what effects it can have (*good* as well as bad), and learn methods for controlling it. Once you can view stage fright as a normal part of a public speaking experience, you are ready to begin building the kind of confidence you need to be an effective speaker.

The potential for public success versus the risk of public failure—this is the conflict that produces stage fright in most people. It is also the source of a special kind of energy that can be controlled and channeled creatively.

UNDERSTANDING STAGE FRIGHT

Of course, you may be one of those people who do not experience stage fright. Some speakers feel as relaxed in front of a large audience as they do chatting with a few friends around the dinner table. If you really feel this way, be happy about it, but do not get overconfident. Being free of stage fright does not automatically make a person a better public speaker than one who suffers from it.

Most People Experience Stage Fright

An old saying goes "misery loves company." If you have been feeling that you are the only one in your class who gets sweaty palms and a queasy stomach at the very thought of giving a speech, you couldn't be more wrong! As a matter of fact, you are part of the majority. Research figures show that over half of the beginning speakers surveyed reported stage fright, and very few experienced speakers were totally free of nervousness. If you were to poll the members of your speech class right now, probably 80 to 90 percent would report some form of nervousness about giving a public speech.

Although the term stage fright is often reserved for public speakers and actors, these same symptoms are also common among tennis and baseball players, concert pianists, and circus clowns—in other words, among most people who must give a public performance of any kind. Nor are these uneasy feelings reserved for inexperienced speakers and performers. Many famous persons, seasoned in appearing before the public, have reported stage fright. Even Sir Winston Churchill, considered one of the most influential speakers of this century, once confessed that he had stage fright when delivering his speeches. The major difference in the effect stage fright has on a beginner and on an experienced speaker comes from how each handles the nervousness once it occurs. Although there is no substitute for platform experience in learning to control stage fright, speakers can start to build confidence with their first speech if they begin correctly.

Why Stage Fright Occurs

The first step in building speaker-confidence is understanding why you usually feel nervous when speaking in public (or even while *preparing* to speak in public). Stage fright affects most people in physical ways —sweaty palms, queasy stomach, dry mouth, excessive perspiration, increased heart rate, shortness of breath. But the beginnings of stage fright are mental, not physical. When you are preparing to give a public speech, a strong psychological **tension** can build up within you. This tension comes from two conflicting realizations: (1) I desperately want to perform well and make a good impression, and (2) I may not be very successful. Your realization that all eyes will be focused on you and that you will be the center of attention intensifies the desire for success and the fear of failure and embarrassment. Most students find it difficult, if not impossible, to take a nonchalant, "so what" attitude about the outcome of speeches they are about to give.

This mental tension carries over to your body, readying you physically as well as mentally to perform well. Just before the start of an important test or athletic event, you have probably experienced this same kind of mental conflict and physical tension. You wanted to succeed so badly you could almost taste it, but you also feared failure and defeat. Once the test or event got underway, however, what happened? Probably you were able to use that tension to think more clearly and perform better. Some coaches of athletic teams check their players' palms before a big game to help them decide on the starting lineup. The players with sweaty palms have the right tension. They are "up" for the game.

Sir Winston Churchill learned to control his stage fright and gave some of the most inspiring speeches of the twentieth century.

Controlled Stage Fright Is Helpful

You can make good use of tension when you are preparing to deliver a speech. Such internal tension causes your muscles to tighten, your heart and breathing rates to increase, and more adrenalin and oxygen to pump throughout your body. The result is that your brain and body muscles become "supercharged." Your body is carrying out its natural function of preparing you to meet a special situation.

Good public speakers can take this result of stage fright and make it work for them by learning how to control it and channel it properly. Well-known speakers have reported that their most successful speeches have been those they were most nervous about beforehand. On other occasions when they were less concerned about making a good impression, or felt overconfident, their presentations fell flat. The simple realization that stage fright is natural before a speech—and actually an aid to sharper thinking—can itself be a means of controlling it. **Controlled stage fright** can then aid you in becoming a successful speaker.

Uncontrolled Stage Fright Can Be Harmful

Inexperienced speakers, unused to feeling the symptoms of stage fright, often think that their dry throat or sweaty palms spell certain doom for their speech. The greater these feelings become the more intense the stage-fright symptoms become. This in turn leads to more worry, which leads to worse symptoms, and so on, and so on. The result is **runaway stage fright.** Its effects are quite different from controlled stage fright and may ruin a well-prepared speech.

Runaway stage fright takes one of two forms. The first form is born of **lack of confidence** and usually strikes before the speech begins. Many times the speaker who experiences this form is actually well-prepared for the speech, but has allowed the symptoms of stage fright to snowball. As a result, self-confidence is at a very low point by the time the speech begins, and this leads to runaway stage fright. The second form arises from poor preparation combined with **overconfidence** and ordinarily does not occur until after the speech has begun. Read in a quote from Mark Twain's famous story how Tom Sawyer suffered great embarrassment when he experienced this form of runaway stage fright.

> Tom Sawyer stepped forward with conceited confidence and soared into the unquenchable and indestructible 'Give me liberty or give me death' speech, with fine fury and frantic gesticulation, and broke down in the middle of it. A ghastly stage fright seized him, his legs quaked under him and he was like to choke.

As you have read, this second form strikes suddenly and takes the speaker by surprise. Inadequate preparation does not always surface during introductory remarks, but it may become very obvious once a speaker has reached the body of the speech. At that point, a moment of forgetfulness is all that is necessary to trigger sudden stage fright.

Since both too little confidence and overconfidence can initiate stage fright, the wise speaker must aim for that critical degree of self-assurance that comes from thorough preparation, mixed with a realization of the unpredictable nature of a public speaking situation.

Stage Fright Feels Worse Than It Looks

Stage fright is a problem that is much more noticeable to the speaker than to others. Beginning speakers sometimes experience the feelings caused by stage fright so intensely they fail to realize that their listeners aren't nearly so aware of their nervousness. The audience can't see or hear your tightening stomach muscles, nor will they ordinarily notice your sweaty palms or dry mouth. They might notice a slight tremor in your voice occasionally or a faster-than-normal breathing rate, but even these symptoms bother the speaker much more than the listeners. Realizing this fact can make a big difference for some stage-fright sufferers.

Chronic victims of stage fright are generally not content to worry only about their possible inability to speak clearly or remember ideas. They like to worry in big bundles, so they also get concerned about what kind of impression their stage-fright symptoms will make on the audience. For such giant-economy-size worriers, it should be comforting to realize that stage fright always feels much worse than it appears to others. Unless speakers foolishly call specific attention to their stage fright by comments such as "I'm so nervous, I'm sure this speech isn't making much sense," the audience will often be unaware that the speakers are nervous.

Application

Focusing on Stage Fright

Give a two-minute impromptu speech about some aspect of speaking in public that gives you stage fright. Explain it in detail, telling why you find it frightening and explaining what you might do to overcome the stage fright. Ask for suggestions from your classmates on other techniques that you might use to control your fear.

CONTROLLING YOUR NERVOUSNESS

Before you began reading this chapter you very likely imagined that the best way to deal with stage fright was to rid yourself of it. By now you know that a limited amount of stage fright can be helpful. The trick is to control that amount—not to get rid of it entirely. The next question, then, is "How do I go about controlling my stage fright?"

Prepare Thoroughly

One effective method for controlling stage fright is to prepare thoroughly for each public speech. Since most stage fright comes from a fear of not succeeding in front of the audience, thorough preparation can guarantee that about 90 percent of your speech will go smoothly. When you are the speaker, you are the person with the greatest control over what occurs during the speech. Make sure you are well prepared.

1. Study your topic.

2. Analyze the needs of your audience.

3. Research and outline the ideas of your speech.

4. Rehearse your presentation sufficiently.

If you do all these things, you will have little reason to fear that something unplanned or unpleasant will happen. Thus you can begin your speech with confidence.

The possibility always exists that something unexpectedly disturbing will occur (a loud noise, a heckler, a fire drill), but such interruptions occur very infrequently. Just keeping in mind this possibility will keep you sufficiently alert, but not allow you to become overconfident.

Thorough preparation can not only give you the right level of confidence *before* your speech begins but also support you once you have started speaking. One of the greatest fears of most beginning speakers is the fear of forgetting part of their speech. Once you have gained some experience at giving speeches, you will realize this is not such a serious problem as it may first seem. For one thing, the audience ordinarily does not know in advance what you intend to say, so even if you leave out a large section of your planned speech, no one is the wiser. (Don't call attention to an omission by mentioning you have forgotten something or by appearing confused.) Second, most speakers have note

By researching her topic thoroughly, this student is building a reliable foundation for herself as a public speaker.

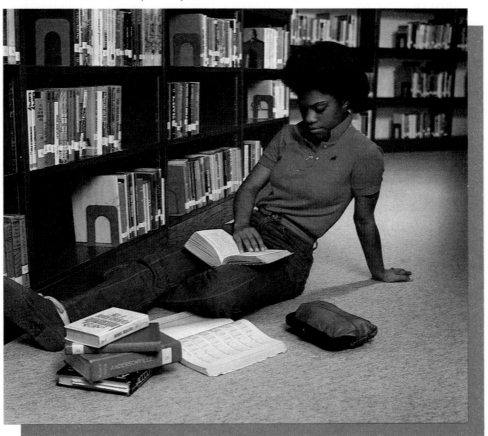

cards available during their speech to help jog their memories if they forget a point. Finally, forgetting is seldom a problem if a speaker has rehearsed thoroughly and correctly. You will see in the next chapter that correct preparation does not mean word-for-word memorization of your speech. If you try to do this, you put a tremendous burden on your memory and are likely to forget.

Relax Before You Speak

Even when thoroughly prepared, many speakers experience physical tension shortly before they are to speak. Some can feel their neck muscles tightening. Others will experience tense stomach muscles. Some may have problems with their facial muscles. Though these are symptoms rather than causes of stage fright, speakers quite frequently find it helpful to relax physically before beginning a speech. Relaxing one's body is a way of convincing oneself that things aren't really hopeless.

Listed here are several relaxation techniques that will help reduce the physical symptoms of stage fright. They should be done as close to the start of a speech as possible, without being noticeable to your audience. Most of these techniques can be done privately just before you join your listeners.

1. Force yourself to yawn widely several times. Fill your lungs with air each time by breathing deeply.

2. Let your head hang down as far as possible on your chest for several moments. Then slowly rotate it in a full circle, at the same time allowing your eyelids to droop lazily. Let your mouth and lower jaw hang open loosely. Repeat this rolling motion five or six times, very slowly.

3. Sit in a slumped position in a chair as if you were a rag doll. Allow your arms to dangle beside the chair, your head to slump on your chest, and your mouth to hang open. Then tighten all muscles one at a time, starting with your toes and working up your body to your neck. Next, gradually relax each set of muscles, starting at the top and working back down to your toes. Repeat this process several times.

Realize Audiences Tend to Be Sympathetic

Audiences are usually sympathetic to the problem of stage fright. Most listeners realize that they could have the same feelings if they were the one at the podium, and they show by their sympathetic treatment of the speaker that they would expect the same charity in return. Audiences want to see speakers succeed, not fail. To the extent that listeners *do* notice symptoms of stage fright, they will usually react in a friendly and encouraging fashion.

CANDIDATE FOR PUBLIC OFFICE

Political candidates must become polished public speakers in order to gain the public favor necessary to win an election. The pressure to succeed drives many candidates to develop speaking skills quickly, often within a few months.

Most candidates experience some of the symptoms of stage fright, especially at the beginning of their campaigns. Those who thoroughly research and study the issues they plan to speak about, however, can face an audience with increased confidence. Altering a talk according to the group being addressed is another excellent technique candidates use to attract an audience's attention. A successful speech to a local businessmen's group, for example, would include a knowledgeable discussion of business-related issues.

Using humor at the beginning of a speech also helps candidates capture audience attention. An audience's enthusiastic response to humor often gives speakers the impetus to continue with more assurance. Effective speakers also practice the use of gestures and platform movement to help them communicate a message more forcefully. Making direct eye contact with listeners and using appropriate gestures are skills that candidates must practice repeatedly to be effective.

Fortunately for political candidates, their campaigning necessitates frequent public speaking. With this additional practice, they can increase their speaking skills by experimenting, rehearsing, and mastering the art of public speaking— abilities that will serve them well throughout their political careers.

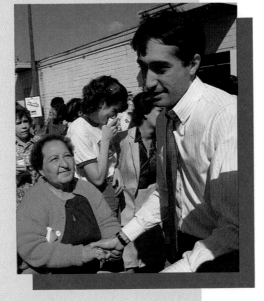

A well-prepared political candidate inspires confidence.

Develop the Right Attitude

If you are like most speakers you are destined to feel some of the symptoms of stage fright before every speech. Since it is probably impossible to prevent these symptoms from occurring, the key to success lies in your mental attitude toward the feelings. Once the butterflies-in-the-stomach and the shaking knees begin, train yourself to think in the following sequence:

1. Since the time for my speech is getting near, what I'm feeling are symptoms of stage fright.

2. This is my body's way of preparing me to meet a special speech situation.

3. Once my speech begins, this tension will serve as a spring to sharpen my thinking and give vitality to my presentation.

If you look upon stage fright as something positive, you are less likely to experience the kind of runaway stage fright that befalls speakers who see it as a totally negative experience. Controlled stage fright will then aid you in becoming a successful speaker.

Concentrate on Your Topic

Many beginning speakers lack confidence because they are thinking too much about themselves: "Will I do as well as that last speaker when my turn comes?" "Should I be making more gestures?" "My mouth feels dry." Instead, begin to develop a positive attitude. Say to yourself: "I have a topic that I really want to share with these listeners. I want to make certain they are informed (persuaded, entertained), and I will do everything in my power to assure that they are." Once you begin truly thinking in those terms, the worst symptoms of stage fright are likely to disappear.

How can you begin developing such an attitude? For one thing, choose your speech topics carefully. Select something you are genuinely interested in and let your speech be an opportunity to share your enthusiasm for that topic with your audience. Don't get up in front of your audience with the feeling "I *have* to give a speech today," but with the feeling "I have a speech to give today!"

Concentrate on Your Audience

While you are actually delivering your speech, search the faces of your audience to make certain they are following your ideas and to see whether the listeners agree with your ideas. If you perceive boredom growing among your listeners, change tactics and attempt to regain their attention and interest.

Of course, in any audience, some listeners will appear more interested than others. It is perfectly all right to give more of your attention while speaking to the interested listeners. Their obvious appreciation for your speech can be a great confidence-builder for you.

Some speakers make the mistake of attempting to interest the most bored or disgusted-looking member of the audience. Nearly every audience will have one or two such people. If you change your tactics to suit them, you may be ruining what was a highly rewarding speech for 90 percent of your listeners. Only when a large portion of your audience is showing signs of boredom or disinterest should you begin changing your approach.

If you concentrate on looking for audience feedback and making an appropriate response to it, you will have little time to think about yourself. As you think less about yourself, your stage fright will be controlled and your confidence will increase.

Inject a Little Humor

Humor has long been used as a means of reducing tension between speaker and audience. Getting a laugh from an audience builds confidence rapidly; a speaker is assured that there is little to fear from the listeners. Once your speech has begun, injecting a bit of humor, particularly near the beginning, relaxes you more effectively than anything else. If not overdone, humor can actually relax your audience as well. When using humor, observe these precautions:

1. Prepare humor thoroughly beforehand, making certain it will be understood and appreciated by this particular audience. A joke that falls flat can destroy a speaker's confidence rather than build it.

2. Use humor mainly during the speech introduction, sprinkling lesser amounts throughout the remainder of the speech.

3. Do not overuse humor.

4. Avoid offensive jokes.

Move About, Use Gestures, and Make Eye Contact

Believe it or not, moving while delivering a speech can help reduce nervous tension as well as the other symptoms of stage fright. Have you ever narrowly missed being in a car accident? If so, you probably noticed that right after your near miss you were trembling. Your body was getting rid of the tension that had built up suddenly when you saw the accident coming. In much the same way, movement of one's body while speaking helps dissipate some of the tension the speaker feels.

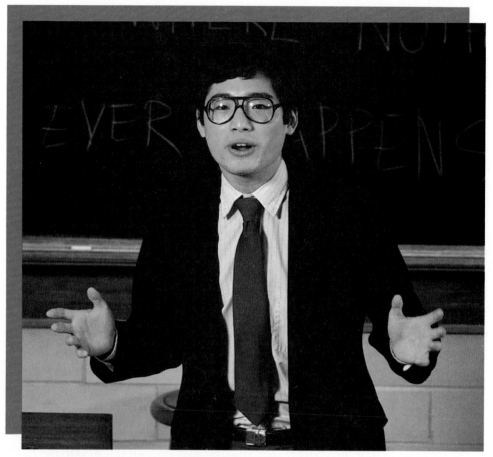

This speaker physically helps his audience make the transition from one idea to another by using gestures and platform movement.

Any movements you make should be suited to the speech and the audience. All kinds of movement will reduce tension, but some forms look pretty ridiculous during a public speech. Beginning speakers, in a subconscious attempt to reduce stage fright, occasionally use movements that tend to distract the listeners from the message. Among these awkward movements several have become fairly common, and might be given names.

The Ping-Pong Pacers constantly pace to and fro in front of the audience until the listeners appear to be viewing a ping-pong tournament. The Lectern Leeches grab the sides of the lectern so tightly their knuckles turn white. The Hair-Tossers, whose hair may not really be in their eyes, regularly toss their heads to get it out of the way. The Pencil-Twirlers manage to draw all eyes to a pencil, paper clip, rubber band, or note card they are folding, spindling, or mutilating as they speak.

Movements that help communicate your message nonverbally are the only kind you should strive to make while speaking. Such movements release nervous tension just as effectively as the distracting ones but have the added advantage of helping you get your message across. Chapter 9 on delivery will present communicative body movements in detail. For the time being, however, notice that they fall into three broad categories:

Total Body Movement   Except for very formal occasions, a speaker should occasionally change positions on the platform. Moving the entire body is called **platform movement.** Such movement looks best when it is made on a diagonal: not directly on a forward-backward axis, nor completely on a side-to-side axis, but between the two. Total body movement is especially appropriate when a speaker is making a major transition in thought patterns or when it is desirable to get closer to one part of the audience where attention seems to be flagging. Movement can also be useful in simply providing variety after a speaker has been in one position for some time. Naturally any amount of total body movement that resembles the antics of a Ping-Pong Pacer is too much.

Gestures   Although some people tend to "talk with their hands" more than others do, most beginning public speakers tend to be too "quiet" with their arms and hands. Practicing specific gestures for a particular point in a speech is not wise. Gestures during a live performance should not look practiced. Gestures should look natural and be natural. One way to achieve this is to use general arm and hand movements during rehearsal. This is likely to loosen you up and lead to similar natural arm and hand gestures during the speech.

Gestures also include movements of the head and face. While speaking, try to move your head frequently to look from one part of your audience to another. You should also vary your facial expression to correspond with the thought patterns of your speech. Again, your movements should be natural.

Eye Contact   Remember that your eyes may be your most effective means of body-motion communication. Many students ask, "Do I have to look right into the eyes of my listeners?" Eye contact is very desirable because of the feeling it gives each audience member that you are speaking to him or her personally. However, if you find in your first few speeches that you get less confused and nervous by simply looking at your audience as a whole and not directly into individuals' eyes, then do so. However, you should make it your goal eventually to look directly into the eyes of several of your listeners.

Application

Humor and Body Movements

Prepare a short speech and give it in class. Your topic should be one that has a humorous side to it. Introduce your topic with a humorous story and sprinkle humor throughout the rest of the speech. Also, make appropriate use of body movements, gesture, and eye contact. After the speech, ask your classmates to evaluate the content of your talk and your use of movement and gesture.

Handle Specific Symptoms of Nervousness

Some symptoms of stage fright may bother you more than others. The chart on page 163 shows several of the more obvious ones with suggestions for handling each. Successfully handling symptoms that you find particularly annoying will help build your confidence.

Speak As Often As You Can

Confidence in public speaking is built more by the experience of giving speeches than by anything else. This class will provide you with several opportunities to deliver speeches, but it may not provide enough experience to make you truly confident of your abilities on the platform. If you genuinely want to feel at ease about public speaking, look for speaking opportunities outside the classroom. Many organizations that you are eligible to join sponsor speech contests each year. The Future Business Leaders of America (FBLA) is one such organization, as is the Future Farmers of America (FFA). Most local Optimist Clubs have speech contests for high school students. Scout organizations give merit badges for public speaking. In addition, your school may have a debating team or a speech club which sponsors tournaments with nearby schools. By getting involved in these kinds of activities you can gain valuable experience in public speaking as well as develop a much greater sense of confidence.

Use Speech Critiques to Your Advantage

Many speech students find both giving and receiving critiques of their classroom speeches awkward. You may be one of those who tolerates a critique of your speech by your teacher, but dislikes your classmates' commenting on your presentation. Perhaps you feel even worse about having to critique someone else's speech, thinking that you may hurt or anger that person.

Symptoms	Solutions
trembling hands and a rattling manuscript	Use 3 x 5 note cards. Place them on the lectern and slide each card to one side after it has been used.
stumbling over words – getting "tongue twisted"	Deliberately slow down your speaking rate until the problem disappears.
the feeling that you cannot get enough breath	Speak slowly. Take longer pauses between sentences. Breathe from your diaphragm through your nose.
unwillingness to look at the audience	In the beginning, do not look directly at individuals. Instead look just above their heads or slightly to one side of their faces. Later, pick the friendliest face in the audience and look first at that person.
excessive perspiration	Ignore it. Do not call attention to it by wiping your hands or forehead.
cold hands and feet	Make some platform movement and gestures.
hoarse or squeaky voice	Before a speech, tape record your rehearsal sessions and concentrate on eliminating vocal problems. If this problem occurs during a speech, ignore it.
dry mouth	Speak slowly to avoid getting tongue tied. Do not lick your lips in front of the audience.
tense muscles	Use platform movement and gestures.
cramps, butter-flies, or stomach noises	Remember that the audience is ordinarily not aware of such symptoms. Ignore them as much as possible.
wanting to return to your seat	Resist this feeling at all costs. The best way to control stage fright is by having experience in public speaking.
feeling inferior	Try dressing for the speech in the outfit that makes you look your best. Naturally, it must be appropriate to the audience and occasion.

Common symptoms of stage fright have practical solutions.

Speech critiques are one of the best ways of teaching you to become a confident and effective public speaker. You learn from your mistakes in giving speeches just as you did when you first took swimming lessons or were on your first softball team. Had your instructor or coach never told you what you were doing right and wrong, you might never have learned to swim or play ball very well. As a matter of fact, you might only have succeeded in deepening your bad habits. What makes a speech class different from a swimming lesson though, is that your classmates are your real audience for your classroom speeches. Learning to adapt to a live audience is a major part of what giving speeches is all about. If your classmates are not allowed to tell what they feel are strong points and not-so-strong points in your speech, you will have a hard time discovering the best ways to relate to other audiences later on.

If what you dislike most about speech critiques is giving them rather than receiving them, remember that you are in a speech class to learn to *listen* as well as to speak. Preparing either a written or an oral critique of one of your classmates' speeches gives you an excellent opportunity to pay close attention to all the details of her or his presentation. You learn listening skills, and at the same time you discover techniques you may want to adopt or avoid in your own speeches.

Of course students just learning public speaking are not yet experts on the art of giving speeches. At times your critiques may include some bad advice. After a fellow student has critiqued your speech, listen carefully for any parts of that critique with which your teacher may disagree. It is your teacher who is the real expert on the subject in your speech class. He or she will be able to balance your classmate's critique with an assessment based on extensive training and experience.

Once you get involved in contest speaking, you also need to consider carefully the critiques of contest judges. Many of their comments will be valid, but judges differ in their approaches to, and perceptions of how speeches should be given. Here again, go over judges' comments carefully with your speech teacher, looking for similar comments from a number of judges. This careful study is the best method for determining the validity of comments.

Finally, remember that everyone who hears your speeches is there to help you improve—your teacher, your fellow students, and contest judges. There is no place in a speech classroom for mean-spirited criticism. When you are asked to give a critique, begin by mentioning the strong points you noticed. Be specific and detailed. Then, in a kind, constructive tone, mention one or two areas where the speaker can improve. When you are on the receiving end of a critique, remember that your critic is trying to help you learn. Such a sharing and caring atmosphere in speech classrooms can help build speaker confidence as much as anything can.

How to Be a Good Speech Critic

- Begin with the positive points. Tell the speaker you found the speech well organized and easy to follow before you say he or she looked nervous.

- Be specific, especially with positive comments. It is much more helpful to say "Your use of humor was very good. The two stories about the giant and the clown really got our attention" than to simply comment "Your humor was good."

- Criticize the speech, not the speaker. Say "The point about the existence of witches needed more proof" rather than "You failed to prove that witches really exist."

- State your reactions as your opinion. Avoid being dogmatic; don't say such things as "You needed to look more toward the right side of the room." Instead, state how you saw it and how effective it seemed to you: "I felt you needed to look toward the right side of the room more. I felt left out because I didn't notice you looking at me."

- Focus on improvement. Suggest how the speaker might improve a specific part of his or her performance the next time. Say "In your next speech, you might want to move a few steps to either side of the podium occasionally" rather than "You didn't move around enough."

- Don't debate your critique with the speaker. Remember, you're not the speech expert. Neither is the speaker. Offer your perceptions and suggestions, then let your teacher clear up any misunderstandings.

- Keep your critique brief. Usually it is best to mention only one or two positive, then one or two negative points. Don't give a speech of your own when you mention each point. State the point concisely, then move on.

- Show empathy for the speaker. Let the speaker know you understand how he or she felt during the speech. A comment such as "I get so nervous I usually talk too fast too" can help build a positive atmosphere about classroom critiques.

Application

Speech Critiques

Practice giving and critiquing impromptu speeches in class. Choose speakers, assign topics, and choose someone to critique each speech as well. The person giving the impromptu speech should focus positively on his or her topic and delivery, and should avoid anticipating the critique while speaking. The person offering the critique should carefully follow the guidelines presented in this chapter. Be especially careful to begin each critique with positive comments. After each critique, the class as a whole can react to and discuss the appropriateness and usefulness of the critique.

6 Chapter Review

■ Summary

Understanding the true nature of stage fright and learning how to control it are two of the most important things you can do as a beginning public speaker.

Understanding Stage Fright Stage fright is a problem that affects the great majority of public speakers, as well as the majority of other people who perform in public. While both experienced and inexperienced speakers suffer from it, those with experience generally handle it more effectively.

Stage fright starts in your mind. A strong psychological tension urges you to do well and at the same time reminds you that you might not do very well at all. This tension triggers physical reactions such as sweaty palms, a queasy stomach, a dry mouth, and shaking limbs. Such symptoms of stage fright can prevent a successful speech if allowed to get out of control. At a controlled level, however, it can be helpful and can actually promote a successful speech by "supercharging" your body and sharpening your thinking.

Controlling Your Nervousness One of the best methods for dealing with stage fright is thorough preparation. Knowing that you are completely ready for a speech can greatly reduce most nervousness. Practicing various relaxation techniques while waiting your turn to speak is helpful in relieving the physical symptoms of nervous tension. If you remember that audiences are sympathetic and that a little tension is good, you will be developing the right mental attitude for public speaking. Concentrating on your topic and the audience rather than on yourself is particularly useful in controlling excess tension. A speaker who is making sure that the audience is "getting the message" has little time to worry about the impression his or her performance is making.

In addition, injecting humor into your speech helps both you and your audience to relax, and using communicative body movements during your delivery dissipates a lot of your physical tension. In the process of learning to handle the specific symptoms of stage fright you will build your confidence. In addition, there is no substitute for actual speaking experience as a cure for stage fright.

Speech critiques can be a useful tool if they are used to benefit the speaker. Be attentive to the critiques of others, using their helpful suggestions. When you are the critic, always be as positive as possible. Be sure that your remarks are kind.

 Vocabulary

Define each term in a complete sentence.

stage fright
tension
controlled stage fright
runaway stage fright

lack of confidence
overconfidence
platform movement

 Checklist

Confidence-Building Skills

1. Use the realization that most people experience stage fright to build self-confidence.
2. Understand why you experience stage fright, and control it by applying the knowledge you have gained in this chapter.
3. Use controlled stage fright as a positive impetus for becoming a good public speaker.
4. Be aware that uncontrolled stage fright can be harmful, and take steps to turn it into controlled stage fright.
5. Control nervousness by preparing your speeches thoroughly and by practicing relaxation before you speak.
6. Make use of audience sympathy to control stage fright.
7. Use humor in your speeches to help you build confidence.
8. Use body movements to help you release tension and become a polished speaker.
9. Speak as often as you can.
10. Learn to use speech critiques as a way to build confidence.

Review Questions

1. Identify two emotions that cause the tension leading to stage fright.
2. Describe how controlled stage fright can help a speaker.
3. Name two causes of uncontrolled stage fright.
4. Name several ways in which stage fright can show itself during a speech.
5. Describe the role of an audience when a speaker experiences stage fright.
6. Describe how thorough preparation for a public speech can reduce nervousness.
7. Describe several methods a speaker can use to relax before giving a speech.
8. Name several attitudes toward stage fright that can help a speaker control it.
9. Describe how physical movements can help to reduce stage fright.
10. Name a way to control each symptom of stage fright.

Discussion Questions

1. Discuss experiences you have had with stage fright in non-speech situations, such as sports events, musical performances, or fashion shows. How did those situations compare to delivering a public speech?
2. With the class, discuss your ideas about what causes stage fright in public speaking situations. If you know of any famous performers who have stage fright, identify them and include their remarks in your discussion. Identify factors that seem to increase tension and self-consciousness. Share your findings and try to identify some common themes.
3. Discuss ways that humor can be used to relax the speaker and to make positive contact with the audience. What precautions should be taken when humor is included in speeches? Make a class list of do's and don'ts for humor in public speaking.
4. Discuss with your classmates any experiences you can recall that involved overconfidence. Do athletic teams sometimes lose the "easiest" game of the season? Have you ever failed a test because of overconfi-

dence? What causes overconfidence? What often results from overconfidence?

5. Discuss your feelings about giving and receiving criticism. Do you object to receiving criticism more from peers than from adults? Do you view all critics in the same way? Do you see value in criticism? Why or why not? What are your thoughts on self-evaluation? When you critique others, do you feel self-conscious? What can be done to deliver a critique in an objective manner?

Critical Thinking

1. **Analysis:** Imagine that you have chosen a topic for a speech that you are really interested in. Moreover, you have spent a number of hours researching your topic and have assembled a large amount of evidence to support the points you will make in your speech. Analyze the effects that this type of preparation is likely to have on stage fright. Have your chances of suffering from stage fright increased or lessened?

2. **Evaluation:** A critique of a speech can benefit both the speaker and the person who offers the critique. How does a critique benefit a speaker? How does a critique benefit the one who gives it? In what ways is the giving of a critique similar to the giving of a speech?

Activities

In-Class

1. Design a poster promoting a campaign to control stage fright. Think of a slogan and promote the idea that this mental monster can be brought under control. Include all of the steps outlined in the text for controlling your nervousness. If someone in your group is artistic, create a character that represents "fear." Choose the best poster and display it in your classroom as a constant reminder.

2. Invite a well-known local person who is frequently in the public eye or someone who is used to public performances to your class as a guest speaker. Try to find someone from the field of sports, from television, or from politics. Prepare a list of questions you will ask to find out (a) whether he or she experiences stage fright prior to or during speeches or performances, and (b) what techniques he or she uses to control stage fright.

3. Since most students report that the greatest problem with stage fright is in the opening moments of a speech, practice getting started by doing the following: (a) Rise from your seat and go to the front of the room. (b) Take a few seconds to observe your audience. (c) Give an introduction for a speech on a topic of your choice. (d) Receive audience reaction. (e) Return to your seat. This "practice" introduction will help you to feel that you have been in front of the audience, at least briefly, before you make a formal presentation. Write your response to the experience in your speech notebook.

4. Review a number of different types of critique sheets for various speech activities. Make certain that you understand the criteria listed. Determine the best critique sheet for public-speaking assignments for this class.

Out-of-Class

1. Read the symptoms of stage fright listed in this chapter. Which of these symptoms do you experience most often? Compose a list for your speech notebook. Put at the top of the list those symptoms that you feel most frequently, and put at the bottom of the list the symptoms that you seldom, if ever, experience. Concentrate on the symptom that causes you the most discomfort and write the suggested solution next to the symptom. Practice the solution. Then move down the list and deal with the next most discomforting symptom. Follow the same process until you have dealt with all of the symptoms on your list.

2. Identify a friend or relative who will be your "silent partner" for this semester in preparing for speeches. Choose someone who will listen to your speeches in rehearsal and will give you both positive feedback and constructive suggestions for improvement. Share your feelings about making a speech and explain the

specific ways that you are working to overcome stage fright. Ask him or her to identify verbal or nonverbal signals that you are sending that may be distracting or that may be signs of nervousness. These signals may be unconsciously sent, and you will not be aware of them unless someone points them out to you. Keep track of your progress in your speech notebook.

3. Learn ways to "psyche yourself up" for the next speaking assignment. Choose a topic that you are really interested in.

Get excited about your speech. Tell other people about your enthusiasm. Walk briskly to the front of the room. Send out positive nonverbal signals throughout the speech. Make yourself and others believe that it was a thoroughly enjoyable experience. Keep a record in your speech notebook of the effects of your enthusiasm. Did it help you make a better speech? Did you feel better about yourself and your performance? Did your enthusiasm reach your audience?

Chapter Project

Put together a videotape or audio-tape presentation on the subject of stage fright. Create a documentary or a docudrama and include

1. an analysis of the nature and causes of stage fright
2. a consideration of positive and negative aspects
3. general suggestions for overcoming nervousness
4. instructions for dealing with specific symptoms
5. testimony on the subject by well-known individuals
6. an evaluation of criticism as a tool for growth

Compose an outline or script for the program. Involve as many members of your class as possible. Rehearse it several times before taping it.

When the tape is complete, make it available to other groups and individuals in your school who participate in public performance. It should be especially welcomed by vocational clubs and special-interest organizations that feature public-speaking contests as a part of their annual activities.

7 Preparing Your Speech

When you have completed this chapter you should be able to:

- Identify ways to choose a speech topic that appeals to an audience.
- Understand and put into practice research skills.
- Prepare a speech outline.
- Recognize the importance of rehearsal in preparation for a speech.

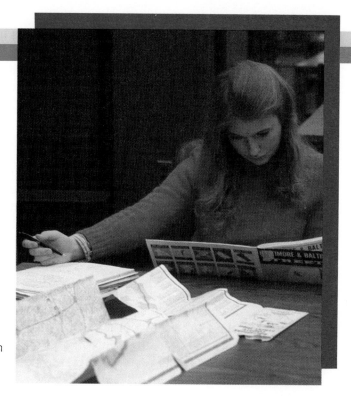

Research and rehearsal are cornerstones of solid speech preparation.

In order to construct a solid and functional house, builders must start with a set of plans. The process of drawing up the plans is, in some ways, as important as the actual construction process itself. Many critical questions must be answered in the plans: "Will the foundation be adequate to support the weight of the house? Are the rooms arranged properly for maximum convenience? Is the structure placed in the best possible position on the lot?" By first building the house in their minds and on paper, the builders can save great amounts of time and money. A mistake at this early stage is easily fixed; mistakes made after construction has started are generally very expensive to correct.

Wise speakers will build their speeches in much the same manner that builders construct houses—first in their minds and on paper. Each speaker's preparation, like the builder's, should answer many critical questions: "What topic fits the occasion and is of interest both to me and to my audience? What strategy best suits the particular audience I will be addressing? Where can I locate the best sources of information and supporting evidence? In what order should I present my ideas?" Without ample time to answer these questions beforehand, a speaker runs a great risk of having the speech crumble into a disorganized jumble of words.

On the other hand, a well-prepared speaker goes into a speech confident of the outcome. This chapter will deal with the preliminary steps in giving a speech—those important steps prior to the actual delivery of the speech that will determine whether the speech sounds smooth and natural or halting and awkward.

FOCUSING ON YOUR TOPIC

The first part of speech preparation involves focusing on your topic. This process starts with your selecting a general subject, then deciding on your general speech purpose. Once this has been done, you focus your topic by narrowing it to fit the particular interests of your audience and the time limit available to you.

Find a Subject That Fascinates You

Begin by searching your mind for a general subject that you find interesting. You should make this decision carefully because the choice of topic can make or break your speech. Write down a list of single words or short phrases naming subjects you find fascinating. At this point you are looking for broad subjects only. Here is a brief sample list:

Airplanes	TV	Equality
Camping	Disease	Space
Nuclear power	College choice	Holidays
The media	Teachers	Vacations
Stereotyping	Cooking	Economics
Health care	Summer jobs	Latin America
Farming	School grades	Computers
Music	Hobbies	Automobiles
Sports	War	Legislation

Sometimes speech students think they must come up with a brand new or highly unusual topic if they want their speeches to succeed. Not at all. As long as you are enthusiastic about your topic, you will be able to generate enthusiasm among your listeners. Throughout history the speeches that have made the greatest impact have been given by speakers totally wrapped up in their topics. Martin Luther King, Jr.'s "I Have a Dream" speech was given by a man whose life was dedicated to attaining civil rights for all citizens of the United States. President John F.

Kennedy's "Ich bin ein Berliner" speech was given by a man who had a deep love of freedom and great admiration for the brave citizens of West Berlin. Similarly, most student speakers who have won national speech contests have been those who chose a topic that genuinely concerned them and not those who simply latched onto any topic just to enter a contest.

Analyze Your Audience

Not every subject that is interesting to you will automatically be of interest to your audience. Classmates who do not sew may be difficult to reach in a speech about dressmaking. You may have problems convincing those with no interest in football that your speech about your favorite football player is electrifying. However, with enough enthusiasm you should be able to make most topics interesting to anyone. As you choose your subject, ask yourself "How can I make this topic interesting and acceptable to all the members of my audience?" Answering this question involves audience analysis, one of the most important steps in speech preparation.

Jesse Jackson reaches his audiences by knowing their needs, interests, and attitudes toward his topic.

When you are just beginning to select your speech topic, **audience analysis** consists of asking yourself a series of questions about any topic you are considering for your speech. Ask yourself questions such as the following:

- Do my audience members already know much about this topic?

- What can I tell them about this topic that they do not already know?

- Will this topic interest some audience members more than others?

- If I take a stand on this issue, will my audience agree with me?

- If they do not agree, what interests or needs do they have through which I might change their minds?

Asking and answering questions such as these about your audience will help you organize your topic for presentation to a specific group of people. Just as in one-to-one conversation, an audience tends to be responsive when members perceive that a speaker has taken their knowledge, interests, needs, and attitudes into consideration.

Audience analysis for a classroom speech is relatively easy. After a few weeks in a speech class you will become acquainted with most of the class members who will form the audience for your speeches. You can readily guess what their interests and attitudes are. Whenever you are unsure, you will have frequent opportunities to ask them directly. You may also find it helpful to discuss your possible speech topics with one or two friends from your speech class. Two or three of you can probably share insights about class members' interests that will prove helpful to each of you in selecting your speech topics.

Once you have chosen your topic, you will need to do more audience analysis than what has been mentioned thus far, especially for persuasive speeches. This further audience analysis is treated in Chapter 11.

Application

Choosing Topics for a Class Speech

The class will divide into several small groups of from five to seven members each. Each group will discuss speech topics that the class would be interested in hearing about. Five topics will be chosen by each group and presented to the class for general discussion. A master list of all accepted suggestions will be prepared and distributed to each student. Keep this list in your speech notebook and refer to it for ideas when selecting a speech topic.

Select Your General Speech Purpose

The general purposes for which speeches are given fall into a fairly small number of categories:

Speeches to Inform   Here your general purpose is to teach your listeners new information. You want them to know more about your topic after your speech than they did before.

Speeches to Persuade   Persuasive speeches are designed to intensify or change listeners' attitudes, beliefs, or behavior patterns.

Speeches to Entertain   Speeches to entertain are given simply for the enjoyment and relaxation of the listeners. They are frequently delivered as after-dinner speeches.

Speeches of Introduction   These are usually brief speeches for the purpose of giving an audience background information on a main speaker they are about to hear.

Speeches of Welcome   These are given when a new person joins a company, a club, or a fraternity, or when a dignitary visits a city or town for the first time. Their purpose is to make the newcomer feel part of the group he or she is joining.

Speeches of Presentation and Acceptance   Here the purpose is to highlight the presentation or acceptance of an award or gift to a deserving individual or organization.

In addition, speeches are given to dedicate buildings, to honor graduates from school, to eulogize those who have died, to say farewell when someone is moving, to demonstrate a product, to motivate groups to perform and achieve, and to inspire an audience.

The two primary speech purposes are to inform and to persuade. Chapter 10 treats the informative speech in detail, and Chapter 11 deals with speeches to persuade. Many of the other types of speeches are covered in Chapter 12. You may want to look ahead to these chapters as you decide on your general purpose for your first speech.

As you look back at the list of general topics on page 174, notice that you can give several types of speeches on the same topic. The topic of "space" for example could become a speech whose purpose would be to persuade or to inform. You could design persuasive speeches on the Challenger disaster, on the costs of the United States space program, or on what parts of space we should explore next. Informative speeches on

This urban ranger's purpose is to inform members of a tour group about the history and design of Central Park in New York City, and to provide facts about the conservation of its natural resources.

the "space" topic could include a comparison of the United States' and the Soviet Union's space technologies, how solid rocket fuel works, or how a black hole is formed. If you want to teach your listeners more than they already know about some aspect of space, you choose the general purpose of informing. If you want to have your audience adopt certain attitudes, or take some action connected with some space topic, you choose a persuasive purpose. The topic of "vacations" can also be used with more than one speech purpose. If you wish to convince your audience to choose a certain country for their next vacation, your purpose is one of persuading. If you simply want to give them helpful hints about how to pack efficiently for a vacation trip, your purpose is to inform. If you hope to amuse them with the story of your vacation on which everything went wrong, your purpose is to entertain. Most topics lend themselves to at least the three general purposes of informing, persuading, or entertaining.

Frequently in a speech class, your teacher will assign a general speech purpose and leave the choice of speech topic up to you. When that happens, you move right from selecting your general topic to focusing on your specific purpose.

Focus on Your Specific Purpose

Once you know your general topic and general speech purpose, you are ready to focus on the specific purpose for your speech. The **specific purpose** is precisely what you want your listeners to know, think, believe, or do as a result of hearing your speech. Imagine that you have selected the general topic of "Airplanes," and your general purpose is to inform. Now ask yourself, "About what specific aspect of airplanes do I want to inform my audience?" Write your answer in a single sentence (called your **purpose sentence**). Here are several possibilities:

- The purpose of this speech is to inform the listeners about the safety of commercial airline travel.

- The purpose of this speech is to inform the audience about the history of commercial aviation.

- The purpose of this speech is to tell the listeners about my most memorable airplane ride.

- The purpose of this speech is to compare and contrast six different styles of commercial aircraft.

Notice that each of these purpose sentences states a specific idea about which a person might wish to speak. A purpose sentence such as "To inform my audience about airplanes" is useless. It is not a sentence. But more important, it shows that the speaker does not have a specific purpose in mind—only a general topic area.

As you go about focusing on a specific purpose, keep in mind the time available for your speech. Some topics are too broad for a short speech. For example, you could not do justice to a topic such as "The World's Major Customs" in a five-minute speech, since you would have time for only a few sentences about each custom. Without time to include more interesting details you would not be informing your listeners of anything they did not already know. Sometimes one part of a broad topic fits better within the allotted time. For example, a subject such as "Major Customs of the Japanese Farmer" could be better covered in five minutes than the topic dealing with all the world's major customs. As you attempt to focus on and narrow your speech topics, you will find it helpful to browse through magazines and newspapers for current subjects that could fit within your time limits. Here is a sample of current topics that might prove narrow enough for a short classroom speech:

The Problems of Commercial Airlines

How to Enjoy the Outdoors

Different Views of Music: Pop, Rock, Western, Jazz

How My Part-time Job Has Helped Me

Are High School Sports Too Competitive?

How to Do Découpage

How High School Students Can Become Politically Involved

What It Means to Be the Principal's Daughter

The Thrill of Water Skiing

Learning How to Cross-country Ski

Where Is the Civil Rights Movement Going Today

Solar Energy Versus Atomic Power

Should the United States Institute Socialized Medicine?

The Confidentiality of News Reporters' Sources Must Be Assured

Do Americans Watch Too Much TV?

The Horror of War: Can Our Generation Avoid It?

How It Feels to Be Stereotyped

All Hail to the Free Enterprise System!

The Day-to-day Life of a Bank Teller

Is There a Cure for Cancer?

Why I Hope to Become an Airline Flight Attendant

Playing the Stock Market: Legalized Gambling?

What Will the Space Program Cost in the Future?

In class, your teacher will usually set the time limits for your speeches. Outside of the classroom, you should always inquire of anyone inviting you to speak: "How long do you wish me to talk?" Once you know the time limit, you can narrow your topic to fit within that limit. Some speakers make the mistake of deciding first how much they want to say, then trying to cram it all, somehow, into a very limited amount of time. This backwards process is much like trying to put toothpaste back into the tube—it's a very frustrating experience. If the time you have available is not sufficient for you to cover a complete topic, choose the most fascinating portion of that topic, which you can cover nicely in the allotted time. In addition, your audience will not come away feeling overloaded with information.

Application

Narrowing Your Topic

Choose three topics from the list of speeches on pages 179–180. Study each carefully to be certain that it is narrow enough for a two- or three-minute speech on the topic. If a topic is not narrow enough, narrow it further. For each topic, write a specific purpose statement that could be used to introduce a speech on the topic.

RESEARCHING YOUR TOPIC

Once you have settled on a topic that is right for you, for your audience, and for the occasion, you need to begin your research. You begin by taking stock of what you already know about your topic, then move to the library and other outside sources of information to complete your research.

Start with What You Already Know

The best way to begin organizing your thoughts is to take stock of what you already know about your topic. For a few speeches—"My Exciting Vacation Last Summer," for example—you will find you already have 90 percent of the information you need to interest and inform your audience. For more meaningful speeches, taking stock of what you already know will only scratch the surface of the total amount of information needed. If you find your topic demands a minimum of research, you may want to outline your speech before doing your research (see pages 194-202 on outlining). However, if you know very little about your topic, you must usually do some preliminary research before you can even begin an outline. Then the research and outlining can be completed together.

At least some research is necessary for nearly every topic to assure the listeners that the speaker has studied the topic. No one is credited with being the only authority on a given topic; even noted scientists and Presidents of the United States regularly use examples, statistics, and the opinions of other people to support their own ideas in their speeches. For example, such a personalized speech as "My Exciting Vacation Last Summer" can be spiced up with statistics noting how many visitors passed through the area you saw or a reference to the time the Queen of England visited the same place. Adding details such as these also helps establish a vivid context for your topic.

Know What You Are Researching

Whether the purpose of your speech is to provide information or to persuade your audience to adopt new views, what you are looking for in your research is **support** for the various statements you will be making in your speech. Support is needed mainly to prove the accuracy of your statements, but it can also be used to illustrate points and make them more interesting. Audiences are accustomed to listening for distinct kinds of support. Among the most common types are facts, statistics, testimony, narrative, examples, and comparisons.

For backing up the accuracy of your statements, facts offer the strongest form of support. A **fact** is an event or a truth that is known to exist or has been observed. A fact is very difficult to contradict or refute, especially if it has been witnessed by a large number of people. Here are examples of facts:

Beethoven's Ninth Symphony was written when the composer was totally deaf.

The population of the U.S. is over 200 million.

Gertrude Ederle was the first woman to swim the English Channel.

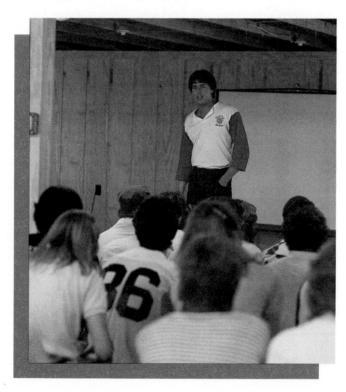

This speaker can enhance his credibility by using reliable facts that support his views.

Notice that a fact is always something that has occurred in the past or is presently occurring. No future event can be used as a fact, since something could happen to cancel or alter it.

Statistics are a second useful form of support for accuracy of statements. **Statistics** are collections of facts stated in numerical terms. They can be used to present facts in percentages, rank order, and averages. The following are examples of statistics:

Roughly 52 percent of the world's population is female, and 48 percent is male.

Americans spend $360 billion a year, or 10.6 percent of our gross national product, for health care. This is more than $1,500 for every man, woman, and child in the country. According to some experts, we may be spending 14 percent of the G.N.P. by the year 2,000.

Another form of support, **testimony,** is the quoting or restating of another person's opinion to support a point. Often the person quoted is a recognized expert in the field. Here is an example of testimony:

As Helen Keller once wrote, "No barrier of the senses shuts me out from the sweet, gracious discourse of my book friends. They talk to me without embarrassment or awkwardness."

Naturally, testimony can consist of quotations of various lengths. In one of his own speeches, Senator Edward Kennedy used a longer example of testimony by quoting from a speech that had been given at an earlier time by his brother Robert:

A speech he made to the young people of South Africa . . . sums it up best . . . "Some believe there is nothing one man or one woman can do against the enormous array of the world's ills. Yet, many of the world's great movements, of thought and action, have flowed from the work of a single man. A young monk began the Protestant Reformation, a young general extended an empire from Macedonia to the borders of the earth, and a young woman reclaimed the territory of France. It was a young Italian explorer who discovered the New World, and the 32-year-old Thomas Jefferson who proclaimed that all men are created equal.

"These men moved the world, and so can we all. Few will have the greatness to bend history itself, but each of us can work to change a small portion of events, and in the total of all those acts will be written the history of this generation . . ."

Testimony is not as strong a form of support for accuracy as facts are since testimony is merely opinion. Even when a quoted source is considered an expert, that expert can make a mistake. However, testimony is frequently very useful, especially if you think your audience is likely to respect the views of the person quoted.

Narrative is supporting material in the form of a story, either real or imaginary. Besides being enjoyable and interesting, narratives are often used in a speech to help make a point that has already been or will soon be supported by facts or statistics. Here is an example of a brief story that might be told by a speaker who wishes to talk about dissatisfaction:

> A story is told of Ali Hafed who sold his farm and set out in search of a diamond mine. He searched over the entire world without success and finally died in despair. Meantime the man who had purchased his farm spotted a glittering object in his creekbed one day and soon became the owner of one of the world's richest diamond mines.

Examples are specific instances or occurrences of a situation or principle you are attempting to describe. Examples may be stated in the form of facts, statistics, testimony, or narrative. Thus examples are general kinds of support that may include any one of several other forms. Three examples are used to support the following sentence:

> Some of this century's most noted speakers have been American presidents. Woodrow Wilson, Franklin D. Roosevelt, and John F. Kennedy are generally considered to have been excellent public speakers.

Examples may sometimes be used effectively to intensify or personalize your ideas. Notice how you are touched by this example of Ralph: "There are many hungry families in our community who could benefit from food donations. Let me tell you about Ralph. Ralph is four years old. He has big brown eyes and a mop of black hair and an empty belly. In all his four years on this earth, Ralph has never once enjoyed three square meals in a single day."

Comparisons involve the equating of essentially unlike ideas or phrases. They highlight the similarities that exist between basically dissimilar situations. Like examples, comparisons may take different forms. They may include facts, statistics, testimony, or narrative. They may also include the speaker's own opinions if the opinions seem to offer a useful means of illustrating the views being presented. The following is an example of a comparison based on opinion:

> The way some people shop at a sale reminds me of a swarm of bees clustered around a hive, each seemingly unaware of all the others crowded about.

After preliminary research, you can begin to build an outline. As you develop main heads and subheads (see page 198 for a discussion of outlining) you will begin to recognize what forms of support you need. This will help you as you proceed with more detailed research. For example, in a speech on "Land Pollution: Desecrating Our Landscape," a main head might read "How Efficient Have We Become at Littering?" Obviously you will need to find an example or some statistics to answer this question. The answer might be:

> Fifty years ago the average American threw away every day a little over two-and-one-half pounds of garbage. Today each of us will create six pounds of trash. . . .

Get to Know Your Library

When a teacher tells a class to "go to the library," many students feel like rats dropped into a maze. They wander around aimlessly, hoping to stumble over a piece of information they are looking for, but with little or no idea how to find the trail that will lead them to it. Once you know the key starting points, however, you can make the library work for you, instead of feeling lost in it.

Start at the library when you need to supplement your knowledge of a topic.

The **card catalogue** holds the master key to locating library information. It is that series of drawers, each holding 3×5 cards in alphabetical order, that you will usually find in or near the central lobby of most libraries. You will find three kinds of 3×5 cards for each book the library owns—a subject card, a title card, and an author card. You first look for a **title card** or an **author card** in the catalogue if you know the book's title or the name of its author. If the catalogue contains a card with the book's title or author, you know that the library owns that book. You then write down the **call number** printed on the left-hand side of the card as your means of locating the book on the library shelves.

When you do not know the title or author of a particular book, but want to find books on a specific subject, such as "clothing," look in the alphabetized drawers of **subject cards** under "clothes" or "clothing." The subject card will give you one or more specific books on the subject with call numbers to help you locate them on the shelves.

Periodicals are also listed in the library's card catalogue. If you are looking for a recent issue of a periodical, you can usually find it displayed on open shelves in the library's periodicals room. If you want an issue from a past year, the call number on the catalogue card will direct you to the book shelves where bound copies of older periodicals are kept.

But suppose you are researching for a speech dealing with American TV viewing habits. You need very specific information such as the number of TV sets purchased each year in the United States, or the kinds of programs most commonly watched. Perhaps your library's card catalogue contains few book or periodical titles that can help you. Or maybe you need to know how many colleges there are in the United States, or when the next total eclipse of the sun is going to occur. You might spend hours searching through individual books and periodicals and still not find such specific information. Now is the time to discover the wealth of information that is available to you through the library's **reference section.** The reference section contains encyclopedias, yearbooks, atlases, indexes, dictionaries, and biographical aids. Here are a few examples of the kind of information you can obtain from them:

Encyclopedias   You may have one of the general encyclopedias in your home, such as the *Encyclopedia Americana* or the *Encyclopaedia Britannica.* Many libraries have these as well as several other general encyclopedias which cover all branches of knowledge. In addition, many libraries contain specialized encyclopedias dealing with certain fields, such as the *McGraw-Hill Encyclopedia of Science and Technology,* the *Encyclopedia of Psychology,* the *Encyclopedia of Education,* the *Encyclopedia of Religion and Ethics,* and *Grzimek's Animal Life Encyclopedia,* among others.

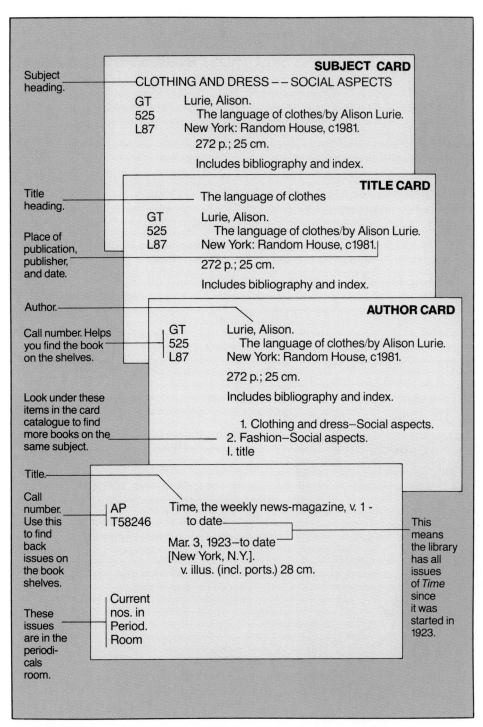

SUBJECT CARD

Subject heading.

CLOTHING AND DRESS – – SOCIAL ASPECTS

GT
525
L87

Lurie, Alison.
    The language of clothes/by Alison Lurie.
New York: Random House, c1981.
    272 p.; 25 cm.

    Includes bibliography and index.

TITLE CARD

Title heading.

The language of clothes

GT
525
L87

Lurie, Alison.
    The language of clothes/by Alison Lurie.
New York: Random House, c1981.
    272 p.; 25 cm.

    Includes bibliography and index.

Place of publication, publisher, and date.

AUTHOR CARD

Author.

Call number. Helps you find the book on the shelves.

GT
525
L87

Lurie, Alison.
    The language of clothes/by Alison Lurie.
New York: Random House, c1981.
    272 p.; 25 cm.

    Includes bibliography and index.

Look under these items in the card catalogue to find more books on the same subject.

    1. Clothing and dress–Social aspects.
2. Fashion–Social aspects.
I. title

Title.

Call number. Use this to find back issues on the book shelves.

AP
T58246

Time, the weekly news-magazine, v. 1 - to date

Mar. 3, 1923–to date
[New York, N.Y.].
    v. illus. (incl. ports.) 28 cm.

This means the library has all issues of *Time* since it was started in 1923.

These issues are in the periodicals room.

Current nos. in Period. Room

The card catalogue contains author cards, title cards, and subject cards that list every book the library has in its collection.

Career Close-up

PUBLIC RELATIONS SPECIALIST

Many companies and public agencies employ public relations specialists to project a positive image of their organizations. To achieve this goal, "PR" specialists inform the public by means of speeches, interviews, and press releases. A PR person from a manufacturing company might write a press release on a new product the company has invented. An oil company PR person might give a talk on the importance of oil in industry. A candidate for a public relations position needs a college degree in liberal arts, public relations, or business administration.

Many of a PR specialist's responsibilities involve public speaking. Most public relations specialists agree that the key to a successful talk lies in its careful preparation. To begin their planning, specialists research the background of each speech and collect the evidence that will support their conclusions. They then select the pattern of speech organization that will best suit their need to convey information and be interesting to their audience. Once the speech has been organized, specialists repeatedly rehearse their talk so that their delivery will be smooth and powerful.

Public relations specialists perform an essential role by providing the connecting link between organizations and the public. Because

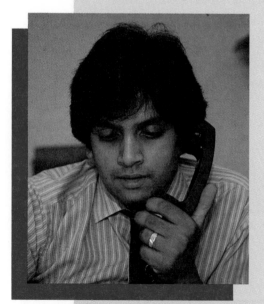

their highly developed speaking skills enable them to portray how an organization is helping people, they serve not only the concerns they represent, but also the public welfare. In addition, PR specialists help ensure that their companies and agencies remain responsive by keeping them informed about the public's needs and interests.

This PR specialist works to create a positive image for a company, based on accurate research.

Yearbooks   These are published annually and contain a tremendous amount of very detailed and concise information on a wide range of subjects. The *Facts on File Yearbook,* for instance, digests all the major national and international news events that occurred in a given year. *The World Almanac and Book of Facts* lists everything from the names of Nobel Prize winners since 1901 to sports records of college and pro teams. If you are interested in statistical information about the social, economic, and political aspects of life in the United States, you can discover such facts as the United States birth and death rates and median family income, broken down by state.

Biographical Aids   The reference section also contains collections of biographical sketches of noted persons, both living and dead. *Who's Who in America, Who's Who of American Women, International Who's Who,* and the *Dictionary of American Biography* are several of the leading sources of biographical information about famous individuals. *Biography Index,* published four times each year, indexes biographical material that has appeared in certain books and periodicals. It is especially helpful if you need information about important living people.

Atlases   Whenever geography is an important aspect of your speech topic, you will want to check an atlas. In addition to the usual maps of the world and each state in the United States, atlases provide you with important information about such matters as the population, politics, climate, energy, and food resources of the various parts of our world and even treat the universe beyond. Two of the best known atlases are *Times Atlas of the World, Comprehensive Edition,* and the *Rand McNally Cosmopolitan World Atlas.*

Periodical Indexes   Once you have a general notion of the direction in which you wish to go with your topic, you will find more detailed discussions of it in periodicals, newspapers, and books. Several handy reference works list articles in periodicals under general subject headings. The *Readers' Guide to Periodical Literature* lists articles in current magazines, such as *Newsweek, Reader's Digest, Time,* and *U.S. News & World Report.* If your topic deals with education, *Education Digest* lists articles that have appeared in education journals. The *International Directory of Little Magazines and Small Presses* lists lesser-known publications, such as literary magazines and scholarly journals that cover a wide variety of topics.

Feel free to browse in the periodical section of your library. Looking at pictures in magazines can stimulate your interest in topics you might not have considered otherwise. Regular reading, especially of magazines dealing with current events and issues, can provide you with a constant source of information on numerous topics. Though you can't be expected to read a dozen magazines every month, becoming familiar with one or two of them and reading them regularly will keep you abreast of current events and serve as a storehouse of support information whenever you need to deliver a speech. Any of the magazines in the list below could be used for this purpose:

Atlantic Monthly	*National Geographic Magazine*
Business Week	*National Wildlife*
Byte	*Natural History*
Commonweal	*Negro History Bulletin*
Creative Computing	*New Republic*
Ebony	*Newsweek*
Field and Stream	*Popular Photography*
Fortune	*Popular Science Monthly*
Harper's Magazine	*Scientific American*
Mechanics Illustrated	*Smithsonian*
Motor Trend	*Time*
The Nation	*U.S. News & World Report*

Stories in newspapers are additional sources of information. Most major news stories are indexed in *The New York Times Index.* Even if your library does not store back copies of *The New York Times,* the stories in that newspaper were probably carried in other major metropolitan newspapers on the same dates as those indicated in *The New York Times Index.*

In addition to the card catalogue and the reference section, many libraries have several other special resources to help you find information for your speeches. One of these is known as **computerized research services.** This service allows you to find obscure or highly specialized information rapidly through the use of computers. What might take hours to find by searching through a number of periodical indexes, for example, can be located in minutes by using computerized indexes known as **databases.** If your library has computerized research services available, you may want to make use of such databases as *Magazine Index, National Newspaper Index, ERIC* (Educational Resources Information Center), *Social Science Citation Index,* and *ASI* (American Statistics Index).

Another special library resource is the documents section. This section contains bulletins and pamphlets published by state and national governments, religious institutions, business organizations, and universities. You may want to check this section of the library for information on certain topics.

Speakers can also find quotations to support their ideas in sources such as *Bartlett's Familiar Quotations, Brewer's Dictionary of Phrase and Fable, Granger's Index to Poetry,* and the *Oxford Dictionary of Quotations.*

Finally, do not forget about reference librarians. Their job is to help you locate materials you need. If you are having difficulty, do not be embarrassed to ask for help.

Find Other Sources of Support

Although the library will often provide you with much of the information you need for a speech, do not overlook other valuable sources of information. Interviews with people knowledgeable about your topic can prove very helpful. If your topic concerns business, why not interview a teacher in the business department of your school or a local business leader? If your speech deals with anatomy, talk to a biologist or a physician. You may want to reread the section on interviewing on pages 96–101 in Chapter 4.

By interviewing officers at the local police station, this student gathers up-to-date information to use in his speech on crime patterns and trends.

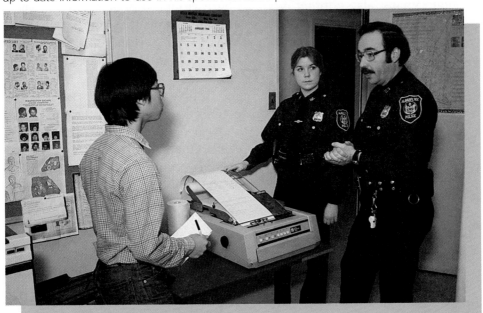

Other frequently overlooked sources of support for speeches are television and radio—particularly news programs. Since the main purpose of local and network news teams is to gather and sort out facts and testimony, their reports are a gold mine of current information with which to support your ideas. Keep up with world and local news and jot down the date of the program as well as the source of the information whenever you hear an item that might prove useful. Since newspapers are available for reading at any time, they possess an advantage over television and radio as sources of supporting materials. If you happen to miss a particular news broadcast, you often fail to obtain the information later. A newspaper can be retrieved and read months after the event has occurred.

Taking your own informal survey of public opinion among friends or neighbors can prove an effective type of support for a speech, particularly when you speak on local issues. Audiences are impressed when a speaker is sufficiently enthusiastic about the issues to conduct such a survey; they enjoy hearing what people living in their own town think about a topic.

When you are speaking on a controversial topic, you can frequently write to special interest groups to obtain information to support one side of an issue. Of course, you need to realize that information sent you by such special interest groups is bound to be biased in favor of their particular position on the issue involved. You can also obtain a great deal of information from government agencies on a wide variety of topics ranging from farming to space. If you do not know where to write to obtain materials, contact your congressional representative's office. Writing away for such information naturally means that you have to start your speech preparation well in advance to allow time for the information to reach you.

Record Your Evidence

As you discover facts, statistics, testimony, and other forms of support for your speech, be sure to write them down. Even though you are not certain you will use a particular piece of evidence in your speech, record it and the source where you discovered it while it is before you. Always take down more than you plan to use to avoid making extra trips to the library or rescheduling an interview.

It is best to establish a consistent system for recording speech evidence. Most speakers prefer to take their notes on 3 × 5 index cards, recording only one item of information on each card. These can be arranged later in the best order for presentation and are easy to handle on the platform. When you discover an item of information you feel might

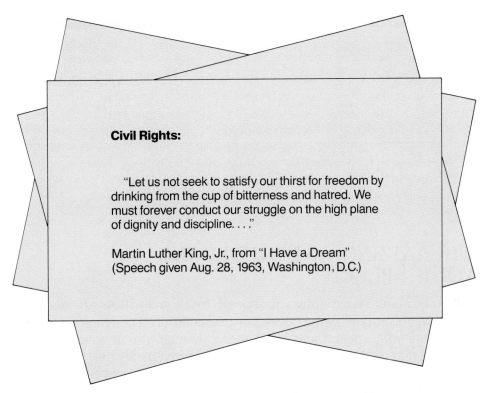

Civil Rights:

"Let us not seek to satisfy our thirst for freedom by drinking from the cup of bitterness and hatred. We must forever conduct our struggle on the high plane of dignity and discipline. . . ."

Martin Luther King, Jr., from "I Have a Dream"
(Speech given Aug. 28, 1963, Washington, D.C.)

A note card should contain a general heading for easy reference, the evidence itself, and the original source of this evidence.

be useful, first record a general heading for it at the top left-hand corner of the card. In the center of the card place the quotation, example, statistic, or fact. Sometimes the evidence may spill over to the back of the card, or even to a second card. Finally, below the evidence, write the source from which you obtained it. Take a moment to study the example of a note card, above.

Typing the cards you decide to use during delivery is useful, since it makes them easy to read on the platform. However, if your handwriting is clear and legible, typing is not necessary.

Even when not preparing for a specific speech, you may find it helpful to keep a general file of favorite topics for future use. You can build a storehouse of information to support these topics by gathering quotations, statistics, and other forms of evidence from books, magazines, newspapers, television, or conversation. A student interested in current events can usually spot information that may prove useful the next time a speech is needed.

Application

ORGANIZING AND OUTLINING YOUR SPEECH

As you go about researching your speech topic, you will also be deciding on an organizational pattern for your presentation. Though you are free to arrange your speech materials in any manner you choose, over the years certain methods of arrangement have proved effective for particular occasions and audiences. Your specific speech purpose will also have a great deal to do with the type of organizational pattern you select. Once your overall pattern has been selected, you are ready to write an outline on your topic.

Select a Pattern of Speech Organization

One common pattern for speeches is the **chronological pattern.** This arrangement proceeds from past to present to future; in other words, the speech develops in the same order that the events developed in time. One of the best known speeches using a chronological pattern is Abraham Lincoln's "Gettysburg Address." Notice how the first portion of the speech is about events that occurred in the past, the middle portion is about events of the present, and the last few sentences express Lincoln's hope for the future:

> Fourscore and seven years ago our fathers brought forth on this continent a new nation, conceived in liberty, and dedicated to the proposition that all men are created equal.
> Now we are engaged in a great civil war, testing whether that nation, or any nation so conceived and so dedicated, can long endure. We are met on a great battlefield of that war. We have come to dedicate a portion of that field as a final resting place for those who here gave their lives that that nation might live. It is altogether fitting and proper that we should do this.

But, in a larger sense, we cannot dedicate—we cannot consecrate—we cannot hallow—this ground. The brave men, living and dead, who struggled here, have consecrated it far above our poor power to add or detract. The world will little note nor long remember what we say here, but it can never forget what they did here. It is for us, the living, rather, to be dedicated here to the unfinished work which they who fought here have thus far so nobly advanced. It is rather for us to be here dedicated to the great task remaining before us—that from these honored dead we take increased devotion to that cause for which they gave the last full measure of devotion; that we here highly resolve that these dead shall not have died in vain; that this nation, under God, shall have a new birth of freedom; and that government of the people, by the people, for the people, shall not perish from the earth.

Of course a speech in chronological order need not always contain all three time periods: past, present, and future. The essential feature of this pattern is that the ideas or events in the speech move forward according to a time sequence.

When the parts of a speech are tied together by space arrangements rather than by time sequence, the organizational pattern is called **spatial.** It is useful in speeches in which the speaker describes a place for the audience. If you wish to give a speech on "My Vacation Trip to Disney World," you might choose a spatial pattern of organization in which the four major sections of the speech would be about *Frontierland, Tomorrowland, Fantasyland,* and *Adventureland.* You would pinpoint the location of each "land" in the overall Disney World layout and describe the features of each section of the park.

A third organizational pattern, called **topical,** is also frequently used. This is a broadly defined pattern in which the subject is broken down into its natural parts. An example would be a speech about "The United States Congress" divided into Senate and House, then subdivided into Democrats and Republicans. A speech on "Modern Modes of Travel" might contain three divisions: monorail, wide-bodied jet, and space shuttle. A speech on "My High School Career" could be divided into sections about the naive freshman, the know-it-all sophomore, the know-nothing junior, and the mature senior. A speech topic may often be divided topically in several different ways. As long as the divisions represent natural parts of the whole topic, the organizational pattern is called topical.

The **problem-solution pattern** is still another pattern used in speeches. Here the speaker devotes roughly the first half of the speech to describing a problem that exists, or is about to occur, and the second half developing one or more solutions. Presidential addresses on national television generally follow this format. If, for instance, the problem is the drug problem in our country, the President might spend the first half of the time proving how serious the problem is and the second half calling on the American people to help him to find solutions. Sometimes speakers misuse this organizational pattern by spending nearly the entire time discussing the problem and then barely mentioning the solution in the final sentences. It is best to devote approximately equal time to the problem and the solution.

Another pattern used especially by salespersons is called **Monroe's Motivated Sequence.** This pattern was originally suggested by Alan H. Monroe for use in persuasive speeches. It consists of five separate steps:

1. The Attention Step
2. The Need Step
3. The Satisfaction Step
4. The Visualization Step
5. The Action Step

The first step is an obvious one. Gaining the audience's attention is always the first task of any speaker. It is a step necessary in every type of speech situation. Once the listeners are paying close attention, the second step for the speaker is to show them that they have needs not being met by the way things are at present. The third step for a speaker using Monroe's Motivated Sequence is to present the opinion or solution that will satisfy these unmet needs of the audience. In the fourth, or visualization, step, the speaker must help the listeners actually see the change that will occur if they adopt his or her views. The final step involves telling the listeners what action they must take to bring about the improvement the speaker has promised. Salespersons, as well as speakers trying to persuade an audience, often use the five steps of Monroe's Motivated Sequence to organize their presentations.

Another organizational pattern, used mainly for after-dinner speeches or entertaining, is called the **string-of-beads pattern.** This pattern consists of a series of stories, jokes, or anecdotes strung out like beads on a string and tied loosely to some weak central theme. The jokes or anecdotes themselves usually carry the main impact in this kind of speech, and the topic or theme is less important. The famous comedian Will Rogers often used the string-of-beads pattern when addressing his audiences. An advantage of this pattern for an after-dinner speaker is its flexibility. Should a speech run overtime, the speaker can easily dispense with several anecdotes without the audience's feeling the speech is unfinished. This pattern does not ordinarily work well, however, for other types of speaking.

Start Your Outline with a Purpose Sentence

A good outline is like a tree without its leaves. All the basics are present in the tree—the overall direction, the necessary support, the division into branches. Only springtime is needed to fill it out with leaves. Your speech outline also needs a basic purpose or direction, supporting materials, and appropriate subdivisions. When time for delivering the speech arrives, you will be ready to fill it out with the necessary words.

If your speech outline is to have any order about it, you must know clearly what your purpose is in making the speech. The best way to begin a clear speech outline is by writing at the top of your outline the purpose sentence you selected earlier. This purpose sentence, remember, states exactly what you hope to accomplish by giving the speech: what you hope your listeners will know, think, believe, or do as a result of hearing your speech. Imagine you wish to tell your listeners something about prisons. You could have a number of different general speech purposes in mind, resulting in some very different specific purpose sentences:

■ The purpose of this speech is to inform my listeners about overcrowding in today's prisons.

■ The purpose of this speech is to convince my listeners that certain kinds of criminals should serve their sentences at home.

■ The purpose of this speech is to entertain my listeners by describing my "queasiness" the first day on my new paper route in the local prison.

Notice that each of these purpose sentences states a specific idea about which a person might wish to speak. A purpose sentence such as "To inform my audience about prisons" is useless. It is not a sentence. But more important, it shows that the speaker does not have a *specific purpose* in mind—only a general topic area. By the time you begin outlining, you must have a specific purpose in mind. The purpose sentence serves to guide you as you complete the outline.

Sometimes speech students think a purpose sentence is a key sentence phrased for use at the beginning of the speech. Though you may often express the same general idea at the start of your speech, the purpose sentence itself is a *written* sentence only meant to guide your outlining process. When a speaker states the purpose aloud to the listeners, it is usually reworded in a much more conversational style.

Develop Main Heads and Subheads

The major divisions of a speech outline are referred to as **main heads.** Ordinarily the fewer main divisions you make of your topic the better. Most speeches should only have two or three main heads, though there are exceptions. A topic with eight or nine main divisions, however, becomes too difficult for the audience to follow or remember and hard for the speaker to fit into the time limit. If it seems impossible to avoid dividing your topic into a large number of main heads, you should consider narrowing the scope of your topic or combining several heads into one.

Suppose you are outlining a speech on "School Vacations." Your purpose sentence could read: "The purpose of this speech is to persuade the audience that our school calendar should include another week of vacation." If this is the case, your main heads might be:

   I. Vacations help us become better students.
  II. Our school has one week less vacation time than schools in neighboring towns.
 III. Our vacations should be the same as those of our friends in neighboring towns.

As shown in the example above, each main head should directly support the purpose sentence and be approximately equal in importance.

Subheads relate to main heads in the same manner that main heads relate to the purpose sentence. They subdivide the main head into parallel parts. Notice how the following subheads A, B, and C support the first main head in a speech titled "Skydiving":

  I. Skydiving is safer than most people imagine.
    A. Only highly qualified personnel may serve as trainers.
    B. Extensive training is mandatory before a "live" jump.
    C. Chutes must be checked and rechecked before a jump.

All subheads under a given main head must be of approximately equal importance.

While it is possible to subdivide further the ideas of the outline under sub-subheads, this is not ordinarily done. Most of the subdivisions below the subheads are reserved for supporting details rather than for concepts or ideas. Notice in the example on pages 200 and 201 how the level below the subheads consists primarily of supporting details (examples, statistics, narratives, comparisons).

Use Complete Sentences for Main Heads and Subheads

Main heads and subheads in speech outlines should be stated as complete sentences. Although experienced speakers sometimes use word or phrase outlines, full sentence outlines are best for beginning speakers. Writing down the basic ideas in complete thoughts forces you to think through the ideas and also helps set them in your memory. This does not mean, however, that the sentences should be long. Actually, you should strive to keep them as brief and simple as possible, as long as they are grammatically complete.

Once you get below the level of subheads, words or short phrases may be all you need in order to remember most of your supporting details. A simple reminder, such as "Narrative about dog" or "Statistics on population," will often be sufficient to remind you of the complete piece of evidence you wish to use.

Notice how the sentences and phrases in the sample outline on pages 200–202 show the relative importance of levels of ideas by the way they are arranged on the paper. As you can see this is done in two ways. First, different letter and number designations are attached to different levels of ideas. Main heads have Roman numerals (I, II, III), subheads have capital letters (A, B, C), supporting details have Arabic numerals (1, 2, 3). Second, the outline shows you at a glance which ideas are more important and which are less important through the use of indentation. Main heads start near the left margin, with the various subheads indented in step fashion to show that each level is less important than the one above. The whole outline becomes a picture of the way in which each idea relates to each of the other ideas.

A Sample Outline

Now that you have considered each part of a speech outline separately, let's put them all together in a complete sample outline. A speech contains three main sections—an introduction, a body, and a conclusion —each of which should always be reflected in corresponding sections of your outline. Suppose, for example, that you have chosen "Playing Tennis" as your speech topic. Your purpose sentence and completed outline might look something like this:

Purpose Sentence	The purpose of this speech is to inform my listeners about the basic techniques used when playing tennis.
Introduction	I. Answer the following multiple-choice question: According to last week's television special, what is the fastest-growing participation sport in this country today? (a) polo, (b) soccer, (c) tennis. A. If you answered "tennis" you were correct. B. If you don't yet play, you're a member of a rapidly shrinking group.
	II. My "vast" experience of three years on the courts only qualifies me to speak to you about the basics.

Body

I. Holding the racket correctly is crucial.
   A. Grasp it as if you were shaking hands with the handle for forehand shots.
      1. Most tennis instructors recommend this technique.
      2. This grip will help keep your shots level.
   B. Use this same grip for serving, except for special types of services.
   C. Turn your hand slightly counter-clockwise from this position for backhand shots if you are righthanded (clockwise if you are lefthanded).
      1. You should be able to lay your thumb flat along the back edge of the grip.
      2. Many players like to support their backhand grip with their other hand.

II. Stance is also very important.
   A. Most beginners face the net directly when hitting the ball.
      1. I did it this way for four months before someone "clued me in."
      2. My shots showed me something was wrong.
   B. The better method is to stand with your side facing the net for forehand and backhand shots.
   C. When serving, you should not face the net directly but on a 45-degree angle.
      1. Notice the pros on television.
      2. Television camera angles sometimes make it difficult to see serving stances clearly.
   D. Sometimes when running for a ball, it is impossible to get in the correct position in time.
      1. I find this especially difficult.
      2. Evonne Goolagong doesn't seem to find it so difficult, however—her strength and agility enable her to make excellent return shots even from "incorrect" positions.

III. The swing is extremely important.
   A. You should begin with a wide backswing that fully engages your back and shoulder muscles.
      1. Using a short backswing will rob your shots of power.
      2. Chris Evert Lloyd's backswing
   B. Try to contact the ball when it is waist high and slightly in front of you.
      1. Keep the ball level.
      2. Avoid "scoop" shots.

C. Keep the racket level as you continue with your follow through.
   1. John McEnroe's form
   2. Tracy Austin's form
D. Except for special shots and serving, the swing should be horizontal, not vertical.
   1. The overhead smash is a special shot for which you use a vertical swing.
   2. The lob, a high and lofting shot, is another special example—it requires a very controlled underhand swing.

Conclusion

I. You probably won't become an overnight Jimmy Connors or Chris Evert Lloyd with what I've told you today.

II. What you can do is start enjoying the fastest-growing sport in America as a participant and not

When the time for delivering your speech arrives, your teacher may allow you to take your outline to the podium. If not, you will want to transfer the major ideas from the outline to note cards. Using 3 × 5 cards makes it easy to insert the same-sized evidence cards you prepared earlier into the deck of outline cards at appropriate places. You then will have only a small stack of cards to handle on the platform. These will include the major ideas of your speech as well as statistics, examples, quotations, and other forms of evidence.

Application

Selecting a Pattern of Organization

Write a purpose sentence for the topic you selected in the previous Application. Then determine the most appropriate pattern of organization for a speech that begins with the purpose sentence you have written. Discuss what appears to you to be the most suitable organizational pattern with your classmates. Consider other patterns that are suggested in the discussion. Be aware of the possibility that different patterns of organization might be appropriate for your topic. After sufficient discussion, select the pattern that you think will work best. Be prepared to explain and defend your choice.

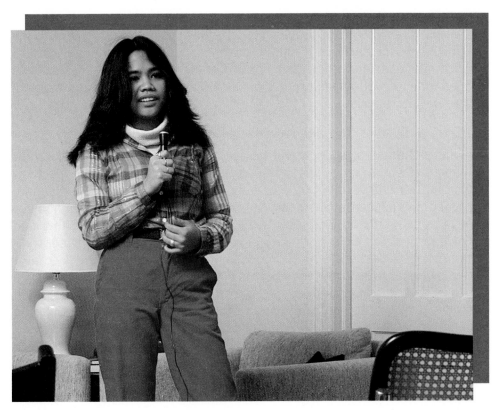

Get comfortable with your ideas and delivery by rehearsing your speech aloud several times during the course of the week.

REHEARSING

Rehearsal is the crowning point of speech preparation. Without rehearsal a speaker is like a beginning golfer entering the U.S. Open after having read all the golfing manuals but never having actually played. Nothing can take the place of thorough practice, and if well done, rehearsal can put you in top form for a successful speech.

Recognize the Importance of Thorough Rehearsal

One or two brief run-throughs does not constitute thorough rehearsal. Start preparing your speech well before the speaking date. Allow time for several rehearsal sessions. Rehearsal that is crammed into one evening is ineffective compared to three or four rehearsal sessions on successive nights.

In order to prepare yourself thoroughly for a speech, you must progress through several rehearsal stages, developing gradually from the stage in which ideas are simply listed on your outline or note cards to the point where they are firmly implanted in your mind. Since people's brains work subconsciously on such ideas between rehearsal sessions, you need time for well-spaced rehearsals if you are to have total command of the speech material.

Find a Place for Rehearsal

Since the actual speech will be spoken aloud, you need a place for rehearsal where you can speak aloud. Simply saying the speech to yourself, or whispering it quietly, only allows you to practice the mental parts of the speech—the ideas. But public speaking demands a number of physical skills as well. You need to rehearse proper breathing and voice projection, clear articulation, good timing, and correct synchronization of words with body movements. The ancient Greek orator Demosthenes is reported to have rehearsed his speeches on the seashore where he had to speak over the roar of the surf. It is also said that he practiced with pebbles in his mouth to make himself conscious of the need for clear articulation. Don't risk choking by using pebbles, but do consider practicing outdoors. It offers a very good place for speech rehearsal since you are forced to speak above the noise of wind and traffic. If you cannot find a suitable place outdoors, the next best place is a room similar in size and acoustics to the one in which you will give the actual speech.

Plant the Pattern of Ideas in Your Mind

Begin by reading your outline over silently to yourself several times, trying to set the **pattern of ideas** in your mind. Often the major segments of the outline will already be fixed in your mind since you are the one who wrote the outline. Your teacher may or may not allow you to use the outline during the actual speech, and even if you are permitted to use it you will want to depend on it as little as possible.

Once you feel you have the ideas firmly planted in your mind, stand up and say the ideas aloud to an imaginary audience. Speak the ideas in whatever words come to you as you are rehearsing. Try to go completely through, filling in details of the outline without starting over. Your speech will be halting at first with long pauses in places, but it will begin to smooth out with repeated practice. The second, third, and fourth times, do not try to say the ideas in exactly the same words you used the first time. Remember, what you are doing is planting the pattern of ideas in your mind, not a memorized pattern of words.

Have your outline or note cards handy (whichever you plan to use during the actual speech), and refer to them if you forget an idea. Run through the entire speech five to ten times or until you are certain you can go from beginning to end without hesitation. This will help establish your pattern of ideas securely in your mind.

Rehearse Alone and with Friends

Most people prefer to rehearse a speech alone, at least until they have it pretty well smoothed out. Once you feel you have the speech under control, however, rehearsing with a friend or two as your audience can improve your preparation. Having a dress rehearsal of this type can give you ideas about possible audience reactions you cannot obtain through a solo rehearsal: Are you speaking loudly enough to be heard in all parts of the room? Do the listeners react in an unexpected way to a particular portion of your speech? Do they follow the organization of your speech? Do they understand all of the message? Do they agree or disagree with all or part of your message? Knowing the answers to these kinds of questions beforehand can allow you time to make changes and produce a better effect on your real audience.

Time Rehearsals

Time yourself as you practice. Using a kitchen timer that shows how much time has been spent and how much is left can be helpful. The timing will probably not be too precise the first few run-throughs, but by your final practice session you should be able to conclude your speech within 30 seconds of your time limit.

For most brief classroom speeches your timing will need to be precise. Later, when you give 20- or 30-minute speeches to groups outside the classroom, timing will still be important, but two or three minutes leeway will probably be permissible. Any speaking you do on radio or television, of course, must be timed very closely and usually demands a manuscript for rehearsal rather than an outline.

Application

Rehearsing Your Speech

For your next speech, make arrangements to record your first practice session. Rehearse the speech several more times to fix the pattern and structure firmly in your mind. Also, practice in front of a mirror to refine your gestures. Tape record the final practice before you present your speech in class. Compare the recording of the first practice with the recording of the final practice. How much did your speech improve?

7 Chapter Review

■ Summary

Speech preparation is the process of building your speech in your mind. Planning it in every detail beforehand can help you avoid embarrassing mistakes during the actual delivery.

Focusing on Your Topic Both your speech preparation and the speech itself will be easier if you choose a subject that fascinates you. Then analyze the background, attitudes, and interests of your audience to determine exactly how to approach your chosen subject. This may call for formal or informal polls, surveys, and perhaps a questioning of the person who invited you to speak. Selecting your general speech purpose means deciding whether you wish to inform, persuade, entertain, or fulfill some other purpose. Once you have done this, put your topic and general purpose into a specific purpose sentence.

Researching Your Topic Thorough research is necessary to discover support for the ideas you will present in your speech. Support takes a variety of forms, the most common of which are facts, statistics, testimony, narratives, examples, and comparisons. Getting to know how to use a library is critical to proper speech research. This means learning how to use the card catalogue and the reference section, as well as seeking help from computerized research services, the reference librarians, and special holdings of your library. Record all your evidence and the sources from which you obtain it on 3×5 index cards.

Organizing and Outlining Your Speech Certain general patterns of speech organization have proven effective for speeches with various purposes. Informative speeches are often organized according to the chronological, spatial, and topical patterns. Persuasive speeches more often follow a problem-solution pattern or Monroe's Motivated Sequence. The string-of-beads pattern is often used for speeches to entertain. Your speech outline should always be guided by a purpose sentence. Every main head in the outline should be a major subdivision of your topic. Subheads give supporting details for each main head.

Rehearsing   All the earlier parts of the speech preparation process are brought together and perfected during rehearsal. Find a place for rehearsal that forces you to project your voice. Use your outline to plant the pattern of ideas in your mind, then speak the ideas aloud to an imaginary audience. Force yourself to speak completely through the outline without backtracking. Repeat your practice at least five to ten times to smooth out rough sections of the speech and to keep it within your time limit. Once you feel confident about solo rehearsal, hold a dress rehearsal with a friend or two.

 ## Vocabulary

Define at least fifteen of the following terms in a complete sentence.

audience analysis	card catalogue	spatial pattern
specific purpose	title card	topical pattern
purpose sentence	author card	problem-solution
support	call number	pattern
fact	subject card	Monroe's Motivated
statistic	reference section	Sequence
testimony	computerized	string-of-beads pattern
narrative	research services	main heads
example	databases	subheads
comparison	chronological pattern	pattern of ideas

 ## Checklist

Speech: Preparation Skills

1. Analyze various topics before choosing one for a speech.
2. Organize and plan your speech carefully ahead of time.
3. Recognize the importance of appealing to your audience.
4. Be aware of the need to research your topic thoroughly.
5. Use the library to advantage as a valuable resource.
6. Outline your speech as part of your preparation.
7. Rehearse your speech, taking care to project your voice.
8. Time your speech as part of your rehearsal.

Review Questions

1. Explain the process involved in focusing on your topic.
2. Explain what you should know about your audience before you begin to prepare your speech.
3. Explain how the time available for your speech affects the topic you choose.
4. Explain the basic purposes of doing research in preparation for a speech.
5. Name some of the sources of supporting material.
6. Explain some typical patterns of organization used in developing a speech.
7. Explain the function of a purpose sentence.
8. Name the best place to rehearse a speech.
9. Explain why it is important to rehearse a speech several times.
10. Name some physical skills you should work on during rehearsals for speeches.

Discussion Questions

1. Hold a brainstorming session in which you identify at least twenty topics that have strong audience appeal to the members of your class. You might examine any list of topics previously developed or begin a new list. Choose someone to list the topics on the chalkboard as they are proposed. Each topic should be thoroughly discussed in terms of audience interest. For a topic to make the list of twenty, the class must agree that it is of obvious interest. Resolve differences of opinion by consensus, compromise, or majority vote. Record the final list in your speech notebook and save it for the future.
2. Conduct a class discussion about whether or not it is preferable to write a speech and then memorize it, or simply to fix a pattern of ideas in your mind and then speak from an outline. What kinds of problems could a speaker with a memorized speech encounter? Does an outlined speech encourage a smoother delivery?
3. Participate in a class discussion on the relative importance of speech content and speech delivery. Is one more

important than the other? How effective is sound content without good delivery? Can you think of examples from your own experience when a speaker used effective delivery techniques but had very little to say? How effective was such a speech? How does one establish a proper balance between content and delivery?

4. Imagine that you have been asked by a local civic group to give a five-minute speech at a luncheon meeting on an important historic building in your town. The only thing you know about this group is that they have an interest in local history. You know absolutely nothing about the building. You have one month to prepare for your speech. Discuss with your classmates the things you would do to prepare for your speech. What would you do before you gather information? What methods would you use to locate information? How would you structure your speech to gain the attention of your audience?

Critical Thinking

1. **Synthesis:** Think about the many commercials you see on television and listen to on the radio. Think about all of the advertisements you see and read in newspapers and magazines. Then identify a product that you believe is worthwhile. It can be something you invent, yourself, or it can be a product you have heard or read about. What would persuade you to buy this product? Would these same things persuade others as well? Use Monroe's Motivated Sequence to develop a commercial or advertisement for this product. Make sure that it contains each of the five separate steps.

2. **Evaluation:** Think of a speech that you have listened to, either in class or somewhere else, which the speaker simply did not rehearse sufficiently. What are the signs of inadequate rehearsal? In what ways does inadequate rehearsal affect content and delivery? Develop a set of standards that you can use to help determine whether or not you or a partner have adequately rehearsed a speech.

■ Activities

In-Class

1. Form small groups of from five to seven. Choose one of the following broad topics: Pets, Hobbies, Summer Jobs, Vacation Sites, Careers, Sports Greats. For each broad topic, identify narrower topics that could be used as topics for five-minute speeches. See how many narrow topics you can identify in thirty minutes. Share your topics with those identified by the other groups.

2. Discuss each of the following audiences. What kind of speech topic would probably be best for each? What kinds of topics would best be avoided?
   (a) a fourth grade class
   (b) a senior citizens' lunch
   (c) a meeting at a convention of chemists
   (d) a garden-club meeting
   (e) a bored student group that is being forced to attend the speech
   (f) an evening meeting of parents interested in learning about the curriculum
   (g) a meeting of people looking for new hobbies

3. Select a speech either from the Appendix of this text or from one of the standard collections of speeches. You should find a speech that can be read in five minutes or less. Identify the original audience for the speech and explain to your classmates whatever other information is needed to understand why the speech was given. Read the speech in class. After you have read the speech, conduct a class discussion about it. What was the purpose statement? Was the introduction effective? How was the speech organized? What kinds of evidence did the speaker use to support his or her main points? Did the conclusion tie all of the main points together?

Out-of-Class

1. Using the list of broad topics on page 174, choose one that you know well and write three possible topics for the subject in your speech notebook. Choose one of these three topics and write a skeletal outline for a speech on that topic. Your outline should include a sketchy introduction, three main heads, and a brief conclusion. Be prepared to discuss your topics and outline.

2. Locate an editorial or a column of opinion in a newspaper that you receive in your home. Paste it on a page in your speech notebook. Divide the page opposite it into two columns. In the first column, write all statements from the example that are opinions. In the second column, write all statements that are facts. In view of the number of facts that your example contains, how persuasive is it? If you were giving a speech on the topic of the editorial or column, would you have enough evidence to support your argument, or would you have to search for more?

3. Identify a topic that you have wanted to find out more about but have not had the time to research. Write the topic in your speech notebook and then write questions about it that you would like to have answered. Research the topic at the library by finding answers to your questions. Once you have conducted your research, use it as a topic for a future speech. Keep all your information about the topic in your speech notebook.

Chapter Project

Working in pairs, choose a topic for an informative speech. Then you and your partner prepare to give five-minute speeches on two different aspects of that topic. Research the topic thoroughly in the library, keeping bibliographic notes of all sources that you investigate.

Write an outline for your speech based on the information you locate through your research. Write pertinent information on note cards. Make certain that your ideas are supported with evidence and coordinate with your partner to ensure that your speeches will complement, not duplicate, one another.

Prepare a folder-packet that includes your outline, note cards, and bibliography. Determine with your partner who should speak first and then deliver your speeches in class. Did the speeches work well together? Submit the packet to your teacher.

8 Choosing Effective Language

When you have completed this chapter you should be able to:

- Explain the difference between written and spoken language.
- Describe the characteristics of clear spoken language.
- Define the terms *concrete words* and *abstract words,* and give several examples of each.
- Define the term *economy of language,* and explain how to use such language in your speeches.
- Define and give examples of figures of speech that you can use to make your speeches interesting.

Boost the impact of your ideas by taking time to choose words and images that express them most effectively.

Words are the garments with which speakers clothe their ideas. Choosing effective language for a speech is like choosing the right clothes for a special occasion. Words can be courageous or timid, commanding or pleading, persuasive or entertaining, hurtful or kind. Their effect on the listeners can be enormous or microscopic, depending on how well the words clothe the ideas. Once when referring to Winston Churchill's speeches to the English people during World War II, John F. Kennedy stated: "He mobilized the English language and sent it into battle." Churchill's words may well have done more for the Allied cause than fifty planes or a dozen ships.

Speeches are made of ideas, but unless those ideas are expressed in carefully selected language, they may be overlooked. In this chapter you will find a number of suggestions that can help you choose the kind of language that will best express your ideas to audiences.

You may ask, "Does this mean I should write out my speeches word for word, then read or memorize them?" No, not usually. Most speech teachers today believe you should learn to give most of your speeches extemporaneously—outlining the ideas, but choosing the precise wording during the speech itself. Linda and Dick Heun, authors of a college speech text, put it this way:

The main reason for not writing out a speech and reading (or memorizing) it is that your focus then would be on your wording rather than your audience's reactions. One unique advantage of oral communication is that you have direct eye contact with your audience and can watch, interpret, and adapt to its reactions.

A second reason for not writing out your speech is that oral style is quite different from written style. In fact, Charles Fox, noted British politician and orator of the nineteenth century, once said, 'Does it read well? Then it's not a good speech.'

On some occasions, of course, you may need to speak from a manuscript. Your teacher may even assign one or more manuscript speeches in this class. But for the most part this chapter's immediate benefit to you will be showing you how to select effective language for those sections of your speech where you want to make the greatest impression—the introduction, the conclusion, and some occasional high points you may wish to read or memorize. In working on the language of these special parts of your speeches, you will also be gaining the skill to put words together effectively when speaking extemporaneously.

You will explore five qualities of spoken language that make it different from written language. Being aware of these differences will help you state your message clearly. Then the chapter will show you ways to emphasize important points in your speech. Speakers must know how to highlight important ideas so listeners will remember them. Finally, you will find a list of certain problems to avoid. The use of effective language involves four points—clarity, emphasis, interest, and caution. By following the suggestions in this chapter, you should find it easier to get your message across to your audience.

DIFFERENCES BETWEEN WRITTEN AND SPOKEN LANGUAGE

The first step in choosing effective language for public speaking is to realize that language that is appropriate for writing is not always appropriate for speaking. In part, this is because the tasks of reading and listening are so different. Readers can set their own pace, stopping and reviewing anything that is hard to understand. Listeners, on the other hand, must try to keep up with the speaker. If they miss an idea, it is often gone for good. Effective language for speaking must therefore be immediately clear to the listener.

In conversation, most people recognize this need to make spoken language immediately clear. In general, spoken language possesses five specific qualities that make it very different from written language:

1. Spoken language makes greater use of short and simple words.

2. Spoken language tends to be more concrete, less abstract.

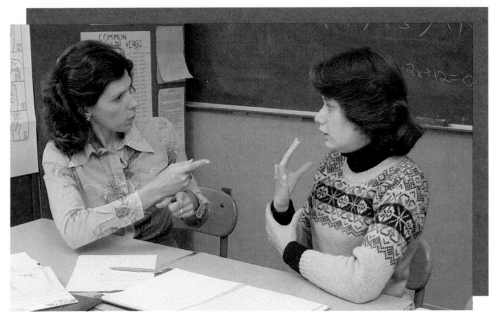

Just as listeners must keep pace with the speaker, the receiver of sign language must keep pace with the signer to understand the message.

3. Spoken language is usually specific.

4. Spoken language makes greater use of restatement.

5. Spoken language generally includes fewer unnecessary words.

The next part of this chapter will focus on these five qualities of spoken language. Although they are a natural part of spoken language, they are too often forgotten when it comes to giving public speeches.

MAKING SPOKEN LANGUAGE CLEAR

A listener runs a much greater risk of missing ideas that are poorly stated than a reader does. If an audience fails to understand even a small part of a speaker's language, that part of the message will be lost to them. The world's great speeches have always been characterized by the clarity of their language. Language for public speaking must be simple, brief, and clear enough that listeners can easily understand it.

Keep Wording Short and Simple

Spoken sentences need to be shorter and simpler than written ones. A great number of long sentences make a speech difficult for listeners to follow. They also make it harder for an audience to pay attention for any length of time. Spoken language calls for short, simple sentences.

Say each of these sentences aloud, then decide which would be easier for a listening audience to grasp quickly:

Lengthy: We have gathered here today in order to explain and detail for you the reasons why one of our very own classmates deserves to be this school's next student council president.

Short: We're here to tell you why our classmate, Sheila Cox, should be our next student council president.

Similarly, spoken language calls for simple words. The use of simple words has long been considered a sign of clear language. Simple words are not always short words, though many are short. Rather, they are those that are among the ordinary vocabulary of your particular audience on any given occasion.

When speaking to your peers, people in your own age group with a similar level of education, your selection of language is relatively easy. Simply choose words you would typically use in conversation. When speaking to a much younger group or a less-educated audience adjust your language level downward appropriately. Watch the listeners' feedback carefully for signs of lack of understanding.

Decide which wording would be better understood by a group of fourth graders to whom you were speaking about computers:

Complex: The type of communications protocol existing between your systems unit and printer may present you with a critical consideration for the proper operation of your computer.

Simple: How your computer talks to your printer may be important to know if you wish to operate your computer well.

If you address a special group with a vocabulary of its own—a sports group, a religious group—it is permissible to use the special words of that group as long as the entire audience will understand the language used. The same is true when addressing groups composed of audience members from a specific region or cultural group. As long as you are a member of that group and nearly all your listeners understand the special regional or cultural terms, you should feel free to use them. Actually, you compliment such an audience by using language that is special to you and them. Do not, however, try to use the regional or cultural language of a special group if you are not a member of the group, or if there are many non-members in your audience.

Use Concrete Language

Language for public speaking must not only be simple, it must also be concrete. **Concrete words** and phrases are the kind that let the listener "see" the idea as well as understand it. A word such as *girl* is concrete since it stands for something that can be perceived by the senses. A word such as *beautiful* is **abstract** (the opposite of concrete), since you cannot see, touch, feel, smell, or taste *beautiful*. Compare the two following sentences and decide which one gives you a clearer mental picture of the ideas expressed.

> *Abstract:*   John seemed nervous, yet determined.

> *Concrete:*   John was shaking, but his jaw was tightly set.

The two sentences express essentially the same ideas, but the second sentence allows you to "see" those ideas. You can't see *nervous*. Now compare these two sentences and decide for yourself which is more concrete and which more abstract.

> The taste in Katie's mouth was like frozen strawberries, slowly melting on her tongue.

> The taste in Katie's mouth was cold and tantalizing.

Application

Using Simple Language

In a two-minute presentation to the class, relate an amusing or interesting story or anecdote. The story or anecdote may be about a real incident that happened to you, or it may be something you heard from someone else. Use language that is clear, concrete, and specific, so that your listeners will listen carefully. After you have finished, discuss your use of language with your classmates. Ask them to identify any parts of your story that might have been unclear.

Use Specific Words

A public speaker also needs to use specific words. **Specific words** are words that refer to a limited class of objects. For example, the word "hobo" is a more specific word than "traveler" since there are many travelers in the world who are not hobos. The class "traveler" is larger than the class "hobo" since hobos are just one form of traveler. A given word cannot be labeled general or specific. It will merely be more general or more specific than some other word. We just said that "hobo" is more specific than "traveler." But "traveler" is more specific than "person," which includes the class "traveler." Notice the progression from general to specific in this list:

galaxies

solar systems

planets

Mars

The trick when preparing a speech is to pick the most specific word you can find to tell your audience just what you have in mind.

Restate Main Ideas

Restatement is a natural speaking device. It assures you that the listener does not miss or forget a part of your message. Writers have less

Consult a dictionary when you need help deciding which word to use. When you prepare a speech, choose the most specific word you can find to tell your audience exactly what it is you have in mind.

need to restate, since the reader can carry out any necessary review by simply rereading a phrase or sentence. Since listeners do not have this opportunity, public speakers typically restate their main ideas a good deal, using somewhat different terms each time to make sure everyone gets the idea.

Notice how Frank Knox, Secretary of the Navy under President Franklin D. Roosevelt from 1940 to 1944, used restatement in a speech in order to make clear his belief that a nation must be willing to fight to preserve liberty and peace:

> The only peace in which the world can put any confidence, for at least one hundred years to come, is the kind of peace that can be enforced by the peace-loving nations of the world. . . .
>
> You cannot preserve liberties such as we enjoy, save by willingness to fight for them if need be.
>
> The currency with which you pay for peace is made up of manly courage, fearless virility, readiness to serve justice and honor at any cost, and a mind and a heart attuned to sacrifice.
>
> We must also remember that it is only the strong who can promote and preserve a righteous peace. . . .
>
> A powerful national defense, especially on the high seas, is a prerequisite of a peace-promoting, justice-loving America. . . .

Remove Unnecessary Words

In daily life, being economical means not wasting money or other resources. In public speaking, being economical means not wasting words. Part of clear speaking consists of using only as many words as necessary to get the message across. Once you have accomplished that—stop! Did you know that on the same day that Abraham Lincoln delivered the Gettysburg Address, another speaker, Edward Everett, gave a speech that lasted nearly two hours? Lincoln's speech, only ten sentences in length, took about two minutes to deliver. Probably you have never heard of Edward Everett or his speech, but Lincoln's Gettysburg Address is known around the world. Part of the reason for the lasting effect of Lincoln's speech was undoubtedly his economy of language. Afterwards, Everett wrote Lincoln a letter in which he declared that he wished he could have done as much justice to the occasion with his two-hour speech as Lincoln had with his two-minute one.

One of the best ways of achieving **economy of language** is by chopping needless words from individual sentences. The speaker who says: "We must take into consideration the fact that this property comes under certain zoning restrictions" could save words (and energy) by shortening the wording: "We must consider certain zoning restrictions on this property." Let's look at several other examples:

Uneconomical: Regarding the situation in the flooded area, we must make a concerted effort to aid the local residents.

Economical: We must try to aid the residents in the flooded area.

Uneconomical: A period of sunny weather set in and remained for a whole week.

Economical: We had sunshine for a whole week.

In each of these examples many of the words in the uneconomical version are not needed. They do not add anything to the meaning of the sentence. They are unnecessary and should be left out.

Application

Economy of Language

Prepare a brief written description of a process that you are very familiar with. It could be a description of how to throw a curve ball or how to service a lawn mower. After you have finished it, reread it carefully, removing all unnecessary words. Now present your description from memory in the form of a short speech. After you have finished, discuss your speech with your classmates. Did they understand the process that you described? Were they aware of any words you used that were unnecessary?

CREATING LEVELS OF EMPHASIS

So far we have considered the importance of using clear language when speaking in public. Language must also help make a speech memorable. Listeners will be more likely to remember your message if you choose language that emphasizes its important points.

Several language devices can be used to create levels of emphasis. Their purpose is to highlight certain parts of your speech and thereby downplay the other parts where they are not used. Among the most common of the devices used to create emphasis are contrast, rhetorical questions, repetition, and climax. Before you consider these devices, however, consider the most basic way of creating different levels of emphasis—the use of variety.

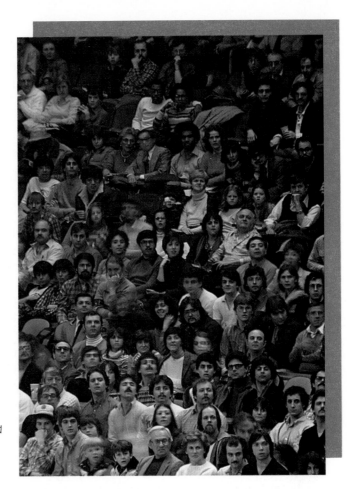

Keep that audience alert. Use a variety of words and sentence patterns to get your message across.

Variety Sets the Stage

Without variety in words and types of sentences, a speech quickly forms a repetitious language pattern. Any kind of regularly recurring pattern quickly distracts an audience, causing them to pay less attention to the speaker's message. But when there is variety in word usage and sentence length, certain points will stand out; others will recede into the background. Thus, language variety can be of great use in creating levels of emphasis.

Varying one's vocabulary, sentence length, and sentence structure can also help maintain listener interest. It can enliven your speech. Speeches which repeatedly use the same words to refer to a given idea soon become monotonous. Speakers who use all short, simple sentences begin to sound like machine-guns clattering. Those who use only long sentences quickly lose the attention and interest of their listeners. A basic key to successful speaking is variety.

Contrast Sticks in the Listener's Mind

The language device called contrast has long been used to make important statements stick in listeners' minds. The following examples come from three speeches by the same person. Do you know who spoke them?

"Let us never negotiate out of fear. But let us never fear to negotiate."

"In the election of 1860 the great issue was whether this country would remain half slave and half free; in the election of 1960 . . . the great issue is whether the *world* will remain half slave and half free."

"Ask not what your country can do for you—ask what you can do for your country."

Each of these uses of contrast by President John F. Kennedy became widely repeated statements. **Contrast,** a language device Kennedy used frequently, begins with two balanced phrases, clauses, or sentences. The words containing the ideas the speaker wishes to emphasize are the only words changed or rearranged in the second part of the statement. Notice how, in the second example above, Kennedy changed only three things: the date *1860* to the date *1960,* the word *country* to *world,* and the verb *would* to *will.* Thus he highlighted what he considered one of the most important issues in the 1960 election year. Had he stated only "The great issue in 1960 is whether the world will remain half slave and half free," his statement would not have carried as much emphasis, nor been remembered as long. Contrast is a language device that seems to stick in the listener's mind. The better your audiences remember some of your key statements, the greater the overall impact your speech is likely to have.

Contrast is not an easy device to create. Ordinarily, speakers do not spout forth well-balanced statements of contrast on the spur of the moment. Such statements usually grow from extended thought and careful planning. Therefore, contrast is usually found when a speaker has had ample time to plan precise language. If you plan to use contrast, you will need to think it out before the speech and then use a manuscript or note cards showing the statements of contrast you wish to make. The time spent is not likely to be wasted. Well-planned use of contrast can prove effective in most speeches.

Contrast, however, is a device that can be easily overused. Since it is generally saved to emphasize one of the major points in a speech, overusing it can stress too many points. The audience may become confused and forget all of them. One or perhaps two well-placed statements of contrast are ample, even in a lengthy speech.

Variety and Contrast

Turn to the Appendix of Speeches at the back of the text. Choose a speech that appeals to you because of its subject matter. Study the speech carefully and take notes on the way its author used variety and contrast. Discuss your speech in class, pointing out the use of variety and contrast. Compare your assessment with those of others who chose the same speech.

Rhetorical Questions Demand Attention

Ideas in a speech can also be emphasized by putting them in the form of rhetorical questions. **Rhetorical questions** are questions that are not meant to be answered out loud. It is difficult, however, for most people to ignore a question put to them. Thus, they will generally try to answer it in their minds. A speaker can sometimes capitalize on this fact by occasionally asking rhetorical questions of the audience. Notice how Dr. Martin Luther King, Jr., used rhetorical questions in his speech "I've Been to the Mountaintop," delivered in Memphis, Tennessee, just before his assassination. He was urging the members of the clergy who were his listeners to join with striking sanitation workers:

> That's the question before you tonight. Not, "If I stop to help the sanitation workers, what will happen to all of the hours that I usually spend in my office every day and every week as a pastor?" The question is not, "If I stop to help this man in need, what will happen to me?" "If I do not stop to help the sanitation workers, what will happen to them?" That's the question.

Dr. King did not expect out-loud responses from his listeners to these questions. Rhetorical questions demand an answer in the mind of each individual listener. They are difficult to ignore.

Repetition Highlights Important Points

Repetition is another effective device for highlighting important points. Listening to TV commercials, you might wonder whether modern television advertising ever makes use of any device other than repetition. Public speakers also make great use of repetition. Sometimes their basic purpose in using it is to persuade, to create an emotional reaction, or to aid listener recall. In many cases, however, the basic purpose is to emphasize important points. When used in this way its effect is like holding up a large sign stating: "Don't miss this! It's one of the most important points of my speech."

Repetition is different from restatement. Restatement (stating the same idea several times using *different* words) aids listener recall, but ordinarily does not drive a point home to the same extent that repetition does. **Repetition** (stating the same idea several times using the *same* words) is much more effective in signaling the important point for the audience. It sounds an emphatic note of insistence that is nearly impossible to ignore. Use repetition sparingly, however. Its overuse is very annoying.

A variation of repetition consists of beginning or ending sentences with the same single word or short phrase. This device, called **parallelism,** was used by President Franklin D. Roosevelt in a fighting speech during World War II:

> From Berlin, Rome, and Tokyo we have been described as a nation of weaklings—"playboys"—who would hire British soldiers, or Russian soldiers, or Chinese soldiers to do our fighting for us.
> Let them repeat that now!
> Let them tell that to General MacArthur and his men.
> Let them tell that to the sailors who today are hitting hard in the far waters of the Pacific.
> Let them tell that to the boys in the Flying Fortresses.
> Let them tell that to the marines!

But repetition should be used sparingly. It serves as a highly effective means of achieving emphasis only as long as it is not overused.

Climax Emphasizes the Last Item in a Series

When a speaker lists three or four items in a series, the item spoken of last carries the greatest emphasis. Suppose you wished, for example, to emphasize how seriously wrong you consider someone's behavior to be. The expected order would look like this: "His behavior is wrong, it is immoral, it is actually criminal." This is called **climax ordering**—moving from less significant to more significant, and ending the series with whichever item is most important. If, in the example above, a speaker were to arrange the items in any other order, the audience would most likely become confused. Since audiences usually expect to hear climax ordering whenever items spoken in a series differ in importance, speakers can emphasize the last item by using it. General Douglas MacArthur, in a speech to the cadets at West Point, used climax ordering two times to describe the "American man-at-arms." They appear in italics in the following excerpt from his speech.

But when I think *of his patience under adversity, of his courage under fire, and of his modesty in victory,* I am filled with an emotion of admiration I cannot put into words. He belongs to history as furnishing one of the greatest examples of successful patriotism. He belongs to posterity as the instructor of future generations in the principles of liberty and freedom. He belongs to the present—to us—by his virtues and by his achievements.

In 20 campaigns, on 100 battlefields, around 1,000 campfires, I have witnessed that enduring fortitude, that patriotic self-abnegation, and that invincible determination which has carved his statue in the hearts of his people.

As is the case with most language devices used for creating levels of emphasis, climax must be used sparingly. Well-placed usage of such devices, however, can make the difference between a poor speech and an excellent one.

Franklin D. Roosevelt used parallelism to memorable effect in his radio speeches to the nation during the Great Depression and World War II.

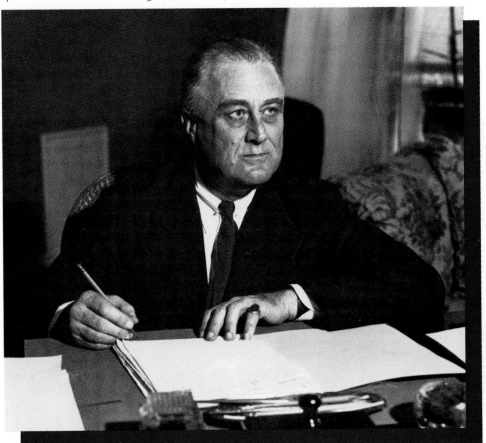

LOBBYIST

Lobbyists represent special interest groups by influencing government policy and legislation at both the national and state levels. Because lobbyists participate at every stage of the lawmaking process, they must have a comprehensive knowledge and experience of how the legislature works. They meet with legislators and their assistants, testify at hearings on bills relating to their group's interests, and work to ensure an important bill's passage.

Because legislators are inundated with requests from interest groups, effective lobbyists must convey clear, concise, and emphatic messages to persuade others to follow their interest group's point of view. Choosing their words carefully, lobbyists rely on powerful, yet simple language to communicate their opinions. They select colorful word images to create unforgettably vivid pictures in the minds of their listeners.

Lobbyists often have only fifteen minutes to testify at hearings or to speak with legislators. Before each appointment, they prepare by streamlining their well-researched position so it can be presented simply. To make each idea memorable, key concepts are illustrated with specific examples, facts, or statistics. Lobbyists also reinforce their presentation by emphatically restating the main ideas.

A lobbyist must deliver a clear and vigorous message to be heard by busy legislators. When lobbyists combine their forceful public speaking with the ability to create vibrant words and images, they wield a powerful tool that leaves lasting impressions on the minds of others.

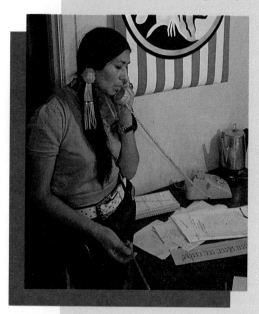

This lobbyist uses crisp, incisive language to make her point.

USING FIGURES OF SPEECH

Language in a speech must sometimes be rich and imaginative; at other times plain and straightforward. The plainer parts help emphasize the richer ones. Few speakers can produce clever, imaginative language constantly, and even if they could the listeners would soon sicken of it. It would be much like eating steak every day, without the faintest hope of some ordinary hamburger now and then. The careful use of imaginative language can, however, add a great deal to your speeches. Knowing ways of creating rich language can help you make your meanings clear to your listeners.

In this section we'll look at several methods of making speech more imaginative, methods that are called figures of speech. **Figures of speech** are phrases and sentences that make a point by stating something that is not literally or exactly true. They rely on such things as comparison, contrast, and exaggeration to make meanings clear.

Similies and Metaphors

Two special forms of comparison, the simile and the metaphor, are frequently used to make ideas memorable for the listeners. A **simile** is a brief comparison of two basically unlike things, using the word *like* or *as*. When Adlai Stevenson lost the presidential election in 1956, he used a simile to express his feelings: "I feel like a little boy who has just stubbed his toe. I'm too big to cry, but it hurts too much to laugh." Very likely, few people would have remembered Stevenson's remark had he simply said, "Well, I'm too old to cry, but I certainly don't feel like laughing either." Instead, Stevenson's simile created a vivid picture that has endured in the public's mind.

A **metaphor** is a more direct comparison of two things than a simile, because it omits the word *like* or *as*. A student speaker used this metaphor:

The Philippine islands are pieces of emerald that were dropped into the South China Sea by some beneficent giant.

The beauty of the Philippines is clearly evoked because the student used metaphor to link the very identity of these shimmering green islands with emeralds. The impact is immediate and powerful. Had the speaker said "The Philippine islands seem like pieces of emerald . . .", the comparison would have been a simile.

Similes and metaphors usually are only one sentence in length. The often-heard retort of a jokester whose joke has fallen flat is a one-sentence simile: "Well, that went over like a lead balloon!" At other times

"My point is, Stalin was about as subtle as a tank."

a simile or metaphor may consist of several sentences. Hubert Farbes won a national high-school speech contest with a speech containing this combination of metaphor-simile:

> For there is a parasite in the minds of men today. It grows like a leech, taking its morbid existence from the strength of its host, warping his mind and character.

If a comparison grows beyond two or three sentences, however, it is ordinarily labelled an extended comparison, or an **analogy.** Similes and metaphors gain part of their impact from being short and pithy.

Similes and metaphors may be used quite frequently in a speech. This does no harm, as long as the speaker does not stuff the listener with such devices. Keep in mind that a substantial portion of your speech must consist of plain food, so that the special treat may be appreciated.

Personification

Personification is a figure of speech by which a speaker gives human qualities to inanimate objects, ideas, or non-human creatures. An effective use of personification was contained in a speech by President Franklin D. Roosevelt. When his political enemies accused him of wasting taxpayers' money by sending a naval destroyer to pick up his dog Fala on an Aleutian island, Roosevelt gave human emotions to the dog in his reply. Notice how he gradually builds up to the personification:

> These Republican leaders have not been content with attacks on me, or my wife, or on my sons. No, not content with that, they now include my little dog, Fala. Well, of course, I don't resent attacks, and my family doesn't resent attacks, but Fala *does* resent them. You know, Fala is Scotch, and being a Scottie, as soon as he learned that the Republican fiction writers in Congress and out had concocted a story that I had left him behind on the Aleutian Islands and had sent a destroyer back to find him—at a cost to the taxpayers of two or three, or eight or twenty million dollars—his Scotch soul was furious. He has not been the same dog since. I am accustomed to hearing malicious falsehoods about myself—such as that old, worm-eaten chestnut that I have represented myself as indispensable. But I think I have a right to resent, to object to libelous statements about my dog.

By focusing attention on the dog's feelings, Roosevelt was able to express some of his own feelings about the charges that had been made, but in a humorous way.

Personification may also be used to set a general mood. Consider the effect of an opening narrative that begins with these words: "It was a dark and gloomy winter's day, with stubborn clouds threatening us every moment. . . ." You might expect suspense, mystery, or intrigue of some sort to follow. Part of the mood is created by the words "stubborn" and "threatening." Since these are qualities of human beings, and not of clouds, attributing them to clouds gives greater liveliness to a speech.

Application

Personification

Write a sentence that includes a personification for each of the following subjects.

1. a movie theater after closing
2. a mountain being climbed by noisy hikers
3. a campfire trying to ignite in wet wood`
4. a train running on mountain tracks
5. a cat trying to avoid a young child

Test your sentences on a small group of classmates. Can they picture each personification? Did each seem appropriate?

Hyperbole

Hyperbole is perhaps the most commonly used figure of speech in everyday conversation. It consists of intentionally exaggerating in order to emphasize a point. Because most of us engage in hyperbole so regularly, much of our everyday use of it has become subconscious. Ordinarily we are exaggerating subconsciously when using common expressions such as:

She's the greatest!

I'm completely exhausted.

I'm dead!

I jogged a thousand miles today.

Such statements are rarely true, of course, but the listener understands that the exaggeration is only intended to underscore the speaker's feelings.

In public speaking, hyperbole must be used sparingly, since in emphasizing too many points, a speaker winds up emphasizing none.

Understatement

Understatement is the opposite of hyperbole. Its purpose is to highlight something by playing down its importance or making what is significant sound insignificant. If a multi-millionaire is asked about the extent of her wealth, she might use understatement in her reply: "Let's just say I'm not terribly worried about where my next meal is coming from."

Irony

Irony is a figure of speech in which the literal meaning expressed by a person's words is the opposite of the meaning intended. If you wished to show your dislike and lack of respect for another person, you might exclaim "Oh, she's a fine person!" with a sarcastic tone in your voice that indicates you mean to convey the opposite of *fine*.

AVOIDING COMMON PROBLEMS

Language can be a public speaker's greatest asset. Unfortunately, it sometimes traps a speaker into saying what is not meant or meaning what is not said. Following are several problems encountered in choosing effective language. A couple of these should always be avoided. Others may prove helpful or harmful, depending on how you use them.

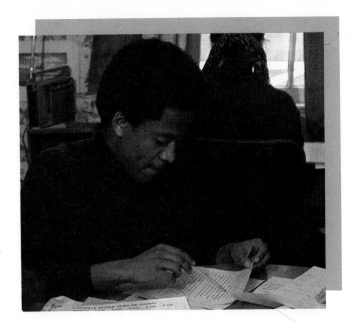

As this student revises his speech, he edits out words that may have strong negative connotations for his audience.

Avoid Unintentional Connotations

All words have a standard, dictionary meaning. This is a generally accepted, objective meaning known as a word's denotation. Words may also have connotations—special meanings for different people or different groups of people. If, for instance, a speaker were to use the word *gold,* the denotation would be "a heavy, yellow metal." The connotation, for some audience members, might include ideas of wealth or beauty. Speakers must be aware of the possible connotations the words they use are likely to carry for the bulk of their audiences. If the connotations are likely to cause strong negative reactions, it is wiser to choose other language.

Use Euphemisms Carefully

Euphemisms are gentle or softened expressions for harsh or unpleasant realities. People often say "He passed on" for "He died." Euphemisms are often helpful, since they allow a speaker to be tactful and avoid insulting an audience. Avoid using them so frequently that your message becomes clouded with soft terms, however.

Avoid Clichés

Clichés are expressions that at one time expressed a truth or idea clearly and briefly, but have become so overused as to be almost meaningless. Examples of clichés are "A stitch in time saves nine," "Where there's smoke there's fire," "Green with envy," and "As pretty as a picture." The use of clichés generally bores an audience. It also causes listeners to lose a certain degree of respect for the speaker, since using clichés makes it appear that the speaker lacks originality.

Don't Stereotype

Stereotyping means assigning qualities to people or objects because they are part of a general group, without considering their individual differences. Stereotypes may be based on a person's appearance, type of employment, nationality, religion, race, or age. "All bus drivers are rude" and "Young people are lazy" are examples of stereotyping. Using words or phrases which stereotype greatly harms a speaker's image. They should always be avoided.

Use Slang Sparingly

Slang consists of contemporary words and phrases that come in and go out of style very rapidly. Because the majority of slang expressions have a short life, using them in your speeches will confuse listeners who have never had a chance to become familiar with them. Some years ago *cool* and *groovy* were "in" words. Today the person who uses them sounds neither "cool" nor "groovy." You should also remember that many slang expressions, current among young people, never get picked up by older people at all.

Be very thrifty in your use of slang even when talking to your classmates. You may wish to use it once in a while to produce an informal atmosphere, for novelty or humor, but beware of using it often in public speaking. As you gain more and more exposure to various types of speeches, notice how little slang good speakers use even in speeches delivered at very informal occasions. Slang dates your speech, and if overused, shows a limited vocabulary.

Shun Incorrect Grammar

Remember, words are the garments with which speakers clothe their ideas. If you use *incorrect grammar,* it is a lot like appearing in public with your shirt on backwards or wearing socks that don't match. It is true that spoken language is often less formal than written language, but that does not mean it can be incorrect. The speaker heard saying "All of us in this room has a stake in this problem", stands out like a person with shoes on the wrong feet. When the voice from the podium announces "He laid down for a nap," listeners feel as they would when looking at someone with green hair. We all make grammatical slips from time to time. It is the speaker who habitually does so who loses the respect of his or her listeners. Here is a chart showing some of the common problem areas in grammatical usage:

Common Problem Areas in Grammatical Usage		
Problem area	**Grammatical explanation**	**Correct usage**
affect/effect	*affect* is usually a verb *effect* is generally a noun	That mistake may significantly affect your career. The movie had quite an effect on me.
beside/besides	*beside* means "next to"; *besides* means "in addition"	John, stand beside Mary. I don't like him; besides, he squints.
between you and I	the object of the preposition *between* is *me*	between you and me
can/may	*can* means "is able to"; *may* means "is allowed to"	He can win the race. She may go to the head of the line.
could care less	should be "couldn't care less" to state that someone was unconcerned	John couldn't care less about Paul's illness.
farther/further	use *farther* for real physical distance; use *further* for other kinds of distance	Cincinnati is farther than Louisville. Nothing could be further from her mind.
irregardless/regardless	always use *regardless*	Regardless of the consequences, I am going ahead.
like	should not be used as a filler word, as in "He was like fifteen years old."	He was fifteen years old.
like/as if	do not use *like* in place of *as if*	You look as if (not like) you are thirsty.
that/which/who	*who* refers to people; *which* and *that* refer to things that are not people	I am the one who called. My car, which is ancient, won't start. I have a parrot that talks.

Errors in grammar may be repeated so often that they *sound* correct even when they are not. Practice proper usage until it sounds right to you.

8 Chapter Review

■ Summary

Words are the garments with which speakers clothe their ideas. Wise speakers choose their language very carefully in order to display their ideas effectively.

Differences Between Written and Spoken Language Language used in writing is different from language spoken aloud. Spoken language contains more short, simple sentences than does written language. It also uses simpler words, is more concrete and specific, has more restatement, and contains fewer unnecessary words.

Making Spoken Language Clear Clarity ranks as the most important quality of spoken language. Clarity means using reasonably short sentences and simple words. It means using concrete and specific language that paints pictures in the listeners' imaginations. It also calls for the restatement of the main ideas in a speech. Finally, it requires the removal of unnecessary words. Language that is simple and direct makes the best impact on an audience.

Creating Levels of Emphasis Language may also be used to emphasize certain points. Varying vocabulary, sentence length, and sentence structure is one way of achieving this. Other devices are contrast—the use of balanced phrases; rhetorical questions—questions that need no answer; repetition—repeating the same words or phrases; and climax—saving the most important item in a series until last.

Using Figures of Speech Figures of speech can help get your meaning across vividly. Comparison, contrast, and exaggeration can highlight ideas and make them memorable. Similes and metaphors compare two essentially unlike things. Personification is a way of giving human qualities to nonhuman things. Hyperbole emphasizes through intentional exaggeration. Its opposite, understatement, highlights a matter by downplaying its importance. Irony makes the literal meaning of the spoken word the opposite of the intended meaning.

Avoiding Common Problems   Language problems to be avoided, or approached cautiously, include unintentional connotations, euphemisms, clichés, stereotypes, slang, and incorrect grammar. Some of these should always be avoided; others can be helpful if used sparingly.

Vocabulary

Define each word in a complete sentence.

concrete words	parallelism	hyperbole
abstract words	climax ordering	understatement
specific words	figures of speech	irony
restatement	simile	euphemism
economy of language	metaphor	clichés
contrast	analogy	stereotyping
rhetorical questions	personification	slang
repetition		

Checklist

Skills of Effective Language Choice

1. Speak in short and simple sentences whenever possible.
2. Use language that your audience will understand.
3. Use concrete language and specific words.
4. Use restatement to help your audience understand your message.
5. Remember that variety in words and types of sentences is essential if your message is to appeal to your audience.
6. Use contrast to help your audience remember what you say.
7. Use rhetorical questions and repetition to gain the attention of your audience.
8. Use figures of speech to help make your speech both imaginative and memorable.
9. Be certain that you use words correctly.
10. Take care to avoid clichés and stereotypes. Use slang sparingly in speeches.

Review Questions

1. Identify five ways in which spoken language differs from written language.
2. Name four characteristics of clear language.
3. Explain the importance of restating main ideas when you are speaking.
4. Explain the best way to achieve economy of language.
5. Name several aspects of language that you should vary to keep your speech lively.
6. Define and give examples of contrast, rhetorical question, repetition, parallelism, and climax ordering.
7. Identify the figure of speech used in each of the following:
   (a) "I feel like a little boy who has just stubbed his toe."
   (b) "He is a prince."
   (c) "Even the stars cry out for justice."
8. Define and give an example of euphemism.
9. Identify five problems to avoid in spoken language.
10. Describe the circumstances in which slang can be used effectively in a speech.

Discussion Questions

1. As a class, discuss each of the following quotations of Winston Churchill:

   (On becoming Prime Minister of Great Britain) "I have nothing to offer but blood, toil, tears, and sweat."

   (On June 4, 1940, speech to House of Commons) ". . . we shall not flag or fail. We shall go to the end . . . we shall fight in the seas and oceans . . . we shall fight on the beaches, we shall fight on the landing-grounds, we shall fight in the fields and in the streets, we shall fight in the hills; we shall never surrender."

   (When the RAF defeated the German Luftwaffe) "Never in the field of human conflict was so much owed by so many to so few."

   Discuss Churchill's use of language. Do you agree with John F. Kennedy that Churchill "mobilized the English language and sent it into battle?" Discuss what President Kennedy meant by those words.

2. Think about a time when you heard a manuscript speech on television. Such speeches are often given by government officials. Even if the speaker uses a teleprompter and looks toward the audience, listeners can still tell that the speech is being read. Discuss why a listener can tell the difference between an extemporaneous speech and a read speech. Does the difference have something to do with word choice or with the way sentences are put together? Why may it be necessary for government officials to read speeches?

3. Eloquence is speaking that is marked by force and persuasiveness. The great speeches of the past are remembered today because they were eloquent statements of the speaker's position. Discuss what eloquence is. In what ways does each of the characteristics of effective language mentioned in this chapter contribute to a speech that is eloquent and memorable?

4. The terms *justice, freedom,* and *education* are abstract terms. But what do these terms really mean? Discuss what each means to you. Compare your definitions with those offered by your classmates. Discuss what you really must do before others have a clear idea of what abstract terms like these mean to a speaker.

■ Critical Thinking

1. **Analysis:** Concrete words communicate exact meanings more readily than abstract words, and specific words communicate more precisely than general words. Explain how general words are different from abstract words. Explain how specific words differ from concrete words.

2. **Evaluation:** When language is used effectively, listeners pay close attention and more easily remember a speaker's message. In which of the three main types of speeches —speeches to inform, persuade, and entertain—is effective language of critical importance? Why?

■ Activities

In-Class

1. Look through magazines that you find in your home and locate some advertisements that you think portray the products they are selling most attractively. Find three very effective ads. Study the language that accompanies each ad. What is it about the language that makes it effective? Analyze the language in each effective ad and share your analysis with your classmates.

2. Work in small groups of from five to seven. Prepare a humorous skit that concentrates on one of the following language features. Rehearse and present your skit in class.
   (a) a skit filled with clichés
   (b) a skit involving hyperbole and understatement
   (c) a skit depicting various stereotypes
   (d) a skit featuring slang
   (e) a skit illustrating incorrect grammar or usage
   (f) a skit using euphemisms

3. Locate a speech either in the Appendix of Speeches in the back of this book, in an anthology of speeches, or in the publication *Vital Speeches of the Day.* Examine the speech carefully from the standpoint of effective use of language. Try to find as many of the effective language features mentioned in this chapter as possible. Report your findings in class.

Out-of-Class

1. In your speech notebook, compose sentences or short paragraphs to illustrate each of the following. Present your work in class and ask for feedback.
   (a) literary contrast
   (b) rhetorical question
   (c) restatement
   (d) repetition
   (e) parallelism
   (f) climax ordering
   (g) simile
   (h) metaphor

2. In your speech notebook, compile a list of current slang terms. Write a brief definition of each. Then consult a person who is from 15 to 20 years older than you. Ask that person to check your list and to tell you how many of the current terms he or she is familiar with. Then ask that person to identify and define as many slang terms as he or she can remember that were popular when he or she was your age. Write these terms and their definitions in your speech

notebook. Report the results in class and discuss what you have learned about the nature of slang terms.

3. Locate a speech in a library source that was given before 1850. Find one paragraph in the speech that is representative of the language used throughout the speech. In your speech notebook, rewrite the paragraph so that it would be understandable to today's audiences. What changes did you make in word choice? Did you make any changes in sentence structure? Be prepared to explain your findings in class.

4. In your speech notebook, write your own fresher expressions for the following clichés. Then write as many other clichés as you can think of. Be prepared to share them with your classmates and to participate in the search for fresher substitutes.
   (a) sink or swim
   (b) the bottom line
   (c) a clean break
   (d) dog-tired
   (e) last but not least
   (f) a whole new ball game
   (g) over the hill
   (h) the bitter end
   (i) pretty as a picture
   (j) cold as blue blazes

Chapter Project

You learned in Chapter 1 that our nation's history has frequently been shaped by the great public speakers who spoke on the vital issues of the day. It is altogether appropriate that students look at important historical speeches to analyze their content and determine what features of the speeches caused them to have political impact. Two such speeches appear in your Appendix: Abraham Lincoln's "Gettysburg Address" and Susan B. Anthony's speech delivered in 1872 on "Woman's Right to the Suffrage."

Working in small groups, consider these two speeches very carefully. Apply all principles of rhetorical analysis that you have learned in this chapter. Determine which features of effective language are present in the speeches and collect examples of each.

When your group's analysis is complete, write it in the form of an oral report and select someone to deliver it to the class.

9 Delivering Your Speech

When you have completed this chapter you should be able to:

- Compare various methods of speech delivery.
- Identify the nonverbal aspects of delivering a speech.
- Explain how to use notes effectively when making a speech.
- Describe the importance of proper articulation and pronunciation.
- Explain ways of dealing with distractions and interruptions when giving a speech.

As a speaker, which method of delivery suits you best: the spontaneity of an extemporaneous speech or the precision of a speech read from manuscript? As an audience member, which would you rather hear?

Delivering a speech is not the same as delivering the mail or a loaf of bread. Generally, the mail and the bread are neither improved nor harmed during the process of being delivered to their destination. On the other hand, a speech can be made much better or much worse by the manner in which it is delivered. Although delivery is not the most essential part of giving a speech, it is very important. Good delivery can make a weak speech seem a bit better. Poor delivery can ruin an otherwise excellent speech. This chapter begins by examining several different methods of speech delivery.

USING DIFFERENT METHODS OF DELIVERY

Over the years, four basic methods for delivering public speeches have developed. One might be called the **manuscript method.** Using this method, speakers write down everything they plan to say to their listeners, then bring their manuscripts to the podium and read them to the audience. A second method, called the **memorization method,** also begins with a written manuscript but differs in that the manuscript is memorized word-for-word and not used during the delivery. Using a third method, the **extemporaneous method,** speakers prepare outlines of the *ideas* of their speeches beforehand, but do not memorize an exact pattern of *words.* They choose the words with which to clothe their ideas as they are speaking. Outlines or note cards may or may not be used. The fourth method, called the **impromptu method,** is used on occasions when people must speak "off the cuff," with no chance for previous preparation. This method demands that the speakers both organize their ideas and choose their words as they proceed through their speeches.

Comparing Methods of Delivery

Each of the four methods has advantages and disadvantages. Let's take a moment to compare them. The manuscript method has an advantage in that there is no danger of forgetting a part of your speech. Unless a sudden wind blows away your manuscript, about the worst thing that can happen is momentarily losing your place while reading. The manuscript method also allows you plenty of time to choose the most effective language for your speech beforehand. Presidents of the United States and other heads of state often read from manuscripts when making major policy statements. This helps assure that they do not make any "slips of the tongue" that could result in embarrassment for their countries or in an international incident. Speeches read from manuscript often sound smoother than those delivered extemporaneously. The use of a manuscript also assures precise timing of a speech, a factor of great importance for televised speeches. Unfortunately, many speeches read from manuscript *sound* as if they are being read. The audience is aware of the manuscript, and it prevents the speech from sounding natural. How many times have you had to listen to a speaker read from manuscript and felt like screaming at the speaker: "Stop reading *at* us and start talking *to* us"?

Memorized delivery has some of the same advantages as manuscript delivery. You may choose the most effective language beforehand, and your speech may be timed precisely. Memorized delivery often sounds prepackaged, however, as indeed it is. Word-for-word memorization also puts a tremendous burden on your memory for any speech longer than four or five minutes. This method of delivery is used rarely nowadays.

The major advantage of the extemporaneous method is that it sounds natural—much like ordinary conversation. Imagine for a moment that you and a close friend are planning to attend a big basketball game. At the last minute your friend is prevented from going, so she asks you to tell her all about the game later. How would you go about preparing your "speech" for your friend? You could make a strong effort to remember all the important plays, the score, the poor calls by the referees (you might even make a few notes to help you remember), but you definitely wouldn't write out your description of the game word-for-word and later read it to your friend. She would get bored listening to your "reading" about the game instead of "telling" her about it. To an audience,

President Ronald Reagan's ability to memorize a speech, and make it sound extemporaneous, resulted in his being dubbed "the Great Communicator."

extemporaneous speaking sounds more like "telling" your speech than like "reading" it. No audience likes a speaker to read a message that can be told. They will usually become bored and lose interest, even if the reader reads well. However, they are very tolerant of a speaker who looks them in the eye and addresses them directly, even if the flow of words is a bit halting.

The extemporaneous method also gives you, the speaker, the best opportunity to make use of positive and negative feedback from your audience. By constantly monitoring the listeners' reactions and making necessary adjustments, you will improve your chances of maintaining a high level of audience interest and enthusiasm. Since the manuscript and memorization methods prevent this, they fall far short of the extemporaneous method of speaking.

The only advantage of impromptu delivery is that it sounds natural— much like ordinary conversation. Its major drawback, of course, is its tendency to sound unprepared. Unless a speaker has had considerable experience at impromptu speaking, this kind of delivery is likely to sound jumbled and awkward.

Combining Methods of Delivery

In Chapter 7, you prepared an outline or a set of note cards to use for reference when delivering a speech. You concentrated on planting a pattern of ideas in your mind, rather than on preparing a speech manuscript to read or memorize. Thus you were really preparing to deliver an extemporaneous speech.

Of the four methods you have been comparing (manuscript, memorization, extemporaneous, and impromptu), extemporaneous delivery appears to have the greatest number of advantages. Many of the best speakers, however, find they are most effective when they combine methods. One of America's greatest public speakers, President Franklin D. Roosevelt, often prepared manuscripts for his major addresses, and then regularly departed from them during delivery, speaking extemporaneously instead. Although this practice annoyed newspaper owners who had sometimes already printed the advance text in their papers, it was

This student combines memorized and extemporaneous delivery with the selective use of note cards. The result is a lively, fluid speech.

extremely effective with Roosevelt's audiences. By combining the methods in this way, he was able to gain the advantages of each, while avoiding their pitfalls.

Combining methods of delivery in this way requires a certain degree of skill and experience. The listeners should not be able to detect which parts are being read from manuscript, which are memorized, and which are being spoken extemporaneously. Combining methods effectively also requires skill in the use of the extemporaneous method, since the extemporaneous parts must sound as fluent and well prepared as the manuscript sections. However, you can begin to use a combination of methods in small ways.

You will probably find it helpful, at this point, to memorize your introductory remarks and your conclusions. Memorizing the introduction gets you off to a smooth start, sounds impressive, and helps build your confidence for the body of the speech. A carefully worded, memorized conclusion can make a lasting impression on the audience and end your speech effectively. Major transition sentences within the body of the speech may also be memorized. Most of the body of the speech can then be prepared using the extemporaneous method. The manuscript method may be used for brief sections of the body where you wish to insert a direct quotation in the original author's language or present a set of statistics too complex to memorize. These kinds of material can be written out fully on 3×5 note cards or a manuscript page and read at appropriate points in your speech. Beware of preparing lengthy sections of the speeches you are now giving by the manuscript or memorization methods, however. Your main concentration should be on learning the extemporaneous method, since it will serve as the backbone for any combination of methods you may later wish to use.

Application

Extemporaneous Speech

Think about a book or a movie that you like and that you feel a friend would also enjoy. Prepare to speak extemporaneously to your friend about it. Jot down some notes and plan the opening and the ending of your talk. Then speak about the book or movie in an informal and conversational tone. When you are finished, ask whether your friend would like to read the book or see the movie. Also, ask if your presentation captured your friend's attention and whether or not it was clear and natural. Jot down useful feedback in your speech notebook.

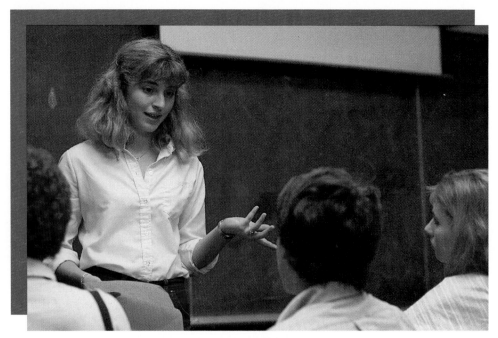

This student extends her message to the audience with face and hand gestures.

RECOGNIZING NONVERBAL ASPECTS OF DELIVERING A SPEECH

People often think of a speech as a set of words spoken aloud. Actually you communicate with an audience as much through nonverbal means as through words. Eye contact, gestures, platform movements, appearance, and the motions you make as you begin and end a speech will "say" a great deal about you and your message to the listeners.

Beginning Your Speech

You may think that your speech begins when you speak the first word. The audience, however, makes judgments about you from the moment you rise from your seat to approach the speaking platform. You nonverbally communicate self-confidence, poise, and leadership, or nervousness, disorganization, and timidity simply by the manner in which you approach the platform and take command of it.

Walk to the platform vigorously, but not hastily. Arrange any notes on the lectern. Turn your face up toward your listeners, and look about at various sides of the audience for several seconds before beginning to speak. This unhurried beginning assures those present of your confidence and command of the situation.

Making Eye Contact

As you speak, establish eye contact with your listeners. Look directly into the eyes of various audience members. This causes most listeners to feel as if you are devoting your attention to them personally in the same way you would if you were conversing with just one person. The greater the proportion of your speaking time you devote to eye contact, the deeper and more positive this impression becomes.

Looking at your listeners also performs a second important function. It makes it possible for you to monitor the feedback. Feedback is simply the total of all the visible and audible reactions of the audience to the speaker. It can consist of yawns, smiles, boos, nodding heads, hisses, questioning looks, and even fidgeting in the seats. When you use extemporaneous delivery, you are largely free to read your listeners' feedback and then adjust your approach to maintain positive feedback.

When making eye contact, look at one audience member for several seconds as you speak, then turn your head slightly to look at another. Don't forget the people at the sides of the room near the front. Because speakers must turn their heads farther to look at them, these listeners are often cheated out of eye contact.

Some beginning speakers report that looking directly at their listeners makes them nervous and confused. If this happens to you, let your teacher know, and he or she will probably suggest that you look at your audience in general for awhile, rather than directly into individuals' eyes. Beware of getting into a habit of doing this, however. Eye contact is so important for both speaker and audience that its lack can sometimes ruin an otherwise good speech. Once you have gained some experience and have learned to relax on the platform, you should be able to maintain real eye contact without difficulty.

Using Gestures

Communicating nonverbally through gestures is a natural part of human communication, yet many beginning speakers freeze up when giving a public speech. Nevertheless, because we all gesture naturally, the urge to gesture will ordinarily return once a speaker has gained platform experience.

Most arm and hand gestures fall into one of four types. **Emphatic gestures** help the speaker stress what he or she is saying. These include making a fist, raising one hand with the palm up, and pointing with the index finger at your audience when saying something such as "It's your responsibility . . ." **Transitional gestures** show that you are moving from one part of your speech to another. They include using your fingers to enumerate points, placing both palms on the podium, and moving both hands, with palms facing each other, from one side to the other in front of you. When a speaker uses **descriptive gestures,** he or she moves the hands and arms to draw pictures in the air. These may indicate the size of an object, such as the "fish that got away," or the general shape of something. Finally, **locative gestures** direct the listeners' attention to some place, object, or person. They are usually made with the index finger or with the entire hand.

Books on public speaking used to include long lists and extensive illustrations of gestures, showing in detail how they should be made. The problem with that approach was that it was like telling a speaker which words to use. Each person has his or her own style of nonverbal communication, just as each chooses his or her own words. When you gesture during a speech, it should be because it feels natural at that point. If, for instance, you are describing a far distant place, and it seems appropriate to extend your arm to indicate how far away it is, extend your arm. If you refer to that same distant place later in the same speech, and this time it does not seem appropriate to extend your arm, you should not do so. It is basically a matter of what feels appropriate at the moment without any lengthy thought about it. While it is helpful for beginning speakers to make some gestures while speaking, it is not good to force gestures. Certainly it is not wise to decide during rehearsal that you are definitely going to make a certain gesture at a particular place in your speech. It would probably look rehearsed if made during the live speech.

Student speakers sometimes ask: "What should I do with my arms and hands when I am not using them to gesture?" Unfortunately, no single answer can be given. As with gestures, basic hand and arm positions must be both natural to you and well suited to the audience and the total speaking situation. Here are some commonly used positions that you may want to consider:

- One or both arms hanging naturally at your side.
- One or both hands resting on (not grasping) the speaker's stand.
- One or both hands held several inches in front of you.

These positions will look quite natural for some speakers but not for others. You can learn from the reactions of your teacher and classmates which suit you best.

Audience members ordinarily pay more attention to a speaker's head and facial gestures than they do to arm or hand movements. Smiles, frowns, nods, and any other movements of the head, eyebrows, chin, lips, or brow can create an impression of a dynamic and enthusiastic speaker, as long as they are appropriate to the spoken message. As with any gestures, head and facial movements must be natural. They must come from your inner enthusiasm about your message and not be practiced or tacked on for show.

Many beginning speakers show too somber a face to their audiences. Of course, some topics demand a serious countenance, but many do not. A speaker describing "How to Shoot Rapids in a Canoe" need not look overly solemn to the listeners. A generally pleasant look, alternating with some facial expressions showing the adventure and thrill of canoeing, will make a better impression on the listeners.

Variety is the spice of public speaking, just as it is of life. Like all other parts of a speech, gestures (whether arm-hand or head-face) must be varied regularly to maintain audience attention and interest. A speaker who makes the same gesture repeatedly distracts the audience with that gesture. Pretty soon many listeners are wondering when the gesture will occur again and are paying little attention to the message. Although he was a first-rate speaker, President John F. Kennedy occasionally overused a gesture with his right arm during his campaign speeches. It became so characteristic of his speaking style that mimics began imitating the movement. But because Kennedy possessed so many outstanding qualities as a speaker, it was easy for listeners to excuse this overworked

"I hear he doesn't like to distract audiences with showy gesticulations. He calls this his all-purpose, subtle-but-stately gesture."

gesture. Unknown speakers, however, must be doubly careful of any gesture that becomes a regular pattern in their speech. While taking care not to overuse any one gesture, remember that using no gestures at all is just as deadly. In addition, a speaker's face should be expressive. Facial gestures such as raising the eyebrows, smiling, frowning, and widening the eyes, indicate your involvement with your topic and generate interest and enthusiasm in your audience.

Using Platform Movement

The way in which a speaker uses platform movement (movements involving the entire body) can also project a certain image to the audience. In Chapter 6 you read about the basic forms of platform movement and the dangers of falling into distracting forms. (Remember the Ping-Pong Pacer, for instance?) The question here is, how can one make the best use of positive forms of movement? Like gestures, platform movement should look and feel natural. The best way to achieve this is to move when there is a reason to move and to remain still at other times. Legitimate reasons to move during a speech are similar to reasons for moving during a one-to-one conversation. Ask yourself: "When do I

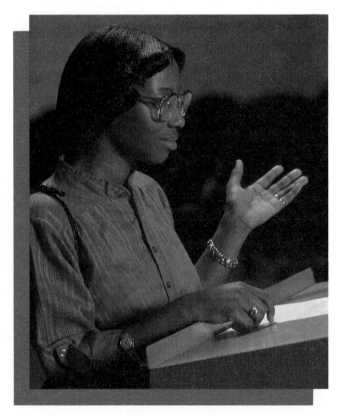

Low-key—yet expressive—hand and facial gestures can be very effective.

ordinarily move about if I'm having a conversation with a friend?" Your answers are likely to include at least two or three of the following reasons:

■ To whisper something confidential or intimate to the other person.

■ To compensate when the listener shifts his or her position.

■ To change to a new topic or to change the mood.

■ To provide variety.

Reasons for platform movement during a public speech fall into the very same categories. You may want to get closer to the audience to show greater confidentiality or intimacy, to compensate for audience members' fidgeting in their seats, to emphasize change to a new topic or section of your speech at major transition points, or to create a bit of visual variety.

Using Notes Effectively

Speaking extemporaneously means having your pattern of ideas clearly in mind as you begin your speech, but selecting your words spontaneously. Many extemporaneous speakers use **note cards** to ensure that they do not forget a major point, or to read an occasional direct quote or set of statistics. You have probably seen speakers who used note cards so effectively you were barely aware the speakers had them. You have also probably suffered through speeches in which the note cards were fumbled, dropped, or even lost. Observing a few tips on the preparation and use of note cards can make all the difference:

■ Cards containing your outline should be very brief, containing only a word or short phrase to remind you of each point in your speech.

■ Cards containing direct quotes or sets of statistics should contain only one item of information each, and should be arranged in the proper order before the speech begins.

■ Be certain to write your source of information at the bottom of cards containing quotations or statistics. Write or type in large, bold characters so that each card can be easily read when resting on the podium.

■ Place the cards near the top edge of the podium so the audience doesn't think you're looking at your feet when you're glancing at your cards.

■ Feel free to hold one or more cards in your hand if you move away from the podium. (Use only 3×5 cards to do this.)

■ Plan not to look at your outline card at all during your presentation. It should be there only as a comforting refuge should you forget a point.

Making the Most of Your Appearance

Much of the appeal of glamorous stars comes from their appearance—the carefully styled hair, the beautiful gowns, the glittering jewels. Speakers, too are often judged as much by how they look as by what they have to say. A speaker's appearance should be suited to his or her personality, the audience being addressed, and the occasion for which the speech is being given. The way speakers dress says a great deal about their attitudes toward their listeners and how much importance they attach to the speech itself. Speakers who radically violate the audience's expectations concerning clothing and general appearance have two strikes against them before they say their first sentence. You can improve your chances of creating a good impression by asking yourself: "What is the most appropriate thing to wear for this particular audience and set of circumstances?"

A speaker's appearance is more than appropriate clothing, however. No matter what your personality, the audience, or the occasion, *neatness* is always necessary when giving a public speech. Even when the most informal mode of dress is called for, neat and clean clothes—together with clean hair, nails, face, and hands—are a must. A sloppy appearance automatically communicates to your audience: "I'm not very interested in giving this speech, so I didn't spend much time getting ready to meet you." Clearly, there is no benefit or advantage to be gained from sending this kind of message to an audience. However, by making the most of your appearance, you demonstrate respect for yourself and esteem for your audience.

Application

Appropriate Dress

Discuss with your classmates how you feel a speaker should dress for the following audiences and speaking situations. Give reasons for your choices.

Audience	Occasion
classmates	pep rally
senior citizens	luncheon
first graders	school assembly
adult business leaders	dinner
family members	family reunion
athletic team	awards banquet

Discuss the negative effects of improper dress for each situation.

Concluding Your Speech

Just as the speech begins at the moment you rise from your seat, it cannot be said to have concluded until you have regained your seat. You do not want to create the impression that you wish to leave the platform as quickly as possible. An unhurried departure is essential. Once you have spoken your final word, pause momentarily while still facing the audience to let the impact of your conclusion sink in. Then walk to your seat in a manner appropriate to your topic.

If your speech was serious in nature, a grave and solemn return is indicated. If the topic was light or entertaining, a more cheerful mode is appropriate. Above all, do not ruin the effect of a good presentation by showing you felt it was a poor job as you depart from the platform. Let the audience be the judge of that. You will learn more about concluding a speech in Chapter 10.

USING YOUR VOICE EFFECTIVELY

A good deal of emphasis is placed on the visual aspects of speech delivery—what an audience *sees*. A large part of the message of a speech, however, is carried by the voice—what an audience *hears*. How you control and use your voice can make the difference between a well received and a poorly received speech. Before you read this section, review "Vocalizing" in Chapter 2 (page 38), to recall the way in which vocal sounds are produced. Then you can proceed to consider a number of different factors involved when using your voice for public speaking.

Speak with the Right Volume

No matter how well organized, researched, and practiced a speech may be, if the listeners cannot hear what is being said, the speech cannot possibly succeed. Although it is possible to speak too loudly for a given room or audience, most beginning speakers have the opposite problem. They speak too softly and cannot be heard in the rear of the room. This may be due to nervousness; more often, inexperienced speakers simply do not realize they are not using sufficient volume.

Volume is controlled primarily by the amount of air a person forces through the vocal cords. By inhaling you obtain a supply of air in your lungs that can then be used to produce vocal tones (sounds) as you exhale, forcing the air across your vocal cords. If you are going to speak very loudly, you must have a considerable supply of air in your lungs. If you need to speak loudly for an extended period of time (as in a public speech), you need a constant, large supply of air. Research has found that people use sixty-six times as much energy addressing a large audience in a large room as they do in ordinary conversation. So the manner in which you inhale while speaking becomes very important. Inhale deeply through your nose, sucking in air by expanding your diaphragm. Upper chest breathing does not provide enough air for an extended sentence in a large auditorium. Diaphragmatic breathing, however, provides plenty. Besides, filling the lower lungs with air does not really take much longer than shallow inhalation.

How you exhale is also important in sustaining sufficient volume. If you let all the air out as you say your first few words, one of two problems will occur. Either the ends of your longer sentences will be too soft to be heard, or you will need to inhale so often you will begin to sound like an air compressor at work. As you gain experience in public speaking, you will learn to pace your exhalation, saving enough air for emphasizing important ideas with extra force.

Variety in volume is important too. A speaker who is constantly loud makes everything sound important. Eventually, nothing sounds important. One who is constantly soft is difficult to hear. Listeners eventually give up straining to hear such a speaker. Important or key ideas must always be spoken with sufficient force so that those in the back row can hear them easily. Transitions to new sections of a speech, the start of the conclusion, and the parts where you wish to be dramatic with a kind of "stage whisper" may be spoken more softly, but should still be audible for listeners in the rear of the room.

Vary Your Pitch

Pitch refers to the tone of the voice on the musical scale. Words or syllables to be emphasized are usually spoken in a higher key. Strong emotion is generally indicated by great differences in pitch among words or syllables that are used together. Think, for example, of the way in which you might pronounce the following sentence: "I certainly don't think that!"

Changing pitch as you speak comes naturally to you in conversation, but beginning public speakers often fail to maintain their pitch variety when speaking from a public platform. Speaking in a **monotone,** with no ups and downs in pitch, can quickly give an audience the impression that the speaker is not enthusiastic or sincere about the topic. Of course, pitch changes should not be affected. The enthusiasm must first be present. Then pitch variety will naturally follow.

Each of you has a general pitch—that portion of your range in which your voice usually hovers when you speak. For public speaking, each person needs to discover his or her optimum pitch, that pitch which can be used most comfortably without strain for extended periods of time. The most comfortable tones are found most often in the lower half of a person's range.

In ancient Greece, Demosthenes practiced speaking over crashing waves.

Watch Your Speaking Rate

Normal speaking rate varies from 120 to 150 words per minute. Some people regularly speak more rapidly or more slowly than others, and nearly everyone varies his or her speaking rate for different situations. Barry Goldwater once said of the late Hubert Humphrey, former vice president and senator from Minnesota: "Hubert has been clocked at 280 words per minute with gusts up to 340."

Many times inexperienced speakers speak too rapidly due to nervousness. If your teacher says you are speaking too quickly, force yourself to slow down by concentrating on the problem. Changes in rate are brought about in two ways: by varying the number and length of pauses between words or by varying the length of time it takes to pronounce each syllable. If you are told that you are speaking too rapidly, the best place to start correction is with your pauses. Some speakers feel they must emit some kind of sound every second they are before their audience. However, a well-timed pause, supported by appropriate gestures, movement, and eye contact can often say much more than several sentences. Pause especially for several seconds between major segments of your speech and more briefly between sentences.

A specific problem, common to many speakers, is called the **vocalized pause.** This is the habit of filling in pause time with "uh," "er," "like," "you-know," or similar non-meaningful sounds. If these sounds become numerous they can be very distracting to the listeners. Here are two methods for handling the vocalized pause.

1. Make a list of transition words to use between sentences and vary them regularly during your speech.

2. Rehearse your speeches with a tape recorder and listen to yourself.

Hearing a great number of vocalized pauses in one's own speech can often motivate a person to concentrate seriously on solving the problem.

Use Crisp Articulation and Correct Pronunciation

As you know, you are capable of producing vocal sounds that are not words. You can use your vocal cords to make sounds like those of a dog or cat, an airplane, automobile, or nearly any sound you choose to imitate. Crisp articulation and correct pronunciation are needed to turn these vocal sounds into recognizable words and verbal symbols.

"Watcha doin ta-day, Sam?" "I dunno. Wudder you?" This kind of talk may communicate very well during informal conversation with your friends, but clearer articulation is definitely called for in a public speech. **Articulation** refers to the way in which the tongue, teeth, palate, and lips are moved and used to produce the crisp, clear sounds of good speech. Most people are capable of producing vowel and consonant sounds clearly, but fall into lazy habits. They become unwilling to exert that extra bit of effort needed to produce clear speech. Unfortunately, when such bad habits are carried over into public speaking, an audience may show little respect for the speaker who sounds sloppy or mushy. When practicing your speeches, therefore, concentrate on moving your tongue, lips, and lower jaw vigorously enough to produce crisp, clear sounds. Be especially careful with consonants that are easily slurred or dropped altogether. Don't use "madder" when you mean "matter," "pacific" for "specific," or "gonna" for "going to."

Pronunciation can also play a role in determining the degree of respect given a speaker by the audience. **Pronunciation** means selecting the correct sounds and the proper syllable stresses. What makes a certain pronunciation correct and another incorrect is usage. Once enough people agree to pronounce a word in a certain way, that becomes the correct way. But you cannot assume that your friends, or even all the people in your school, have cornered the market on correct pronunciation. The two best sources for discovering the accepted pronunciation of words are (1) the dictionary and (2) the prominent speakers of the day, such as national news commentators and noted government officials.

Career Close-up

INTERPRETER

Interpreters translate spoken passages from one language to another. They listen carefully to what one speaker is saying and then quickly translate it into the language of the other speaker. Employed by many government agencies, hospitals, and corporations, interpreters are needed wherever people speaking different languages communicate. Although educational requirements in this field vary, applicants often are required to have a bachelor's degree in foreign languages.

These specialists use their voices skillfully to communicate well. They articulate distinctly so that they will be understood and maintain enough volume to be heard by everyone. Skilled interpreters develop the ability to adjust their speaking rates faster or slower according to the speed of those needing translation. Even when there is pressure to translate more quickly, interpreters must be wary of speaking so fast that they cannot be understood. To help with delivery in these situations, an experienced interpreter inhales deeply into the diaphragm so that there is enough air to complete a thought without losing articulation or volume.

Interpreters must be efficient non-verbal communicators to interpret the facial expressions, gestures, and other body motions of those from different cultures. They also must use nonverbal communication to help convey translated information. As interpreters apply both forms of communication to the delivery of their translations, they fulfill a vital role by enabling people to communicate who otherwise would be prevented from doing so.

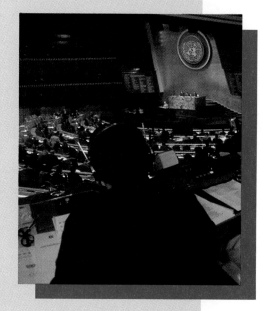

The interpreter attends to both verbal and nonverbal communication.

If you need to use proper names or technical terms in a speech, be certain you know the accepted pronunciation before beginning your rehearsal. Using the correct sounds and stresses during rehearsal will usually assure correct pronunciation during the live performance. When you pronounce unusual words with authority and without hesitation, your audience is likely to be impressed by the thoroughness of your speech preparation and to feel you have genuinely earned the right to speak to them.

Pause Effectively

Beginning speakers often have difficulty with pausing. Some rush ahead like a speeding train with no pauses at all; others fill their pauses with meaningless sounds, those vocalized pauses mentioned under speaking rate; still others pause in the middle of thoughts rather than at the end. Your teacher will work with you in correcting any such pausing problems you might have.

As you correct pausing problems, you will also want to discover ways to make pausing work for you to improve your speech. The well-known

Mark Twain knew the value of a well-timed pause and used it to great effect in his public speaking.

American writer, Mark Twain, who gave many speeches during his life, once said: "The right word may be effective, but no word was ever as effective as a rightly timed pause." Especially in speeches to entertain, a pause of just the right length in just the right place can result in more thunderous laughter than a lengthy story.

There is no quick way to learn how to pause effectively in public speaking. It is mostly a matter of timing and comes primarily from experience. When listening to experienced speakers, notice when they pause and for how long. Pay attention to their audiences' reactions. Practice pausing when rehearsing your own speeches. Use pauses when you wish to create a dramatic effect, when you want to signal your listeners you are changing thoughts, or when you wish to create laughter. Be aware that what usually seems like a three-minute pause to a beginning speaker is actually about three seconds in length. When pausing for laughter from your audience, do not continue with your speech until the laughter has subsided. On the other hand, do not wait until several seconds after the laughter has died down to continue, lest you lose momentum or create the impression that you wanted more laughter than you received.

Application

Vocal Delivery

At least five members of the class should volunteer to read the following excerpts from noted speeches. When all speakers have finished, the class should decide which speaker had the most effective vocal delivery.

> You ask what is our aim? I can answer in one word. It is victory. Victory at all costs—victory in spite of all terrors—victory, however long and hard the road may be, for without victory there is no survival.   *Winston Churchill*

> A nation is formed by the willingness of each of us to share in the responsibility for upholding the common good.   *Barbara Jordan*

> It is rather for us to be here dedicated to the great task remaining before us—that from these honored dead we take increased devotion to that cause for which they gave the last full measure of devotion—that we here highly resolve that these dead shall not have died in vain—that this nation, under God, shall have a new birth of freedom—and that government of the people, by the people, for the people, shall not perish from the earth.   *Abraham Lincoln*

SPECIAL PROBLEMS OF DELIVERING A SPEECH

Delivering a speech frequently involves dealing with special problems and situations. Among these are the use of a speaker's stand and microphone and coping with distractions and interruptions. Practice at handling these matters can aid you when you encounter them as a speaker.

Using the Speaker's Stand

In the majority of places where speeches are given a **lectern** (speaker's stand) is available. One can probably be found in your school's speech classroom. On occasion, however, you may encounter a situation in which a lectern is not available. Therefore, you need to know both how to use a speaker's stand effectively and how to get along without one.

The basic purpose of a lectern is to hold a speaker's notes or manuscript. It was never intended to serve as a support for speakers with weak backs or as a hiding place for those with wobbly knees. A person

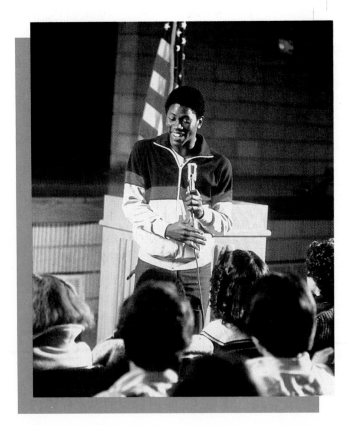

This student is prepared to speak with or without a lectern or microphone. He has learned to use both, but depends on neither.

who uses the speaker's stand to lounge upon or to hide behind immediately reveals apathy or extreme nervousness to the audience. Allowing one or both hands to rest on the stand occasionally is acceptable, as long as one does not *grasp* the stand so desperately that the knuckles turn white. You should never place your foot on the base of the stand either. Your foot should be flat on the floor behind the stand. In general, the less the lectern is grasped, leaned on, caressed, or tapped on, the better the overall impression will be.

Usually the top surface of a lectern is tilted at an angle to allow a speaker to read note cards or manuscript pages with ease, but at the same time keep them out of sight. The best way to handle papers, when using a lectern, is to lay them on the stand at the start and *leave them there throughout the speech.* The audience should be as unaware of your notes as possible, so you must avoid picking them up and putting them down or carrying them in your hands. In addition, cards or manuscript pages should be brought to the lectern in a prearranged order. Try to avoid using paper clips or staples that will require removal or the flipping of pages. When the top card or page has been used, you want to be able to slide it gently and quietly to one side, exposing the next card or page. Picking up a stack of cards in order to place the used one on the bottom of the stack can be very distracting to the listeners, as is the flapping of stapled manuscript pages over the front of a speaker's stand.

Your teacher may ask you to give at least one of your classroom speeches without using the lectern. This can help prepare you for later occasions when no lectern is available. If you want to use note cards but know you will have no stand on which to place them, remember that the easiest size to hold is a 3×5 card. As each one is used, you can quietly slip it to the back of the deck, making the next card ready for reference. A full-sized manuscript is more difficult to handle without a speaker's stand. Thus, if you intend to read from manuscript, you should always find out whether or not a stand will be available.

One advantage of having no lectern when you are using note cards is the additional freedom you have to move about on the platform. Not feeling tied to the stand allows you to walk a few steps more often, reducing your tension and generating greater audience attention.

Adjusting the Microphone

When you are speaking to more than 80 people, or are in a room where the acoustics are poor, you will find a microphone helpful. A microphone must be properly used, however, if it is going to enhance the communication rather than harm it. The first step in its proper use comes before the speech begins. Test the microphone if at all possible! Probably more speeches have gotten off to weak starts because of untested, faulty microphones than because of any other single cause. It only takes a moment to make certain (1) the microphone is turned on, (2) there is no electronic feedback, and (3) it is set at the proper distance and height.

Students often ask: "How far should the microphone be from my mouth?" Microphones vary somewhat, but an average of 10 to 12 inches (25 to 30 centimeters) works well for most microphones. Of course you must keep this "mouth-to-mike" distance fairly constant while speaking. You cannot weave or move your head very much, or your voice will begin to fade in and out like a siren. One advantage of a **lavalier microphone,** the kind that hangs around your neck, is greater freedom to move about on the platform.

Occasionally a speaker will look at the microphone rather than at the audience. This can create a comical effect, since it appears to the audience that the speaker is addressing remarks to the microphone rather than to them.

Certain consonant sounds are easily distorted if spoken with too much force into a microphone. Some of the worst offenders are *t, p, b, s, sh, z, g, k,* and *d.* You will want to avoid blasting your listeners or using too much force when uttering these sounds.

Since the presence of a microphone makes certain demands upon a speaker, it is wise to rehearse with a live microphone, particularly before your *first* microphone speech. If at all possible, secure the room or auditorium in which the microphone will be used for a practice session. Run through your speech several times with the microphone on, and have another person stand or sit at various locations. Even an untrained listener can tell you whether you are coming across clearly or not. Your speech teacher may be the ideal person to help you during such a practice session if his or her schedule permits.

Dealing with Distractions and Interruptions

During the delivery of a speech unexpected events sometimes occur that cannot be planned for beforehand. Although the list of such potential distractions and interruptions is large, it is a rare speech in which more than one such problem arises. Speakers, therefore, should not fear that a string of major disasters is likely to occur every time a speech is to be delivered. On the other hand, being aware of the problems that may arise can prepare you to deal with one confidently if it does occur.

Some interruptions distract the audience's attention only briefly. Noisy jets may fly over the building. A latecomer may interrupt to find a seat. You may lose your place or stumble over words, or people may cough or shuffle their feet. These do little harm to the listeners' basic interest in you and your topic. The best way to handle such noises and distractions is to pause briefly until the room is quiet, then proceed as if nothing had happened. Making a comment about this kind of interruption simply increases the distraction and usually does more harm than good.

Other interruptions—the kind that create a major breakdown in the audience's concentration on your speech—need to be handled differently from minor distractions. If a group of people arrives late, for instance, and their attempts to find seats distract a good portion of the audience, the speaker should fall silent and remain quiet until the entire group is settled. The speaker may even aid people in finding seats by pointing out empty chairs, thereby shortening the length of the disturbance. Should a loud noise begin and appear likely to continue for the remainder of the speech, the speaker should first attempt to be heard over the noise, or ask the audience to move closer to the speaker's stand, if possible. If it proves impossible to overcome, the speaker may have to abandon the attempt to deliver the speech.

If a heckler should begin to yell at you from the audience, handle the situation with dignity and poise. First, remember that the audience came to hear *you* speak, not the heckler, and their sympathy is basically with you. For a time it is usually best to ignore a heckler, attempting to be heard in between the interruptions. If the heckler's comments are too frequent or too loud to permit the audience to hear you, members of the audience may attempt to quiet the heckler themselves. As the speaker you should provide sufficient time for this to occur, since a heckler soon loses heart when it becomes obvious the audience does not support the disturbance. Only when all this has failed should you address the heckler directly, with a calm and dignified comment, such as: "Sir (or Madam), I will be happy to try to field any questions or comments from the audience as soon as I have finished my prepared remarks." Under no circumstances should you ever engage in a shouting match with a heckler, since this gives the intruder precisely what was hoped for—a major share of your audience's attention.

Application

Dealing with Distractions

Discuss with your classmates ways in which a speaker might handle embarrassing or unexpected distractions such as dropping notes, forgetting an important part of the speech, being interrupted by unruly audience members, being interrupted by a fire drill, and hitting the microphone by mistake. Then select students to role-play each situation and the strategy you have developed to deal with it. Make appropriate notes in your speech notebook for future reference.

9 Chapter Review

Summary

The way a speech is delivered is quite important. Good delivery will improve almost any speech, while poor delivery will ruin an otherwise excellent one.

Using Different Methods of Delivery   A speaker may choose from four different methods for delivering speeches—manuscript, memorization, extemporaneous, and impromptu. While each has certain advantages and disadvantages, the most helpful one for a beginning speaker to master is the extemporaneous method, where the pattern of ideas is prepared beforehand, but the exact wording is chosen during delivery. Once speakers have gained some experience with this method, they can begin experimenting with various combinations of the methods until each speaker discovers his or her own most effective style.

Recognizing Nonverbal Aspects of Delivering a Speech Remember that your speech begins when you rise from your chair and approach the speaker's platform. Move vigorously, but not hastily; arrange any notes you may have; and look at your audience for several seconds before speaking. Other nonverbal aspects of speech delivery include eye contact, gestures, platform movement, and appearance. Finally, you should remember that your speech is not truly over until you have regained your seat. When you have concluded your speech, look around your audience, then leave the platform in a confident, unhurried manner, and return to your seat.

Using Your Voice Effectively   Since being heard is basic to giving a speech, learn to breathe deeply and maintain enough volume to be heard easily in all parts of the room. Vary your volume, pitch, and rate to create interest or change a mood. Articulation and pronunciation both play an important part in forming sounds into recognizable words and verbal symbols. Avoid "lazy-lips" and know the correct pronunciation of each word and name in your speech. Use pauses effectively as well.

Special Problems of Delivering a Speech As a speaker, you must know how to deal with a number of special situations. First, you must know how to handle a lectern, as well as how to get along without one. A speaker's stand is a convenient place to lay notes or a manuscript. When one is not available, notes must be held inconspicuously in the hands. You must also be able to handle a microphone. You should rehearse with it and test it shortly before the speech. If distractions or interruptions occur during a speech, they must be handled calmly and with poise. If the interruption is minor, it is usually wise to ignore it; if it creates a major disturbance, you must handle it decisively.

 ## Vocabulary

Define each term in a complete sentence.

manuscript method
memorization method
extemporaneous method
impromptu method
emphatic gestures

transitional gestures
descriptive gestures
locative gestures
note cards
monotone

vocalized pause
articulation
pronunciation
lectern
lavalier microphone

 ## Checklist

Speech-Delivery Skills

1. Be aware of the best methods of speech delivery and employ them when you give a speech.
2. Combine methods of delivery for greater effectiveness.
3. Be aware of the nonverbal aspects of speech delivery and use them effectively.
4. Use note cards efficiently and unobtrusively.
5. Be poised, confident, and well-groomed when speaking.
6. Speak with proper volume and pitch. Be sure not to speak too rapidly or too slowly.
7. Use clear articulation and correct pronunciation.
8. Use pauses effectively in your speeches.
9. Learn to use a lectern and a microphone properly.
10. Develop effective ways of dealing with distractions and interruptions when giving a speech.

Review Questions

1. Name the four different ways to deliver a speech.
2. Identify the method that requires planting a pattern of ideas in your mind.
3. Describe the parts of a speech that should be memorized.
4. Describe the use of manuscript in speech delivery.
5. Name the most important reasons for keeping eye contact with an audience.
6. Explain the value of variety in a speaker's facial expressions.
7. List several reasons for using platform movement.
8. Describe several ways to end a speech.
9. Name and define four aspects of vocal delivery.
10. Describe the proper way in which to use a lectern.

Discussion Questions

1. As a class, discuss which of the four methods of speech delivery would be most appropriate for the following situations. Note: A combination of methods might also recommend itself. (a) The mayor of a city talks at a press conference about an agreement just reached with the city's sanitation workers. (b) A candidate accepts a political party's nomination for the office of governor. (c) A sales manager analyzes last year's performance at a sales meeting. (d) A woman is asked by a television reporter on the street for her assessment of a new housing law.
2. Discuss the role of gesture in speaking—from the audience's point of view. What kinds of gestures would distract an audience? What kinds of gestures would the audience find natural and barely noticeable? What role does variety play in gesture?
3. Discuss the use of a lectern during a speech. What benefits does the speaker receive from using a lectern? What are the disadvantages? Would you prefer to speak with or without a lectern?
4. Discuss the importance of learning to pause effectively while speaking. What effect can a well-timed pause have upon an audience? What happens to an audience when a speaker delivers a speech at a rate that never varies?

5. Discuss the distractions that are likely to occur in a classroom during a speech. What kinds of distractions can a speaker learn to live with? What kinds of distractions are truly troublesome? What can a speaker do when faced with major distractions?

■ Critical Thinking

1. **Analysis:** Of all of the principles of good delivery, which are the most difficult to master? Which come more naturally to the beginning speaker? Arrange a list in the order of difficulty from most difficult to least difficult.

2. **Synthesis:** Imagine that you have only one side of a 3 × 5 index card on which to list the most important delivery advice to speakers. The card will be attached to the speaker's lectern. What advice would you list? Make maximum use of this very small space. Put your most important piece of advice first.

■ Activities

In-Class

1. Prepare a brief introduction and conclusion of a speech. Memorize both. Then perform the following activity in class: (1) Walk from your seat to the front of the room and stand behind the lectern or at the place from which you will speak. (2) Establish eye contact with your audience. (3) Deliver the prepared introduction to your speech. (4) Pause briefly. (5) Deliver the prepared conclusion of your speech. (6) Return to your seat. Your classmates will react and provide feedback on your delivery.

2. Select a descriptive passage from your literature anthology or from some other source which can be read in approximately one minute. Read the passage aloud several times. Then read the passage and make a tape recording of your reading. Listen to the tape three times. Each time you listen to it, focus on one aspect of vocal delivery. First, listen for

rate and pausing. Then listen for variety in pitch. Finally, listen for articulation and pronunciation. Write a brief evaluation of each aspect of your vocal delivery. Then play the recording in class. Ask your classmates for their reactions and suggestions.

3. Select a speech in the Appendix of Speeches and study it carefully. Jot down the main ideas in the speech on note cards. Make certain that you arrange the cards in the proper order. Then practice using the cards to summarize the speech to a group of from five to seven classmates. Do not attempt to give the speech word for word. Simply provide the basic information that is in the speech in your own words. As you summarize the speech, the other students in the group will compare your information with the actual speech. Discuss the quality of your performance with the other members of the group.

4. Choose a small group of students who will work together to devise a variety of interruptions that could arise during a speech. Each individual in the class will then deliver a part of a speech that was developed or given earlier and attempt to deal with the variety of interruptions offered. The class will then discuss and evaluate each individual speaker's response to the interruptions.

Out-of-Class

1. Attend a public speech. Carefully observe the speaker's eye contact with the audience, and answer the following questions in your speech notebook. (a) What approximate percentage of time did the speaker look at the audience rather than at notes? (b) Did the speaker use a pattern of eye contact that started at some point in the audience and then moved to another point? (c) Did the speaker ignore any part of the audience? (d) Did the speaker respond in any way to audience feedback? How did the speaker respond?

2. Develop breath control by doing the following two exercises every evening before going to bed or upon rising in the morning. (a) Inhale slowly and steadily, filling your lungs with air as much as you can. Now begin counting from 1 to 25 while exhaling slowly, controlling your breath with each number that you say. Repeat this activity until you can count from 1 to 25 on a single

breath of air. (b) Lie flat on the floor and place a relatively heavy book on your stomach, just below your rib cage. Inhale and exhale, causing the book to rise and fall with your breathing.

3. As rapidly as you can, say each of the following tongue twisters three times in succession. Go only as fast as accuracy will allow. Time yourself on each tongue twister to see if your articulation improves. Return to this activity from time to time. Remember that you must articulate accurately for a time to count. Keep a record of your progress in your speech notebook. (a) Sally Sunshine sews her socks. When Sally Sunshine sews her socks, the seams she sews seem sealed like stocks. (b) Peter and Paul play paddle ball. Peter plays perfectly as does Paul. A perfect pair, playing paddle ball. (c) Mary Macer makes many messy meals. Since most of Mary Macer's meals are messy, Mary Macer's mother makes Mary make her meals less messy. (d) Brother Brather bothers Mother. Mother bothers brother Brather. Brother Brather's brother, Baffer, baffles Brather and his mother.

■ Chapter Project

Deliver a three- to five-minute speech on the topic "A Person Worth Knowing." The person might be someone you actually know, a person who is known for some accomplishment, or a historical figure. Gather whatever information you need about the person, write and memorize an introduction and conclusion for your speech, prepare notes and an outline for an extemporaneous delivery, and rehearse your speech carefully before delivering it in class.

While you are speaking, your fellow students in the audience will complete a critique sheet on your speech. Your verbal and nonverbal performance will be rated. The critique sheets will be given to you. Check them carefully to determine what aspects of speaking you can work on in the future. Take note in your speech notebook of those areas that need improvement.

Types of Public Speaking

unit 4

10 Speaking to Inform

11 Speaking to Persuade

12 Other Kinds of Speaking

10 Speaking to Inform

**When you have completed this chapter
you should be able to:**

■ Identify the main characteristics of a speech that is meant to inform.

■ Explain how to gain audience attention and build interest in your topic during the introduction of a speech.

■ Describe how to maintain attention, react to feedback, and execute smooth transitions during the body of an informative speech.

■ Identify the types of visual aids that are available.

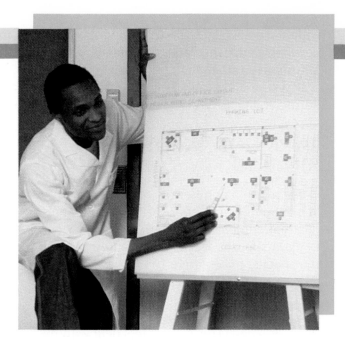

Communicating new facts, ideas, or plans is the one objective common to all informative speeches.

Occasionally a speech may be given to inspire, to entertain, to introduce someone else, to accept an honor given, or to eulogize a person. The Appendix of Speeches at the back of the book presents models of some of these different types of speeches for you to study. Most speeches, however, are given for one of two basic reasons: to inform or to persuade. This chapter discusses informative speaking. Chapter 11 is about persuasive speaking Chapter 12 covers other kinds of speaking.

When you give a speech to inform, your basic purpose is to provide the listeners with information they do not already have. Even though the audience may have some general knowledge of your topic before you begin, an **informative speech** will impart new knowledge or more in-depth information on that topic.

Speeches given to inform serve many useful functions in everyday life. Reports at business meetings, classroom lessons and demonstrations, reports to labor unions, tours through state and national parks, speeches given at civic clubs—all are examples of informative speeches. Notice that a speech is considered informative whenever the speaker's *primary* purpose is to impart new knowledge. In some cases a speaker may have a mixed motive. Along with imparting new information the speaker may also wish to persuade listeners by influencing their beliefs, attitudes, or behavior. Teachers, for example, often speak with such mixed motives. Along with showing you how to work with decimals, a math teacher might wish to persuade you of the importance of knowing how to work with decimals. Since the teacher's main purpose in speaking is to impart new knowledge, however, you would call this math lesson an example of informative rather than persuasive speaking.

If you are like most people you will give many speeches to inform during your life. Let's take a look at four types of informative speeches.

TYPES OF INFORMATIVE SPEECHES

There are a number of ways to classify types of informative speeches. Your teacher may choose to use different names for these types or a different number of types. He or she may assign only one or two kinds for in-class speeches. Those presented here, however, will include most of the specific informative topics you and your classmates choose.

Speeches About Objects

Speeches about objects deal with anything you can see, feel, hear, taste, or smell. These speeches deal with particular items in our physical world. As used here, the term "objects" includes persons living or dead, animals, places, plants, and structures. Here are several *general* topics you could use for a speech about objects:

space travel	Albert Einstein
Statue of Liberty	computers
dinosaurs	*Hamlet*
the human brain	Ronald Reagan
Venus' flytrap	guitars
chestnut trees	Monticello

In order to focus on your *specific* informative purpose, you next need to select a particular aspect of your topic and state it in a purpose sentence. Here are a few examples:

- My purpose is to inform my audience what to look for when buying a home computer.

- My purpose is to inform my audience of the major accomplishments of Ronald Reagan's presidency.

- My purpose is to inform my audience about the architectural style of Thomas Jefferson's home, Monticello.

- My purpose is to inform my audience about the anatomy of the human brain.

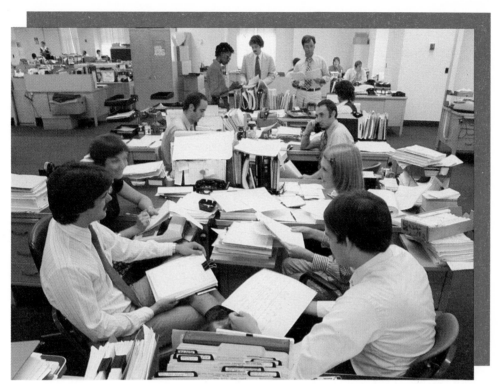

Sharing information with coworkers is a vital part of most businesses.

Speeches about objects may be given in chronological, spatial, or topical order. The organizational pattern you choose will depend upon your specific purpose for giving the speech. If your purpose is to trace the background or history of an object, you will choose chronological order:

My purpose is to inform my audience about the development of the computer industry in the United States.

If you wish to deal with your topic primarily from a geographical viewpoint, you will use spatial order:

My purpose is to inform my audience about the layout of Thomas Jefferson's estate, Monticello.

Often speeches about objects lend themselves more readily to the topical pattern of organization:

My purpose is to inform my audience about the major functions of the human brain.

Speeches About Events

An informative speech about an event may be about anything that either has happened or is happening, or that is regarded as happening. Here are some examples of general topics:

Mardi gras	architecture
football	the Boston Massacre
the Great Depression	fads
acid rain	gold mining
tornadoes	earthquakes in Mexico
famine in Africa	child psychology

As with informative speeches about objects, you need to focus on some specific aspect of your topic:

■ My purpose is to inform my listeners about the devastating earthquakes in Mexico during the past century.

■ My purpose is to inform my audience about famine currently ravaging parts of Africa.

Speeches about events often fall into the chronological pattern of organization, as in the above cases. When your purpose is to focus upon the causes of events rather than upon their history, a causal pattern of organization may be called for. Such a pattern would be appropriate when your purpose sentence reads like these:

■ My purpose is to inform my listeners why Mexico has experienced such devastating earthquakes during the past century.

■ My purpose is to inform my audience about the causes of the current famine in parts of Africa.

Speeches About Processes

A process is a related series of events that lead to a specific result or product. The following process speech topics have already been focused into specific purpose statements:

■ My purpose is to inform my audience about how to make the basic shots in tennis.

■ My purpose is to inform my listeners about the basic steps in the process of making bread.

- My purpose is to show my audience how to make high-quality photographs with a simple camera.

- My purpose is to teach my audience how to perform several basic moves in karate.

Note that with some speeches about processes, the purpose is only to have the audience understand the process. In others, it is to enable the listeners to perform the process themselves. Many speeches about processes require the use of visual aids. Selecting and properly handling visual aids is discussed later in this chapter.

Usually, informative speeches about processes are arranged in chronological order. Occasionally, when you want to focus on the principles or techniques involved in the process rather than on the steps, you may want to use topical order.

Speeches About Concepts

Speeches about concepts are more abstract than those about objects, events, or processes. Concept speeches include those dealing with beliefs, theories, ideas, and principles. Here are three examples of purpose sentences for speeches dealing with concepts:

- My purpose is to inform my listeners about the basic tenets of democracy.

- My purpose is to inform my audience about the major principles of mathematics.

- My purpose is to inform my audience about the guiding principles of nonviolent resistance.

Speeches about objects are usually arranged in topical order. A less frequent approach is that of comparing and contrasting competing schools of thought on the topic.

BEGINNING AN INFORMATIVE SPEECH

Many speech authorities consider the introduction the most important part of any speech. Listeners quite often base their opinions about a speech on their first impressions. Thus, the quality of the introduction may determine the effect of an entire speech. Because of the importance of an introduction, a large portion of this chapter is devoted to ways you can make your introductions most effective. There are five important things to remember when introducing an informative speech.

Gain the Audience's Attention

Perhaps the first and most important way you can use an introduction is to attract the audience's attention. If a speaker fails to gain the listeners' attention at the beginning of a speech, it is highly unlikely that the speech will ever fulfill its purpose. Audience members will mentally test a speaker for the first few moments of a speech. If the material sounds dull or uninteresting, their attention will quickly turn to other matters—a homework assignment or what will be served for supper. So one of the speaker's first tasks is to demand the listeners' attention by using special material as an **attention device.** Over centuries of speech-making, certain types of material have proven effective and become widely accepted for this purpose.

One of the most widely used attention devices is **humor.** Nearly everyone enjoys a good joke, so most audiences will automatically pay attention to a speaker who uses humor. Humor that is closely related to one's speech topic, the occasion, or the audience is usually more effective, however, than just a standard joke. The speaker who relates a funny incident that serves as a smooth transition into the main body of the speech will not lose the listener's attention as soon as the joke is over. This was the approach used at the start of a speech on the safety of commercial airline travel:

> Last week, shortly after the takeoff of a Boeing 727 at Chicago's O'Hare Field, the passengers heard a voice over the intercom: "Ladies and gentlemen, you are priviledged to be the first passengers on an historic flight. There is no pilot or co-pilot in this aircraft. Your entire flight today, from takeoff to landing is being controlled by a system of electronic tapes from the ground. You need not worry in the least. These tapes have been thoroughly tested, and have been found to be completely foolproof . . . foolproof . . . foolproof . . . foolproof . . ."

This lighthearted opening to his subject gave the speaker a natural opportunity to turn his audience's attention to the more serious issues involved in airline safety.

Some people are more effective at being funny than others. Before attempting to use humor in a public speech, ask yourself whether you are an effective humorist. If you are able to make friends laugh in private conversation or at a party, you have probably developed an ability to be humorous. If you seldom get a laugh when you wish to, it is wiser to wait until you have had a chance to develop this technique before using it in a speech introduction. Attempting humor in a public speech, and then having it fall flat, can deflate the speaker's confidence and often does more harm than good.

Nothing relaxes a group like a good joke. As an attention device for a speech, humor that relates to the topic can help build the audience's interest in it.

If you are one of those people who is an effective humorist, you may be strongly tempted to overuse humor in your public speeches. Do not give in to this temptation. Humor acts as a spice in public speaking—a little bit is helpful; too much can destroy the "flavor" of your speech. Audiences respect a speaker who can be both humorous and serious, but if the purpose of the speech is to inform, the listeners expect to be informed, not merely entertained. Use humor sparingly as an attention device.

Finally, make sure any humor you use is in good taste. Though some members of your audience may laugh at offensive humor, their respect for you will decrease. Since a speaker's character in the listener's eye has always been considered one of his or her most potent means of influence, a joke that is offensive will be harmful rather than helpful. It will diminish you in the minds of your audience and make it that much harder for you to gain their serious attention.

An attention device similar to humor is the **anecdote.** A story does not need to be funny in order to be fascinating and to secure the attention of an audience. Speakers who use anecdotes in their introduction are almost sure to capture their listeners' attention. As with humor, a story that has a natural connection with the speech topic is far better than one without any connection.

Notice the effective way in which one speaker gained audience attention by starting with the following anecdote in a speech on cardio-pulmonary resuscitation:

> You may have read the story, in last Wednesday's paper, about Joe Bowers and Susan Atkins. Joe was swimming at the Northside Swim Club, doing laps for exercise. Susan, an eighteen-year-old lifeguard at Northside, had just taken her seat in one of the guard chairs as Joe Bowers started his laps.
>
> No one saw it happen. Maybe Joe was daydreaming, or maybe he just misjudged the end of the pool. When Susan spotted him, he was lying on the bottom in the deep end, after ramming his head into the wall. With a blast of her whistle, warning the other guard, Susan tore to the end of the pool and pulled Joe to the surface. Once they hauled him out, Susan started CPR while the paramedics were on their way. The newspaper called Joe Bowers very lucky; it called Susan Atkins a hero.

Avoid the temptation to make the story too detailed or too lengthy. Many stories need to be shortened and adapted to a particular speech, especially if the entire speech is rather short. A five-minute story as an attention device in a ten-minute speech is too long. Keep in mind the general rule that speech introductions should usually account for only about ten percent of the total speech.

The **common ground technique** is another widely used means of gaining listener attention. When using this device, speakers begin by identifying hobbies, interests, careers, experiences, or preferences that they share in common with their listeners. They might note similarities in political or religious background, ethnic heritage, or interest in certain sports. The common ground technique includes anything that highlights the fact that speaker and listeners share common interests. When Princess Margaret of the United Kingdom visited the Kentucky Derby and was asked to present a cup to the owner of the winning horse, she began her presentation speech by noting the similarity between the Kentucky Derby and the English Derby.

The common ground technique gains listener attention most effectively when the similarities between the speaker and listeners are greatest. If there are few real likenesses between you and your listeners on a given occasion, you would be better off choosing another attention device. Do not try to force weak similarities.

The attention device called **shock technique** is used to demand quick, almost instantaneous attention from an audience. Shock technique consists of mentioning an unusual, frightening, or hard-to-believe fact, statement, or statistic. It usually is used at the very beginning of a speech.

Using shock technique to get your listeners' attention is like giving them a poke in the ribs to wake them up to your topic.

The idea is to blow away any mental "cobwebs" in your listeners' heads and startle them into instant mental alertness. Thom Mayer, a student speaker, made excellent use of the shock technique in a speech on "The Population Bomb":

> If I were to tell you that there are 3.6 billion people on the earth, with more arriving at the rate of 132 per minute, these figures would probably do nothing more than bore you. If, on the other hand, I were to say "There's a bomb in this room and it could explode at any second!" it is likely that I would have your attention, and you would realize the urgency in what I had said. The cold facts, however, are that the bomb I warned you about and the figures I cited are actually one and the same thing. That bomb is known as the Population Bomb, and it is ticking right now in this room and all over the world.

Not only did Thom Mayer assure listener attention from the first words of his speech, but the statistics led naturally into the main body of his speech on overpopulation. As with humor and narrative, the shock technique works best when it is closely tied to the main message of the speech. Speakers using the shock technique must always have evidence to prove the shocking statements they make.

Suspense is another device useful for developing rapid listener attention in an introduction. Usually suspense is developed by withholding one's theme or topic from the audience for several moments and by hinting at its importance or uniqueness. A speaker who is building suspense talks "around" the topic for several moments, teasing the audience into trying to guess what the topic will be. Marie Ransley, a student speaker, used suspense in the following manner at the beginning of a classroom speech:

> "Warning: the green slime is here." It sounds like a creature out of a grade-B horror movie. But unfortunately it's more real than that. The *New York Times Magazine* warns: ". . . a monster has been loosed among us. In . . . countless incidents around the world, one can almost hear the sloshing of the algae as they grow and expand like the mucid mutations of the late-night horror movies, crawling everywhere and smothering life beneath the slime of cells gone berserk."
>
> Yes, algae is the monster and the immediate victims are the country's lakes.

When used as an attention device in an introduction, suspense must be built quickly. A brief amount of suspense makes an audience curious and expectant, but suspense drawn out beyond several moments rapidly loses its effect. The listeners begin to resent the speaker for not "letting them in on" the speech topic.

Application

Choosing Attention Devices

Think of five topics for informative speeches. Choose the two that interest you the most and write three different introductions for each. Use the devices presented in this chapter. Try them out on a partner to determine which is the most effective for that particular topic. Begin a collection of interesting stories, anecdotes, and startling and unusual facts that could be used in speech introductions. Keep these in your speech notebook for future use.

Build Interest in the Topic

Besides gaining the listeners' attention, a speaker should build their interest in the speech topic during the introduction. Some topics are naturally more fascinating to certain audiences than others are. A speaker who has analyzed the audience beforehand will know whether she or he must build audience interest in the topic.

Building interest in one's topic is not the same as gaining attention, but many of the same devices may be used to accomplish it. Earlier in this chapter it was mentioned that humor as an attention device works best if it is easily tied to the speaker's topic. Telling a humorous incident unrelated to your topic may gain your listeners' attention, but it does nothing toward building their interest in your topic. A topic-related joke, however, can fulfill both these important functions at once. The same principle holds true for the anecdote and for the common ground, shock, and suspense techniques.

There are other methods of building interest in the speech topic which have also been found effective. One is the practice of starting the speech with questions related to the topic. A speech dealing with furniture-making, for instance, might begin with a series of questions: "Do you know which is the hardest wood in existence? Do you know which is the most expensive hardwood still used for making furniture? Which is the most commonly used wood for furniture construction?" You read in Chapter 8 that these are called rhetorical questions. The speaker does not expect an "out-loud" answer from the listeners. Rather, it is intended that the listeners will mentally try to answer the questions. The speaker thereby generates attention and builds interest in the speech topic. Occasionally, speakers will ask *real* (not rhetorical) questions, which they expect audience members to answer aloud. This can sometimes be done by a show of hands or by inviting specific listeners to answer aloud. This technique can build topic interest as well as arouse attention, but it is a bit risky. Since the speaker may not receive the expected answer, he or she may be caught off guard and become confused. If you plan to use real questions, prepare to react to various kinds of responses.

Another interest-building technique consists of beginning a speech with a quotation that highlights an important aspect of your topic. Audiences are usually interested in the thoughts of others, particularly if quoted from some well-known or well-beloved person. One way to build listener interest in a patriotic speech, for example, would be to introduce your topic with John Kennedy's famous quotation "Ask not what your country can do for you,—ask what you can do for your country." The use of a quotation from the Bible or another religious work in introductions has long been a favorite interest-building device of members of the clergy. The quotation identifies the general topic area for the listeners and creates a mild suspense about how the speaker will develop the particular topic within the area.

Directly challenging your audience is still another means of building topic interest. When you ask rhetorical questions that challenge your audience to formulate answers, for example, you generate interest in your own answers as well. You build interest by directing a real challenge to your listeners—by including them.

Preview the Topic

On the covers of many paperback books you will find intriguing hints about the contents of the book. These are meant to help sell the book. A speech introduction serves a similar function prior to the main body of the speech. Audiences have learned to expect the speaker to "clue them in" on the speech topic, its purpose, and often the main points that will be covered. Thus, previewing the topic is a significant function of most speech introductions.

The most obvious and straightforward method of previewing the topic consists of simply stating your speech purpose to the audience during the introduction. Sometimes, however, this type of introduction may fail to fulfill the other important functions of an introduction at the same time. An introduction that merely previews the topic, without at the same time generating attention and building interest in the topic, might be labeled a clear but dull introduction. Notice how this introduction to a speech on modern laboratories begins by focusing the listeners' attention, builds their interest in the speaker's subject, and finishes by previewing the topic for the audience:

> If you are like me, you hate going to the dentist. Even the remote chance that he might find a cavity, followed in rapid-fire order by the pain of the novocaine needle, the siren-like whine of the dreaded drill, and later by the leathery lip which won't allow you to eat with dignity—all this sends shudders through most of us. If you have ever done really serious time in the dentist's chair, say for a root canal or to have a full crown fitted, you probably look upon dental science as a science barely emerging from the Neanderthal Period. Even some of the tools the dentist waves before your eyes remind you of prehistoric instruments, looking about as subtle as stone-headed axes as they are forced inside your gaping mouth.
>
> The truth is, though, that dentistry is a very modern, high-tech science in which measurements must be made in tens of thousandths of a millimeter. Every day, researchers and technicians in dental labs deal in minute expansions and contractions of plasters, wax, gold, and plastic to assure that dental patients will enjoy perfectly fitting dental products. Today I want to share with you some of the facinating "high-tech" insights I gained while working in such a dental lab last summer.

Again, as you can see, the previewing of the topic is a very important function of the introduction in speeches given to inform. Because the principal purpose of the speech is to teach, the speaker must make sure the message is received. To insure audience understanding, good public speakers use several opportunities to restate their message. Previewing the topic in the introduction is the first opportunity to give the listener the basic message in a brief form. If the members of the audience hear the topic previewed in the introduction, are told the complete message in the body of the speech, and then hear the message summarized in the conclusion, most of them are likely to receive the message.

Apply the Message to the Audience

A fourth function of the introduction is a natural follow-up to previewing the topic. As soon as you tell your listeners what you propose to talk about, show them how that topic applies to them. Applying the message to the listeners means showing them what they stand to gain from hearing the message, why the topic should be of particular interest to them, and why it has significance for them.

Louis Housman applied his message in a speech on "Older Americans" by showing that the speech dealt with a significant topic and by implying that his listeners stood to gain from hearing about this topic:

There are 31 million Americans 60 years and older. They constitute the single largest minority in the nation.

This minority, since 1900, is growing at twice the rate of our total population.

The way in which these older Americans are viewed by society as a whole, by younger persons, and by themselves, has important implications for all of you concerned with the well-being of older persons.

Bring the message home to your listeners by linking it to their interests, needs, and concerns.

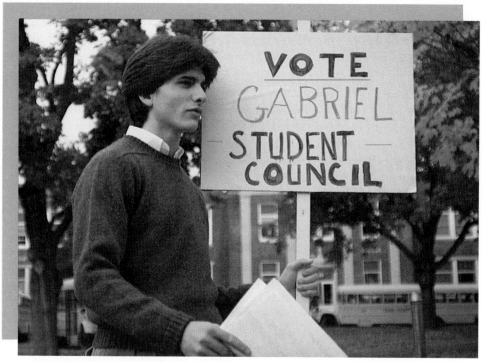

Name recognition alone rarely establishes ethos. This student would be a more convincing candidate if he listed relevant credentials.

Establish Ethos

The ancient Greek rhetorician Aristotle claimed that three forces influenced an audience—the speaker's logic, appeals to the listeners' emotions, and the character of the speaker. He wrote that the speaker's character, which he called **ethos,** was the most powerful of the three. Although Aristotle was writing about persuasive speaking, and though some modern speech authorities would disagree with his ranking of the three elements, no one would claim that the speaker's character and credibility are unimportant, even in informative speeches. You have undoubtedly noticed how you accept what some people tell you much more readily than you accept the words of others. Ethos is also the basis for the old adage among salespersons: "You have to sell yourself first."

Since listeners more readily accept information from a source they believe and have confidence in, establishing one's ethos is an important task for a public speaker to accomplish during the introduction of an informative speech. Of course, not all speakers need to begin by establishing their expertise and sincerity. Well-known personalities or speakers fortunate enough to be introduced to their audience by someone else are usually wiser to accept their reputation in modest silence. Most speakers, however, must themselves fulfill the job of convincing the listeners of their knowledge, sincerity, and likability. When this job is left up to you, as it will be in most of your speeches, you should establish your ethos early, preferably during the introduction.

Ethos exists in the minds of your listeners. It consists of their inward answers to three unspoken questions: "Is this speaker thoroughly familiar with the subject?" "Is this speaker being completely open and honest with me?" "Do I enjoy listening to this speaker?" Many of the techniques useful for gaining audience attention and building interest in the speech topic may also aid in building speaker ethos. Humor, for instance, usually increases an audience's enjoyment when listening to a speaker. Devices such as anecdote and the shock technique can show listeners the speaker has done research and is informed about the topic.

Several specific techniques for building ethos can be used on occasions when you feel a special need to "sell your credentials" to your audience. One of these is straightforwardly mentioning some of the research and preparation you did for the speech. This can be worked into your introduction not in a bragging way but simply to show the listeners you have earned the right to speak to them. A similar technique of ethos-building consists of mentioning some experience you have had that qualifies you as an "expert" on your topic. Here is an example of such an ethos-builder:

> "Perhaps the process by which soft drinks are bottled sounds like an awfully dry and humdrum topic for a classroom speech. Last year I probably would have considered it boring too, but my job last summer in a bottling plant showed me that, far from being humdrum, it's exciting and sometimes even dangerous. This afternoon I'd like to share with you some of the experiences. . . ."

Such an introduction, besides building interest in the speaker's topic, shows the listeners they are listening to an eyewitness—someone who has earned the right to speak to them on this particular topic.

On occasions when you are introduced to the audience prior to your speech, you ordinarily will not want to attempt much, if any, ethos building of your own at the start of your speech. Usually a simple "Thank you, Bob" or "Thank you for that kind introduction" is all that is needed. If the introducer has been extremely flattering, you may want to insert a humorous comment to show modesty, such as "My generous introducer got so carried away, I found myself sitting here trying to imagine who was going to give this marvelous speech!" If, on the other hand, your introducer should fail to give you enough credit, you should modestly supply some of the missing facts yourself during the speech introduction.

This should be done very matter-of-factly, as an attempt to fill in some information the introducer overlooked. Here is an example:

> Thank you, Sharon, for that introduction. Something Sharon did not mention was my two years as a Little League umpire. I bring this up because that experience gave birth to many of the ideas I will be expressing in my speech tonight.

IMPARTING THE MESSAGE OF AN INFORMATIVE SPEECH

The central part of an informative speech, sandwiched between the introduction and conclusion, is called the body of the speech. The body contains the essential message of the speech, completely developed. The speech outline, of course, plots the speaker's individual approach to the topic, and the way in which the subject unfolds during delivery is unique to each individual speaker and speech occasion. Still, certain general rules must be followed while imparting the message if the informative speech is to have its maximum impact.

Maintain Attention

A basic function of the introduction is to gain the initial attention of the audience. Gaining attention at the start, however, does not automatically give the speaker a guarantee of unbroken attention for the rest of the speech. Since people's attention usually focuses on one person or idea only briefly and shifts constantly from one object to another, a public speaker must make a constant effort to keep the listeners focused on the message.

Most of the attention devices that are useful during the introduction of an informative speech may also be sprinkled throughout the speech to maintain listener attention. A humorous anecdote, an occasional story, a set of shocking statistics, or a bit of suspense during the body of the speech can regain flagging attention and renew audience interest.

Careful preparation regarding nonverbal attention-factors can also help to capture audience attention effectively. The way your audience is seated is one of these nonverbal attention-factors. Speakers have found that audience attention generally remains at a higher level the closer the audience members are to one another. Audience members generate attention among themselves, thus relieving the speaker of part of the task of keeping their attention. Whenever you find yourself facing a sparse or scattered audience, with numerous empty chairs between your listeners, invite the audience to sit more closely together in front rows. Maintaining their attention throughout your speech will prove considerably easier.

A second nonverbal attention-factor relates to listening conditions. The more you, the speaker, can assure comfortable conditions for effective listening, the more likely you will be to have the continuous attention of your audience. Whenever possible, arrive at the speaking location before your audience to arrange for proper listening conditions.

React to Feedback

As you proceed through your speech, be alert to audience reactions and respond to them whenever necessary. Reacting to audience feedback is not a technique a beginning speaker can acquire all at once during a first or second speech. It is an important skill to develop, however, since a public speech involves two-way communication just as a conversation does. Not to show any reaction to audience feedback may cause some listeners to feel you are ignoring them. Many audiences may find this lack of response insulting.

In order to respond to feedback, you must first learn to interpret it. As you begin giving speeches you will notice that some listeners react more vigorously than others do. Some people will appear more interested,

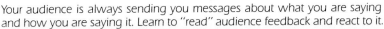

Your audience is always sending you messages about what you are saying and how you are saying it. Learn to "read" audience feedback and react to it.

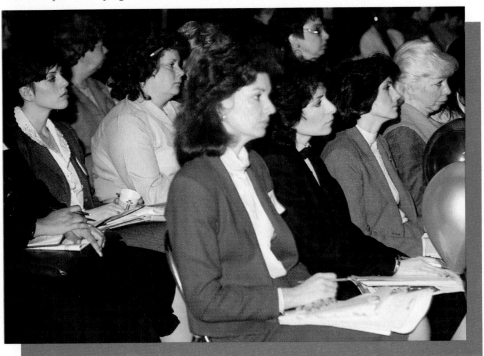

more alert, and more intense in their reactions. Pay closer attention to these individuals as you speak, and look for signs of understanding, puzzlement, agreement, or disagreement in their faces, in their posture, and in their eyes. Once you have developed the ability to recognize positive and negative reactions, you can begin to adjust your message, language, and delivery techniques a bit to lessen negative reactions and increase positive forms of feedback.

Adjust especially to an audience reaction if it comes from a sizable proportion of your listeners. If only one or two listeners frown, for instance, their action may only mean that they did not understand or did not agree with something you just said. However, if thirty or forty percent of your listeners frown, whatever you just said probably needs repeating or clarifying.

Make Smooth Transitions

A **transition** is like a switch on a railroad line. It allows a speaker to change from one aspect of the topic to another. Well-planned transitions go unnoticed by the listeners but give them an impression of a smoothly flowing speech. Not planning one's transitions results in jerky shifts from one main point to another, making the speech sound like a series of disconnected mini-speeches.

Transitions between major points (the main heads of your outline) may consist of only a sentence or two that relates what you have just finished saying to what you will say next. Transitions between minor points (subheads) can often be made with just a word or phrase, such as "First . . .," "Second. . . ." In either case they all must be thoroughly planned and rehearsed, not left to chance. Word-for-word memorization may be useful when rehearsing transitions to assure they will tie the parts of the speech together clearly.

Speakers commonly plan major transitions (those between main heads) by selecting a key word or phrase to make one point point and then using it again to make the next point. Notice how President John F. Kennedy, in his inaugural address, linked the past to the present by focusing on the past and present tenses of the verb *summons* in a transition:

> Since this country was founded, each generation of Americans has been summoned to give testimony to its national loyalty. The graves of young Americans who answered the call to service surround the globe.
>
> Now the trumpet summons us again—not as a call to bear arms, though arms we need—not as a call to battle, though embattled we are—but a call to bear the burden of a long twilight struggle, year in and year out, "rejoicing in hope, patient in tribulation"—a struggle against the common enemies of man: tyranny, poverty, disease and war itself.

The transitions that President John F. Kennedy crafted into his inaugural address created a powerful feeling of momentum.

A typical transition accomplishes three purposes: first, it summarizes the point you have just finished; second, it tells the listeners what you will cover next; finally, it shows the relationship between the two. Usually a good transition does all of this in one or two sentences. For example, if you were giving a speech telling your classmates about your summer job as a hospital volunteer, a transition between your first and second main points might state: "In addition to helping people in need as a hospital volunteer, I also gained valuable job experience." Here are several other examples:

- Increasing the amount of money spent on education is only one part of the solution. The other part is to ensure that the money is spent wisely.

- Now that we have explored the ancient origins of astrology, let us turn to its modern popularity.

- So much for the present; what about the future?

- We've seen what high protein diets can do for you. What about high carbohydrate diets?

Your teacher may ask you to write your transitions out word-for-word in your speech outline and memorize them. Clearly stated transitions give listeners one of their best means of keeping track of your speech.

Avoid Becoming Too Technical

Imagine you are listening to one of your classmates giving a speech explaining the disorder known as "autism" in children. You hear him say:

> Autism is a severe communication and behavioral disorder occurring in infants and characterized by ritualistic response to environmental stimuli. Symptoms include an inability to utilize language meaningfully and an inability to process information about the environment. Half of all autistic children are totally mute; those who have limited capacity for verbalization tend to repeat mechanically any aural stimuli to which they are exposed. Other common symptoms are a vacant, withdrawn facial expression, fascination with mechanical objects, and resistance to environmental alteration.

Chances are you wouldn't pay attention to the speech very long. Even if you tried to pay attention, you might wind up with a severe headache within five minutes! What is wrong with such a speech? The speaker is using too much **technical language.** His information is quite accurate, but he is expressing it in language understood by trained psychiatrists. If our student speaker were willing to tackle such a technical subject for his informative speech, he needed to understand it thoroughly first, then put it into simple language that his audience could understand. He might have done it this way:

> Imagine this: You are the parent of a beautiful little boy. He may not speak at all, ever; half of all autistic children don't. If he does speak, he may just croon the same word over and over in a singsong voice, perhaps a word you've said to him a minute or so earlier. Much of his time is spent rocking his body, back and forth, back and forth, endlessly. He lives almost entirely in his own world, inside his own head. But that doesn't mean he's not aware of what's going on around him. Beware of changing something in his room or moving his toys around! He may become frantic and fly into a tantrum.

In listening to this second version, you would be able to understand it easily. The only technical word was "autistic," the word the speaker was defining.

In addition to avoiding language that is too technical, you will want to watch out for selecting informative speech topics that are too technical. Remember what you studied about your audience on pages 277-288 in

PARK RANGER

The National Park service was established in 1916 to conserve certain areas in the United States for the enjoyment of future generations. Park rangers serve as guides and answer questions for visitors to the various National Parks. Although park rangers primarily conduct tours (up to ten per day), they also give talks and slide presentations for schools, senior citizens, and other organizations. To qualify for a position with the National Park Service, a park ranger needs at least two years of a college program with a history major, including courses in English composition and speech.

Park rangers are knowledgeable about their site and can speak about its history in a way that will be intriguing. This information must be updated with material researched in libraries or the site's archives. Regardless of their experience, rangers regularly rehearse their talks to ensure that they will flow smoothly, even as new information is added.

Effective park rangers do more than merely recite facts, however. They include colorful details in each talk to maintain their listeners' interest. Because each audience is so varied, rangers begin with anecdotes that everyone can relate to. This helps focus the group's attention. To express enthusiasm, rangers vary the pitch of their voices and maintain eye contact with listeners.

The park ranger's ability to speak spontaneously to meet the interests of different audiences results from superior speaking skills and the careful preparation of talks, which rangers prepare themselves. Because of this expertise, rangers successfully immerse visitors in the drama of our nation's past, thus fulfilling the goal of the National Park Service.

This park ranger involves listeners in living history.

this chapter. You can probably make almost any topic understandable to any audience to a certain degree, but highly technical topics demand first that you be an expert in the area, then that you take great pains in simplifying your language to ensure audience understanding. Usually it is not possible to simplify a very technical topic for a five-minute classroom speech. This doesn't mean, of course, that you should never choose a classroom topic more technical than "How to Bake a Cake." At the same time, be wary of trying to give a five-minute speech on "The Theory of Quantum Mechanics."

Personalize Your Speech

People are interested in people. Probably nothing maintains the attention and interest of an audience as well as having a number of stories, examples, and humor involving people. The speaker who frequently brings people into his or her speeches is **personalizing** the speech.

Suppose you are speaking about the effects of radiation—the kind of radiation emitted by such ordinary items as microwave ovens and video display terminals. You could give your listeners tons of statistics showing how many people are affected by such radiation each year, and how many additional health care dollars it takes to treat them. *Some* statistics of that sort would be very helpful. But if you want to be certain of regaining your listeners' wavering attention following a string of numbers, give them an example with a person in it:

> Becky Krimson worked for the Citizens National Bank of Chicago. Throughout her three-year period of employment there, Becky often complained of headaches, dizziness, fatigue, and loss of hair. Her boss said she occasionally suffered partial memory loss, while her co-workers frequently complained about Becky's emotional instability. Upon a visit to her doctor she was given some pills, told to take a few days' rest, and sent home. At the time Becky did not know that the video display terminal she worked with at the bank was zapping her with radiation, and that rest and pills could not cure her symptoms.

Personalizing your speech does not mean you must always use real people as examples. You might create a fictional person who is meant to stand for the "average" individual in certain circumstances. In so doing, you are able to present your information in story form rather than as a string of statistics. One student speaker created Vladimir, a typical Russian child, for a speech on life in the Soviet Union. He was able to show his listeners how the Russian school system differs from ours by tracing Vladimir's progress through his years of schooling.

Personalizing Your Speech

Search through an anthology of speeches or the magazine *Vital Speeches of the Day.* Find a speech in which the speaker has made a genuine effort to personalize it. What kinds of stories or examples did the speaker use? Were they based on fact or were they fictional? How did they help the speaker get important points across to the audience? Compare the personalized examples you found with those that were found by others.

CONCLUDING AN INFORMATIVE SPEECH

Speech conclusions are typically brief, accounting for only about five percent of the total speech. However, the conclusion may represent the most important part of many speeches. Since the audience hears the conclusion last, they are likely to remember it the longest. You should use as much care preparing your conclusion as you did your introduction. Like introductions, speech conclusions accomplish several key purposes in speeches.

Signal Your Conclusion

Audiences typically expect speakers to do certain things for them during speech conclusions—summarize the main points, reinforce the central idea, and psychologically close the speech. Before listeners are able to pick out these guideposts, however, they must know when the conclusion of the speech begins. Therefore your first job in concluding a speech is that of giving your audience a clear signal that you are about to conclude.

How do you send this signal? One of the simplest ways is by beginning your conclusion with signal words, such as "In conclusion," "In closing," "My purpose has been," "Let me end by saying," "Let me leave you with," or "Finally." A second way is through subtle changes in your wording and your manner of delivery. By an extra long pause prior to your conclusion, by changes in vocal tone, volume, and pacing, or by moving a few steps as you start your conclusion, you can signal the end of your speech. Your wording, too, becomes "larger," more grand in tone as you return to the general theme with which you began the speech. Without actually saying "in conclusion," you signal your audience that you are about to close. Notice how effectively Kathy Weisensel, a student speaker, concluded her speech dealing with misconceptions about the victims of mental retardation:

> While misconceptions are slow to pass away, they must surely die. Our nation's retarded are not mentally ill, totally ineducable, or incapable of happy and productive lives.
>
> I know, in a deeply personal way, the pain that these misconceptions inspire. But I also know that the world is changing. I have a deep faith that you and others of our generation will reject the senseless and destructive stereotypes of the past. As Bernard Posner has said: "The young people of the world seem to be forging a new set of values. It appears to be a value system of recognizing the intrinsic worth of all humans, retarded or not, . . . a value system of acceptance: of accepting life as it is, and people as they are."
>
> Thank you for your acceptance.

Summarize the Main Ideas

The **summary** is the main part of a speech conclusion. Though a conclusion may have other functions as well, its principal function is summarizing the major ideas, especially in an informative speech. Summarizing means presenting the basic message again in very brief form. This is generally accomplished by using the device called restatement—repeating the same ideas, but in different words. Observe how Mary Nielsen summarized an informative speech on bats.

> This, then, is the bat. This ugly creature whose appearance makes it very easy to hate. This creature that belongs to the same biological class as people. A much maligned creature who has been used by storytellers and entertainers to inspire fear and horror in their audiences for centuries. A creature that has been the victim of half-truths and exaggerations. Now, however, scientists are beginning to understand the worth of this creature —its place in nature and in the laboratory. Perhaps nobody will put a bumper sticker on a car stating, "Have you hugged a bat today?" but maybe now we can learn to understand them.

In this student's summary, the main ideas of the entire speech were again presented in brief form. Even without reading the entire speech, you were able to know the topic of the speech and its main points.

Reinforce the Central Idea

Since your conclusion is your last chance to impress the central message of your speech upon your listeners, you will often try to do this in several ways. A summary, of course, typically restates the central idea, but often simply restating it fails to "brand" it into the listeners' minds.

Ending with a **quotation** is an additional means of ensuring that the audience will remember your speech. Here, for instance, is how Randy Larsen concluded a speech on the growing use of lasers in surgery:

> But even with these problems, the laser's future seems bright. We hear so much about military "Star Wars" technology; it's encouraging to know the laser has life-saving capacities as well. Dr. Janos Voros believes, "The laser will revolutionize surgery." In some areas, it already has.

Closing quotations are especially effective when they relate closely to the central message of the speech, and are brief.

A **dramatic statement** that you yourself make up is another way of impressing your basic message upon the listeners as you conclude. In a speech on suicide prevention, a student made striking use of this technique when she concluded:

> My friend is back in school, participating in activities she never did before—and enjoying life. I'm happy and proud to say she's still fighting for her life and even happier she failed to kill herself. Otherwise, I wouldn't be here today trying to help you. You see, *I* am my 'friend,' and I'm more than glad to say, I've made it.

Naturally, her audience was stunned by this dramatic conclusion. Probably none of them soon forgot the basic message of her speech.

Another method by which to reinforce your speech's central idea in the conclusion is by referring back to your introduction. Since the introduction nearly always contains a preview of the speech's purpose, a reference back to it in the conclusion serves to implant that purpose firmly in the listeners' minds. A speaker who opened her speech by stating that "Disney World in Florida is really not a Mickey Mouse organization; it is truly big business!" concluded her speech in the following way:

> I hope I have given you a sense of the scope and complexity involved in running the Magic Kingdom. Were you allowed to see behind the scenes— behind the fairyland to the maze of computers, behind Donald Duck and Goofy to the army of interviewers screening job applicants, behind Cinderella's Castle and the Monorail to the planners and risk takers who constantly pour millions of dollars into this fantasy world—you would recognize that Disney World is by no means a Mickey Mouse operation. It is truly big business!

Psychologically Close the Speech

Audiences not only want to *know* a speech is over; they want to *feel* it is complete too. Did you ever have to leave an exciting basketball game shortly before it ended? You were probably left with a feeling of incompleteness that was not erased by later reading the final score in the newspaper. Speech audiences expect speakers to tidy up any loose ends during their conclusions. In addition to restating the main points and refocusing on the central idea, speakers frequently should finish by involving their listeners in the topic one more time.

One way of doing this is by issuing a *challenge* to your audience. Gale Klappa, vice president of Southern Company Services, Inc., closed a speech on attitudes toward the media by asking for her listeners' help:

> I hope you'll join me in that effort. I hope you, too, are concerned—that you want to turn public anger and outrage toward the media into admiration and respect.

A second way is to ask a **rhetorical question.** Rhetorical questions can involve the audience at least as effectively when used in your conclusion as in the introduction. When used at the end of a speech, they often linger in the listener's mind because no answer was provided. They can cause individual listeners to keep trying to provide themselves satisfactory answers well after the speech has ended. If you are a person who is always late, would you later re-think this student speaker's closing rhetorical question?:

> So remember, people who are always late aren't just disorganized. There are three possible reasons for repeated lateness: first, they could be trying to defy authority; second, they could be trying to gain power over the other person; and, finally, they could be trying to live up to stereotypes about groups of people. Could any of these reasons describe you?

A final method of psychologically closing a speech is by repeating a **theme** or **slogan,** first mentioned in the introduction. This technique is much like that of referring back to your central purpose, except here you are trying to plant a brief statement in the listener's memory—a theme or slogan that will vividly recall your speech to mind. Preachers frequently use this approach when they begin a sermon with a Bible verse, then close by repeating it word-for-word.

Whichever techniques you use to close your speeches, remember every informative speech needs some form of conclusion. Never end with your last main point. The audience expects you to "put it all together" before you sit down. Conclusions need not be lengthy—as a matter of fact, they should almost always be brief—but they must always be there!

Making Conclusions Work

Working in groups of four or five, decide on a speech topic and purpose. Discuss at least four possible conclusions for the speech and then write them down. Be prepared to explain the type and purpose of each conclusion. Take turns reading each one aloud, pausing in the most effective places and stressing the most important sections. Discuss with the group how well each conclusion fulfilled its purpose.

CONDUCTING A QUESTION-AND-ANSWER PERIOD

At the conclusion of your in-class informative speeches, your teacher may ask you to remain at the lectern for a brief question-and-answer period with the class. This gives class members an opportunity to ask about points in your speech that are unclear to them. They can ask for additional information or simply delve more fully into your topic. Question-and-answer periods are also helpful for you in several ways. For one thing, they provide an opportunity for you to learn to think on your feet by forcing you to form answers without preparation beforehand. This should not alarm you if you know your subject thoroughly. A second reason for practicing question-and-answer periods stems from their frequent use following speeches given outside of the classroom. A large number of informative speeches given to civic clubs, church groups, or business groups call for the speaker to respond to questions from the audience about the speech topic.

Invite Questions

You will generally know whether or not a question-and-answer period is likely to follow a speech. Some clubs and organizations consider such a session traditional. Or you may anticipate your topic arousing enough interest to cause a number of audience members to ask questions. Whenever you expect a question-and-answer period to follow a speech, it is a good idea to invite such a session when you begin your speech. Mentioning at the start that you will be happy to respond to any questions when you have finished gives the listeners a chance to develop questions during your talk. When a speaker ends the speech with "Now, are there any questions?" without giving any prior warning, the audience is caught off guard and often cannot form any significant questions quickly.

Once a question-and-answer session has begun, the speaker must be as impartial as possible in recognizing listeners who have questions. Naturally, preference should be given to the first hands raised over the later ones and to those who have not yet asked a question over those who have already had a turn. If there is a pre-arranged time limit for questions or if you feel that the audience is getting bored or that the questions are becoming repetitive, you can provide a warning that you are about to close the session. For example, you might make a comment such as "I believe we have time for only two more questions. I'll recognize the woman in the second row, then the man in the rear."

Answer Questions

If you are thoroughly prepared and knowledgeable about your speech topic, you will be able to answer most questions easily. Occasionally, of course, a question will be raised to which you do not know the answer. When this occurs, simply respond "I'm sorry, I can't answer that question." For informative speeches you will not appear to be avoiding the question, but merely indicating a lack of knowledge on your part. Audiences do not expect speakers to be all-knowing on any topic, so using this response occasionally causes no one embarrassment.

In the next section you will learn about using visual aids during your speeches. If you have used one or more of these visual aids during an informative speech and someone asks a question related to a visual, be certain it is again brought into full view of the audience before responding to the question. This allows listeners to perceive your answer through two channels, verbal and visual. You may also wish to point to a particular part of a visual while responding, if the question relates specifically to that part.

When you are asked a question requiring both a direct answer plus some explanation, provide the direct answer first, then the explanation. Usually the questioner is more interested in the factual answer than in a list of reasons or causes, and making the person wait for the core of the answer can irk the questioner. Occasionally, you may feel there is strong justification for reversing this order, but ordinarily give the direct answer first followed by the explanation.

Finally, be complete and concise in answering questions. Avoid, on the one hand, single word answers such as "Yes" or "No." On the other hand, once you have answered the question, stop. Do not be tempted to ramble on with fascinating information that strays too far from the topic and which may only bore your listeners. If the matter is fairly technical in nature and requires some explanation for a complete answer, by all means give the explanation, then stop. Often there may be several others anxiously waiting to ask a question that is very special to them.

This lively audience enjoys the opportunity to question a speaker who has engaged their interest and stirred their curiosity.

USING VISUAL AIDS

Dr. Ray Birdwhistell, one of the foremost scholars in nonverbal communication, claims that words account for only thirty-five percent of what we communicate; the remainder is largely accomplished by body motion. Though the figure may be exaggerated, it emphasizes an important concept for public speakers. As a public speaker, you can accomplish communication through what the audience *sees*, as well as through what the audience *hears*.

Visual aids have been found very helpful both for the speaker and the listeners, especially during informative speaking. For the speaker they provide a natural excuse to move about on the platform, to gesture, and to point. They can also help the speaker to remember details of the presentation. If the speaker is giving a demonstration, they may be an essential part of it. Members of the audience find that visual aids deepen their perception and understanding of the speaker's message and help them remember the details of the speech.

While visual aids, well used, can better a speech in a number of ways, they can also turn a speech into a disaster if a speaker attempts to use them without thorough preparation and practice. Because speaking with visual aids involves doing two things at once—maintaining the verbal flow and handling physical objects—it is never easy. So more careful preparation is called for than for a speech without visual aids.

Deciding When to Use Visuals

One of the first questions that will arise is "How do I know when to include visual aids in an informative speech?" During this course, your teacher may answer that question for you by saying "Your next speech should include visual aids." This is especially likely to happen if you are asked to give a demonstration. On other occasions, however, you will have to decide for yourself whether one or more visual aids should be used. Ask yourself these two questions: "If I use a certain visual, will its presence make it easier for me to get my point across? Will using a certain visual make the point more meaningful for my audience?" If the answer to either question seems to be "Yes," then you should include the visual. Suppose, for example, that you are asked to give a speech on "How to Thread a Motion Picture Projector." Using a sideview drawing that shows the working parts of a projector, or even better, an actual projector to thread with film as you talk, will save you an enormous number of words and much time. If you are giving a speech on "My Trip to the Grand Canyon," using several color slides will surely deepen the impression on your audience.

Once you have decided to use visual aids in a speech, beware of the temptation to overuse them. Visual aids in public speaking should always remain in the role their name implies—aids. Once they become the main center of audience interest and attention they have ceased to be aids and have turned a speech into a presentation of the visuals themselves. Using five or six of your best slides as visual aids in a speech on "My Trip to the Grand Canyon" greatly enhances your speech, but showing twenty-five or thirty slides during a six- to eight-minute presentation means you are no longer giving a speech with visual aids; you are giving a slide show with a brief commentary.

Types of Visual Aids

At times you will want to use a series of visual aids, at other times only one will be necessary. It all depends on your speech topic and the relationship of the visual aids to it. Following are brief descriptions, with examples, of visual aids that are available to a speaker.

Charts A drawing showing the relationships among the parts of a whole is a **chart.** The drawing usually includes lines and words and can deal with almost any subject. One commonly used type of chart is the *line-staff* chart showing the relationships among members of an organization. An example appears below.

Graphs A second common type of visual aid is the **graph.** Graphs picture large amounts of information (usually quantitative or numerical) at a single glance. They consist primarily of lines with occasional words and numbers. One frequently used type is the line graph on page 304. When the area under the peaks and valleys in a line graph is darkened to provide greater visual contrast, the graph is called a profile graph.

A sample line-staff chart

A sample line graph

A sample bar graph

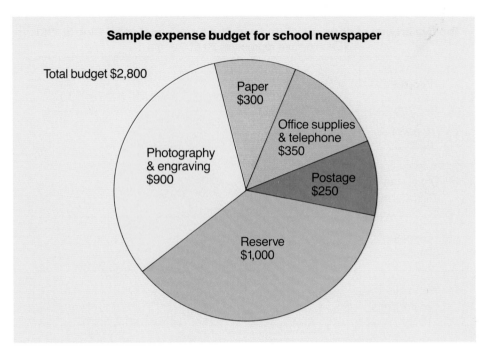

Sample expense budget for school newspaper

Total budget $2,800

Paper
$300

Office supplies
& telephone
$350

Photography
& engraving
$900

Postage
$250

Reserve
$1,000

A sample circle or pie graph

The bar graph, shown on page 304, is another form of line graph, often used to show the same kind of information.

A circle graph, or pie graph as it is sometimes called, is used to indicate parts of a whole. A typical circle graph is shown above.

Picture graphs are similar to bar graphs in basic design, but include pictorial materials to heighten visual appeal. Since they demand more artistic ability, they are more difficult and time-consuming to prepare. At the top of page 306 is a picture graph.

Diagrams   Like a chart and a graph, a **diagram** is used to show the relationship of a part to a whole. Diagrams, however, generally rely more on drawing and less on words and numbers than charts and graphs do. Diagrams may range from very simple line drawings to very complex pictures with shading and perspective. The figure at the bottom of page 306 is an example of a diagram.

Maps   A **map** shows information that is geographical in nature. Some maps are used simply to indicate location, whereas others show location as it relates to elevation, weather at a given time, agricultural production, or any number of other items. The figure on page 307 is a map showing land use in China.

A sample picture graph

A sample diagram

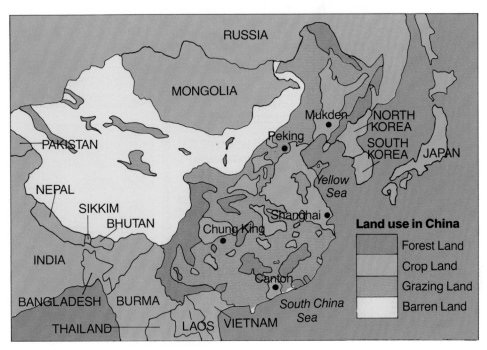

A sample map

Posters   A relatively easy type of visual aid to prepare is one consisting of print or lettering on a **poster.** Lists of important points in your speech, key phrases, slogans, and humorous sayings can all be visually presented through print. Simply printing the main ideas of a speech on a large sheet of paper and showing it to the audience does not make an effective visual aid, however. Printed visual aids should be genuinely attention-getting or essential memory aids. The lettering must be imaginative, with attention given to spacing, color, size of letters, and their type style.

Cartoons   Cartoons turn humor into a visual aid. A **cartoon** is simply a funny or satirical drawing used to make a point. Though cartoons demand a certain artistic ability to be effective, their impact on an audience can be great when they are well prepared.

Pictures   Whether simply printed or in the form of a photograph, slide, filmstrip, or film, a **picture** can be a very effective visual aid. Two cautions, however, must be observed when using pictures. First, they must be large enough to be easily seen by the whole audience. If necessary, they must be enlarged through projection. Second, the pictures themselves can easily become the center of attention and

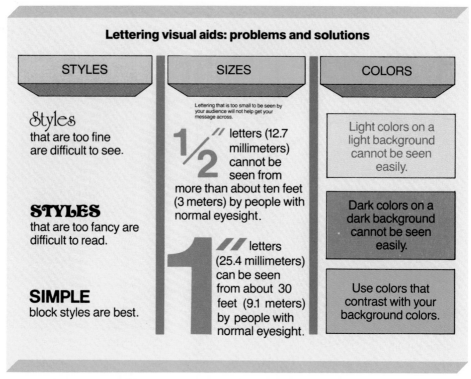

Lettering visual aids: problems and solutions

STYLES	SIZES	COLORS
Styles that are too fine are difficult to see.	Lettering that is too small to be seen by your audience will not help get your message across. ½″ letters (12.7 millimeters) cannot be seen from more than about ten feet (3 meters) by people with normal eyesight.	Light colors on a light background cannot be seen easily.
STYLES that are too fancy are difficult to read.	1″ letters (25.4 millimeters) can be seen from about 30 feet (9.1 meters) by people with normal eyesight.	Dark colors on a dark background cannot be seen easily.
SIMPLE block styles are best.		Use colors that contrast with your background colors.

Following these guidelines will help you produce an effective visual aid.

distract the audience from the speaker and the message. They must, therefore, be used sparingly. When these cautions are observed a picture can, indeed, be worth a thousand words.

Objects The visual aids discussed thus far are two-dimensional. A three-dimensional **object,** however, will make a deeper impression than a picture or representation. One of the great sales advantages of an auctioneer is being able to present the object being sold as he or she talks. Thus using a collection of Indian arrowheads, rather than drawings of them, as visual aids in a speech will gain greater audience attention and interest. At times it may be possible for audience members to handle as well as to see actual objects.

Models Sometimes, an object is too large to be conveniently brought to a speech presentation. Then a scaled-down version, called a **model,** may be used instead. A two-foot (58.8-centimeter) plastic model of a rocket, for example, enables the speaker to show parts and views not possible with either a real rocket or a two-dimensional drawing. Models of many large objects may not be readily available, but often an inexpensive one can be made from cardboard or papier-maché.

Cutaways   A model with a section of the outer covering removed to show interior parts is called a **cutaway.** A model of an internal combustion engine, with part of the casing removed to show the valves and pistons, would be an example of a cutaway.

Handouts   Something prepared ahead of time to give to each member of your audience is a **handout.** It can contain explanations, directions, maps, charts, or other material. Handouts are especially useful to present information to your audience that they will want to refer to after your speech is over. Be sure to have enough copies of your handout available so that each member of your audience can have one.

Handouts and the other visual aids mentioned here are not the only types of visual aids available; they are simply the ones most commonly used. Anything that can visually support the speech and is appropriate for the speaker, audience, and occasion may be used as a visual aid.

Preparing Speeches Using Visual Aids

Because speeches containing one or more visual aids are more difficult to deliver than speeches without visual aids, precise preparation and practice is called for when aids are to be used. Speakers usually prepare their own visual aids, but even in cases where the visual is readily available (objects, for example) careful rehearsal of the speech with the visual is essential to achieve perfect timing and handling.

A first principle regarding the selection and preparation of any visual aid you plan to display is that it must be capable of being seen easily from all parts of the room. Elementary as this may seem, it is one of the most frequently violated rules regarding the use of visual aids. For graphic visuals such as charts, graphs, diagrams, maps, cartoons, and posters, this means that letters, numbers, and lines should be large and heavy and have sufficient contrast with the background on which they are mounted to be easily seen by all audience members in the back rows. The best way to ensure this is by stepping to the back of the room in which the speech will be given and checking the visual during its construction. Pictures cut from newspapers or magazines are rarely large enough for even a classroom audience of thirty people to see details without projection. Snapshots almost always require projection. Occasionally actual objects or models are too small for easy viewing of details. Remember, however, that it is only necessary for the audience to see whatever degree of detail you consider important. If minute details of the visual are not essential to your speech, then it is not essential that they be large.

A second necessary element in a visual aid is that it be neat and attractive. It need not be a work of art, but it should never be sloppy. One of the major problems with drawing a visual on a blackboard or easel while you are speaking is that most people who are not artists cannot produce a visual in a neat and attractive way under pressure. Preparing well-proportioned visuals ahead of time, on the other hand, can greatly enhance your prestige with your audience. It gives listeners the impression that you were concerned enough about the reception of your speech to take pains to create attractive visual aids. When preparing them, the stress should be on neatness, but don't overlook the opportunity to highlight important items through the use of various colors and varied media. Felt tip pens, crayons, pre-made lettering, ink, and many other elements can be combined to produce a visual that is both informative and appealing.

You will also need to plan prior to the speech how to display the visual aid. Small objects, models, and cutaways can be held in the hands and shown to the audience with relative ease. Most good graphic and pictorial aids, however, will be so large that holding them while speaking will appear clumsy and awkward to the audience. If an easel is available, it can be very useful in displaying this type of visual, as long as you make sure that it is placed at the proper angle to be seen from all parts of the room. When an easel is not available, you may want to bring masking tape to help you properly display the visual. When displaying it by attaching it to the wall, be certain it is placed high enough so that the audience can see it. You should also make sure it is far enough from the lectern, so your body will not block the listeners' views. Finally, if you decide to lean the visual against something—an easel, the lectern, or a blackboard—you must use cardboard that is heavy enough to remain in place without being held.

Naturally you will need to point to various details on your visual at certain points in your speech. Pointing with your hand often means your arm blocks part of your audience's view of the visual. Thus you should use a pointer if at all possible. When using a pointer, hold it in whichever hand is closer to the visual so you do not have to reach across your body to point. Look at the visual only long enough to locate the spot to which you wish to point. Then, with your pointer held on that spot, turn your eyes immediately back to your audience. If your visual is such that you will be pointing to it repeatedly, continue holding the pointer in your hands during that portion of the speech in which you are making frequent reference to the visual. If, on the other hand, you plan to refer to the visual at only a few widely separated times during the speech, lay the pointer aside and pick it up again the next time it is needed.

Visuals, such as the map that this weather reporter is using, should support the spoken presentation—not overpower it.

Two other important matters to consider are the point at which you first wish to display a visual and the length of time you will want to continue to display it. If the aid will be referred to off and on throughout most of the speech, you want to show it to the audience when you first make reference to it and then let it remain in view until the speech is completed. If the visual is to be referred to only once, or for the final time long before the speech is completed, you should put it aside or cover it immediately after your last reference to it. Otherwise, it will distract the listeners by remaining in view. Visuals mounted on cardboard may be turned face down on a desk or table. Objects, models, and cutaways can be covered with a piece of cloth.

In order for a speech involving visual aids to look smooth and professional, you must practice coordinating the verbal and the visual elements. Practice when to first display the visuals, how to display them, for what length of time, and when and how to remove them from view. Be sure that your body does not block the audience's view of visual aids.

Some visuals are used to make a single point in a speech. If you plan to use one or more visual aids of this type, be certain to give the audience sufficient time to view it. Inexperienced speakers often work hard to produce a neat, attractive visual, then lose its effectiveness by displaying it for only two to three seconds. If the audience is going to have just one opportunity to see a visual, they will ordinarily need about ten to twelve seconds to familiarize themselves with its content. It is perfectly acceptable to display an aid in silence for several seconds after explaining it to the audience.

Demonstration Speeches and Visual Aids

A common purpose for giving an informative speech is to demonstrate a process or procedure to an audience. If your speech purpose is to show your listeners how to do something, how to make something, or how something works, it may be labelled a **demonstration speech**. Many demonstration speeches demand the use of visual aids.

To teach your listeners to *perform* a process themselves, arrange the steps in the process sequentially, demonstrating each step in order. For this form of demonstration speech, aids such as objects, models, and mock-ups usually prove more effective than graphs, charts, and diagrams. Don't overlook your own body as an effective visual aid. A talk on how to do aerobic dance, for example, demands no other aid than your demonstrating some of the steps during the speech.

When teaching listeners how to do something, keep the number of separate steps in the process to a minimum. If the process has more than five separate steps, try to group the steps into stages. This will aid the listeners' memories. Likewise, avoid handling too many separate aids. Use one, two, or three key aids to demonstrate the process.

When the purpose of your demonstration speech is to have your audience *understand* a process, you have greater choice in how you arrange the steps. Arrangements such as easy-to-difficult, order-of-importance, known-to-unknown, and chronological order may be used. To demonstrate three methods of thawing a frozen pipe, for example, you might use an order of most-preferred to least-preferred:

1. Heat the pipe with a torch.
2. Pour boiling water over cloth wrapped around the pipe.
3. Wrap the pipe with electrical heat tape.

Graphs, charts, and pictures may often be just as useful as objects and models when you wish your listeners to understand a process. A picture or drawing of a torch heating a frozen pipe, for instance, should prove just effective as, and easier to handle than an actual torch.

When giving demonstration speeches, student speakers sometimes fall into the trap of allowing the "demonstration" part to steal the show. That is not a speech supported by a visual demonstration; it has become a demonstration, supported by a few remarks.

Using Equipment with Visual Aids

Some visual aids can best be presented through the use of some form of equipment—an overhead projector, an opaque projector, a videotape unit, a movie projector, or a slide projector. When equipment is to be used, rehearsing with the equipment is as crucial as rehearsing with the visual aids themselves. Most projectors require a darkened or semi-darkened room, so you must be certain this can be arranged before choosing a visual requiring projection. Many times it is best to arrange for a friend or classmate to run the equipment during your speech and to turn the lights on and off at the proper times to relieve you of having too many responsibilities all at once. Naturally, such preparations must all be rehearsed in advance.

The day of the speech itself, carefully set up the equipment and check it prior to the speech. Don't assume that the projector bulb is all right or that the videotape player is working properly. More good speeches have probably been ruined by burned-out bulbs than by any other single cause. Finally, it is wise to plan how you will handle the situation if a piece of equipment malfunctions during your presentation. Perhaps you can prepare handouts in advance to use in case other materials cannot be used. It may be possible for you to explain verbally the material you had planned to display. Remember that audiences are usually sympathetic, so don't panic.

Application

Considering Visual Aids

Watch several television commercials. Take notes on the visual aids that are used and observe how the speakers use them. Discuss with your classmates the most effective visual aids that you saw. Explain how the speaker used them to get the commercial's message across. Could you improve on the choice or use of visual aids in the commercials that you watched? How?

10 Chapter Review

▇ Summary

The main purpose of speeches given to inform is to impart new knowledge to the listeners.

Types of Informative Speeches Informative speeches may be classified into four types. Speeches about objects deal with anything you can see, feel, hear, taste, or smell. Speeches about events tell about anything that has happened, or is happening, or is regarded as happening. Speeches about processes treat related series of events that lead to specific results or products. Speeches about concepts deal with beliefs, theories, ideas, and principles.

Beginning an Informative Speech The introduction to an informative speech should gain audience attention, build interest in the topic, preview the topic and apply it to the audience, and establish the ethos of the speaker. The speaker should draw upon several attention devices to carry out these functions.

Imparting the Message of an Informative Speech Several functions must be fulfilled during the main part of a speech. A speaker should maintain audience attention by using attention devices and by checking seating arrangements and listening conditions. A speaker must also react to audience feedback and make smooth transitions during the speech. Finally, it is important to avoid becoming too technical. Personalize the speech regularly.

Concluding an Informative Speech The conclusion of an informative speech should summarize the major points made during the body of the speech. It should also signal the conclusion for the audience, reinforce the central idea of the speech, and psychologically close the speech.

Conducting a Question-and-Answer Period Be prepared for a question-and-answer period and promise to answer audience questions.

Be impartial in recognizing questioners and aware of any time limit for the session. If you do not know the answer to a question, say so. If a question relates to a visual aid, display it while answering. Answer questions directly, completely, and briefly.

Using Visual Aids Use visual aids only to clarify a point or make it more meaningful. Choose the most appropriate types of visual aids and be sure that they can be seen easily from all parts of the room and are neat and attractive. Rehearse with each visual to find the best method for using it.

Vocabulary

Define each term in a complete sentence.

informative speech	technical language	graph
attention device	personalizing	diagram
humor	summary	map
anecdote	quotation	poster
common ground technique	dramatic statement	cartoon
shock technique	rhetorical question	object
suspense	theme	model
ethos	slogan	cutaway
transition	chart	handout

Checklist

Skills for Speaking to Inform

1. Be aware of your basic purpose in speaking to inform.
2. Use a purpose sentence.
3. Learn to focus on a specific aspect of your topic.
4. Formulate a good introduction.
5. Use attention devices to gain audience attention.
6. Apply your message to your audience.
7. Attend to audience feedback.
8. Use smooth transitions.
9. Use language that your audience will understand.
10. Prepare properly if you plan to use visual aids.

Review Questions

1. Identify the primary purpose of an informative speech.
2. Name several functions that an introduction fufills.
3. Describe several devices you can use to capture the audience's attention during your introduction.
4. Describe the main purpose of the body of an informative speech.
5. Identify the nonverbal factors that can affect the audience's attention to a speaker.
6. Describe the importance of the conclusion of a speech.
7. Name the different parts of a summary.
8. Identify some two-dimensional and three-dimensional visual aids.
9. Describe when visual aids should be used.
10. Describe the use of visual aids during the question-and-answer period after a speech.

Discussion Questions

1. As a class, discuss possible topics for each of the four categories of informative speeches. Focus upon topics that would be of interest to your age group at the present time. Try to identify at least ten topics in each category that are of interest to the class.
2. Discuss possible openings for a speech that explains how in the future the sea will be a greater source of human food than it is now. How might you gain the audience's attention in such a speech? What devices might you use to build interest during the introduction?
3. Discuss how you might personalize a speech on any of the topics that you have identified earlier. What kinds of experiences would you turn to in order to introduce a real person into your speech?
4. As a class, pick an informative speech topic about a process. Discuss the kinds of visual aids you might use in a 10-minute speech on this topic. What kinds of aids would help both the speaker and the audience? How could you use visual aids to develop and maintain audience interest?

Critical Thinking

1. **Analysis:** Under what circumstances would it be appropriate to invite questions from the audience after an informative speech? How knowledgeable about the topic should the speaker be? What procedure should the speaker follow if asked a question that she or he cannot answer?

2. **Evaluation:** Imagine that you are giving a speech on the longest rivers of the world. Each time you introduce a river, you use a beautiful slide of the capital city of the country through which the river flows. How necessary and effective are these visual aids? What aids might help an audience during a speech on this topic?

Activities

In-Class

1. Work in groups of from five to seven. Select a topic from either the sample speech topics in Chapter 7 that are suitable for informative speeches or the topics that you identified during the discussion questions. Suggest as many effective attention-getting devices as you can to introduce the topic. Try to include examples of each of the techniques studied in this chapter. Select someone to compile the list and present it to the class as a whole for reaction and feedback from classmates.

2. Work in groups of from five to seven. Each group will design a critique sheet that allows for rating the use of visual aids. The sheet should rate the selection, the construction, and the use of visual materials. Assign one group member to explain the form to the class. The class will then select the best features from each group's sheet. A usable critique sheet for visual aids can then be developed and used to evaluate future speakers and speeches.

3. Work in groups of from five to seven. Each member of each group will tell an anecdote based upon personal experience or upon a story from

someone else. Each group will then select the most interesting anecdote and present it to the class as a whole. Discuss how each anecdote might be used to build interest in a speech. Be sure to identify the topic of an informative speech that the anecdote could be used with.

Out-of-Class

1. Examine the speeches in the Appendix of Speeches at the back of this book or in one of the standard speech collections in your library. Find a speech introduction that you believe is striking and engages the attention of the audience. Copy the introduction in your speech notebook. With an understanding of the speech's original audience in mind, write an analysis of the introduction, pointing out why it would immediately get the audience's attention. Be prepared to present your findings in class.

2. Using the Appendix of Speeches at the back of the book, a standard anthology of speeches, or *Vital Speeches of the Day,* examine the conclusions of at least four speeches. Then answer the following questions in your speech notebook. (a) How do the various speak-

ers introduce their conclusions? (b) Which of the speeches examined contains the best summary of the points made in the speech? Copy the summary. (c) Do any of the speeches end with a quotation, a dramatic statement, or a rhetorical question? Give examples. (d) What percentage of the speeches refer back to the introduction in the conclusion? Be prepared to present your findings in class.

3. Assume that you will give an informative speech on one of the following topics: "Alligators and Crocodiles," "Breeds of Cats," or "Living Costs in Major American Cities." Think about the visual aids that will help your audience learn more about the topic. List and describe the visual aids you would use in your speech notebook. Be prepared to present your list in class and to add other aids suggested by your classmates.

4. Choose a topic for an informative speech that was presented in the text or identified in one of the various activities devoted to topic selection. Find a topic that you know little or nothing about. In your speech notebook, write a series of questions that audience members are likely to ask about the

topic before they hear the speech. Be prepared to discuss with your classmates how this question-writing technique might be usable in speech preparation.

Chapter Project

Prepare an eight- to ten-minute demonstration speech in which you explain either how to do something or how something works. Choose a topic that you already know something about and that lends itself to the use of visual aids. Follow these steps: (a) Organize the body of the speech into an outline. (b) Write an introduction that gets the attention of your audience. (c) Carefully consider the structuring of the body of your speech. (d) Compose a carefully thought-out conclusion. (e) Memorize the introduction, important transitions, and the conclusion. (f) Prepare your visual aids, referring to the checklist in this chapter as you do so. (g) Be prepared to participate in a two- to five-minute question-and-answer period following your speech.

11 Speaking to Persuade

**When you have completed this chapter
you should be able to:**

- Describe the difference between informative and persuasive speaking.
- List characteristics of positive, neutral, disinterested, and opposed audiences.
- Explain how evidence and reasoning work together to create logical persuasion.
- Define and explain what is meant by responsible persuasion.

When speaking to persuade, your aim is to influence or change the thinking or actions of others.

Much of public speaking has as its primary purpose providing information to listeners—informing them about subjects the speaker knows more about than they do. But another purpose which accounts for a great number of speeches is that of persuasion. A speech given to persuade has as its primary goal the influencing of the attitudes, beliefs, or behavior of the listeners. Political figures try to secure votes through persuasive speaking. Lawyers use persuasion to secure a jury's decision. Legislators speak persuasively for or against a pending bill. All citizens have numerous opportunities for persuasive speaking. You might want to convince members of your PTA to take a certain stand on the school budget, tell your city council why you believe they should vote for an ordinance you favor, or explain to other members of your investment club why you feel a certain stock should be bought. All would be exercises in persuasion.

Each one of the general principles of public speaking discussed in earlier chapters applies to persuasive speaking. Persuasive speaking, however, is more difficult than speaking to inform. It demands additional skills which will be discussed in this chapter.

TYPES OF PERSUASIVE SPEECHES

Persuasive speeches are given in situations in which two or more points of view about a topic are in conflict. The speaker tries to convince those who disagree that his or her point of view is the correct one.

Another way of saying this is that persuasive speeches are given when there is some *question* about which view is correct. Three types of questions give rise to persuasive speech situations: questions of fact; questions of value; and questions of policy.

Questions of fact deal with occurrences and the reasons that they have happened, are happening, or will happen in the future. Here are several examples of purpose sentences for persuasive speeches dealing with questions of fact:

- My purpose is to persuade my audience that a major earthquake will hit California within the next fifteen years.

- My purpose is to convince my audience that there should be increased security in airports.

- My purpose is to persuade my audience that automobile airbags can save thousands of lives over a ten-year period.

- My purpose is to convince my listeners that the Chernobyl nuclear accident will have a major health impact in the United States in coming years.

Notice that each speech purpose deals with occurrences about which there is some element of doubt. If it were now a solidly proven fact that Oswald acted alone in the Kennedy assassination, there would be no reason for anyone to give a persuasive speech on the subject. The same is true of the topics that relate to the present, such as political terrorism, and of course to those dealing with the future, such as a California earthquake, since nothing in the future can yet be considered an established fact.

Is DNA research morally justifiable? What are the ethical responsibilities of journalists? These are **questions of value.** Though such questions involve matters of fact, they go further. They also call for judgments about right and wrong, ethical and unethical, good and bad, proper and improper. "How many journalists are there in Washington, D.C.?" is purely a question of fact since it involves statistics. However, a question such as "What are the ethical responsibilities of journalists regarding more medical care for the elderly?" goes much further since it demands a moral judgment. A person's answer to this second question depends not only on his or her knowledge about medical care for the elderly, but also on his or her moral values. Notice how the following purpose sentences for speeches of value also require this kind of judgment:

- My purpose is to persuade my audience that the original *Star Wars* is a classic movie.

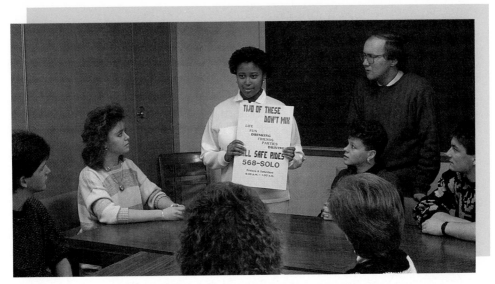

This student is highlighting facts for a publicity campaign whose purpose is to persuade others not to mix drinking with driving.

- My purpose is to persuade my listeners that the state should have a better food-stamp program.

- My purpose is to persuade my audience that in the long run it still pays to buy American-made cars.

Questions of policy deal with whether certain courses of action should be taken. They include matters of both fact and value within themselves, but go beyond them to consider what should or should not be done. A question such as "What steps should be taken to control the problem of car theft?" demands both that the audience know certain facts about car theft, and that they consider it wrong. Once this is established, the speaker can go further to advocate that one or more solutions be carried out. Here are some examples of purpose sentences for speeches dealing with questions of policy. Notice that most such sentences contain the word "should":

- My purpose is to show my audience that a permanent site should be established for the Olympic Games.

- My purpose is to persuade my listeners that stricter controls should be placed on genetic research.

- My purpose is to convince my audience that the U.S. government should adopt a tougher policy to deal with terrorism that affects American citizens traveling abroad.

THREE SOURCES OF PERSUASION

Before people will believe, think, or do something, they must *want* to do it. **Persuasion** is simply a means by which one person can cause another to *want* to believe, to think, or to do. You adopt new beliefs, attitudes, and actions constantly. Think for a moment why you might decide to see a certain film, admire a certain singer, or learn to drive a car. Basically, each decision is made only when *you want* to make it. Whenever someone else tries to convince you to decide a certain way, that person is using the process of persuasion.

Over 2500 years ago, the ancient Greek, Aristotle, wrote a book on persuasion called the *Rhetoric*. The *Rhetoric* is still considered by most speech scholars to be the most influential book written on the subject. In it, Aristotle stated that there are three primary sources by which people can be persuaded: **pathos,** which means the listeners' own personal drives, needs, and desires; **ethos,** by which he meant the way in which an audience perceives the character and personality of the speaker; and **logos,** meaning the listeners' own thinking processes. Persuaders must concentrate on each of these factors. They must know their listeners'

Aristotle found persuasion to be based on pathos, ethos, and logos.

324

needs, establish their own prestige when attempting to influence an audience, and build logical arguments that their listeners can follow. A knowledgeable, sincere, logical speaker stands a good chance of successfully persuading others.

Application

Types of Persuasive Speeches

Divide the class into three groups. Each group will choose five topics that are suitable for a persuasive speech. For each topic, develop a purpose sentence that deals with a question of fact, a question of policy, and a question of value. You should be able to develop all three sentences for each topic. If you have difficulty, explain your problem when the groups come together to discuss the topics and purpose statements as a class. Keep these purpose statements in your speech notebook for future persuasive speeches.

PATHOS: ANALYZING THE NEEDS OF YOUR LISTENERS

Most people like to consider themselves very logical creatures. They prefer to think they make decisions and behave in certain ways based solely on logic. But if they were to make an honest analysis of the reasons for much of their behavior and many of their decisions, they would probably be forced to admit that they are sometimes not logical at all. Unlike Mr. Spock of *Star Trek,* people frequently believe, decide, or act in particular ways simply because they want to or need to, rather than because reason or logic points to these choices.

If you plan to persuade people, you must appeal to the needs and desires of your listeners as well as to their brains. Some people consider this beneath the dignity of a persuader. This is not the case at all, as long as the needs and desires to which you appeal are legitimate, and you honestly believe in the cause you are promoting.

Discover the Needs of Your Audience

The effective persuader seeks out the special needs and attitudes of each audience prior to a speech in order to plan the strategy most suited to that group of listeners. Remember the section on audience analysis in Chapter 7? Knowing the particular needs and attitudes of an audience is especially important when you are speaking to persuade. In a persuasive speech the success or failure of your entire speech can depend on how well you know your audience beforehand.

Audiences may have hundreds of special needs and attitudes depending on the subject of a given speech and the listeners' previous experiences with the topic. These many different needs can be grouped according to how they affect the audiences' reception of you and your topic. An audience's attitude toward you and your topic will fall somewhere on a scale between "very positive" and "very negative." Essentially, audiences fall into four basic categories: the positive audience, the neutral audience, the disinterested audience, and the opposed audience. Each has a different set of needs and must be approached differently by the speaker. You will want to try to place your audiences' pre-speech attitudes as carefully as possible on this scale.

The **positive audience** is one that already agrees with your basic persuasive purpose. If you are speaking to librarians about the need to raise money for the local library, most of your listeners are likely to be in favor of your idea before you begin. If you are speaking to students about the need to oppose a curfew for young people in your community, most of your audience will again be likely to support your idea. Of course, this is the easiest type of audience to persuade. Your only persuasive task is to deepen their feelings about the topic. Their basic need is simply for a "recharging."

The **neutral audience** has a different need. They are neither for nor against your topic—they simply do not know very much about it. Their basic need is for information that will make it possible for them to form an opinion. Suppose you are trying to sell a brand new dishwashing detergent, and the people in your audience have never heard of it before.

Scale of audience attitudes

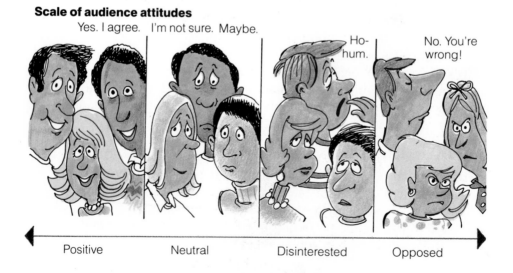

Positive   Neutral   Disinterested   Opposed

If you are going to persuade them to buy it, you must first give them some information about it. You might, for example, tell them that it washes more dishes per bottle than brand X, it smells better than brand Y, it cleans better than brand Z, and it is easier on the hands than all three!

The **disinterested audience** knows about the topic but couldn't care less. They consider it a dull issue or an unimportant one, not particularly relevant to them or their needs. This kind of audience needs to be "electrified." They need to be shown the seriousness of the problem, the closeness of the danger, or the way in which they will be affected. Before they can be persuaded to do anything, they must be motivated to care.

The **opposed audience** is the most difficult kind of audience for a persuasive speaker to face. It is composed of people who disagree with your stand on the topic. They feel as strongly about the issues as you do, but they have opposing opinions. Sometimes they may distrust you simply because you hold a viewpoint different from theirs. Their need is first for open-mindedness, then for conviction. You must first succeed in getting a fair hearing for your side, then attempt to convince them of your viewpoint.

How do you discover whether you will be facing a positive, neutral, disinterested, or opposed audience? Usually by the same methods mentioned under "Audience Analysis" in Chapter 7 starting on page 175. Ask the person who invites you to speak about the attitudes and needs of the listeners. Ask friends and acquaintances who know your future audience members. Talk to other speakers who have addressed the same group in the past. In each case, ask questions designed to tell you about the attitudes of the audience toward your topic and about their needs in relationship to the topic.

If you are planning a speech that strongly advocates greater freedom for editors and reporters on your school newspaper, appropriate questions to ask about members of your future audience might include the following:

- How many of my audience members will be fellow students?

- How many will be teachers and school administrators?

- What is the attitude of our organization of parents and teachers towards the school paper?

- Are there certain opinion leaders among the group? If so, what are their views on freedom of the press?

- Have any of the audience members been bothered in the past by insistent school reporters?

- Do some of the school administrators feel our school press is too liberal in its editorial views?

Questions of this kind should enable you to make an educated estimate of the attitudes and needs of the particular audience you will be facing. Once you know those attitudes and needs you can begin planning your persuasive strategy. Strategies differ, depending on the type of audience.

Use Different Approaches for Different Audiences

For the positive audience, your job is a relatively easy one—keep them happy or make them even happier! Since the positive audience already is in basic agreement with you, you have probably been invited to speak either to rededicate or remotivate them or talk about means rather than ends. A common example of a speaker facing a positive audience is that of a coach giving a pep talk to a team before the big game. The team members form a positive audience in the sense that they share the same goal as the coach—they all want to win. The coach's job as a speaker, then, is not to convince them that they should win, but to "psych them up" and to convince them that certain tactics will work better than others. Speeches of this kind, given to positive audiences, are sometimes referred to as **inspirational speeches.**

The neutral audience needs information. Certain kinds of information, especially factual information, can be convincing in itself, particularly when fact is piled upon fact. The strategy for handling a neutral audience, then, is one of presenting the listeners with information from which they can reach only one conclusion—the conclusion you want them to reach. Beth Simmons, a high school student, shows how to apply this strategy in her speech called "It's Hard to Be Human."

From early America's melting pot to today's claim that "Everybody Needs Milk" our differences have been homogenized to produce an era of paper people. Now you take a society, fold it into convenient sizes, cut carefully, unfold, and PRESTO! Nameless, faceless, expressionless silhouettes meaninglessly holding hands.

Whoever you are, the message in any fortune cookie is universally didactic. If you need a friend, phone dial-a-smile to hear continuous laughing for three minutes, only interrupted by a voice reminding you that it is just a recording. It's easy to become satisfied with having things done for us by our computers and tape recorders. And, just as easy, to slip into the efficiency of automatic communication.

Notice how Beth Simmons used specific examples and experiences common to most of her listeners. In this manner, she increased her chances of persuading her audience to agree that it is difficult to be an individual in an increasingly impersonal world.

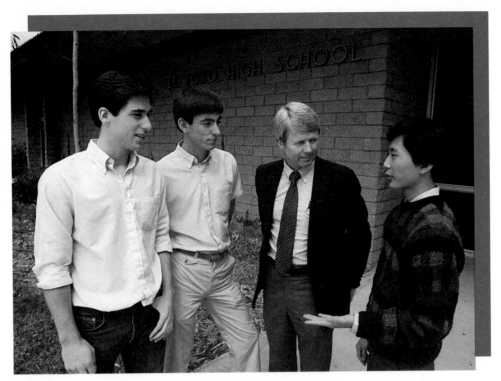

If this speaker is going to persuade his neutral listeners, he will have to provide information that leads them to accept his conclusion.

Facing a disinterested audience is harder than facing a neutral one. When an audience is aware of an issue, but considers it unworthy of any mental strain on their part or too dull to bother getting excited about, the speaker's main persuasive task is somehow to light a fire under those listeners. Often this can be done by showing the audience how the topic will affect them directly. President Ronald Reagan used this technique when appealing to his listeners' basic need for survival in a speech calling for a stronger U.S. defense capability:

> For 20 years the Soviet Union has been accumulating enormous military might. They didn't stop when their forces exceeded all requirements of a legitimate defensive capability. And they haven't stopped now. . . .
> As an example, the United States introduced its last new intercontinental ballistic missile, the Minuteman III, in 1969 and we are now dismantling our even older Titan missiles. But what has the Soviet Union done in those intervening years? Well, since 1969 the Soviet Union has built five new classes of ICBM's, and upgraded these eight times. . . .

Dealing with the opposed audience requires a double strategy. First, the listeners must be "softened up" to the point where they will really listen to your arguments and consider them fairly. Second, you must present sound evidence to back your position. Imagine that you have discovered some "shady dealings" during your school's most recent election for class officers. You plan to expose these practices in your next classroom speech, to be titled "Whatever Happened to Integrity?" You know you will face an opposed audience, since most of the members of your speech class were very active and involved in the election process either as candidates or campaign workers. Starting your speech with a direct attack on the issue would be an almost certain way to lose that kind of audience right at the beginning:

> Student politics and student government in this school are riddled with graft and corruption. The recent election showed me quite clearly that we cannot trust either the winners or the losers. In an election where vote buying occurred and campaign workers tampered with ballot boxes. . . .

Such an opening will only deepen the negative feelings of an opposed audience. Even with facts to back up your claims, it is unlikely that you would achieve a fair hearing for your case. A better approach for this kind of audience would be:

> This school has always had good student leadership. I think you will agree that since our first year here we have been fortunate in the people we have elected as our class officers. I know many of you are dedicated to good student government here, as I am. I was very surprised and shocked, therefore, to discover some irregularities in our recent election process. Please listen as I recount some facts that have come to my attention. . . .

This approach may not persuade your listeners to believe you any more than they would have with the first approach, but at least, in the second case, your audience is likely to listen to your arguments and consider them. If the arguments you then present in the body of the speech are strong enough, the listeners may actually be persuaded.

Of course, positive, neutral, disinterested, and opposed audiences do not always occur in pure form. Many times an audience is composed of people who disagree among themselves. When an audience is made up of positive listeners and neutral listeners, the speaker's task is not too difficult. Giving persuasive information to such a group satisfies the neutral listeners and recharges those who already agree. The same approach can also be used effectively with an audience of neutral and opposed listeners but should be preceded in this case by some "mind-opening" tactics before presenting the factual information. For a disinterested and opposed group, the approach suggested for opposed listeners alone may prove effective. Perhaps the worst combination to face is an audience of positive and opposed listeners. Here, too, the safest approach might be to use the strategy for opposed listeners. By appealing mainly to them, you may gain some converts from your opposed listeners and are unlikely to lose any of the positive ones. The next section will present specific kinds of evidence that can be useful in dealing with these different types of audiences.

Application

Reaching Your Audience

Choose a purpose statement that was developed in the previous Application. Explain to your classmates how you would present this topic to a positive audience. Then identify techniques you would use for a neutral audience, a disinterested audience, and an opposed audience. Ask for reactions and feedback from your classmates.

ETHOS: ESTABLISHING YOUR PRESTIGE

In Chapter 10 you read that the ancient Greek rhetorician Aristotle used the term *ethos* to describe a speaker's prestige. He felt it was the most powerful form of proof a speaker could possess. No matter how logical a speaker, no matter how well that speaker appeals to the needs of the listeners, if those listeners do not respect the speaker's character, there is little chance of successful persuasion. Thus, as a speaker, you must establish ethos, especially when attempting to persuade an opposed audience. This is done by showing listeners you are well prepared and competent, by being sincere in what you say, and by appearing genuinely interested in your audience.

Competence: Let Your Preparation Show

If a persuader ever hopes to convince listeners of anything, that speaker must show a high degree of **competence** and **confidence.** Audiences do not follow frightened or hesitant speakers. Only speakers who know their topic thoroughly and feel confident in their preparation are likely to succeed at persuasion. If your preparation has been shallow or haphazard, you will find it almost impossible to convince your audience of anything. Abraham Lincoln's well-known saying applies aptly to persuasive speaking: "You can fool some of the people all of the time, and all of the people some of the time, but you cannot fool all of the people all of the time." Incompetence and lack of confidence will usually become obvious to most audiences after a very short period of time.

While audiences seldom fail to notice incompetence, they may occasionally fail to recognize a truly competent speaker. If no one points out a speaker's knowledge, preparation, and ability to the listeners, they can misjudge the true qualities of that speaker. Sometimes a speaker's competence is mentioned when someone introduces him or her to the audience before the speech begins. In such introductions the audience is informed about the speaker's qualifications to speak on the topic. When a speaker has already established a national reputation in a given field or is well known to a local audience, it is unnecessary to remind listeners of the speaker's competence. Unfortunately the speakers most needing this kind of "prestige-boosting," the unknown or inexperienced speakers, are the ones who least often receive it. This leaves them with the task of building their own ethos during their speeches.

One of the most effective methods of assuring your audience of your competence is to let your speech preparation show during the speech. This can be accomplished in several ways. One way is by frequent use of evidence and supporting materials. The use of facts, survey results, statistics, and quotations from known authorities in the field says several important things about your knowledge and preparation. First it assures the audience that you are not simply "putting your mouth in motion." Listeners who hear sufficient amounts of evidence will recognize that you have backing for what you are saying and are not merely expressing your own unsupported opinions. Second, referring to outside sources of evidence shows the audience you have taken the time and effort to discover that evidence. Even though they may be an opposed audience, they will admire you for doing thorough research to support your point of view. They will realize you have earned the right to speak to them about your topic.

A second way of showing your competence is by referring to your own experience with your topic, particularly during the introduction of your speech. Audiences have learned to expect this kind of self-competence building from unknown speakers and do not consider it bragging, as long as it is done in a subtle and sophisticated manner. Notice how this student speaker established his competence by referring to direct family experience at the end of his introduction:

> Have you ever attended a Special Olympics competition? Do you know what the Special Olympic Games are? They are modeled on the International Olympic Games, but competition is limited to people with some form of developmental disability. Their purpose is to give these people

their day in the sun, as they compete against one another in 100-yard dashes, the long jump, discus throwing, and many other track and field events. Their motto is "Let me win, but if I cannot win, let me be brave in the attempt." Why do I know so much about the Special Olympics? Because my little brother has competed in them for the last four years.

In addition to focusing his audience's attention on his topic by the use of two rhetorical questions, the speaker established his competence by relating his personal connection with the Special Olympics.

You can also show experience or preparation by mentioning a part-time job you have had, by describing an informal survey you have taken, or simply by saying, "While researching for this speech, I noticed . . ." So long as you do not overdo this kind of reference, your ethos will grow in the minds of your listeners.

Sincerity: Don't Fake It!

Sincerity is the second part of a speaker's prestige. Like competence, it must be genuine to make a lasting positive impression. Insincere speakers can impress audiences for a time, but eventually most are exposed as "fakes." What is meant by **sincerity** in persuasive speaking?

Politicians like Senator Edward Kennedy know that audiences have built-in fake detectors and are unlikely to forgive insincerity.

SOCIAL WORKER

Social workers are employed by public government agencies, private agencies, or hospitals. They are often assigned to families. Welfare workers visit homes, interview family members, and make decisions for promoting the family's welfare. Educational requirements for social workers include a bachelor's degree followed by a Masters in Social Work (MSW) program.

Interviews are among the most important form of contact with clients. Each interview is prepared carefully, with questions planned in advance. Experienced social workers report that when they are sufficiently prepared they feel more confident and can listen more attentively to their clients. To gain the family's trust and respect, they begin the first interview with positive comments. This technique allows clients to feel more at ease.

While a sincere desire to help people is essential, a social worker cannot be successful without the ability to listen carefully and communicate convincingly with clients. Social workers must possess a repertoire of persuasive strategies so that they may select the technique most likely to convince clients that the prescribed course of action is best for them.

Social work can extend well beyond securing such basics as food and shelter for clients. To serve clients fully, social workers must often intervene persuasively on their behalf with groups and agencies that provide education, job training and placement, counseling, medical care, or other services. Such advocacy is effective only when social workers gather and present relevant information in a clear, well-reasoned manner.

This social worker speaks persuasively to clients and service groups.

Basically, it means that the speaker's motives for advocating a particular attitude, belief, or behavior must originate from a genuine concern for the best interests of the audience rather than from self-interest.

If a politician speaks to the people about a solution to a problem during an election year, the listeners sometimes find it hard to believe that the politician is attacking the problem unselfishly. A natural question in their minds is "Is the purpose of this speech to help solve the problem or to assure election?" A politician speaking under such circumstances needs to make a special effort to convince the audience of her or his sincerity. Audiences will more readily accept a speaker they consider somewhat incompetent than a speaker they consider insincere. The slightest hint of insincerity will turn many listeners against a speaker instantly.

A few public speakers are gifted with *charisma.* Charisma is difficult to define, but it often enables speakers who have it to influence and dominate their listeners in a way that ordinary speakers cannot. Charismatic speakers seem to be taken almost at face value as sincere and possessing great credibility. They are highly captivating and can often carry their audiences away with their words. Because they wield such power over their listeners, speakers who possess this gift have a special responsibility to use it wisely. To use it for wrong purposes not only harms the particular audiences that hear such a speaker; it also breaks down the trust that must exist between speakers and listeners everywhere if persuasion is to continue to be a means by which decisions are made in a democratic society.

Good Will: Show a Genuine Interest in Your Audience

Audiences will be more open and receptive to a speaker who shows an interest in them or good will toward them. Particularly with opposed audiences, persuaders need first to open the minds of their listeners to assure a fair hearing for their side of the issue. Getting an audience to like you as a person can lead to its members liking and accepting your arguments.

One commonly used method of showing an interest in one's audience is the practice of expressing appreciation for the invitation to speak to the group. The first thing ordinarily done by many speakers is to voice an appreciation for the privilege of addressing the audience.

Closely related to thanking one's audience is complimenting them. If you genuinely believe "This club represents the leaders in our community," then do not hesitate to tell the club. If you consider your audience to be a fair-minded group of people of sound judgment, tell them that, especially if your topic is likely to demand that they be fair as they listen: "This group has a reputation for being open-minded and fair in its decisions. I feel confident you will listen to what I have to say today in that same spirit." An opening such as this compliments the listeners and challenges them to be fair-minded as they listen to your speech.

Another way to show interest in your audience is to speak directly to various individuals in the group. If you are well acquainted with members of your audience, you may want to call them by name during your introductory remarks: "I see my friend Charles Stevens here today. I'm glad you could be here, Charlie." This sort of public recognition flatters Charles and probably puts him in a more receptive frame of mind toward you and your message. But calling audience members by name can be risky. If you call one friend's name, you'd better call all of your friends by name; otherwise, those left out may feel slighted. If you see twenty-eight of your friends in the audience, however, you'd better avoid such a roll call! Take care also not to identify someone as a friend if that person is only a nodding acquaintance. This comes across as false and insincere.

To show interest in your audience in another way, you might identify interests and experiences you and your listeners have in common. The use of the common-ground technique (see page 280) is a good method for demonstrating a genuine interest in your listeners as people. Audiences appreciate this. Effective use of humor (see page 278) also makes the speaker seem a likable person. If you can make your listeners laugh with you, they are more likely to listen receptively to your serious, persuasive message.

Application

Analyzing Ethos

Think of an individual whom you admire. Put together a list of words that describe this person. Think of what the person does and says that leads you to choose such words. How many of these qualities are discussed in this chapter? How can you use your knowledge of what you admire to develop your own ethos?

LOGOS: BEING LOGICAL

Have you ever been in an argument with someone and found yourself saying, "You're not being logical!" If you have, you probably still remember how frustrated you felt because the other person wouldn't argue according to the rules of logic. People frequently make decisions

Only valid evidence and correct reasoning will persuade the judge.

based on their needs and desires, but they like to feel they have decided logically. A persuasive speaker's job is to show listeners through logic how to fulfill their needs and desires. Logic, then, is a powerful tool of persuasion.

Use Valid Evidence and Correct Reasoning

Being logical in persuasive speaking means using valid evidence and correct reasoning. **Evidence** is the raw material with which you must begin. **Reasoning** is the process of putting this raw material together into a logical argument, which in turn may be used to reach a logical conclusion. The process of building a logical argument to use in a persuasive speech can be compared to the way in which mighty rivers are formed. Rivers begin in the mountains and hills in tiny rivulets and creeks (evidence), which then flow together (the reasoning process) to form larger streams. Finally, these larger streams run together in a mighty river (the conclusion). Imagine that you wish to persuade your fellow townspeople that your city desperately needs a new hospital. In the diagram on page 338, the creeks represent your evidence, the paths taken to form streams represent the reasoning process, and the entire process results in a river—your conclusion.

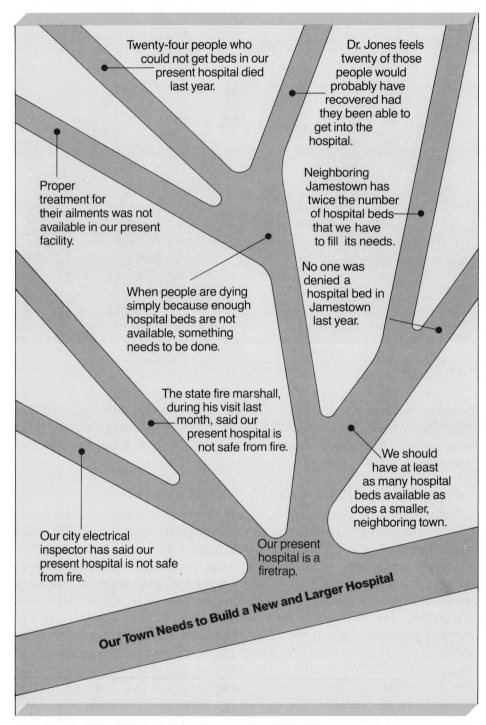

These streams of evidence and reasoning flow logically toward the conclusion: Our town needs to build a new and larger hospital.

To reach this conclusion, you must begin with good evidence. In Chapter 7, you studied a number of different types of evidence that can be used to support your arguments: facts, statistics, testimony, narrative, examples, and comparisons. The most persuasive evidence you can use generally consists of facts or statistics. Testimony, when the opinions are based upon facts, is also a very persuasive type of evidence. Notice how, in the diagram on page 338, the pieces of evidence are either statements of provable fact or opinions that can be backed by facts. Since support for a conclusion almost always begins with such evidence, a good persuader must be certain of the correctness of the evidence which is used throughout the argument.

Once you have chosen your evidence, use the process of reasoning to make sure that the evidence flows together logically to produce the conclusion you wish to reach. If you have given equally persuasive facts for and against your conclusion, you cannot expect your audience to agree with your conclusion. If your conclusion is based on three arguments but you have supported only one of them with evidence, you will also have difficulty in convincing your audience. If your evidence is weak or contrary to the practical experience of the audience, you are again likely to fail. To succeed, your reasoning must show how each piece of evidence works with the other pieces of evidence, how all of them together lead to one very definite conclusion—the conclusion you wish the audience to reach.

Make Your Evidence Suit Your Audience

Different forms of evidence are especially suitable for certain kinds of audiences. The chart on page 340 gives the four basic types of audiences and the kinds of evidence that are effective with each.

The positive audience needs recharging, not convincing. Anecdotes, examples, and comparisons seem most effective with such listeners. The neutral audience lacks information. They find examples helpful, but are likely to be more impressed with facts, statistics, and testimony. The disinterested audience must be given facts and statistics. They must be shown that a serious problem exists or is about to become critical and that it affects them. The opposed audience needs all the tools at the speaker's command. A speaker is wise to start with humor, common-ground devices, or compliments. An anecdote can also work well at the beginning. Once the listeners have decided to give the speaker a fair hearing, these can be followed with the harder forms of evidence (facts, statistics, examples, and comparisons). Mixed audiences react best when the speaker analyzes their needs correctly, then applies the various kinds of evidence in the best proportions. Correct reasoning is important no matter what type of audience you face. Logical reasoning is especially important, however, when facing an opposed audience.

Type of Audience	Kinds of Evidence
Positive	Narrative, Examples, Comparisons
Neutral	Facts, Statistics, Testimony, Examples
Disinterested	Facts, Statistics
Opposed	Narrative, Facts, Statistics, Examples, Comparisons

Identify the audience before gathering your persuasive evidence.

Application

Using Logic That Will Suit Your Audience

Look in your local newspaper for articles about organizations in your community. Locate information about two organizations and issues that are of interest to them. Imagine that you were invited to make a persuasive speech before each group. Make a chart that shows the kinds of evidence that would be most effective for each group.

Use a Logical Framework

Two of the speech patterns discussed in Chapter 7 provide an especially logical framework for persuasive speeches. These are the problem-solution pattern and Monroe's Motivated Sequence. You may want to review that section of Chapter 7, giving particular attention to these two patterns. Both offer certain ideas that may be useful in developing a logical strategy for your own persuasive speeches.

Whatever pattern you use, your persuasive speeches must have an introduction, a body, and a conclusion. These three basic parts of a speech, which were discussed in Chapter 10, serve similar functions in almost every speech. However, a special emphasis should be given to several specific functions in persuasive speeches. In the introduction, building your ethos becomes particularly important. In the body, it is essential to use valid evidence and correct reasoning. In the conclusion, you must reestablish your ethos and clearly indicate the response you desire from your audience. As you can see, building ethos, or establishing **prestige,** is especially important in persuasive speaking.

BEING RESPONSIBLE

Persuasive speaking is, in many ways, more difficult than speaking to inform. It demands detailed audience analysis, considerable research, and a well-planned strategy for building your prestige, particularly in the face of an opposed audience. For these reasons and others, persuasion has long been considered the highest level of public speaking. A speaker who can effectively persuade wields great influence over the minds of others. With this influence comes heavy responsibility as well.

Persuasive speaking is one of the major ways in which decisions are reached in a free society. The President of the United States attempts to persuade the American public to adopt a plan for fighting inflation. Members of Congress attempt to persuade one another to vote for or against the passage of an important bill. Business leaders work constantly to persuade customers to buy. Citizens have the opportunity to persuade each other to vote for particular candidates in each election. Responsible persuasive speaking is necessary if such a society is to function well.

Centuries ago, the Roman rhetorician, Quintilian, defined the ideal orator as "a good man skilled in speaking." In doing so, he placed major focus on good character as the primary requirement for effective persuasive speaking. Being a responsible persuader does not guarantee you will always be right in what you advocate to an audience, but it does mean you honestly *believe* you are right. If you try to convince your neighbors to vote against a property tax increase, for example, you should sincerely believe that a tax increase is unwise at the moment, and not just wish to avoid paying higher taxes. If you are asking a group of people to vote for you, you should believe honestly that you are the best-qualified candidate, and not wish simply to increase your own personal power.

Responsible persuasion can mean different things to different people. For centuries, however, most persuaders have agreed on certain ethical standards, without which the process of persuasion loses much of its value. At the top of the list is the belief that any form of deception is wrong. You should be honest. Don't present false evidence. Don't present the ideas of others as if they were your own. Don't appeal to the emotions of your listeners without any basis in fact. Don't pose as an authority if you are not. These forms of deception are considered both irresponsible and unethical. Responsible persuasion means telling the truth as you have discovered it.

11 Chapter Review

Summary

The primary goal of persuasive speaking is to influence the attitudes, beliefs, or behavior of the listeners. To do this, a speaker must combine the skills needed to give an informative speech with a number of additional skills that are special to persuasive speaking.

Three Sources of Persuasion   Persuasive speaking involves making an audience want to think, believe, or do something they might not have done otherwise. The three major factors that are most likely to influence people are their own needs, their own thinking processes, and the character and personality of the speaker. Thus, a persuasive speaker must appeal to personal needs and logic, while stressing his or her own prestige.

Pathos: Analyzing the Needs of Your Listeners   To appeal to listener needs, you must first discover what those needs are. Knowing whether you face a positive, neutral, disinterested, or opposed audience —or some combination of these four—can help you determine what strategy to use.

Ethos: Establishing Your Prestige   The speaker's prestige (ethos) has long been accepted as a powerful, persuasive influence. In order to achieve this kind of prestige a speaker must be seen as competent and sincere and must clearly act with good will toward the audience. Methods of building speaker prestige include making frequent references to evidence, noting your experience in the topic area, being convinced of the truth of your viewoint, using the common-ground technique, and showing sincere appreciation of your audience.

Logos: Being Logical   Logical appeals consist of the proper use of evidence and reasoning. Evidence is the raw material upon which arguments are based. Reasoning is the process of putting evidence together into larger conclusions which in turn prove the main points of your speech. Certain forms of evidence may prove more effective with different kinds of audiences. Anecdotes, examples, and comparisons work well with positive audiences. A neutral audience is generally most impressed by statistics, facts, and testimony. Disinterested listeners also need facts and statistics. The opposed listener usually requires all forms of evidence at the speaker's command.

Being Responsible   The ability to persuade others is a powerful tool and carries with it a heavy responsibility. Decisions in a free society are regularly reached through persuasive speaking. Therefore, those who wish to persuade must not only know the best techniques but must practice them ethically. Any form of deceit in persuasion will be discovered and does harm to the democratic decision-making process.

 Vocabulary

Define each term in a complete sentence.

questions of fact	logos	confidence
questions of value	positive audience	sincerity
questions of policy	neutral audience	good will
persuasion	disinterested audience	evidence
pathos	opposed audience	reasoning
ethos	competence	prestige

 Checklist

Skills of Persuasive Speaking

1. Realize the primary goal of a persuasive speech.
2. Know when to use a particular type of persuasive speech.
3. Understand the three primary sources of persuasion.
4. Show your audience that you are competent and confident.
5. Be sincere and show good will toward your audience.
6. Use valid evidence and correct reasoning.
7. Use evidence that suits your audience.
8. Be responsible when speaking to persuade.

Review Questions

1. Name the primary goal of a persuasive speech.
2. Name the factors that cause people to adopt attitudes, beliefs, or behavior patterns.
3. State why audience analysis is especially important for a persuasive speaker.
4. Describe the chief characteristics of each kind of audience: positive, neutral, disinterested, opposed.
5. Name the approach a speaker should use to persuade each kind of audience.
6. Name and define the two components of logic.
7. Describe the differences between evidence and reasoning.
8. Describe the types of evidence that are especially suited to each type of audience.
9. Describe three ways in which you can establish your prestige as a persuasive speaker.
10. Name the characteristics of a responsible speaker.

Discussion Questions

1. Discuss the role that persuasion plays in a free society. In what sense is the right to persuade at the heart of the democratic process? What is the connection between persuasion and the right to speak out? Under what circumstances could persuasion be used for harmful purposes?
2. Discuss the responsibilities that accompany the right to persuade. Why is responsibility a key factor in evaluating a persuasive speaker? In what ways must the persuasive speaker be responsible? Why did the Roman orator Quintilian say that the persuasive speaker is "a *good* man skilled in speaking"?
3. Discuss the importance of evidence and reasoning in the persuasive process. How does the prestige of the speaker affect evidence and reasoning? Can the prestige of the speaker ever be a substitute for evidence and reasoning?
4. Discuss the role of the listener in the persuasive process. What should the listener concentrate upon? Does the listener have responsibilities as a target of persuasion? What might they be?

5. Discuss the challenges that the persuasive speaker faces when the audience is disinterested. What techniques can the speaker use to interest such an audience?

■ Critical Thinking

1. Comprehension: Can a speech be both informative and persuasive? How? Can it be persuasive without being informative? How? Can a persuasive speech be informative without being persuasive? How?

2. Analysis: Think of the many commercials that you have seen on television. How do ethos, pathos, and logos operate in these commercials? At which of these sources of persuasion do many commercials seem to be aimed?

■ Activities

In-Class

1. After a brief period of preparation, present a two-minute persuasive speech in which you advance one argument to support your position. Choose a topic that you have already thought about a great deal. Support your argument with at least three types of evidence. Your speech should also present sound reasoning and strong emotional appeal. Present your speech first to a group of from five to seven. Receive feedback and make any necessary adjustments. Then present your speech to the entire class.

2. Conduct a class discussion about credibility. Agree on a list of at least five public figures who possess credibility. Then determine what it is about the people that makes them credible. What characteristics do these people have that cause you to think well of them and to believe them? What role does appearance play in your feelings? What role does their status or position play? What role does past performance play? Try to assemble a list of characteristics that credible people possess.

3. As a class, decide upon a persuasive topic that everyone is knowledgeable about and can support. The class might agree, for example, that recreational programs should be offered in the schools on Friday evenings. Then divide the class into three groups. One group should prepare an introduction for the speech as if it were to be given to a friendly audience. The next group should prepare an introduction for a disinterested audience. Finally, the third group should prepare one for an opposed audience. Present the introductions to the class as a whole. Discuss the merits of each introduction that is presented.

4. Select two members of the class to improvise a skit in which one of them plays the customer and the other the sales representative in an automobile dealership. They should act out a scene in which the sales representative tries to persuade the customer to purchase the car. After the skit, discuss the message that it contains for persuasive speakers. Pay particular attention to how the salesperson tried to make the product appealing to the customer. As you analyze the exchange that took place, keep the following question in mind: "Whose benefit appeared to be most important during the exchange?"

5. As a class, identify at least three issues that are being discussed in your community at this time. For each issue, develop a question of fact, a question of value, and a question of policy that could give rise to persuasive speeches about the issue. Then compare the questions developed with the written arguments and speeches that have already been made about each issue.

Out-of-Class

1. Visit at least three stores to examine and request information about a product that has to be explained (a VCR, for example, or a home computer or camera). Listen closely to the sales presentation that each salesperson makes. What level of credibility did each salesperson possess? Did the salesperson use logical appeals, or emotional appeals, or both? Did the salesperson let it be known that the product would benefit you? How was this done? Write a report about your experience in your speech notebook.

2. Identify an attitude or conviction that you once had that is now changed dramatically. For example, you might have once thought that summer jobs were to be avoided, but you now feel that a useful summer job would be most desirable. What was your original attitude? What is your current attitude? Who caused you to change your thinking, or what facts and arguments altered your belief? Write an account of this change in attitude in your speech notebook. Be sure to identify its causes as fully as possible.

3. Certain contemporary speakers are widely acknowledged to possess the magical quality of "charisma." Identify one speaker who possesses that quality, in your opinion. Identify the things the person says and the way the person says them that suggest charisma. What kinds of actions and statements do you expect that person to make? Do you have high expectations about that individual? Briefly summarize your impressions and observations in your speech notebook.

4. In your speech notebook, keep a log of the times you personally use the process of persuasion during a single day. Log both one-to-one exchanges and group presentations. Do not overlook minor efforts to persuade parents, brothers and sisters, friends, and teachers. Also, keep a log of the times that other people attempt to persuade you during an ordinary day. Be prepared to bring both logs to class to compare with those of your classmates.

Chapter Project

Prepare a five- to seven-minute persuasive speech that will be delivered in class extemporaneously. Choose a topic on an issue that you feel strongly about and that you believe will interest the student audience. Research your topic thoroughly, gathering as many types of support as possible. Keep your evidence on note cards and outline your speech, perhaps using Monroe's Motivated Sequence as an organizing principle. Write an introduction and a conclusion and memorize them. Rehearse the speech at least five times and deliver it in class.

12 Other Kinds of Speaking

**When you have completed this chapter
you should be able to:**

- Explain the general purposes of speeches for special situations.
- Define the specific purposes of several kinds of speeches focused on persons.
- Define the purposes of several kinds of speeches for special occasions.
- Describe the essential difference between impromptu speaking and other kinds of speeches covered in this chapter.
- Deliver an impromptu speech in class.

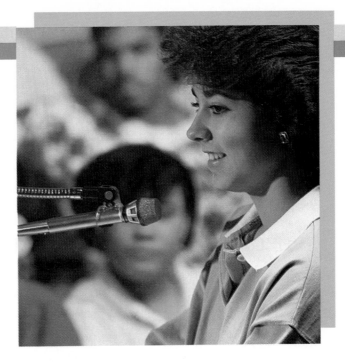

Special events, such as commemorating a new gym or graduating from high school, call for special kinds of speeches.

"Ladies and gentlemen, it is my great pleasure and distinct honor to introduce . . ." "How do I find the words to thank you adequately, my friends for so many years . . ." "Today is a sad day for those of us who knew and loved her, but for Betty it is a day of glory and unending joy . . ." "So, as you leave these halls of learning and step into the wider world of danger and opportunity . . ." Each of these lines comes from speeches given every day—speeches of introduction, speeches of acceptance, commemorative speeches, commencement speeches. Though informing and persuading are the two primary purposes for which public speeches are given, you will be faced with many occasions on which you are expected to introduce a speaker, honor a fellow worker who is leaving, express a public "thank you" for a gift, deliver a keynote speech at school, or give an impromptu speech without advance warning. This chapter will give you some suggestions about these special kinds of speech situations under two categories—speeches focused on persons; and speeches for special occasions. Although you will find elements of informing and persuading in nearly all of these special situation speeches, that is not their primary purpose. Typically their chief purpose is to inspire, to challenge, to honor, to entertain. They are given to make us feel good about ourselves and those around us.

Because the purpose of such speeches differs from that of informative and persuasive speeches, you must focus on different speaking skills when giving special situation speeches. All of the skills of researching, finding supporting materials, organizing your speech, building ethos, and the like, certainly remain important. However, in most speeches for special situations, you will want to put more focus on your speech skills of language usage, memory, and delivery. Vivid language is important to inspire the audience and to make the speech occasion a celebration. Well-chosen words help you to highlight the formality and seriousness of most special situation speeches. Memorizing brief, but key portions of these speeches also adds impact to the speaker's delivery. Reading even short portions from manuscript detracts greatly from the listeners' feelings about the speaker's sincerity.

SPEECHES FOCUSED ON PERSONS

Has it ever occurred to you to ask yourself, as you sat through what seemed an unending funeral oration or a tedious commencement speech, "Why do we bother with such speeches at all"? They can seem endless and boring to those not directly involved with the person or people being honored, but when it is your grandfather being honored, or your own graduation ceremony, it usually means a great deal more. We honor those who have achieved great things because we value what they have accomplished. We could privately hand a terrific swimming coach who is leaving our school a watch or a plaque without saying a word. That would honor the coach to some extent, but a public speech accompanying the plaque makes it an occasion. The coach is more fittingly thanked with the gift *and* the speech, and those who hear the speech are again reminded of the importance of those qualities the coach showed—kindness, patience, leadership, and concern for her swimmers.

Though there are several additional types of speeches that focus on persons, probably those given most frequently are speeches of introduction, speeches of presentation, speeches of acceptance, and commemorative speeches honoring persons. You should know the purpose of each of these kinds of speeches and some guidelines for delivering them.

Speeches of Introduction

Speeches of introduction are intended to say to the audience "You will benefit from listening to this speaker." They should also tell the speaker "This audience is anxious to hear your speech." The two major purposes facing someone who introduces a guest speaker, however, are:

- To build enthusiasm for the guest speaker by establishing his or her credibility.
- To build audience interest in the guest speaker's topic.

While this trophy represents a winning record, a speech honoring these players is a tribute to their efforts as individuals and as a team.

Too often those giving speeches of introduction make little or no preparation and simply read a few lines from a speaker's résumé to the audience. Such an approach does little to fulfill either of the basic purposes, and cheats both the guest speaker and the audience. Following a few guidelines when preparing a speech of introduction can make a tremendous difference.

First, keep speeches of introduction brief. They typically last from thirty seconds to three minutes. If the speaker is already well-known to the audience, thirty seconds is enough. An extreme example of a too-long introduction occurred during World War I. When Lord Balfour, Britain's Foreign Secretary, was to give a major speech at a rally in the United States, the speaker who introduced him gave a 45-minute oration on the causes of the war. When Lord Balfour finally got the opportunity to speak, he said: "I'm supposed to give my address in the brief time remaining. Here it is: 10 Carleton Gardens, London, England." Imagine the embarrassment of his introducer!

Second, be absolutely accurate. Start with your pronunciation of the speaker's name. Nothing can more surely destroy the impact of an otherwise superb speech of introduction than to mispronounce the main speaker's name. If you think you might forget it, have it in front of you in writing. If it is a difficult name to pronounce, be certain to learn the correct pronunciation beforehand, then practice it. Be certain that you know the basic facts about the speaker's background. Since speeches of introduction are brief, you should have no problems with memory. However, if you think there is any chance you may forget an important fact, or reverse the order of some facts, bring a brief outline on a note card with you to the podium.

Next, suit your level of formality to the occasion. Obviously, you would be more formal and restrained were you selected to introduce one of your teachers as the main speaker for a PTA meeting, than you would when introducing him or her to lead a roast for a departing school principal. Your language would undoubtedly be more formal and serious in the first case, as would the whole tone of your introduction. For the roast, a more informal approach would be appropriate.

Make the speaker you are introducing feel good. Not only are you trying to generate enthusiasm in the audience, you also want your introduction to serve as a springboard from which the speaker can launch an inspiring speech. Be factual about his or her accomplishments and show how the speaker's background and experience have prepared him or her to speak with authority on this topic. Be wary of overdoing it. Don't embarrass the speaker with excessive praise. Be especially careful not to praise his or her speaking skills. Telling the audience that they are about to hear one of the greatest speakers of the last decade starts the poor speaker off with little or no chance of succeeding. Finally, don't reveal personal incidents of the speaker's life that could be embarrassing. Sometimes this is done in an attempt to get a laugh: "Why, I've known Seth Mobley since he was the dumbest kid in the fifth grade. How he ever managed to become a lawyer is still a mystery to me!" The audience may laugh, but Seth won't come to the podium feeling good about himself and his speech.

The introducer should also show the listeners the relationships among the speaker's background, the chosen topic, and the audience's interests. This is the basic job description of an introducer. An introduction that simply lists the accomplishments of the speaker and stops, fails to fulfill its basic purpose. What each audience member wants to know from an introducer is "Why will this speaker, speaking on this topic, be interesting to me?" A competent introducer shows why the speaker's background qualifies him or her to speak on this particular topic, and why it will prove interesting to this particular audience. Too often, an introducer fails to discover in advance what topic the speaker plans to talk about.

This makes it difficult to tie the speaker's topic and the audience's interests together. The wise introducer will always check with the main speaker several days before the speech occasion to learn not only what the topic will be, but what approach the speaker plans to take.

Finally, work to build a feeling of expectation and drama among the members of the audience. Speeches of introduction are similar to an appetizer before a meal. Both tease the taste buds in anticipation of the main course to come. Probably the most common technique for doing this in speeches of introduction is that of saving the name of the main speaker until the end of the introduction. This works best, of course, when the speaker is not already well-known to most members of the audience. At any rate, introducers use this strategy to make the speaker's name the high point of the introduction. In those cases in which most of the audience already knows the speaker, it is best to concentrate on discovering little-known facts about the speaker's background and to focus on the topic. It is also effective to mention lesser-known facts about the speaker's background that relate to his or her knowledge and expertise on the topic.

Generating a sense of expectation and drama requires a well-rehearsed speech of introduction. Many introducers neglect to rehearse a single time because they are "just" the introducer. The brevity of speeches of introduction seems to lull many people into a false sense of preparedness. Though there is little chance of forgetting, remember that the effectiveness of such speeches relies on language usage, memory, and delivery factors. Each of these requires thorough rehearsal.

Application

Speeches of Introduction

Plan and deliver a speech of introduction for one of the following occasions.

1. a sports superstar speaking at a high-school assembly

2. a representative from a major university addressing your class about planning for college

3. a recruitment officer speaking at a career day about opportunities in the military

4. a magician performing at an elementary-school assembly

5. a police-department safety officer speaking to a driver-education class

Speeches of Presentation

Frequently, when people receive gifts or awards, there is need for a **speech of presentation.** Typical examples include awards ceremonies at the end of a school year; the Tony, Emmy, and Oscar awards; and those countless occasions when gifts are presented to friends who are moving, retiring, or completing a term of office. The primary purpose of a speech of presentation is, of course, to honor the recipient. Secondary purposes (when necessary) include explaining the purpose for which an award is being given and praising the losers in cases where there has been competition for an award.

Speeches of presentation are short, usually lasting no more than four or five minutes. In delivering very brief speeches, for example, when presenting a gift, the presentor typically asks the recipient to stand near the podium during the presentation speech. Then the award is presented. During longer speeches of presentation, ranging up to four or five minutes, the recipient remains seated until the speech is completed. As in the case of speeches of introduction, the presentor should take care not to overpraise and risk embarrassing the recipient. It is usually best to restrict your remarks primarily to the actions or qualities of the recipient for which the award is being given.

An often-used pattern of organization for a speech of presentation consists of three parts. The speaker 1) describes the award and reads any engraved message with which the audience is not familiar; 2) indicates the values the award attempts to honor; and 3) shows how the actions and character of the recipient reflect those values. The order of the three parts may vary. Often a presentor will intertwine a description of the values with a recounting of the actions and character of the recipient. The description of the award may come first or last. No matter what pattern of organization is used, the chief purpose of a speech of presentation is to honor the recipient. Notice how effectively actor Gregory Peck honored Danny Kaye for his service to others:

It's a long trip from Brooklyn to Buckingham Palace, and it's a far piece from Beverly Hills to an obscure village in Bangladesh. Danny Kaye has made both journeys, sustained by his remarkable gifts, his grace, and his intelligence. He has been a star of the first magnitude since his remarkable talent exploded on the Broadway stage in *Lady in the Dark* in 1941, and one who has had a high sense of priority: His wife, Sylvia, and daughter, Dena, have always come first in his life—and then, in no special order, his work, the world's children, and great music.

For UNICEF (United Nations International Children's Emergency Fund), he continues to travel the world, bringing joy and hope to children on all the continents, and initiating programs to save them from hunger and give them a better chance in life. He has been doing this for years, with no pay and without fanfare. No trumpets. No headlines. His reward, the laughter of children.

As forbearing and skillful as he is with children, so he is with symphony orchestras, groups of seventy or eighty highly disciplined artists. He cannot read music, yet he has conducted major orchestras all over the world with musicianship that is sensitive, completely serious, and, at times, likely to veer off alarmingly into the hilarious. Danny's irrepressible *joie de vivre* makes his concerts joyous occasions for musicians and audiences alike. Bach and Mozart have no better friend. Nor have the orchestras and their pension funds. Nor have we.

And thus, for his prodigious labors for the children of the world, for the wondrous people who make music, the Board of Governors proudly gives the Jean Hersholt Humanitarian Award to a "Citizen of the World" who does honor to our profession—Mr. Danny Kaye.

Speeches of Acceptance

If you have watched such ceremonies as the Academy Awards, the Emmys, or the Tonys on television, you know that acceptance speeches can take many forms and can vary in length from a simple "thank you" to

An award honors the recipient for accomplishment. When receiving an award, be prepared to give a brief and gracious acceptance speech.

a lengthy monologue. **Speeches of acceptance,** in their ideal form, however, have the simple purpose of thanking both those bestowing the award and those who helped the recipient gain it. If you have any doubt whether or not you are expected to give a speech when accepting an award, ask the presentor for advice. Most audiences respond favorably to a speech of acceptance, as long as it is *brief.* Unless it is clear that the award is expected to serve as the introduction for a major speech, keep acceptance speeches to no more than two or three minutes. Also bear in mind that an acceptance speech is given for the audience's benefit. It is an acknowledgement that the award has been accepted and appreciated.

Sometimes you will be taken by surprise by the presentation of an award. When that happens, you have no choice but to speak impromptu (See *impromptu speaking,* on page 368.). Whenever you think there is a reasonable chance that you might receive a gift or award, prepare a brief speech of acceptance in advance. Be certain to thank everyone involved in both presenting and helping you attain the award. You may also modestly mention your commitment, and that of others, to the values and actions for which the award is given, but place the focus on the values and actions, not on yourself. The speech that follows is Danny Kaye's acceptance speech given after the presentation speech, quoted on pages 354–355, by Gregory Peck. Notice that Mr. Kaye's speech is brief, humble, and gracious.

> I am terribly excited to be given this great honor. And I'm so delighted that I find myself, as we say, trembling. If I were any more delighted, I think I'd be in an institution.
>
> However, I feel a little bit guilty about all the praise that Greg lavished on me. It was really no hardship at all. Really. I am crazy about children. I am crazy about conducting, and I am crazy about flying.
>
> I am definitely not crazy about disease or famine or neglect. But, then, neither are any of you. And we, all of us in our profession, share a long and wonderful tradition of doing something about it—of giving of our time and our talent wherever and whenever needed—without prejudice, without stint. That's one of the reasons that I am so very proud of our profession and so proud to be one of you.
>
> I share this award with you, with all of you, and I give thanks to the memory of Dag Hammarskjold and Maurice Pate, with whom I started to work for UNICEF about twenty-eight years ago. And to Gene Ormandy, who put a baton in my hand, my little nervous hand, and made me an offer I couldn't refuse—to stand in front of a symphony orchestra and conduct. Wow! That's the greatest feeling of neurotic power in the world. You ought to try it!
>
> My special thanks to the Board of Governors. I love this and I love you. Thank you.

Commemorative Speeches

Commemorative speeches remain among the most inspiring and best remembered in our country's history. Abraham Lincoln's Gettysburg Address, Edward Kennedy's speech at his brother Robert's funeral, and Ronald Reagan's speech following the Challenger disaster served to implant the memory of brave people in our minds and to inspire us to reach for the ideals for which they stood. Though commemorative speeches sometimes recall events rather than persons, here we will look at those that are focused exclusively on persons—testimonial speeches and eulogies.

Testimonial speeches are given to honor living persons. Their purpose is to praise someone or to celebrate an occasion focused around persons. You may hear testimonial speeches given in the form of toasts at weddings and retirement dinners, as speeches of farewell and appreciation when a boss or co-worker is moving away, or as roasts for those successful and well-liked in their careers. They may range in length from a toast of a few seconds to a roast with a dozen or more speakers taking five to ten minutes each to honor an individual with tongue-in-cheek humor. Most often they are given in connection with a dinner, or at least when food is being served—for example, at a wedding reception.

The testimonial speaker deals in feelings, not facts. He or she tries to stir emotions, not thoughts. Though the speaker may narrate some scenes from the life of the person being honored, the purpose is to generate respect, admiration, appreciation, and best wishes for the future. The speaker will evoke joy, laughter, celebration, and sentiment from the audience while honoring the special person. Testimonial speakers depend heavily on the creative use of language. If an informative speaker can be compared to an essayist, the testimonial speaker is like a poet. A good testimonial speaker chooses language rich in connotation and steeped in emotion to create a warm and positive mood fitting the occasion.

When humor is used, as is the case at roasts, its purpose should always be to honor the individual for whom the roast is given. Occasionally speakers at roasts, keen on getting laughs from the audience, will relate a funny incident that is truly embarrassing. Such an approach does not honor the person, and usually harms the speaker's image in the audience's eyes, even though the listeners will laugh at the joke. If you are asked to speak at a roast, pick humor that you know will genuinely amuse the roastee as well as the audience. If you have any doubt, either ask the roastee privately beforehand, or skip that particular story.

Eulogies are commemorative speeches, given usually to honor those who have died. Though they are most often delivered at a funeral service, they may be given weeks, months, or even years later. As with testimonial speeches, their purpose is to honor and praise an individual. An equally important purpose of eulogies is to comfort and uplift the listeners who feel the loss of a loved one or a great person. The eulogist has a difficult task since emotions of sorrow and loss are usually high in the audience. The eulogist must respect those feelings while attempting to inspire those present by recounting the virtues of the deceased.

The eulogist typically picks out several of the most noble and praiseworthy attributes of the deceased and extols them with examples from the person's life. The eulogist may also call upon the listeners to remember and imitate those virtues. However, the essence of a eulogy is to honor the person who has died. As with testimonial speeches honoring the living, the most important tool for the eulogist is lofty language. Great care must be taken to select words and phrases that are noble, dignified, and moving. Notice how Adlai Stevenson, one of this country's most eloquent speakers, used such language at a memorial service for Sir Winston Churchill.

> Today we meet in sadness to mourn one of the world's greatest citizens. Sir Winston Churchill is dead. The voice that led nations, raised armies, inspired victories and blew fresh courage into the hearts of men is silenced. We shall hear no longer the remembered eloquence and wit, the old courage and defiance, the robust serenity of indomitable faith. Our world is thus poorer, our political dialogue is diminished and the sources of public inspiration run more thinly for all of us. There is a lonesome place against the sky.

Because the eulogy depends so much on eloquent language, it is often written in advance, then delivered from manuscript or memory. Experienced speakers will occasionally use a combination of read, memorized, and extemporaneous delivery with excellent effect. The following example of a eulogy was given by a student in a public speaking class, honoring her grandfather. It exemplifies the best features of a dignified and moving eulogy:

My Grandfather
Kim Lacina

Every day people are born and people die. Human beings come into this world and leave it—most without their names being immortalized in any history books. Millions of people have lived and worked and loved and died without making any great claims to fame or fortune.

But they aren't forgotten—not by their friends, not by their families. And some of these people, some very special people, are not forgotten

COACH

Coaches of sports teams at any level direct participants through the entire competitive experience. They must be experienced players of the sport they are coaching and must be familiar with its strategies and regulations. Above all, coaches need excellent communications skills, since they not only deal with the players on their teams, but with the public as well.

Often coaches must deliver speeches of acceptance or presentation. To prepare for these speeches, coaches list the topics they plan to discuss on a note card. When they deliver their speech, the note card helps to focus their thoughts. To convey their enthusiasm more powerfully, coaches memorize their introductory and concluding remarks to maintain direct eye contact with the audience. As part of their final preparation, they rehearse their speech using the note card as their only aid.

During speeches of presentation, coaches honor individual players and those inner qualities that contributed to the success of the individual and the team. By recognizing team members, coaches reinforce the characteristics and values they have been stressing all season.

Coaches who are successful public speakers add an invaluable dimension to their coaching abilities. By honoring athletes, coaches inspire others to emulate their admirable qualities. When rousing the team before a competition, the coach's choice of words and spirited delivery stimulate players to greater achievement. In these ways, a coach's speaking ability enables him or her to help young athletes realize their potential.

This coach is skilled at giving speeches that inspire and honor others.

even by those who hardly knew them. My grandfather was one of these very special people.

What made him so special? Why is he remembered not only by friends and family but even by casual acquaintances? Very simply, because he was the essence of love. More than that, he was the essence of what I think of as "active" love. Just as his heart was not empty, his words were not empty.

He didn't just speak of compassion. During the Great Depression he took homeless people off the street into his home when they needed a place to sleep. He gave them food when they needed something to eat. And though he wasn't a rich man by any means, he gave them money when they had none. Those people off the street will remember the man who had enough love in his heart to share with them all that he had.

He didn't just speak of tolerance. During the 1960s, when his peers were condemning those "long-haired hippies," I can remember riding in the car with my grandfather, picking up dozens and dozens of those "long-haired hippies" who were hitchhiking, and going miles out of our way to give them a ride somewhere. Those men and women will remember the man who had enough love in his heart to bridge the gap between his world and theirs and to practice the spirit of brotherhood.

And he didn't just speak of courage. He proved his courage time and time again. He proved it to a little girl who was trapped in the basement of a burning building. He pullled her out of the flames and gave her back her life. And that little girl, now a grown woman, will remember the man who had enough love in his heart to risk his life for a person he didn't even know.

He also proved his courage, in a more personal way, to his family. In 1966 he was told he had leukemia and only a year to live. He immediately started chemotherapy treatment, and I don't know which is worse—the effects of the disease or the effects of those treatments. In the ensuing year we saw his hair fall out, we saw his skin turn a pasty shade of gray, and we saw him lose so much weight that he seemed to shrivel up into half the size he had been. We didn't want to see him go out that way.

And we didn't. He fought that disease with all his strength and all his courage. And despite the pain he endured, he never complained. I think about him when I catch myself complaining about my "tons of homework" or a "terrible headache," and suddenly that homework or that headache doesn't seem so terrible after all.

He lived through that first year, and he lived through eight more. And that disease never stopped him from working, and it never stopped him from caring. All through those years of suffering, he continued to show compassion and tolerance and courage.

He died in 1975. And though he left this world without ever making the pages of a history book, he still left the world a great deal. He left to the people who knew him a spirit to exemplify life—a spirit of unconditional, selfless, and truly inspiring love.

Commemorative Speeches

Write and deliver a commemorative speech—either a testimonial or a eulogy. Your primary purpose will be to inspire, to challenge, or to honor. You may select as your subject a historical figure, a famous person, or someone known to you personally. Plan your speech to be from three to five minutes long. Focus on making your language and delivery appropriate to the purpose and person you have chosen.

SPEECHES FOR SPECIAL OCCASIONS

Various kinds of public occasions are highlighted by speeches. Graduation ceremonies, large meetings and conventions, dedication ceremonies, and some public lectures employ a speech as a focal point of the event. Generally, the purpose of such speeches is to commemorate the meeting or ceremony that is taking place. We will look briefly at five kinds of special occasion speeches: keynote speeches, commencement speeches, dedication speeches, public relations speeches, and speeches to entertain. Finally, we will consider a special way of delivering speeches— impromptu speaking.

Keynote Speeches

Meetings or conventions of many large organizations begin with a **keynote speech.** Most Americans are familiar with the keynote addresses delivered near the opening of the Democratic and Republican conventions every four years. In addition to these political speeches, keynote addresses occur regularly at business and professional conventions ranging from those of the American Medical Association to those of the National Association of Teachers of English. Keynote speeches serve several purposes. First, they rally the members of the organization around its central goals and purposes. Since such large organizations typically meet only once a year, the keynote address opens each new convention by renewing the enthusiasm and commitment of the membership to its values and purposes. Second, they provide a common theme or focus for the particular meeting that year. The speaker will sometimes need to stress the specific goals and issues facing the organization in the upcoming year. On other occasions the need may be to sound a call for unity if the organization is threatening to splinter apart. Still other circumstances may demand that the keynote address focus on a crisis facing the organization and stress the importance of this year's convention in meeting it. Finally, since a keynote speech usually provides the central focus for a convention, it also commemorates it. Such speeches later come to stand for the themes or highlights of past conventions.

The keynote speaker is usually either a well-respected member of the organization, or some well-known person from the outside who has great credibility with the members. The keynote speaker's job is that of a cheerleader, molding the members into an enthusiastic and involved group.

Commencement Speeches

Commencement speakers often have a difficult time keeping the attention of their listeners. Graduation ceremonies are often held outdoors in late spring or in a sweltering gymnasium packed with graduates, teachers, families, and friends. Nearly everyone in attendance wants to be there, but not for very long!

Commencement speeches both celebrate an occasion and honor the graduates. Their purposes are to applaud the accomplishments of the students while in school, recognize the contributions of those who

This commencement speaker strikes a lively balance between the past and the future, memories and challenges, humor and seriousness.

362

helped them, and tell the graduates of the challenges ahead. Since the word "commencement" means a beginning, most commencement speakers spend the bulk of their time inspiring the graduates to meet their new challenges and responsibilities. Typically a commencement speaker gives a great deal of advice about the future. However, too much stress on advice and the future can quickly wear the audience's patience thin. A graduation ceremony is also a celebration and a time to honor the graduates. When that part gets lost amid an undergrowth of endless advice, especially in a hot and crowded gym, the speaker can quickly lose the attention of the audience.

For several years, you are more likely to sit in the listener's chair at commencement speeches than you are to stand behind the podium. However, you may find some real benefit from giving a commencement speech in class. Try the following application.

Application

Giving a Commencement Speech

Imagine that you have been invited to give the commencement speech at the graduation of the elementary school that you attended. Prepare notes for a three- to five-minute speech in which you briefly congratulate the graduates and those who assisted them. Spend some of your time telling the students how to get the most out of the years ahead of them. Use your own experiences in junior and senior high school to provide helpful and useful anecdotes for the graduates. Be prepared to give your speech in class and to compare your advice with that given by your classmates.

Dedication Speeches

Several dictionary definitions of the word "dedicate" read: "To set apart for any special use, duty, or purpose; To commit (oneself) to a certain course of action or thought; To open or unveil (a bridge, statue, etc.) to the public." Thus cities dedicate new city halls, schools, libraries, and parks. Citizens dedicate the opening of the annual United Way fund drive. Clubs dedicate their founding.

Public speeches make up the major part of dedication ceremonies. They serve to highlight the meaning of a new creation that is being dedicated, or a new endeavor that is being started. The dedication speaker focuses the listeners' attention on the goals and values that the new creation (building, bridge, piece of artwork) represents, or that the new endeavor (fund drive, new organization, Olympic Games) stands for. The length of **dedication speeches** may vary, depending mainly on the scope of the new creation or endeavor and on the expectations of the audience. Sometimes only one speaker will address those gathered for the ceremony; at other times there will be a series of briefer speeches.

When dedicating a new school gymnasium, for example, a speaker might briefly outline the history of the building project and mention the names of key school board members and administrators whose vision and planning resulted in the completed structure in which the audience is now seated. The speaker's main thrust, however, would be to stress what the new gym will mean to the school in the future. The speaker would note the importance of physical education in a school curriculum, then paint a picture of the stampede of eager students who can now begin to enjoy the new gym for generations. The speaker might recall the importance of "a sound mind in a sound body," then depict the pure fun that will now begin to come from basketball games, tennis, pep rallies, and dances. As with other speeches for special occasions, the speaker's success will depend largely on clear and lofty language, memorization of key passages, and a direct and dynamic delivery.

Public Relations Speeches

Do you remember any television commercials of several years ago? Certain restaurant chains were building their images as bigger and better than the competition. Today, business and industry spend a great amount of time and money on image building. They do it not only through television, but also by regularly sending their executives out on the lecture circuit. Carl Terzian, a consultant in executive speech training has noted that

> A growing number of executives not only are enthusiastically acknowledg-
> ing lecture requests, but are actually seeking them out. Influencing others
> is very rewarding. Some employ the platform to champion the cause of
> industry; to create a healthier business climate; to generate sales; to
> proclaim ambitious corporate goals; to promote an image . . .

In addition to corporations' increasing use of **public relations speeches,** or speeches that promote their companies, government service and educational institutions are also using this approach to maintain contact with the public and to promote a positive image.

Unlike the other special occasion speeches we have looked at, the public relations speech has a strong persuasive purpose. However, that purpose is not to sell a particular product or a specific service. Rather it is to promote an overall positive image of the organization. Such

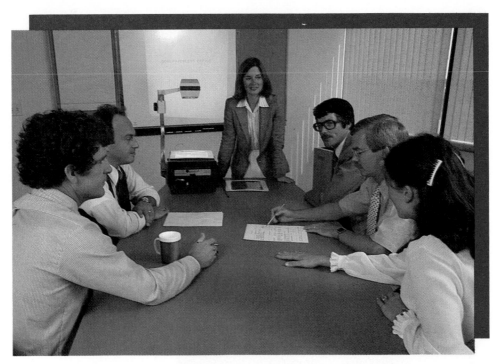

This public relations speaker is responsible for promoting her company's purpose and usefulness.

speeches often include a broad informative purpose as well, since promoting a positive image frequently demands giving the listeners facts about one's company.

A public relations speaker typically makes three general points. He or she outlines the goals and purposes of the organization; shows the audience how those goals tie in with their needs and values; and indicates how the organization can help people. At times, the public relations speaker may not only represent his or her own organization, but an entire group of similar organizations. For example, the speaker who works for a national retail chain may address the question "How can large retail chains recapture the spirit of the old country store?" Such a topic does not directly promote the company's products, or the products of other retailers, but it does help the consumer in the audience see giant chains as reaching for a more personal, down-home brand of service.

Speeches to Entertain

Many speakers, when delivering informative or persuasive speeches, use humor effectively. Only when the primary *purpose* of a speech is to cause the audience to relax, smile, and enjoy the occasion, however, do we label it a **speech to entertain.** Speeches to entertain are frequently called "after-dinner speeches," since they often form a program of entertainment following a banquet or meal. The after-dinner speech should have a theme or focus. Though the focus need not be as sharp as that of an informative or persuasive speaker's, there should be a central theme that the audience can pick out.

A comedian giving a monologue, on the other hand, can hop rapidly from one subject to another. The entertaining speaker cannot. Joe Creason, the late writer for the Louisville *Courier Journal,* often gave a highly entertaining speech dealing with a brand of humor that he found to be special to Kentucky. Though the humorous stories he related dealt with widely different situations, the theme that glued the speech together was "There is a special brand of Kentucky humor that is unlike that in other states."

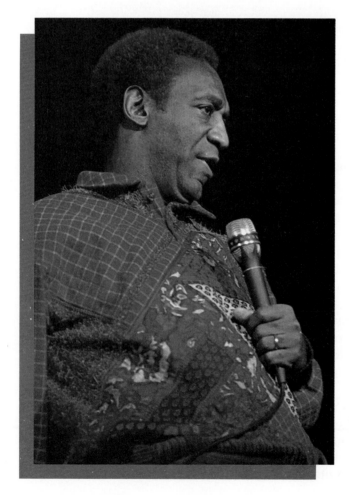

When speaking to entertain, Bill Cosby uses his unique humor to buoy a central theme that may be serious.

Originality should also mark a good speech to entertain. While speakers may insert material read or heard elsewhere, they should develop the general subject matter, the specific theme or focus, and much of the specific material of the speech themselves. Think for a moment of professional entertainers whose humor you especially enjoy. In most cases, each of them has developed his or her personalized approach to getting laughs. One tells funny stories on himself or herself; another focuses regularly on certain topics such as money problems or politics; a third always works with another person and uses dialogue to entertain the audience. An entertaining speaker, too, needs to develop an original, individual style and approach that suits his or her personality. Much of the speech material should also be developed by the speaker. The entertaining speaker who simply tells the audience a series of stock jokes will usually not entertain very well. Good sources for humorous topics often come from looking at a familiar subjects from an unusual vantage point. Many topics that are usually looked at seriously have a humorous side when you search for it. Could you develop an entertaining speech from these topics and speech titles?

Topic	Entertaining Theme
Summer jobs	"Summer jobs for high schoolers: The daily diary of the American nightmare."
Taking tests	"What tests *really* mean to teachers."
Camping out	"Petrified in a pup tent: The night the rattlesnake came in from the cold."

Of course some of your specific stories and examples will have to come from other sources. Audiences do not expect every sentence in a speech to entertain to originate from the speaker's personal experience. If you develop an overall approach and style that fits you, and use a great deal of original material, your listeners should enjoy the speech. Many entertaining speakers will take a humorous story they have heard or read and retell it as if it happened to them or to some member of their audience. If this does not embarrass anyone in the audience, it is an effective technique. Consult your library if you need some good sources of humorous material.

As with other special occasion speeches, language and delivery are important in speaking to entertain. In making language choices, aim for vividness—words and images that paint pictures in the listeners' imaginations. Of course, your language should also be light, and appropriate for a relaxing occasion. Memorize as much of your material as you can, especially punchlines. Reading a punchline to an audience is far less effective than maintaining eye contact while speaking it. In addition, an extemporaneous delivery contributes a feeling of relaxation.

Nonverbal communication is an important part of delivery in speeches to entertain. Timing is particularly important. Knowing when to pause, and where to emphasize a point often makes a difference in whether your audience "gets it" or not. When the listeners laugh, wait until the laughter has subsided before you go on. Do not be discouraged if your audience does not laugh as often as you hoped or at the precise points you expected. Plan during rehearsal how you will react if several of your funniest lines should fall flat. Finally, remember that your job is basically to make your listeners relax and enjoy themselves. That does not always mean they have to be laughing nonstop.

Impromptu Speaking

The types of speeches for special occasions mentioned so far in this chapter (keynote, commencement, dedication, and public relations speeches) are just that—types of *speeches.* **Impromptu speaking,** on the other hand, is a *method* of speaking—a way of delivering any kind of speech. In Chapter 11 we compared impromptu speaking with manuscript, memorized, and extemporaneous delivery. We called it the kind of delivery one must use when called upon to speak with no advance notice and with only a moment or two for immediate preparation. In reality, you are giving an impromptu speech each time a teacher calls on you suddenly to "tell us what you think" in the midst of a class discussion. After you graduate, you will occasionally be asked to make a point or react to what someone has said in a public meeting or gathering. Ordinarily you will be asked to speak only about subjects with which you are fairly familiar. Sometimes you can do so informally, from your seat; at other times you will be expected to speak from a podium. Whatever the situation, the first rule to keep in mind is DON'T PANIC! When you realize that you have actually given a number of impromptu speeches in the classroom without knowing it, you can have confidence in your ability to speak off the cuff to other groups. Audiences don't expect impromptu speeches to be polished orations. They just want to hear your thoughts spoken in whatever language comes to you. They also do not expect to hear a lengthy impromptu speech. Listeners are nearly always sympathetic with public speakers, no matter whether they have had time for preparation or not. They are especially sympathetic with those speaking impromptu.

Though the flow of your words may not be as smooth as you would prefer when speaking impromptu, you can manage to sound well-organized. Here is a simple four-step plan of organization that will help you collect and present your thoughts, and that you can apply to most impromptu speaking situations:

1. State the point you are answering (if you have been asked to respond to a previous speaker).

2. *State* the main point you wish to make. You do not need to elaborate on your point.

3. Support the main point with appropriate examples, statistics, and testimony.

4. Summarize and restate your main point. (If your speech has been less than a minute in length, you may want to omit this step.)

In cases in which you are not responding to a previous speaker, simply eliminate step 1 and use only steps 2, 3, and 4.

Many of the impromptu "speeches" you are asked to give are really brief "statements" during meetings or conversations with friends. When, in a meeting of your school's yearbook staff, someone asks you: "Jamie, what 'look' do you feel the overall layout should promote this year?" everyone else falls silent waiting for your answer. That answer, however brief, is an impromptu speech. More formal occasions may call for more formal delivery and perhaps a longer speech, but they are essentially no different from the answer to the question about layout. Use the many opportunities that arise to give brief impromptu responses, take advantage of using the organizational pattern suggested above. Then, when you are asked to give a "bigger" impromptu speech, you will be an old hand at the basic method.

Application

Speeches to Entertain

As a class, plan an imaginary banquet that celebrates a specific event or occasion or honors a specific person. The banquet may mark the end of a sports season or a debate season, honor the birthday of a famous person, or acknowledge someone for a special contribution to your school or community. Prepare a list of speakers and assign students to introduce them. Simulate the banquet and have students introduce the speakers. If appropriate, awards may be given and accepted.

12 Chapter Review

■ Summary

Public speeches are given daily to honor persons and to celebrate special occasions. The primary purpose of such speeches is neither to inform nor persuade, but to inspire, challenge, honor, or entertain.

Speeches Focused on Persons Speeches of introduction are intended to build both audience enthusiasm for the main speaker and interest in the topic. They should be thoroughly prepared—but brief— and they should relate the main speaker's topic to the audience.

Speeches of presentation honor the recipient of an award and may also serve to explain the reasons for making the presentation. Recipients often make a brief acceptance speech, but should ask the presentor whether this is appropriate. Humility, brevity, and graciousness should characterize speeches of acceptance.

Commemorative speeches fall into two major types: testimonial speeches and eulogies. Testimonial speeches praise living persons or celebrate occasions focused upon persons, and they evoke joy, laughter, celebration, and sentiment. Eulogies are given to honor the dead and to console the living. They are often written in advance and delivered from manuscript or memory.

Speeches for Special Occasions Speeches given to mark special occasions include keynote speeches, commencement speeches, dedication speeches, public relation speeches, and speeches to entertain.

Keynote speeches often open large conventions or meetings of government, business, and professional groups. They serve to rally the members around the organization and commit them again to its goals.

The purpose of commencement speeches is to honor graduating students by noting their accomplishments, recognizing the contributions of those who have aided them, and elaborating on the challenges ahead.

Dedication speeches depend on clear and lofty language to highlight the meaning of a recent creation or a new endeavor. The speaker's job is to focus attention on the goals and values of the event.

Unlike most special occasion speeches, the public relations speech has a strong persuasive purpose: to promote a positive image of an organization. Public relations speakers typically outline the goals and purposes of their organizations, show how these tie in with the needs and values of their listeners, and indicate how their organizations can help.

Speeches to entertain, often called "after-dinner speeches," serve to relax an audience with humorous stories and vivid language. They differ from a comedian's monologue in that they have a theme or focus.

Impromptu speaking—speaking with no advance notice—is a method of speech delivery. In order to give an organized impromptu speech, speakers state the main point, give supporting evidence, and then summarize and restate the main point.

 ## Vocabulary

Define each term in a complete sentence.

speeches of introduction	keynote speeches
speeches of presentation	commencement speeches
speeches of acceptance	dedication speeches
commemorative speeches	public relations speeches
testimonial speeches	speeches to entertain
eulogies	impromptu speaking

 ## Checklist

Skills for Other Kinds of Speaking

1. Know the different purposes of speeches that relate to persons.
2. Be prepared when giving even the briefest speech.
3. Be accurate in pronouncing names and giving facts when you introduce a speaker.
4. Remember to suit your level of formality to the occasion.
5. Build feelings of expectation and drama in your audience.
6. Be poised when giving an impromptu speech.
7. Realize the fact that the testimonial speaker must appeal to the emotions of the audience.
8. Know the value of public relations speeches in business.

Review Questions

1. Describe the general purposes for which special situation speeches are usually given.
2. State why special situation speeches demand emphasis on the speech skills of language usage, memory, and delivery.
3. Name five types of special situation speeches that focus on persons.
4. Describe the specific purpose of each of the five kinds of speeches focused on persons.
5. State the appropriate length for each of the following kinds of speeches: introduction, presentation, acceptance, and testimonial.
6. Name five kinds of speeches for special occasions.
7. Describe the specific purpose of each kind of speech for special occasions.
8. Describe how public relations speeches and speeches to entertain differ from keynote, commencement, and dedication speeches.
9. State how impromptu speaking differs from everything else covered in this chapter.
10. Identify the first rule to remember when you are asked to speak impromptu.

Discussion Questions

1. What qualities characterize an admirable person? Each person in the class will name someone whom he or she admires and then provide three reasons why that person deserves respect. The person named may be living or dead, someone who is well known, or someone who is a personal aquaintance. Discuss the characteristics that all of those named have in common. What kinds of speaking occasions could this information be used in? What would be the purpose of speeches made to mark what these individuals represent or have accomplished?
2. Commemorative speeches are often made to honor special occasions, such as Independence Day and Veteran's Day. What special occasion is overlooked and should be honored? Discuss historical events you think should be honored because of their importance.
3. People are often honored in speeches of presentation be-

cause they have done things that have great historical significance, or they have made a worthwhile and obvious contribution to society. Are there any individuals and groups that you know of who work quietly and without fanfare, but who accomplish things of real value? Discuss overlooked and silent heroes who would be excellent people to honor with awards.

4. Discuss the tone that should be maintained in a eulogy. Should it be consistently somber and remind listeners of the sadness of the loss? Or may it also celebrate and recall the actions of the person being eulogized?

Critical Thinking

1. **Analysis:** Compare and contrast the impromptu speech and the extemporaneous speech. In what ways are they alike? In what ways are they different? What do listeners have a right to expect of an extemporaneous speaker? What should they expect of an impromptu speaker?

2. **Synthesis:** Imagine that you are in a position to give a public relations speech on behalf of an organization that you are connected with. It might be your school or a social, civic, or religious organization that you belong to. What three general points would you make in your speech? What kinds of things would you say in order to develop a positive image of the organization?

Activities

In-Class

1. Work with a partner. Invent a special award that will be presented in class. The award may be given for a genuine achievement, or it may be given for humorous reasons. One of you will present the award. The other will play the part of the recipient. Decide which role each of you will play. The pre-

senter will then plan a presentation speech and the recipient will prepare an acceptance speech. Present your speeches in class.

2. As you probably know, a "roast" is an event in honor of someone, during which humorous speeches are given that draw attention to the person's supposed faults. As a class, choose someone to roast. It might be a classmate, another student in your school, or a staff member. Be sure to choose someone whom everyone in the class is familiar with. Then work in groups of from five to seven. Each group must prepare a humorous speech that concentrates on some of the personal traits of the person being honored. Remember that the speeches are made in the spirit of good fun. Be sure that nothing is said to insult or embarrass the person being honored. Do whatever interviewing might be necessary to discover information about your subject. Choose someone from your group to give the speech in class.

3. As a class, develop a number of topics that are suitable for impromptu speeches. Some might deal with popular entertainment or sports figures. Others may be abstract concepts like "fairness" or "embarrassment" that the speaker will have to define. Still others may be drawn from recent newspaper headlines. Write each topic on a 3 × 5 index card and put the cards in a bag or box. Each student will go to the front of the class, draw a card, read the topic to the class, and speak on the topic for no longer than two minutes. The class will provide feedback and may wish to vote to determine the best impromptu speaker.

4. As a class, identify someone in your school or local community who is worthy of an "Unsung Hero Award." Instead of an individual, you might choose to honor an occupational group that performs a community service. Individuals and groups should be thoroughly discussed when they are proposed. Reach a consensus about the individual or group to be honored. Then discuss in detail the reasons why the person or group deserves to be honored. Appoint a small group of from five to seven to prepare a testimonial or presentation speech. You may consider honoring the person or group in class or at a school assembly.

Out-of-Class

1. Check standard speech anthologies or *Vital Speeches of the Day* to locate a commemorative speech. In your speech notebook, analyze the speech in depth, pointing out how it meets the criteria presented in this chapter. Be prepared to read the speech in class and to present an oral report of your analysis.

2. Assume that you have an opportunity to deliver a public relations speech on the value of training in speech communication. Choose a specific audience for your speech, such as a group of students who are considering taking a course, a civic group made up of owners of small businesses, or a parent-teacher organization. In your speech notebook, outline and assemble notes for your speech. Be sure that your speech presents the goals and purposes of a speech course, shows how the goals cater to the needs of those who will take the course, and demonstrates how such training will pay dividends in the future. Be prepared to give your speech in class. Describe the makeup of your imaginary audience before you begin.

3. Choose a famous historical figure, one whom you have always been interested in and whom you always wanted to find out more about. In your speech notebook, write a eulogy for this individual. Gather whatever information you need from standard biographical sources. Choose your language carefully and arrange your content for maximum emotional impact. Be prepared to deliver your eulogy in class.

Chapter Project

Choose a topic for a five- to seven-minute speech that is designed to entertain. Be sure to choose a topic that you personally find humorous. Outline your speech and gather whatever material you need to enhance the humorous content. Write and memorize the introduction, the conclusion, and the important transitions between sections. Rehearse the speech as frequently as you need in order to be at ease with it. Be prepared to deliver your speech in class.

Debate and Parliamentary Procedure

unit 5

13 Debate

14 Parliamentary Procedure

13 Debate

**When you have completed this chapter
you should be able to:**

- Explain the major differences between debate and discussion.
- Analyze a debate proposition.
- Find evidence to support logical reasoning when building a debate case.
- Describe different strategies that can be used by each side in a debate.

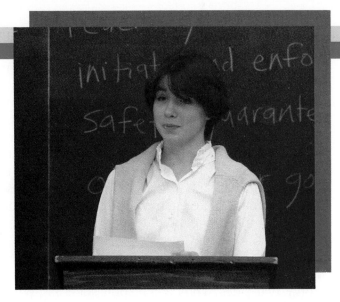

Opposing views are aired, examined, and resolved through the medium of debate.

The ancient Greeks were among the first to recognize the value of placing ideas in open competition in order to arrive at decisions about important matters. This same practice is followed today in legislatures and law courts. Debating is perhaps the most challenging form of oral communication in which you can engage.

The benefits you gain from participating in debate are many. Among the most important are the stimulation of your interest in current issues, the development of your critical thinking ability, the sharpening of your communication skills, and improvement in research abilities. In addition, you learn how thoughtful, positive, and orderly change may be brought about in a democratic society. Without the opportunity to decide matters and reduce conflict among ourselves through the clash of ideas, we would often be left with little choice but the clash of arms.

This chapter will introduce you to debate as a decision-making process and as a means of persuasive argument. Although this chapter will focus on **formal debate**—the kind used in school contests—you should be aware that any time you argue the strengths of two political candidates with your neighbor, speak for or against increasing the school budget, or take a stand on the energy issue, you are debating informally.

THE NATURE OF DEBATE

The formal debates held in schools and colleges throughout the country are contests. Each can, in fact, be seen as a mental tug-of-war. There is an issue to be decided with two sides holding opposite views. At the end a judge will usually decide who is the winner. The purpose of formal debate is to determine the set of arguments which seem more convincing by testing both sides under pressure. No other form of oral communication discussed in this book has these characteristics. Conversation is certainly not a contest. It is built on a basis of cooperation. Group discussion is also built on cooperation. It is not a contest but a cooperative search for the truth about a matter. Nor is public speaking a contest. Instead the speaker informs or persuades the listening audience. Only debate pits one side against another in order to discover the best answer through mental and verbal battle. By bringing the best evidence on each side out in the open, debate enables those listening to judge wisely as to the best solution, the best candidate, or the best course of action.

The Clash of Ideas

Not every issue is debatable. Debate is restricted to issues that have only two sides. Thus a question such as "What should be done about inflation?" is not debatable. There may be numerous answers. In order to assure only two sides in a debate, and a direct clash of ideas between the two, debate issues are stated in the form of a **proposition.** A formal debate proposition is a statement that can be answered by yes and no. It also generally demands that some specific action be taken or not taken. Here are two examples of debate propositions:

> Resolved, that the United States should adopt a system of national health insurance.

> Resolved, that more on-site job experience be incorporated into the high-school curriculum.

A well-worded formal debate proposition has several features:

1. It is worded as a statement, not a question.

2. It is worded to permit only a *for* and *against* response.

3. It is worded so that each side has an equal opportunity to argue its position successfully. In other words, the proposition is not slanted to favor one side.

4. It is worded to address a current, controversial issue.

5. It is worded to call for a change from present policy.

6. It is worded using specific, concrete language that does not make judgments about the topic.

Using these guidelines to write a debate proposition will help define an issue, which then may be supported or opposed.

Application

Writing Debate Propositions

The class will divide into four groups. Using the guidelines presented in this chapter, each group will write three debate propositions. The class as a whole will then select the five propositions that are judged best. These will be used later in the chapter.

The Opposing Sides

The two sides in a formal debate are called the **affirmative** and the **negative.** Each side may be represented by any number of speakers, but usually either one or two people argue each side. The affirmative has two basic tasks: attacking the way things are at present (the **status quo**) and arguing that a specific change should occur. Suppose the debate proposition reads "Resolved, that compulsory education should end after the eighth grade." The affirmative side must show that there are serious problems with the present requirement that young people stay in school until age 16 or older. They must also argue that many of these problems could be solved by allowing people to leave school after the eighth grade. The basic structure of an affirmative argument might go like this:

> There is a serious problem (or series of problems) caused by the present situation.

> The affirmative proposes an alternate plan of action that will solve the serious problems of the *status quo* and will be in and of itself beneficial.

The affirmative side in a debate is the side proposing a change from present policies. Thus, it has the responsibility of proving that a problem exists and that the solution stated in the proposition would work better than the present system. This affirmative responsibility is called the **burden of proof.** Just as in court trials, where defendants are presumed innocent until the prosecution proves them guilty, so in a debate the *status quo* is presumed the best way of continuing until the affirmative proves another plan better.

The basic task of the negative side in a debate is to disprove, or **refute,** the attacks on the *status quo* made by the affirmative side. The negative side must prove the *status quo* is satisfactory or that the plan for change proposed by the affirmative side will not work.

The opposing sides take turns presenting their arguments. Because the affirmative side is the one proposing a change from present conditions, it always presents the first and the last arguments. In some debates both sides are also given the chance to **cross-examine,** or question, the other side about their statements. Various debate formats permit different arrangements of affirmative and negative speakers. These formats are explained in detail later in the chapter; however, three such arrangements are shown on page 383.

PREPARING TO DEBATE

Formal debate, with a set order of speakers and usually an audience, demands careful preparation. This means you must carefully analyze the debate proposition. You must prepare sound evidence and reasoning to build an organized case. Then you must plan with your debate partner so that you will work well together. All of this takes time. Political candidates will tell you that they never prepare for a debate overnight. You, too, must prepare carefully in advance.

Analyze the Proposition

Your first step in preparing for any formal debate is to begin with the proposition. It is the written source that dictates the direction the debate must take. Analyze it carefully. Decide upon the words or phrases which need to be defined, and write down the definitions you consider fair. The first affirmative speaker will begin the debate by defining the terms. If the negative considers certain definitions to be unfair, it should provide its own definitions in its first speech.

Discover the background that has caused the proposition to become a debatable issue. Find out as much as you can about the opinions on both sides of the question. It doesn't matter whether you will be taking the affirmative or negative side of the debate. You will need to know the possible arguments of the opposition as thoroughly as you do your own in order to plan how to handle them.

Focus on the **issues.** The issues in a debate are the major points of disagreement. They are the key arguments on which acceptance or rejection of the debate proposition hangs. In most debates there will be only three or four main issues. Often you can discover major issues by asking questions such as these about the topic:

■ Are serious problems being created by the present system? Can these problems be better solved by some other approach?

■ What other approach, if any, would better solve the problems? Is such an approach feasible? Practical? Too expensive?

■ Is the proposed solution the best solution?

Standard format	Speaking time
First affirmative constructive speech	10 minutes
First negative constructive speech	10 minutes
Second affirmative constructive speech	10 minutes
Second negative constructive speech	10 minutes
First negative speaker's rebuttal	5 minutes
First affirmative speaker's rebuttal	5 minutes
Second negative speaker's rebuttal	5 minutes
Second affirmative speaker's rebuttal	5 minutes

Cross-examination format	Speaking time
First affirmative constructive speech	8 minutes
First negative speaker cross-examines	3 minutes
First negative constructive speech	8 minutes
Second affirmative speaker cross-examines	3 minutes
Second affirmative constructive speech	8 minutes
Second negative speaker cross-examines	3 minutes
Second negative constructive speech	8 minutes
First affirmative speaker cross-examines	3 minutes
First negative speaker's rebuttal	4 minutes
First affirmative speaker's rebuttal	4 minutes
Second negative speaker's rebuttal	4 minutes
Second affirmative speaker's rebuttal	4 minutes

Lincoln-Douglas format	Speaking time
Affirmative constructive speech	6 minutes
Negative cross-examination	3 minutes
Negative constructive speech	7 minutes
Affirmative cross-examination	3 minutes
Affirmative speaker's rebuttal	4 minutes
Negative speaker's rebuttal	6 minutes
Affirmative speaker's rebuttal	3 minutes

Three common arrangements for debate include the standard format, the cross-examination format, and the Lincoln-Douglas format.

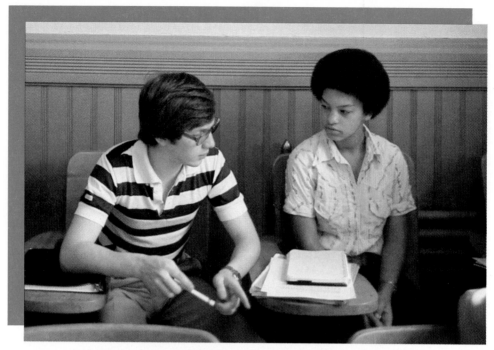

Having anlayzed the debate proposition independently, these partners now focus on building, outlining, and supporting their case together.

■ Will another solution to the problems have certain disadvantages? Will these disadvantages be as serious as those of the proposed solution or the present system?

Once you have located the main issues of the proposition, you are ready to begin to build a case. Then you must work with your partner, and support your case.

Build a Case

In debate, the term **case** refers to a team's total argument on any given proposition, set down in writing. There are at least two methods for outlining a debate case, either of which can be effective, depending on the side you will be debating and on your own personal preference.

A **brief** is a full outline of your case, written in complete sentences. It contains, as main heads, what you consider the major issues in the case. The subheads are the evidence and proof for those issues. Specific examples, quotations, and statistics are sometimes written out fully as sub-subheads. They may also be placed on individual evidence cards and then referred to by number in the brief. Affirmative teams usually find it easier to prepare a case in the form of a brief than negative teams do.

Since the negative often does not know the specific plan the affirmative will use, preparing a complete brief is difficult. However, negative teams sometimes prepare several briefs. During the debate, the negative chooses the one that presents the case that works best against the issues raised by the affirmative team.

The second method of preparing a case is to outline it on evidence cards. This is often simpler for negative teams. Particular cards may be inserted into the case, deleted, or rearranged, depending on the approach taken by the affirmative. The method for building a case on evidence cards consists of numbering the individual pieces of evidence (one on each card) in the order in which they will be presented during the debate. Additional evidence cards must be handy for use whenever the opposition inserts an unexpected issue into the debate. Thus, evidence cards are more flexible and adaptable than a complete brief.

The brief includes all the debater's analysis and reasoning. Evidence cards contain only the evidence. Inexperienced debaters will probably find it helpful to prepare both. Preparing a brief like the model on page 386 firmly establishes the logic of the case in one's mind. The evidence cards are simpler and easier to handle during the actual debate.

Whether you prepare your own case on evidence cards or by writing a brief, it is important that you plan what your opponents are likely to say in response to your arguments as you proceed. As you build your case, be constantly alert to discover the best refutation to each of your points. Put yourself in the other side's position, and research their probable answers as you look for support for your own case. In this way you will be best prepared to meet their responses during the actual debate.

Work with Your Partner

Just as attorneys often work in teams to represent a client, so do most school debates involve two-person teams. Teamwork in preparation, and consistency in the team's presentations, are very important in debating. If you are going to debate with a partner, prepare for the debate with that partner. This does not mean that each of you cannot do research independently. However, the overall planning of your strategy, deciding on the major issues, writing the brief, and rehearsal must be done as a team. Each person must be certain which issues the other will deal with. Each must know how the team will handle unexpected points brought up by the opposition. Thorough rehearsal also gets you used to your partner's speaking style and ensures that all parts of the case mesh properly. Nothing can hurt a team's chances of winning a debate as much as a contradiction or disagreement between members.

During the actual debate, listen carefully as your partner is speaking. Everything you say should agree with your partner's presentation. Any

INTRODUCTION

"Resolved: that (state the proposition) _____

_____ ,"

  I. The justification for the debate (cause for discussion)
    A.
    B.
    C. (And so on)
  II. The history of the question
    A.
    B.
    C. (And so on)
 III. Definition of potentially controversial terms
    A.
    B.
    C. (And so on)
 IV. Waived issues
  V. Conceded matters
 VI. The main issues of the debate
    A. To be established by the affirmative
      1.
        a.
        b.
      2. (And so on)

    B. To be established by the negative
      (developed in the manner just shown)

DISCUSSION

  I. First main contention   for
    A. First subcontention _____ for
      1. Evidence _____ and
        a. _____ and
        b. _____ for
          (1) _____ for
            (a) _____
    B. (And so on)
  II. Second main contention (developed in the manner just shown)
 III. (And so on)

CONCLUSION

  I. Since _____ , and
  II. Since (include as many points in summary as there are main
    contentions) _____
    Therefore, (repeat proposition by affirming or denying it).

This model brief shows the basic order and structure to use when outlining a case for debate.

disagreement between team members must be resolved either before-hand or privately during the debate. You will need to recognize one of your team members as leader. When a disagreement arises during a debate about the team's strategy, the matter must be settled quickly. There is not time for extended discussion. After a brief private exchange of views on the matter, the recognized team leader should decide.

Support Your Case

The kinds of evidence and reasoning that you use to support a debate case are the same as those used for support in a public speech. Begin by reviewing "Know What You Are Researching" on page 182 and "Get to Know Your Library" on page 185 in Chapter 7. Then review "Logos: Being Logical" on page 336 in Chapter 11. These will remind you of places to look for evidence. They will also show you how to put that evidence together to form a convincing argument.

Working with Evidence   How much evidence is sufficient? There is no magic answer to this question. It would be nice if you could be sure that a combination of three direct quotes, four sets of statistics, and two individual examples would always beat an opponent. But since, in debate,

Know what evidence you need, look it up in your library, and build it into the logical framework of your case.

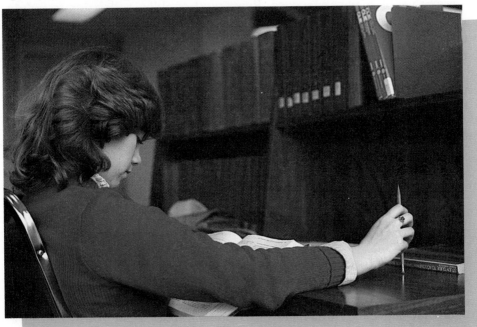

the team with the greater amount of sound evidence usually wins, the wise team will gather as much evidence as possible.

The methods of recording evidence for use in debate are slightly different from those of recording evidence for a public speech. For one thing, a public speaker will ordinarily not record much evidence beyond what will actually be used during the speech. A good debater, however, should have on hand about three times the number of evidence cards expected to be used in the debate. This is always necessary because neither team knows beforehand what kind of approach to the topic the other side will take.

Quotations, statistics, and examples are recorded on 3×5 cards, as for a public speech. For debate, each card heading should list the way in which the card can be used and the debate issue to which it relates. The quotation, statistic, example, or other evidence is recorded under the heading. At the bottom you should note the exact source from which you obtained the information. On page 389 is an example of an evidence card from a debate about ways to reduce crime. The first part of the heading, "Plan Meet Need," shows that this piece of evidence could be used to help refute one of the possible solutions the other side might propose. The rest of the heading shows that the card deals with the plan to give lie-detector tests to more suspects in order to reduce crime.

Using Reasoning   Reasoning is the mental process of forming logical conclusions from one's evidence. Through reasoning, a debater builds an affirmative or a negative case. Reasoning enables a debater to refute arguments of the opposition during a debate. For centuries, several forms of reasoning have been considered valid. Among these are induction, deduction, cause to effect, effect to cause, and analogy.

Induction is reasoning from specific facts or cases to general principles. Here a person begins by stating a number of facts that are similar. If these similarities are consistent enough, the reasoner concludes that they represent a general principle. For example, if you wish to prove that having smoke alarms in homes can save lives, you could give statistics for the last five years comparing the number of deaths caused by fires in homes with smoke alarms versus the number in homes without smoke alarms. From these statistics you could conclude that having smoke alarms in homes can save lives.

In **deduction** you reason from general principles to specific cases. In using deduction, a debater attempts to prove a specific case is true because it falls under a general principle or law. Thus, if you wished to show that an affirmative team's plan should be rejected because it could lead to greater inflation, you would start with the general principle, "Any plan that causes greater inflation is undesirable." Next you would give evidence to show that the plan of the affirmative side would cause higher prices. Your conclusion, then, is "this plan will very likely lead to more inflation. Therefore, it should be rejected."

Reasoning from what began something to its result is reasoning from **cause to effect.** If you show that one event will take place as a result of another event, you are using cause-to-effect reasoning. In attempting to prove that jury trials should be done away with, one of your arguments could be that serving on juries causes hardship on the jurors. The cause would be serving on juries. The effect would be hardship on the jurors.

Reasoning from a result back to what started it is reasoning from **effect to cause.** In arguing the other side of the jury system topic, you would be using effect-to-cause reasoning if you showed that the excellent record of court decisions in this country is largely due to the jury system.

An **analogy** is a comparison. When using analogy, you prove the truth of something by showing its similarity to something else. For example, in debating the safety of nuclear power plants you might argue: "Building and operating a nuclear power plant today is about as safe as lighting one's campfire within three feet of a wooden keg of gunpowder. As long

This model evidence card shows how to record information.

```
PLAN MEET      Guilty-knowledge (lie-detector)
NEED:          test not always possible

               "...the guilty-knowledge test (with
               a polygraph) cannot be used in all
               cases.  The police have to have
               enough privileged information to
               design a test."




which means:   Lie detector test cannot be used in
               all cases because police sometimes do
               not have access to information they
               need to prepare questions for the test.




David T. Lykken, Professor of Psychology at the University
of Minnesota, Psychology Today, March, 1975, p. 58
```

as you exercise extraordinary caution, everything is fine. But take your eyes off that fire for just a few minutes, and the results can be unbelievable!"

For reasoning to be successful, of course, it must be supported by sound evidence. If you think of reasoning as a steel bridge that can carry an argument from start to finish, evidence can be seen as the individual girders that support the bridge itself. Without the support of examples, statistics, and quotations, the structure of reasoning collapses. Beware of going into a debate armed with reasoning, but without having researched enough evidence to support that reasoning.

Application

Using Evidence and Reasoning

Analyze one of the debate propositions selected in the previous Application. Discover one major issue of the proposition, gather at least four pieces of evidence for it, and write each piece of evidence on a separate index card. Then prepare a brief, or outline, for a well-supported argument on this issue.

USING DIFFERENT STRATEGIES

Each side in a debate is responsible for certain tasks. You read about these tasks on pages 381 and 382. How each side goes about fulfilling their responsibilities depends on the strategy each chooses to use, as well as the format of the debate.

Fulfilling Responsibilities of the Affirmative Side

The first task of the affirmative in carrying its burden of proof is that of presenting a **prima facie case.** A *prima facie* case means an overall argument that would convince any reasonable judge who has not yet heard the response of the other side. Say the proposition being debated is "Resolved, that the federal government should provide a guaranteed annual income for all U.S. citizens." If the affirmative fails to show that harm comes from U.S. citizens not being guaranteed an income, and merely claims it would be helpful for everyone to have the money, it has failed to present a *prima facie* case. The argument is too weak to deserve a response. In such an instance, a judge could decide in favor of the other side even before hearing any of its arguments.

The affirmative side always opens a debate. If you are the first speaker for the affirmative, you should begin by stating the debate proposition. You should also define any terms in the proposition that need definition. Then you must present your proposal for change by proving that there are serious weaknesses in the *status quo*. These are often needs that are not being met (or cannot be met) by the present approach to the problem. If the debate proposition calls for changing the jury system, for example, you might argue that the present jury system causes undue hardship through lengthy delays. You might also argue that the present jury system is terribly expensive. Once a speaker from the other side has had a chance to respond, the second affirmative speaker generally presents the team's plan for change. This speaker shows the advantages of the plan over the *status quo*. In this case, the second affirmative might argue for a team of six professional jurors whose experience would enable them to decide cases much more efficiently, thus hastening trial dates and saving money in the long run.

The responsibilities of the affirmative team are frequently divided along the following lines:

First affirmative	*Second affirmative*
States proposition	Presents affirmative plan
Defines terms	Shows advantage of plan
Attacks *status quo*	Summarizes entire affirmative case

If there is only one debater on each side, then all of the above tasks fall to the single affirmative speaker.

This form of affirmative argument based on need → plan → advantages has long been the most common approach to building an affirmative case. It has usually been called the **needs case.**

In recent years, however, a slightly different type of affirmative reasoning has often been used instead of the needs case. This other form of affirmative case is called the **comparative advantages case.** Instead of the typical need → plan → advantages form of arguments, this affirmative case consists of agreed goals → plan → comparative advantages. With certain debate topics, it is sometimes more useful than a needs case. An example would be a debate proposition that reads, "Resolved, that the state's sales tax should be abolished." In using a comparative advantages case to debate this topic the affirmative would begin by calling upon the negative to agree that everyone should be allowed to keep as much of their personal income as possible to spend as they see fit. The negative can hardly disagree with that idea. It would be an **agreed goal.** The debate then revolves, not around the goal of personal economic freedom, but around a comparison of two means by which to achieve that goal. The affirmative would then argue that their plan—for example, to reduce certain state services—would prove better for citizens than paying the sales tax to get those services. A good affirmative debater will carefully analyze a debate proposition. Then the debater will decide which strategy—a needs case or a comparative advantages case—will work better for a given topic.

A comparative advantages case generally calls for a division of speaking responsibilities quite different from that used with a needs case:

First affirmative	*Second affirmative*
States proposition	Responds to attacks of first negative speaker
Defines terms	
Presents goals negative will have to agree with	Reinforces plan
Presents plan for meeting goals	
Outlines advantages of plan	

Fulfilling Responsibilities of the Negative Side

The basic task of the negative side is to disprove the attacks on the *status quo* made by the affirmative. There are several ways the negative may do this. Any one of these may win the debate for the negative if done well enough. One way is by attacking the affirmative's arguments of need. The negative may claim that the *status quo* is completely satisfactory or that the affirmative has failed to prove it unsatisfactory. There is no need for a change.

Another possibility is for the negative to center its attacks on the affirmative plan. Here the negative argues that the affirmative plan would create problems more serious than those currently being experienced under the *status quo*. This is usually the best strategy to use against an affirmative comparative advantages case.

A third option is the **need-plan wedge case.** When using this approach, the negative does not attack the affirmative's need or plan directly. Rather the negative attacks the logical link between the two. The negative argues "even if the need the affirmative claims did exist (which is doubtful), and even if their plan were a workable one (which is doubtful), their plan is incapable of satisfying the need they have outlined."

A fourth approach, and perhaps the most common one, is called the **running-refutation negative case.** Here the negative side attacks all parts of the affirmative case. It claims that the *status quo* is handling the situation satisfactorily and that the affirmative has failed to show a need for a change. It also argues that the affirmative plan is not workable, that the plan would not produce any significant advantages, and that it might produce some disadvantages.

Unlike the affirmative side, which begins the debate knowing its own strategy, the negative has the disadvantage of having to wait until the debate has begun to decide its specific plan of attack. However, this does not mean the negative cannot prepare beforehand. Thorough preparation for the negative consists of researching all of the major issues the affirmative might use. Then the negative must prepare a response to whatever kind of case the affirmative might choose. The affirmative team's strategy will become evident during their first speech. Then the negative side can insert its most appropriate proofs and its most appropriate case.

The duties of the first and second negative speakers differ according to how the affirmative case is presented as well as according to how they decide to disprove the affirmative case. If the affirmative uses a needs case, the first negative speaker will generally refute the affirmative needs. The second negative will generally attack the plan and its advantages. If the affirmative has chosen to use a comparative advantages case rather than a needs case, the negative response will be different. In that case, the first negative will generally attack the affirmative advantages. These will have been heard in the first affirmative speech. The negative will usually try to show that the affirmative plan cannot produce the advantages claimed, that the advantages are not significant, or that they can be gained without the affirmative plan. The second negative will generally refute the plan itself and try to show it to be unworkable. The argument will usually be that the plan will produce disadvantages that outweigh any advantages.

Having prepared to refute an array of possible affirmative arguments, the responsibilities of the negative speakers might be summarized as in the following list:

If the affirmative uses a needs case:

First negative
Agrees with or redefines affirmative's definitions

Refutes affirmative's needs

Second negative
Attacks affirmative plan

Refutes advantages

If the affirmative uses a comparative advantages case:

First negative
Agrees with or redefines affirmative's
   definitions

Attacks advantages of affirmative plan

Second negative
Attacks affirmative plan

Debate Formats

Many different formats can be used for conducting debates. The format that is used depends on the time available, the seriousness of the issue, and the number of debaters on each side. Here the discussion will focus on three formats widely used in high school debates.

In the **standard format** two different kinds of speeches are made by each of the two speakers on each team. Each speaker gives both a constructive speech and a rebuttal. The **constructive speeches** are lengthy, usually ranging from eight to ten minutes each. They are used to present and develop the major points of each team's case. **Rebuttals** typically last four to five minutes each. They are used to refute the opposition's arguments and to answer objections to one's own case.

In the standard format this is the order of speakers:

Speaker	*Number of minutes*
First affirmative constructive speech	10
First negative constructive speech	10
Second affirmative constructive speech	10
Second negative constructive speech	10
First negative rebuttal	5
First affirmative rebuttal	5
Second negative rebuttal	5
Second affirmative rebuttal	5
Total time	60

Notice that the order of affirmative and negative speakers switches in the rebuttal period. This is done to assure that the affirmative team both opens and closes the debate.

The **cross-examination format** also has two speakers representing each side. In this format, cross-examinations follow immediately after each constructive speech. A member of the opposite team attempts to expose weaknesses in each speaker's arguments by asking questions for

TRIAL LAWYER

Lawyers interpret our increasingly complex body of laws. To accomplish this task, they must have a firm knowledge of the law and the legal system. Attorneys also need to communicate effectively with all types of people, and understand the process of debate. Law candidates must obtain a bachelor's degree followed by a law degree. Graduates then must pass the bar examination in the state in which they plan to practice.

As trial lawyers, attorneys must collect and carefully prepare the evidence needed to present a convincing case. They confer with the opposing lawyer to compare facts and to detect the other's strategy. Trial lawyers often rehearse their presentation to ensure that their delivery will be as sound as their preparation. In the courtroom, trial lawyers engage in debates as they represent their clients.

In such cases, lawyers must know how to search for weaknesses in the opposing lawyer's case. These flaws can be used to reveal an opponent's faulty reasoning, thus strengthening their own case. When both sides present their final argument, effective lawyers select only the most convincing facts, testimonies, and conclusions from the trial so that the judge or jury will be persuaded to decide in their client's favor.

Trial lawyers who master the art of debate are better able to champion the legal rights of their clients. Even more than that, when lawyers add a persuasive, well-documented presentation to their conscientious interpretation of the law, the rights of everyone in our society are better protected.

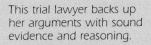

This trial lawyer backs up her arguments with sound evidence and reasoning.

the speaker to answer. High school cross-examination periods usually last about three minutes. The order of speakers in the cross-examination format is shown in the list below. Note that debates following the cross-examination format differ from debates following the standard format in only one respect: Each constructive speech is followed by a cross-examination period.

Speaker	Number of minutes
First affirmative constructive speech	8
First negative speaker cross-examines	3
First negative constructive speech	8
Second affirmative speaker cross-examines	3
Second affirmative constructive speech	8
Second negative speaker cross-examines	3
Second negative constructive speech	8
First affirmative speaker cross-examines	3
First negative speaker's rebuttal	4
First affirmative speaker's rebuttal	4
Second negative speaker's rebuttal	4
Second affirmative speaker's rebuttal	4
Total time	60

The times for each presentation in both the standard and the cross-examination format may be shortened to insure that a debate will fit within a class period. In tournament competition, however, the times indicated should be strictly observed.

Another debate format that is often used in competitions is called the **Lincoln-Douglas format.** It gets its name from the famous debates between senatorial candidates Abraham Lincoln and Stephen A. Douglas in 1858. In Lincoln-Douglas-style debates, each side is represented by only one speaker. This style of debate, as it is usually practiced, is little more than a modification of the standard cross-examination format.

This exciting style of debate usually deals with a proposition of value rather than one of policy. The propostion "Resolved that the recently passed five-cent sales tax on gasoline should be revoked" would be inappropriate for Lincoln-Douglas debate because it is a proposition of policy. However, the proposition "Resolved, that the recently passed

Lincoln and Douglas debate the issues during the Illinois senate race of 1858.
Lincoln lost, but won the presidential election two years later.

five-cent sales tax on gasoline will prove beneficial to our country" would fit this format well.

Lincoln-Douglas debate is less formal and more philosophical than most other styles. It depends more on analysis and reasoning and less on evidence. Since it does not deal with a policy proposition, no plan is called for in the affirmative case.

Lincoln-Douglas debate provides challenges and advantages to the individual debater that cannot exist when there are two people on a side. The challenges come from being alone and therefore totally responsible for arguing your side of the case. The advantages are that you do not have to coordinate your case with anyone, either during preparation or during the actual debate. You are forced to do your own research and preparation, two of the great benefits debate has to offer, and you alone can claim whatever credit your win-loss record shows.

Participation in Lincoln-Douglas-style debate provides excellent preparation for the typical forms of informal debate that occur in everyday life. Most of the informal debates that you will engage in at home or on the job will have only one person advocating each side of a question. However, debates involving opposing teams do sometimes occur in everyday life, and therefore most people can benefit from gaining experience both in standard-format and Lincoln-Douglas-format debates.

In debates following the Lincoln-Douglas format, the order of speakers is as follows:

Speaker	Number of minutes
Affirmative constructive speech	6
Negative cross-examination	3
Negative constructive speech	7
Affirmative cross-examination	3
Affirmative rebuttal	4
Negative rebuttal	6
Affirmative rebuttal	3
Total time	32

MEETING THE OPPOSITION

Once a debate begins, your two primary tasks are to present your own case in the most favorable light possible and to refute the arguments of the opposition. This section will discuss methods of testing the evidence and reasoning presented by your opponents, the process of note-taking during a debate, cross-examination techniques, and delivery of debate speeches.

Look for Weaknesses in the Opposition's Evidence

The foundation on which any argument rests is its evidence. A good debate team will first be certain that its own evidence is both true and valid. Then, as the debate progresses, it will constantly look for weaknesses in the opponents' evidence.

Have your opponents presented sufficient evidence? Occasionally, debaters make statements they wish to have accepted as fact, but provide no supporting evidence. These statements are called **unsupported assertions.** Obviously, unsupported assertions represent the weakest form of argument. Suppose your opponents claim "Socialized medicine has worked effectively in other countries. There is no reason it cannot work effectively in the United States as well." They have made an unsupported assertion. Unless your opponents supply at least several examples of particular countries where socialized medicine has been effective, you should vigorously attack their argument as an unsupported assertion.

It is obvious that without evidence it is impossible to win a case, but remember that the quality of a debater's evidence is just as important as the quantity. As you listen to an opponent's constructive speech, try to ascertain which pieces of evidence presented are questionable and open to attack during rebuttal. Here are several questions you can ask yourself to test the quality of your opponents' evidence:

- Is my opponent's source of evidence reliable? Is the person who is being quoted someone who is trustworthy? Knowledgeable in the field? Unprejudiced on the matter quoted?

- Are the statistics being presented sound? Have they been carefully gathered? Are they being reported accurately? Is the sample valid? Do the people questioned in the sample accurately represent the entire population?

- Are the opposition's examples appropriate? Has each individual case been reported by an eyewitness? Are there enough individual examples to support the debater's conclusion?

- Is the evidence being offered up-to-date? On certain debate topics, where rapid change is not occurring, older evidence is acceptable. On a topic such as the energy crisis, however, statistics and examples from 1970 are no longer valid.

- Are there major pieces of evidence that contradict or invalidate the evidence presented by my opponents?

While the delivery may sound convincing, always test your opponents' evidence and reasoning.

Watch Out for Faulty Reasoning

Sometimes debaters use sound evidence but still arrive at the wrong conclusion through faulty reasoning. Here are a few questions that can be used to test your opponents' reasoning:

- When reasoning by induction, has the opposition given enough examples? For instance, can a debater who cites three examples of dogs that have bitten children logically conclude "dogs make dangerous pets"? Obviously not.

- When arguing by deduction, have my opponents considered all reasonable alternatives? Consider this argument from a debate on socialized medicine: "To improve health care in this country we must institute a system of socialized medicine." The flaw in this argument is the failure of the debater to consider alternative solutions (other than socialized medicine) for improving health care, such as methods for easing the shortage of doctors in some areas of the country.

- When arguing by cause and effect, has the opposition shown that an event was actually *caused* by a preceding event or did it simply occur later? Suppose someone said, "We had baked apples for dessert last night and everyone in the family got sick. We'll never eat baked apples again." This person has blamed the baked apples when they may not have been the cause of the illness at all.

- When arguing by analogy, did my opponents overlook any essential differences in the two things being compared? A Russian once claimed to an American visitor that his system of government was as democratic as ours by arguing that they held elections, just as we do. The American found the flaw in the analogy and retorted that in the United States there is more than one party from which the voters may choose their candidates.

Take Notes and Keep a Flow Sheet

During a debate, you should take notes of your opponents' arguments. Be sure to include notes about any weaknesses you find in their evidence or reasoning. Include only those key points you want to respond to. In a typical debate, your opponents will bring up a much greater number of arguments than you will have time to answer. The approach of one high school debater was to begin a speech: "The negative team has asked us to answer a long list of questions. We are more than happy to do so, so here goes: yes, no, no, maybe, you've got us there, maybe, no, yes, yes. . . ." Although this method may have secured a laugh from the judge, it probably did not win the debate for its user. A good debater will respond only to key arguments that apply directly to the case.

One useful method for selecting the key arguments to refute is to construct a flow sheet as the debate progresses. A **flow sheet** is your own summary outline written in a continuous manner to show how the arguments on each issue progress throughout the debate. It is written during the debate, usually in vertical columns on a large legal pad or art pad. Each column represents one speech that is given. If you record, in brief sentences or phrases, the essence of each argument—and the response to it in a subsequent column—you will have a picture of the debate at any point along the way.

Keep track of your opponents' arguments by taking notes on their main points, their line of reasoning, and their supporting evidence. This will also help you clarify the strengths and weaknesses in your own case.

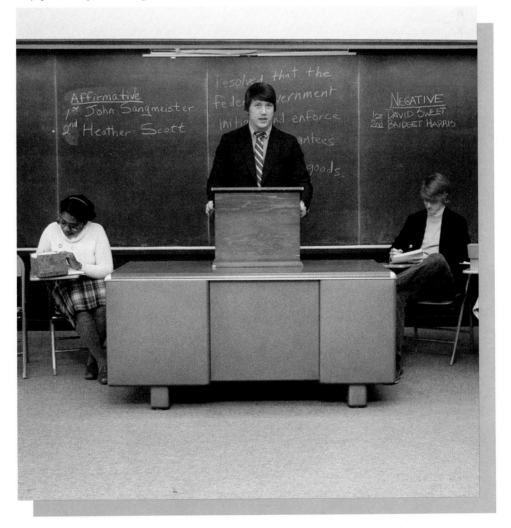

A partial flow sheet from a debate on energy in the United States

1st. Aff. Con.	1st. Neg. Con.	2nd. Aff. Con.
	Theme	
	Status quo can solve any problems.	
	Topicality	
	NO PLAN TO SOLVE	
	Sig.	
	NO QUANTIACATION of SOLVENCY	
	Harm	
	- Economic harms are not pragmatic	→ reserves are not reliable
	- SQ can decrease dependence Fossil Fuels	
I. U.S. is dependent on oil (must import)	Oil demand is decreasing	→ Exxon evidence is biased
A. Are dependent.	We have enough	
B. Imports will increase (36% needed)	Alaska's Oil North Slope Oil }	→ Must compare to Arab reserves
	- Present System can Decrease Dependence	
II. Harms (personal)	→ No harm to Arab investment	→ Doesn't apply
A. Purchasing power decreasing ($45 - $60 bill)	→ Doesn't hurt economy	→ Bad housing (deaths?)
B. Oil Crisis likely (only have enough reserve for 60 days)	→ OPEC can't afford embargo	
C. Problems will continue		→ Oil prices will increase
III. Harms (other)	→ A. No sig impact	
A. Trade deficit is caused by oil.	B. Deficit must allow for investment	
B. Will get worse.	C. Deficit doesn't devalue dollar	**PLAN**
IV. Harms (economic)		I. National Coal Gasification Board
A. The dollar devaluates		II. Enforcement
B. Link - (Economy is tied to Energy.)		III. Funding
C. Inflation leads to higher oil prices		ADV: Less pollution
		A. 65% sulfur and ash removed
D. Inf. will continue		B. Coal can't be undermind by OPEC

A partial flow sheet from a debate on energy in the United States

2nd. Neg. Con.	1st. Neg. Reb.	1st. Aff. Reb.
——————→ X	No Sig?	
——————→ X (plan in 2 AC is unfair)	No Ink	
——————→ X	No Impact to Harm	
——→ Energy demand is slower		
——→ Best (only) evidence given ———————		—→ Aff. evidence is better
		—→ X
——————————————→ goes both ways		
——→ Difficult link —————→ X		
——————————————————→ X		
——————→ X		
——————→ X		
* Trade deficit not shown to be the same as devaluation of the dollar		
——————→ Extra topical —→		can't deny the advantage.

A flow chart enables you to see the arguments you have not responded to thus far in the debate and helps you select arguments for refutation that seem to be key points. Another advantage of keeping a flow sheet is being able to see which of your own arguments your opponents have been able to refute. The part of a sample flow sheet illustrated on pages 402 and 403 will give you an idea of how yours can be constructed.

Make Effective Use of Cross-examination

The brief cross-examination periods included in many high-school debates can be the most exciting part of a debate. These questioning sessions, modeled on courtroom cross-examination, give each team a chance to expose weaknesses in the opposition's case through clever questioning. Though skill at cross-examination requires some experience, here are suggestions for both the questioner and the respondent to consider:

For the Questioner

Prepare general questions on each of the major issues before the debate. During the debate, try to tie your questions as closely as possible to the specific arguments actually used by your opponents.

Never ask a question for which you think the opponents might have a strong answer. If their response is strong, you only score points for the opposition by giving them a free chance to state it.

Keep questions brief and clear. Do not attempt to confuse your opponent with long or complicated questions. You will also confuse the judge.

Demand brief answers. You cannot demand a simple yes or no. If the respondent begins to give a little speech, however, you may cut it off.

Do not comment on the responses you receive during the cross-examination period. This should be done in your, or your partner's, later speeches. You may, however, use follow-up questions during the cross-examination period.

For the Respondent

Be constantly on guard. The purpose of the questioner is to make your case look weak and foolish.

Remember that you do not have to answer an unreasonable question. If you are asked, "Are all your examples as bad as that one?" you may point out that this is a loaded question and refuse to answer it.

Keep your answers brief, but complete. You cannot be forced into single word answers. Briefly giving a reason or qualification for your answer is always permissible.

If you do not know the answer to a question or are not familiar with the context of the question, say so immediately.

If you do not have a strong answer to a particular question, it is better to yield the point immediately rather than offer a weak response. A weak response gives the questioner a chance to make you look bad with a series of embarrassing, follow-up questions.

Speak Persuasively

All the rules for public speaking and persuasion explained in Unit 4 apply in debate. Since a debate is a special kind of speaking situation, a few special rules need to be mentioned.

You are trying to convince the judge, not your opponents. Direct your arguments and your eye contact to the judge.

Be thoroughly familiar with your evidence cards. This will enable you to maintain a large measure of eye contact with the judge while reading them.

Do not develop the tendency of many debaters to try setting a speed record. A good speaking rate for any kind of persuasive public speaking is also a good speaking rate for debate. The judge is not interested in how many arguments you can squeeze into eight or ten minutes, but in how effective your arguments are.

Do not forget the value of gestures, platform movement, and facial expressions. Be dynamic and forceful in your delivery.

Maintain variety in vocal expression. Changes in pitch, rate, and volume give persuasive impact to your message.

Never allow yourself to get angry with your opponents. No matter how outrageous they seem, stick to the issues. Do not attack the debaters.

Application

Keeping a Flow Sheet

Keep a flow sheet for a debate. You may actually attend the debate, listen to it on a recording, or hear it read by students in class. Note each major argument in the debate, and the opponent's response to it, in the proper column on your flow sheet. At the end of the debate, compare your flow sheet with those of your classmates. Did they interpret the arguments as you did? Take a class vote on which side won the debate. Briefly discuss the value of keeping a flow sheet. Discuss arguments that might have been made by either side in the debate but were not.

13 Chapter Review

■ Summary

Debate is perhaps the most challenging form of oral communication. It is used daily in courts and legislatures as a means of arriving at decisions about important issues. It has also been used in schools for centuries as a means of training for responsible decision making.

The Nature of Debate   A formal debate begins with a proposition —a statement that something should be considered or done—that is answerable by both yes and no. There are only two sides in a debate. The affirmative upholds the proposition by proving that a problem requiring change exists in the *status quo* and that its plan for a solution would work better than any other. The negative argues against such a change by refuting the affirmative's arguments. A judge decides the winner.

Preparing to Debate   Preparing to participate in a debate demands careful analysis of the debate proposition, the writing of a fully outlined case, close work with your debate partner, gathering sound evidence, and the development of clear reasoning. Analyzing the proposition includes deciding what terms need definition, obtaining background information about the proposition, and focusing on its major issues.

Using Different Strategies   The affirmative side always opens a debate by first presenting a *prima facie* case—an overall argument that would convince any reasonable person who has not also heard the negative side. The affirmative may use a needs-case strategy, present a plan to meet those needs, and then show the advantages of that plan. Another approach is the comparative advantages case, in which the affirmative presents goals on which both sides can agree, followed by a plan it attempts to show is better than the negative's approach.

The negative side must disprove the attacks of the affirmative. They may attack the affirmative's claims of need, its plan, or the logical link between the needs and plan. A fourth way is to attack all parts of the affirmative case. This is called the running-refutation negative case.

Meeting the Opposition When a debate begins, you must continually test your opponents' evidence and reasoning and also take careful notes on a flow sheet to determine how the arguments on each issue are progressing. Never ask a question during cross-examination if you know there is a strong answer. Keep questions brief and clear, and demand brief answers. Respondents should always be on guard. They should keep their answers brief and admit immediately if they do not know an answer.

Vocabulary

Define each term in a complete sentence.

formal debate	induction	running-refutation
proposition	deduction	negative case
affirmative	cause to effect	standard format
negative	effect to cause	constructive speech
status quo	analogy	rebuttal
burden of proof	*prima facie* case	cross-examination format
refute	needs case	Lincoln-Douglas format
cross-examine	comparative	unsupported assertion
issue	advantages case	flow sheet
case	agreed goal	
brief	need-plan wedge case	

Checklist

Debate Skills

1. Understand the kinds of issues that are debatable.
2. Be able to debate the affirmative and negative sides.
3. Prepare carefully for a debate by analyzing the proposition.
4. Focus on the issues—the major points of disagreement.
5. Learn to use two methods for outlining a debate case.
6. Learn to work with a partner in debate.
7. Learn several different formats for conducting debates.
8. Use correct reasoning and self-control in debates.

Review Questions

1. State the purpose of formal debate.
2. Describe how debate issues are stated.
3. Identify the characteristics included in a well-worded debate proposition.
4. Identify the steps you should take in preparing to debate.
5. Name five forms of reasoning that may be used to support a case.
6. Name three things you should do during a debate to prepare yourself to meet the opposition during rebuttal or cross-examination.
7. Describe the responsibilities of the affirmative side in a debate.
8. Describe the responsibilities of the negative side in a debate.
9. State the differences among the standard format, the cross-examination format, and the Lincoln-Douglas format.
10. Describe how a questioner should proceed during a cross-examination.

Discussion Questions

1. Discuss the role of debate in American society. Where is debate used? How important is it in the political process? What impact has television had on the role of debate?
2. Select one of the debate propositions from an Application. Discuss the various arguments that could be developed on both the affirmative and negative sides of the issue. Which side of the issue would you prefer to argue? Why?
3. Discuss the following statement: "Resolved, that the brutal game of football should be abolished." Is this a well-worded debate proposition? If not, how could it be reworded to become one?
4. Discuss the elements that must be present before a *prima facie* case can be made. Refer to one of the propositions developed in the Applications. Give an example of an argument that does not constitute a *prima facie* case. Then develop an example that does meet the standards of a *prima facie* case.

Critical Thinking

1. **Analysis:** Assume that you are asked to debate the following proposition: "Resolved, that an increase in the state sales tax would provide better services to the state's citizens." Develop an affirmative or a negative case for this proposition.

2. **Evaluation:** Assume that you are serving as a judge for a debate. Make a short outline of the things a judge needs to be alert for during the arguments. How would you use what you have learned about debate to decide on a winner?

Activities

In-Class

1. As a class, select a policy issue and develop a properly worded debate proposition for it. Then work with a partner to prepare a case for either the affirmative or the negative side of the proposition. Analyze the question, plan your arguments, and gather evidence to support your viewpoint. If you are to argue the affirmative side, check your case to be sure that it meets all basic requirements. If you are to argue the negative side, decide on the best strategy to refute the likely arguments of the affirmative. Debate the proposition in class with two-person teams on opposing sides, and with the class serving as judge. Which pro and con strategies worked best? Why?

2. Invite a local attorney to speak to the class on the role of debate in the legal profession. Ask this person to explain in detail how a trial is conducted and what kinds of arguments are admissible. Ask questions about rules and standards of evidence—including what they are, how they may differ according to the type of case being tried, and what criteria are used to determine whether or not any given piece of evidence meets their stated requirements. Ask your guest to explain how a court case can be lost even though the evidence presented is sound.

3. Work in groups of from five to seven to develop a debatable proposition. Decide whether to argue the affirmative or the

negative side of the issue and then gather evidence to support your case. Use your evidence to support an inductive, deductive, cause to effect, or effect to cause argument, and an analogy. Decide as a group which argument best supports your side and share your best argument with other groups.

Out-of-Class

1. Conduct research on both the Lincoln-Douglas debate of 1858 and the Kennedy-Nixon debate in the 1960 presidential campaign. In what ways has debate been affected by the technology of television? What aspects of debate have remained constant? How do you feel about the role of personal style and appearance in the debate process?

2. Develop a debate proposition of your own and choose either the negative or affirmative side of the question to work on. Find as much evidence as you can and record each piece on a separate card. Identify each card for use in a debate round. Start an evidence file that you can use in a class debate. Add additional evidence to your file as you collect it.

3. Watch television programs that use a debate format. Note the types of topics chosen for discussion. In your speech notebook, evaluate the effectiveness of each program. Summarize each discussion and decide whether or not the format that was used allowed for adequate coverage of the topic or debate proposition. Be prepared to share your evaluations with classmates and to offer suggestions for how these television debates could be improved.

4. Attend a formal debate. In your speech notebook, keep a flow sheet that shows how the arguments progressed. If possible, speak to some of the participants and find out how they conducted their research and planned for the debate. Summarize this information in your speech notebook.

5. Prepare a set of cross-examination questions for use in one of your classroom debates. Develop questions that you think the opposition will find difficult to answer. Make certain that your questions are brief and clear, and touch upon major issues of the debate. Be ready to adapt your questions to meet the changing needs of the live debate situation.

◼ Chapter Project

As a class, choose a debatable proposition and conduct a mini debate tournament in either the standard debate format or the Lincoln-Douglas format. Students may debate either individually or in teams. Each student or team will debate two rounds, one affirmative and one negative. Arrange for a judge who will decide the winners of each round. Undefeated debaters will meet other undefeated debaters. Eliminations will continue until two debaters or teams remain. The debate between these two final individuals or teams will determine the winners of the class championship.

14 Parliamentary Procedure

When you have completed this chapter you should be able to:

- Explain the purposes of parliamentary procedure.
- Describe several of the basic principles of parliamentary procedure.
- Explain the duties of the chair.
- Describe the purposes of each of the types of motions.
- Explain the order in which motions may be made.

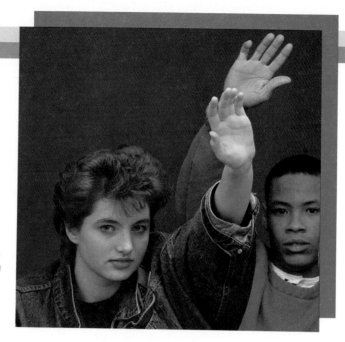

An equal voice and vote on every issue under discussion are among the rights provided by parliamentary procedure.

Have you ever attended a meeting with more than five people present? Have you been frustrated by everyone talking at once? Did it seem to take forever to arrive at a decision? **Parliamentary procedure** is a set of rules designed to reduce that kind of frustration. Probably you have attended meetings of clubs, student government organizations, or other groups that use these rules to conduct their business. Parliamentary procedure makes discussion at such meetings more efficient and productive. The rules are also designed to protect the rights of the individual. These include the right to be heard, the right to remain silent, and the right to full and free discussion of every issue presented. While parliamentary procedure provides for majority rule, it also protects the rights of the minority.

Parliamentary procedure did not suddenly spring into existence fully developed. Years ago a few basic rules were formed in the early English Parliament. They were gradually expanded and changed to fit the needs of that growing body and other democratic groups and societies where it came to be used. Today a number of standard codes of parliamentary procedure are in wide use throughout the world. *Robert's Rules of Order, Newly Revised* and *Sturgis Standard Code of Parliamentary Procedure* are the two most commonly used in this country. This chapter will not make you a **parliamentarian** (an expert on parliamentary procedure). It will, however, explain the fundamentals of parliamentary procedure. Copies of these codes are readily available for anyone who wants to learn more.

BASIC PRINCIPLES

Several fundamental principles form the basis of parliamentary procedure. Once you have these in mind, all of the lesser rules, regulations, and motions will seem logical.

One Question at a Time

Order can be maintained in a group by debating and voting on only one issue at a time. The members may not always vote on an issue before moving on to another one. But this principle dictates that they must dispose of a pending issue *in some way* before considering another.

Majority Rule

In bodies following parliamentary procedure, each member automatically agrees to abide by the decision of the majority. A **simple majority** is at least one more than half the people who voted. In special situations at least two-thirds of those voting must vote favorably in order for the issue to pass.

Protection of Minority Rights

Voting members of an organization who make up the minority group on an issue are not necessarily wrong. Voting with the **minority** means only that on that particular vote less than half the members agreed with them. The rules of parliamentary procedure protect the rights of the minority. One of the rights protected is the right to continue to be heard and to try to change the minds of members in the majority group.

Equality of Rights and Responsibilities

In a body that follows parliamentary procedure, everyone is equal. Each has an equal right to speak or to remain silent, to vote or not to vote. At the same time each has the same responsibility to take an active part in discussion, to cast her or his vote, and to serve as an officer of the organization when called upon to do so. Though some members may be more active than others in exercising their rights and in fulfilling their responsibilities, all are equal in their possession of those rights and responsibilities.

Free Debate

Free debate is essential to enable members of an assembly to vote intelligently on issues. Parliamentary procedure attempts to guard open discussion of every issue, so long as a reasonable number of those present want it to continue. Motions to limit debate or to cut it off entirely require consent of two thirds of the members to pass. Free debate also means that ordinarily only one person may speak at a time, and only after having obtained the floor by recognized procedures.

HOLDING A MEETING

Parliamentary procedure provides a number of very specific rules for holding meetings. These rules allow meetings to be efficient, productive, and democratic. They regulate the way meetings are announced and the number of members who must be present to conduct business. They also regulate the manner in which the business is conducted and the duties of the presiding officer.

Notice

When an organization plans to hold a meeting, notice must first be given to all of the members. **Notice** means that all of the members are told about the meeting far enough in advance so that they can plan to participate. Ten days' notice is normal. Failure of the officers to give adequate notice can invalidate decisions made at a meeting. If it can be proven that the officers conspired to hold a "secret meeting"—thereby preventing certain members from participating—they can be removed from office. Notice should ordinarily be given in writing. It is often routinely given for regularly scheduled meetings by mailing out to the membership beforehand the list of items to be discussed (the **agenda**) with the date, time, and place of meeting.

Quorum Requirements

Once the time for the meeting has arrived, the presiding officer must determine whether a quorum is present before calling the meeting to order. A **quorum** is the number of members that *must* be present before any meeting can be held or any official business conducted. Though each organization can set its own quorum requirements in its bylaws, the standard requirement is a majority of all members in good standing. Suppose an organization had 100 members in good standing on its membership role. Following the standard requirement, that organization would need 51 members present before it could hold an official meeting and conduct any official business.

An organization may, of course, set its quorum requirements at less than a majority in its bylaws. This assures that business may be conducted when attendance is low. However, it is dangerous to set the quorum too low. This would make it possible for a very small minority to set policy and decide important matters for the entire organization. Setting quorum requirements too high should also be avoided. It might become difficult to secure enough attendance to conduct business.

Order of Business

The **order of business** for a meeting is an agenda. This is a listing of the various items of business in the order in which they will be taken up during the meeting. This is generally the agenda followed:

1. Call to order

2. Reading and approval of the minutes of previous meetings

3. Reports of officers, boards, and standing committees

4. Reports of special committees

5. Unfinished business

6. New business

7. Announcements

8. Adjournment

Following the call to order, this student reads the minutes of the previous meeting, which then must be approved for completeness and accuracy.

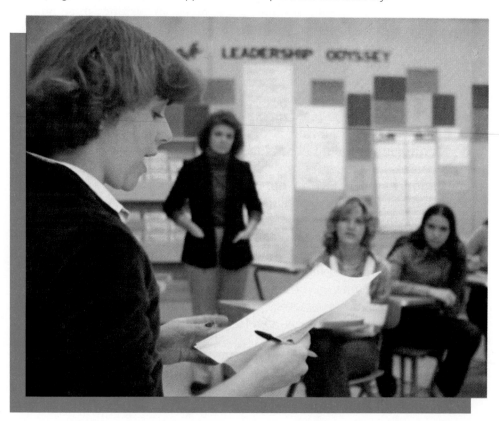

Ordinarily, an organization will follow this regular order of business unless its bylaws call for a different order. Occasionally, though, if a special reason exists it is possible to shift around certain items.

Application

Value of Parliamentary Procedure

Interview members of at least two different school committees or other local organizations that use parlimentary procedure. Ask if the use of parliamentary procedure helps that organization get its business done. Does it permit the participation of all members? Does it allow the minority to be heard? How? Does it save time by enabling the group to focus continually on the issues? What characteristics do the members feel are necessary to serve competently as chair? Discuss your findings with your classmates.

Duties of the Chair

The **chair** is the name given to the person presiding over a meeting of an organization. Ordinarily this duty is exercised by the president of the organization. The vice-president usually presides if the president is absent. The chair has the same right to vote that any other member has. A number of other duties are also fulfilled by the person in this position.

Maintains Control   The chair's main task is to maintain control over the meeting, continually making sure that each member's rights are protected. The chair is not the ruler of the assembly, however; she or he serves the organization.

Maintains Order   The chair must maintain order at all times. He or she should prevent debate that takes the form of personal attack rather than a discussion of the issues. The chair must also guard against the railroading of matters through to a vote without time for sufficient thought and discussion. Sometimes members of a group try to prevent a vote on an issue by making long speeches to waste time. This is called **filibustering.** The chair should discourage such stalling tactics and must always restore order at the first sign of any form of disturbance.

Acts Impartially   The chair should not take sides on issues being discussed. If, on rare occasions, the chair wishes to speak for or against a particular measure, another officer should be asked to preside for as long as the chair takes part in debate. If the chair possesses information about a matter that is unknown to the other members, he or she may state such information impartially without relinquishing the chair.

Recognizes Speakers Impartially   The chair must be especially impartial in allowing members to speak. This process, which is called **recognizing** members, follows certain rules. When a particular member has made a motion, the chair should always give that member the right to speak first about the proposal. Then, the chair should alternate between those speaking against and for the topic. If there is uncertainty about who is in favor and who against, the chair should ask before permitting a member to have the floor. The chair should also recognize those who have not yet had a turn to speak on the subject before those who have already had an opportunity.

Assures Understanding   The chair should be sure that every member understands each matter being discussed. All members should know what they are voting on and what effects their vote will have.

Keeps the Meeting Moving   The chair must insure that the meeting moves along at a good pace. Members will then be more likely to pay attention and be enthusiastic. At the same time, the chair must not deny members their parliamentary right of full discussion.

As you can see, the chair must be constantly alert in exercising these duties. Much of the responsibility for a productive meeting rests squarely on the shoulders of the presiding officer.

Application

Using Main Motions

Select a classmate to chair a meeting about proposals for a class trip. Each proposal must be presented as a main motion and may be discussed only after it is seconded. Each main motion must be voted on before another can be presented. Permit several classmates to serve as chair during the meeting.

Methods of Voting

There are several ways in which members may show how they wish to vote on an issue. These methods of voting include voice votes, rising, raising hands, roll calls, and secret ballots.

The most common method of voting is a voice vote. The chair usually calls for a voice vote by saying "All those in favor say aye," and then "All those opposed say no." If the vote is a close one, or if the motion requires a two-thirds vote to pass, the chair may instead ask members to rise or to raise their hands. The wording is similar: "All those in favor please rise (or raise your hands)." This is followed by a count of the votes in favor. Then the chair asks those opposed to rise or to raise their hands.

Roll-call votes are required in the bylaws of some organizations. A roll call may also be necessary if guests who don't have the right to vote are present at the meeting. A roll-call vote is announced by the chair in the following way: "Those in favor will answer aye as their names are called. Those opposed will answer no. The secretary will call the roll."

Voting by secret ballot is required in elections of officers and when voting on important issues. The chair should be sure that each member has a ballot and understands how aye and no votes are marked before the vote is taken.

MOTIONS

When a meeting is being conducted according to parliamentary procedure, business is handled through the making of **motions.** A motion is a formal suggestion or proposal made by a member for consideration and action by the group. Before any new business can be discussed in a parliamentary meeting, someone must make a motion. Without a motion on the floor the group cannot accomplish anything. It is as if they were all sitting in an automobile ready to start a trip and no one bothered to turn the ignition key.

Once a motion is made, the members must act on it in some way. They may vote for it or against it. They may postpone consideration of it. They may refer it to a committee or handle it in any of several other ways. But they may not simply forget about it.

How Motions Are Made

What should you do during a meeting when you wish to make a motion? First you must obtain recognition from the chair to speak. This may be done by holding your hand in the air until you are called upon by the chair, standing until recognized, or whatever the local custom demands. The chair will recognize you by calling your name or by pointing to you. Then you may state your motion. Always begin with the words "I move." Never begin with "I suggest" or "I recommend" or "I think that we should." The words "I move" are a signal that you are making a motion—a formal proposal that you wish the group to debate and act upon.

Formal motions require a **second,** which is an indication by one other member of the assembly that he or she wishes to see the matter debated and acted upon. This is accomplished by someone's saying "Second" or "I second the motion" immediately after it has been made. Though a second is usually made by a member who agrees with the intent of the motion, it is not necessary that the seconder agree. The second only indicates that she or he also wishes to have the matter considered and acted upon. The seconder may actually intend to vote against the motion.

Immediately following the second, the chair restates the motion by saying "It has been moved and seconded that we (do such and such)." Then, if it is a debatable motion, the chair says, "Is there any discussion?" This restatement by the chair officially puts the motion on the floor and makes it a **pending motion**—a motion that is under consideration.

Here is an example of a motion being made:

Liz, *a member:*	*(raises hand)*
Chair:	Liz.
Liz *(rises):*	I move that we hold a pancake breakfast to raise money for the scholarship fund. *(Liz sits down.)*
Nick, *a member:*	I second the motion.
Chair:	It has been moved and seconded that our club hold a pancake breakfast to raise money for the scholarship fund. Is there any discussion?

Motions are divided into four types. These are main motions, subsidiary motions, privileged motions, and incidental motions. Let's look at each type of motion and some of the rules governing them.

Main Motions

Main motions are those which deal directly with the items of business being considered. They are directly concerned with the issues before the group. Here are a few examples of main motions:

"I move that this club donate $100 to our college scholarship fund."

"I move that we initiate a new membership drive immediately."

"I move that we raise our local dues by $1.00, starting May 1."

"I move that we accept Evan Lee as a new member of this board, to complete the unexpired term of Wanda Malik."

Main motions introduce items of new business to an assembly. They must ordinarily be made first, before any of the other classes of motions would make any sense. Main motions are the foundation of parliamentary business.

Main motions require a *second* before they may be debated. They are debatable motions, and they require a simple majority vote to pass. A simple majority means fifty percent plus one of those present and voting. Suppose thirty members are present for a meeting, and only twenty decide to vote on a particular motion. The majority required to pass that motion would be eleven. When the vote is taken, the chair must always ask for both the affirmative and the negative sides of the vote.

Subsidiary Motions

Subsidiary motions allow members to change the nature of main motions or to handle them in some way other than ordinary debate and a vote. They allow such things as postponements, amendments, and limitations on debate. Following are seven commonly used subsidiary motions in the order in which they may be made following a main motion. You will see the purpose of each, whether each is debatable, and what size vote is required to pass each. Subsidiary motions are always proposed after the main motion to which they apply. They must be debated and voted on before the group returns to debate on the main motion.

Postpone Indefinitely   The purpose of making the subsidiary motion to **postpone indefinitely** is to prevent any further discussion or voting on a pending main motion. By not allowing the main motion to come to a direct vote, you can assure that it will be defeated. Assume, for example, that the following main motion is pending: "I move that this club donate $100 to our local college's scholarship fund." A member who wishes to see this motion defeated might get recognition to speak and state, "I move that we postpone this motion indefinitely." If there is a second, this subsidiary motion may then be debated and voted upon. If a simple majority votes in favor of the motion to postpone indefinitely, the main motion to donate the $100 is defeated or killed. If the majority votes against postponing indefinitely, the assembly returns to the debate on the main motion.

Amend   The purpose of a motion to **amend** is to change a main motion in some way. Again assume the pending main motion is to donate $100 to the college scholarship fund. Someone may propose an amendment such as "I move that we change $100 to $50 in the main motion" or "I move we add 'by this coming weekend' to the main motion." Although amendments may change a main motion, they must be **germane** to the main motion to which they apply. Being germane means they must be logically and directly connected with the subject of the main motion. Suppose someone tried to amend the main motion to donate $100 by

"All those in favor of the motion to refer publicity planning to committee, raise your hands."

adding "and raise the salaries of all our club officers." The chair would have to rule the amendment out of order since it is not germane. Raising the officers' salaries is not directly connected with the matter of donating $100 to a scholarship fund.

As is the case with all subsidiary motions, debate and voting on an amendment occur before returning to the main motion. A simple majority vote is required to pass an amendment. If an amendment passes, the assembly returns to debate on the amended version of the main motion. If the amendment fails, the group debates on the main motion in its original form.

Refer to Committee   The motion to **refer to committee** is used when a group wants to save time by allowing a small sub-group to discuss a complicated matter. It is also used when the assembly wishes to insure privacy on a delicate matter. Referring to a committee can put off a decision until later, or it can defeat a matter if the committee is hostile. This motion may be made in the simple form: "I move that we refer this motion to a committee." When makers of this motion wish, they may include any pertinent details they desire in the motion. Details may include how many members should be on the committee, who the members should be, and when the committee should report back to the main assembly. Another detail could be whether the committee may only recommend action or whether it has the power to make a decision for the entire assembly. If a motion to refer to a committee passes, any such details not given in the motion are then decided by the chair of the assembly.

The motion to refer to a committee may be debated briefly. Debate is restricted to selection of the committee, instructions to it, its membership, and duties. A motion to refer to a committee requires a simple majority vote to pass.

Postpone Definitely   Whenever it is desirable to put off consideration of a pending motion, with the intention of bringing it up again at a later time, a motion to **postpone definitely** should be used. Unlike the motion to postpone indefinitely, the motion to postpone definitely includes a specific time when the pending matter will again come up for consideration. Suppose the main motion to donate $100 is pending. Someone might move "to postpone consideration of this matter until after we have heard our annual budget report at the next regularly scheduled meeting." This motion to postpone definitely assures that the motion on the $100 donation will again be on the table following the budget report at the next meeting. Matters may also be postponed definitely until a time later in the same meeting in which the motion is made.

The motion to postpone definitely, as is the case with all formal motions, requires a second. It may be debated briefly. Debate is restricted to the reasons for and the time of postponement. It requires a simple majority vote for passage.

Limit or Extend Debate   The motion **to limit or extend debate** either restricts the time to be devoted to debate on a pending motion or removes any limitation placed upon it. Its most common use is to limit, rather than to extend debate, however. There are a number of ways to make such a motion:

"I move that we limit debate to a total of fifteen minutes."

"I move that we limit debate to one minute per speaker."

"I move that the debate on this motion cease at 2:30 p.m."

Since the very purpose of the motion to limit debate is to restrict further discussion, the motion to limit debate itself may be debated only briefly. Debate must be restricted to the type and time of the limitation. Because limiting debate violates a basic principle of parliamentary procedure—complete and free discussion of every issue—this motion requires a two-thirds majority to pass.

Vote Immediately This motion, if it passes, instantly cuts off debate on a pending motion and brings it to a vote. Assume that the main motion to donate $100 has been placed on the floor for debate. Either right away, or after some discussion on it, a member gets recognition and says: "I move that we **vote immediately** on this motion." The purpose could be to prevent further discussion which the member feels would damage her or his side of the case. The purpose could also be simply to move business along more speedily. In any case, if there is a second, the chair stops debate and immediately takes a vote on the motion to vote immediately. Since its purpose is to stop debate, it is not a debatable motion. Also, since, like the motion to limit debate, it cuts off further discussion, it requires a two-thirds majority to pass. If it passes, the chair then takes an immediate vote on the pending motion. If it fails, the assembly returns to debate on the pending motion.

Postpone Temporarily The subsidiary motion to **postpone temporarily** sets aside consideration of a pending matter until some time later in the same meeting. It is sometimes called a motion to lay on the table. It differs in two ways from the motion to postpone definitely. First, its effect applies only during the same meeting in which it is made. If a matter postponed temporarily during a meeting is not again brought up later in that same meeting, it dies. Second, no definite time is stated in this motion for again discussing the postponed matter.

One reason for making a motion to postpone temporarily is to secure more information about a pending matter before voting. Another reason is to set aside an unwelcome motion in the hope that it will not be brought up again. This motion is not debatable. It requires a simple majority vote to pass.

Application

Using Subsidiary Motions

As a class, select five students to role-play members of your school system's board of education. The members will elect a chairperson and conduct a school board meeting. The class as a whole will decide on agenda items before the meeting begins. The board members will introduce main motions and use subsidiary motions as needed to deal with all business thoroughly and efficiently. After the meeting, the class will discuss the board's performance. Did all members get a chance to voice their opinions? Were all agenda items taken care of efficiently? Were the rules of parliamentary procedure followed correctly?

Privileged Motions

Three motions are considered to be of such an urgent nature that they form a class called **privileged motions.** Unlike subsidiary motions, they do not relate to the items of business before the assembly. They refer instead to the organization and its members. Because of their urgent nature, they may be made and considered ahead of any of the other classes of motions. They are the motions calling for question of privilege, recess, and adjournment.

Question of Privilege Though called a motion, the **question of privilege** is really a request made by a member and granted or denied by the chair. A question of privilege may be made to secure immediate action on some urgent matter that relates to the comfort, convenience, rights, or privileges of the assembly, or one of its members. It may also be made to secure permission to make an urgent motion while some other matter is pending. The following example shows how a question of privilege may be presented:

Member:	Mr. Chairman, I rise to a question of privilege.
Chair:	State your question of privilege.
Member:	I ask that we send someone to check the public records in the courthouse before we vote on this current matter.

If the courthouse records are likely to have a direct bearing on the assembly's decision on the pending matter, the chair would probably grant such a request.

Recess If a motion to **recess** passes, it calls a halt to a meeting without ending it. A motion to recess must always include a time when the body will resume the meeting. Though recesses are usually brief, they can last for days. The time of the recess cannot extend beyond the time for the next regularly scheduled meeting of the group, however. The motion to recess requires a second. It may be debated briefly regarding the time or need for the recess. It needs a simple majority vote to pass.

Adjournment Passage of a motion to **adjourn** ends a meeting. Unlike the motion to recess, which only calls a halt in a meeting, the motion to adjourn legally concludes a meeting. When members of an assembly meet again following an adjournment, they do not take up at the point where they left off on their agenda (as in the case of a recess). Rather they begin a new meeting with a new agenda. Business that was interrupted or left unfinished by an adjournment comes up on the agenda of the next

HEALTH SERVICES ADMINISTRATOR

Health services administrators supervise and coordinate a hospital's numerous departments. They are responsible for managing personnel, executing public relations activities, and preparing the hospital budget. A career in this profession requires a master's degree in one of these fields: hospital administration, public health, or business administration.

The hospital's board of directors, the most important group the administrator works with, determines the hospital's operating budget. The administrator must present the hospital's financial needs to the board to receive the necessary funding. Many hospital boards use parliamentary procedure to conduct their business. Effective administrators use this set of rules to their advantage in order to communicate the hospital's most pressing needs.

Because parliamentary procedure dictates that participants be notified of upcoming meetings, administrators can utilize this time to research and prepare any essential information. During meetings, their phrasing and timing of motions may be so exact that discussion is encouraged or discouraged according to their needs. When the administrator's position on an issue is opposed to the board's, parliamentary procedure guarantees him or her the opportunity to state the hospital's position completely without interruption.

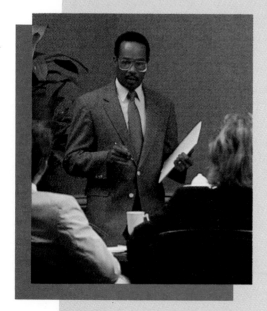

By itself, a competent use of parliamentary procedure is not enough to achieve budgetary goals. However, when the administrator's ability to speak persuasively is combined with an expert use of parliamentary procedure, obtaining the funds necessary to maintain high standards of health care becomes more likely.

This administrator gains support through skilled use of parliamentary procedure.

meeting under the heading "Unfinished Business." Since it would defeat the purpose to debate a motion to adjourn, it is not debatable. It requires a simple majority vote to pass.

Incidental Motions

The last type of motion relates to procedures having to do with the conduct of parliamentary business. Some of these are true motions, requiring a second and a vote. Others are simply requests, granted by the chair. Here are the names, purpose, and vote required (if any) of the eight most common **incidental motions:**

Appeal   An **appeal** motion allows a member who disagrees with a ruling by the chair to put that ruling to a vote. This is a true motion requiring a second and a simple majority vote.

Suspend the Rules   A motion to **suspend the rules** is also a true motion. It allows the assembly to set aside some procedural rule so the members can do something not ordinarily allowed by that rule. Only procedural rules may be suspended. Suppose the bylaws of an organization call for a particular order of business, but the officer who should make the next report has not yet arrived. A member may make a motion to suspend the rules and allow that officer to report later so the group may proceed with other business in the meantime. Such a motion would require a second and a two-thirds majority vote.

Object to Consideration   This allows an assembly to avoid debate and a decision on a pending motion. The assembly may believe it to be embarrassing or unprofitable, or may have some other good reason for not wishing to consider it. Since it completely avoids consideration of an issue if it passes, **object to consideration** is a motion requiring a second and a two-thirds majority to pass.

Point-of-Order   This is a request used to call to the attention of the chair and the assembly that an error is being made. Perhaps a procedure is being violated. A member must gain attention by calling **"Point of order"** immediately after the error has occurred. After stating what she or he believes the error to be, an immediate ruling is given by the chair. No vote is taken.

Parliamentary Inquiry   **Parliamentary inquiry** is a request that gives a member an opportunity to ask the chair questions about parliamentary procedure dealing with a motion under consideration at that time. Because it is a request addressed to the chair and not a motion, it does not require a second. The chair answers the inquiry, so no vote is necessary.

Withdraw a Motion **Withdraw a motion** enables a member who has made a motion to remove it from consideration before a vote is taken. Such a motion may be withdrawn by simple request of its maker if (a) the chair has not yet restated the motion to the assembly or (b) the chair has restated it, but no one objects to its being withdrawn. If just one member objects in the second case above, however, the request to withdraw becomes a motion requiring a simple majority to pass.

Division of Question A **division of question** is used to separate a motion having two or more independent parts into separate motions for purposes of separate debate and voting. This is ordinarily a request, granted by the presiding officer, unless a member objects. Then, like the motion to withdraw a motion, it must be voted upon and requires a simple majority to pass.

"I move that we amend the motion." Members of this committee must, according to the order of precedence, debate and vote on the amendment before resuming discussion of the main motion.

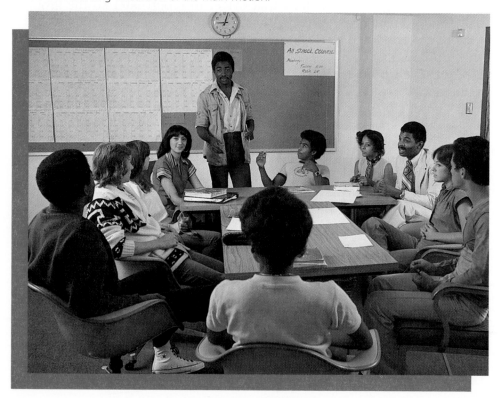

Division of Assembly   If a vote has been taken by voice, and anyone is unsure about which side has the majority, a member may request a **division of assembly.** This is simply a method of retaking such a vote by a show of hands or by having members rise in their places to be counted. Such a request is ordinarily granted by the chair as long as there is a reasonable question about the outcome of the voice vote.

Precedence of Motions

All of the motions discussed, except the incidental motions, must be dealt with in **order of precedence.** This is a ranking system that tells you the order in which you must vote on each of the motions. There are two rules that govern the order of precedence:

1. When a motion is pending, only motions above it in the order of precedence may be made.

2. When motions have already been made, they must be debated and acted upon in the opposite order from that in which they were made. In other words, the motion made most recently is acted upon first.

Earlier in this chapter when you read about the different kinds of motions, they were presented in the order in which they could be introduced. The order of precedence reverses that order and lists the motions in the order in which they would be acted upon. This reversal reflects the need to work back to the main motion. It guarantees that the main motion will be addressed only when all other motions that affect it have been dealt with. The order of precedence looks like this:

Privileged Motions	**1.** Adjourn
	2. Recess
	3. Question of Privilege
Subsidiary Motions	**4.** Postpone Temporarily
	5. Vote Immediately
	6. Limit Debate
	7. Postpone Definitely
	8. Refer to Committee
	9. Amend
	10. Postpone Indefinitely
Main Motion	**11.** Any Main Motion

The first rule of precedence means that only motions of higher rank may be made while another motion is pending. Suppose, for example, that a member has made the main motion to donate $100 to a scholarship fund. While this main motion is pending, someone else moves to amend the amount to $50. This motion to amend is permissible, or in order, since the motion to amend (9) is of higher rank than the main motion (11). During the debate on the amendment, however, someone attempts to make a motion to postpone indefinitely (10). The chair must rule this motion out of order. This means it cannot be made at that time. This is because the motion to postpone indefinitely (10) is of lower rank than the pending motion, amend (9).

The second rule of precedence means that members must always first dispose of the last motion made. Then they can proceed backwards to the first one proposed. Suppose, for instance, they start with a main motion. A member proposes an amendment to the main motion. Then someone moves to limit debate. The assembly must first decide on

Rules governing motions with order of precedence					
	Can Interrupt?	Requires Second?	Debatable?	Amendable?	Vote Required?
Privileged motions					
1. Adjourn	no	yes	no	no	majority
2. Recess	no	yes	yes^r	yes^r	majority
3. Question of privilege	yes	no	no	no	none
Subsidiary motions					
4. Postpone temporarily	no	yes	no	no	majority
5. Vote immediately	no	yes	no	no	two-thirds
6. Limit debate	no	yes	yes^r	yes^r	two-thirds
7. Postpone definitely	no	yes	yes^r	yes^r	majority
8. Refer to committee	no	yes	yes^r	yes^r	majority
9. Amend	no	yes	yes	yes	majority
10. Postpone indefinitely	no	yes	yes	no	majority
Main motions					
11. The main motion	no	yes	yes	yes	majority
(r = restricted)					

Rules governing motions with order of precedence

Rules governing motions with no order of precedence					
Incidental motions	Can Interrupt?	Requires Second?	Debatable?	Amendable?	Vote Required?
Appeal	yes	yes	yes	no	majority
Suspend rules	no	yes	no	no	two-thirds
Object to consideration	yes	yes	no	no	two-thirds
Point of order	yes	no	no	no	none
Parliamentary inquiry	yes	no	no	no	none
Withdraw a motion	yes	no	no	no	none
Division of question	no	no	no	no	none
Division of assembly	yes	no	no	no	none

Rules governing motions with no order of precedence

whether or not to limit debate before returning to debate on the amendment to the main motion.

The incidental motions have no order of precedence. They may be made at any time they are appropriate and must be acted upon immediately. The chart on page 430 and the chart above on this page summarize these and other motions. Used together, these charts should provide you with all the basic information you will need in order to deal with motions made during a typical meeting.

Application

Practicing Parliamentary Procedure

As a class, set up an imaginary club or governmental body and conduct a meeting. Begin by establishing an agenda. One group wishes to pass as many motions as possible. The other group wishes to postpone action on as many motions as possible. Elect a chairperson and begin the meeting. Adjourn after 30 minutes and discuss the experience.

14 Chapter Review

◼ Summary

Parliamentary procedure is a set of rules designed to streamline the conduct of business at meetings and at the same time protect the democratic rights of the participants. It began in the English Parliament and has developed over the years as a set of basic principles.

Basic Principles Parliamentary procedure is based on five principles: only one question may be considered at a time; the majority rules; the rights of the minority are protected; all members share equal rights and responsibilities; and every issue may be subjected to free debate.

Holding a Meeting Holding a meeting according to parliamentary procedure begins with giving notice. This means informing members about the meeting, usually about ten days in advance. When the time for the meeting arrives, the chair must determine whether a quorum is present before beginning. The usual order of business consists of the call to order, approval of the minutes, reports of officers, reports of standing and special committees, unfinished business, new business, announcements, and adjournment. During a meeting the chair's duties include keeping order, recognizing members to speak, insuring that all members understand the issues, and moving the meeting along. Methods of voting include voice votes, rising, raising hands, roll calls, or secret ballots.

Motions Business is handled during meetings by the making of motions. Motions are formal proposals made by members for consideration and action by the assembly. Motions fall into four major types. Main motions deal directly with the issues before the assembly. They are the foundation of a parliamentary meeting. Subsidiary motions allow members to change the nature of main motions, or to handle them in some other way than by ordinary debate and a vote. Privileged motions relate to urgent matters dealing with the organization and its members. Incidental motions have to do with procedural matters and the conduct of parliamentary business. Order of precedence determines the order in which each motion must be addressed.

Vocabulary

Define at least 15 terms in complete sentences.

parliamentary procedure	refer to committee
parliamentarian	postpone definitely
simple majority	limit or extend debate
minority	vote immediately
notice	postpone temporarily
agenda	privileged motion
quorum	question of privilege
order of business	recess
chair	adjourn
filibustering	incidental motion
recognizing	appeal
motion	suspend the rules
second	object to consideration
pending motion	point of order
main motion	parliamentary inquiry
subsidiary motion	withdraw a motion
postpone indefinitely	division of question
amend	division of assembly
germane	order of precedence

Checklist

Skills Of Parliamentary Procedure

1. Be aware of the purpose of the rules that govern parliamentary procedure.
2. Make use of published codes of parliamentary procedure.
3. Apply the basic principles of parliamentary procedure at meetings whenever possible.
4. Learn the specific rules of parliamentary procedure.
5. Learn and apply the duties of the chair.
6. Know the various methods of voting by which members may show how they wish to vote on an issue.
7. Follow proper procedure for making motions.
8. Learn the differences among the various kinds of motions.

Review Questions

1. Name the five principles that form the basis for parliamentary procedure.
2. Name the two most commonly used codes of parliamentary procedure.
3. Define a simple majority.
4. List several guidelines for responsible membership in an organization.
5. Define the term *quorum*.
6. List the usual order of business for a meeting.
7. Name the duties of the chair.
8. Identify the four types of motions used in parliamentary procedure.
9. State the purpose of each of the four types of motions.
10. State the order of precedence for these motions.

Discussion Questions

1. Discuss the contribution that parliamentary procedure can make to the functioning of a democracy. What fundamental democratic principles does parliamentary procedure help to safeguard? How might these be jeopardized if the principles of parliamentary procedure were not adhered to?
2. Discuss the use of parliamentary procedure in organizations to which you belong. Do most of them use parliamentary procedure? How can you encourage organizations to do a more efficient job of conducting business? What problems might occur regularly in organizations that do not use parliamentary procedure in their meetings? How would these problems be solved?
3. Discuss the duties of the chair or presiding officer. Why is this job so important? What personal qualities should a presiding officer possess in order to chair a meeting effectively?
4. Discuss the circumstances under which it is advisable to table a motion. What are the possible outcomes of tabled motions? How can this device be used by the minority to strengthen its position?
5. Discuss the responsibilities that members of a parliamentary group have. What must members do to ensure that the group operates effectively and efficiently?

Critical Thinking

1. **Analysis:** Assume that a legislative body sets its quorum requirements at ten percent of its elected members. Would such a requirement promote the serious consideration of issues? What effect would such a requirement have upon an established majority?

2. **Evaluation:** Imagine that all debate has ended on an important issue in a legislative assembly. A vote is called for, and the chair decides upon a voice vote. It is very difficult to determine which side has a majority, but the chair rules that the motion is defeated. Comment on the chair's action. What should the chair have done, instead, under the circumstances?

Activities

In-Class

1. Select members of the class to make brief reports on the following topics. Be prepared to add to the information supplied or to correct mistaken information.
    (a) which motions are not debatable, and why
    (b) why certain motions are classified as "privileged"
    (c) what a chair should do to ensure impartiality
    (d) the proper use of a motion to amend and the limitations of this type of motion
    (e) why some motions require a two-thirds majority to pass while others require a simple majority
    (f) the necessity of careful planning when formulating by-laws for an organization
    (g) the procedure for indicating that proper procedures have not been followed
    (h) the procedure for registering disagreement with the chair on the chair's rulings

2. Imagine that your class is a state legislative body. Decide on three laws that will be debated during a meeting. Establish an agenda for the meeting and elect a chair. During the meeting, attempt to use as many types of motions as possible. Remember to rise to a point of order if either the

chair or a member violates a rule of procedure.

3. As a class, discuss what the minority tries to accomplish at a meeting. What tactics does the minority use to accomplish its goals? If you were a member of the minority when an important proposal was being discussed, what rules of parliamentary procedure would you use to gain the most exposure for your cause?

4. During a mock meeting to determine how to spend surplus money in the student activities' fund, take turns with various class members serving as chair. After the meeting, discuss the problems and successes each of you had while acting as chair.

Out-of-Class

1. At the next formal meeting of an organization to which you belong, practice the correct use of the motions explained in this chapter. If the organization does not currently use parliamentary procedure in its meetings, point out the benefits that such rules would bring to the organization.

2. Attend a meeting of a local government board, a town or city council, or a school board. Note the way in which parliamentary procedure is used during the meeting. Summarize what took place at the meeting in your speech notebook. Be prepared to report your findings to the class.

3. Find examples in U.S. legislative history where the filibuster rule was used effectively either to prevent, postpone, or draw attention to an issue. Why do you think the filibuster rule became a part of parliamentary procedure? Share your examples and conclusions with the class.

4. Decide upon a course of action that you would like to see taken by a real or imaginary organization. Describe in your speech notebook how you would gather support for your proposals. Draw up whatever motions might be necessary to get your proposals approved. If you belong to the organization, try to implement your plans according to the rules of parliamentary procedure.

5. Research the history of parliamentary procedure. Find out who Henry Roberts was and examine a copy of Robert's *Rules of Order*. Prepare a brief oral report on parliamentary procedure, including the reasons for its development and eventual adoption, and deliver it to the class.

■ Chapter Project

Select a group of students to develop a public-information program about parliamentary procedure. The program could be presented at a school assembly or at a meeting of an interested organization. The class as a whole should decide upon both a format and an outline for the demonstration, and should prepare charts or any other visual aids needed to enable the presenters to communicate clearly. The program could take one of any number of forms, such as a series of short lectures, a combination of lecture and demonstration, or a docudrama that reenacts the history and present-day use of parlimentary procedure. After everything is prepared, the group of presenters should give a performance for the class and then request reactions and feedback. Incorporate valuable suggestions for improvement into the program before presenting it to the public.

Mass
Communication

unit 6

15 Radio and Television

15 Radio and Television

**When you have completed this chapter
you should be able to:**

- Explain how radio and television are different from other types of communication.
- Discuss the development of radio and television and the impact these media have on people's lives.
- Discuss the verbal and nonverbal requirements for radio and television performers.
- Describe special communication skills necessary for different types of radio and television performers.
- Describe some of the jobs that are part of radio and television production.

Radio and television—unparalleled in their ability to reach millions of people—represent a new dimension in communication that is insulated from the effects of immediate audience feedback.

Mass communication, whether in the form of newspapers, books, movies, radio, or television, differs from all other types of communication. It is designed to reach large audiences who are not usually physically present and who can "turn off" the senders at will.

The importance of mass communication can be seen in the history of Lincoln's Gettysburg Address. When President Lincoln spoke his Gettysburg Address in 1863, the audience that heard his words was very small compared to the number of people who later read the speech in newspapers, magazines, and books.

Mass communication in these written forms has been available for hundreds of years. Recent technological advancements have not only improved the methods of producing written forms of mass communication but have also made possible the development of electronic forms of mass communication. Through the **electronic media** of radio and television, large audiences can now not only hear and see something happening on the other side of the world, but can also witness it at the moment it occurs. Radio and television have become, by far, the two most effective means of mass communication available.

THE NATURE OF RADIO AND TELEVISION

One reason for radio and television's success is their capacity to attract enormously large audiences. It is estimated that many American families own as many as six radios, including those in cars, and that 99 percent of the homes in the United States have at least one television set. Over 80 percent of the population listens to the radio at least once a day, and many people spend several hours each day watching television.

Radio and television have also made it possible for countless numbers of people to share a single experience. In 1969, over 600 million people throughout the world heard men speak from the surface of the moon. By 1984, close to one and one-half billion people watched the Twenty-third Summer Olympics in Los Angeles.

Another important characteristic of radio and television is their ability to communicate over long distances in very short amounts of time. Think about it. Radio and television have made it possible for someone to hear live music from New York City and to see a football game as it is being played in Dallas, Texas—all without ever leaving the confines of a living room in Boston, Massachusetts. Because radio waves travel at the speed of light, or about 186,282 miles (299,792 km) per second, it is even possible for people listening to the sounds of a live concert being broadcast from another state to hear the sounds a split second before the sounds reach the back of the room in which they are being made. Radio and television can bring you into direct and immediate contact with other people and places all over the world.

Perhaps the most significant aspect of radio and television is the amount of control the audience has over the media. With radio and TV, the listener is not part of a "captive" audience. If you do not like what is being communicated, you can simply flick a switch and change the message. Furthermore, if you do not wish to hear or see any message at all, you are equally free to remove yourself quickly and easily from what is being communicated, or simply to shut the medium off altogether.

THE DEVELOPMENT OF ELECTRONIC MEDIA

The electronic media have developed within the last hundred and fifty years. Before the invention of radio and television, long distance communication of sound required the use of wires such as those used in telegraph and telephone service. The gradual development of the "wireless"—as the early radio was called—marked the beginnings of important changes in the way people could communicate. Continual developments in technology have produced rapid changes in the use of electronic media and the effect they have on people's lives.

A Brief History of Radio

No one person or country can be credited with the invention of the radio. In the late nineteenth and early twentieth centuries many scientists and inventors working in the fields of electricity and magnetism

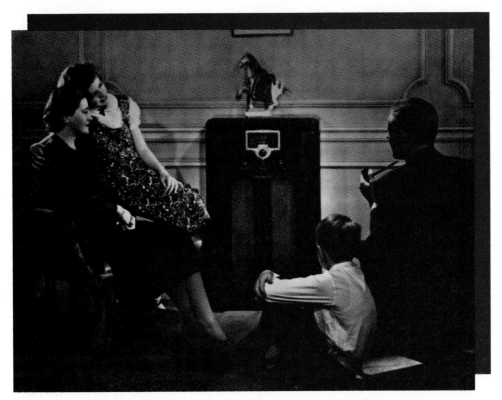

The novelty and impact of early broadcasts were such that families often gathered to *watch* the radio as favorite programs were aired.

contributed to its development. In 1897 a British patent was obtained for "communication using electro-magnetic waves." In that same year, the first permanent radio installation was established in England.

At first, radio could only transmit coded sounds as the telegraph did. But, by the early twentieth century, radio operators were communicating with each other in words. One of the most important uses of early radio was providing a direct communication link from ship to shore and from ship to ship. In 1912 the survivors of the sunken Titanic were rescued because of their radio distress calls.

In the 1920's, radio began to capture the interest of the American public. By 1923 over five hundred separate radio stations were broadcasting on a regular basis. In the 1930's and 1940's, countless families gathered around household radios to hear voices being transmitted through the air and into their kitchens or living rooms.

Radio became "big business" as well as "show business" when individual companies bought time on radio stations to advertise their products and produced their own live comedy, variety, and musical programs to attract audiences. Soap manufacturers developed continuing drama programs for broadcast during the daytime that have been known ever since as *soap operas.* Situation comedies were also first developed through radio. News and sports programs were broadcast regularly. Joe Louis's championship boxing matches were so popular that movie theater operators would often stop the film in order to broadcast the program for their audiences.

A Brief History of Television

Almost as soon as people learned how to transmit sound through the air over long distances, experiments to do the same with pictures were begun. As with radio, no one person can take all the credit for the invention of television. Rather, a series of independent discoveries over a relatively short period of about thirty years made television possible. Although experiments with television began as early as 1884, progress was slight until the discoveries made between 1920 and 1950. In 1923 the first television camera suitable for broadcasting was introduced. By 1929 complete television systems were available, and by 1939 America was broadcasting television on a regular basis. The American public, however, did not respond very eagerly to this new invention. Few television sets were sold in the late 1930's and early 1940's because of the public's attachment to radio and the expense involved. After World War II ended in 1945, interest in television increased greatly. By 1950, the great television boom was in full swing. It wasn't long before the medium of television had completely overtaken radio in popularity.

One of the reasons television proved to be so popular was the way it was able to incorporate the best of both film and radio. Like a movie, TV was visual. Like a radio broadcast, TV was immediate. With television, people found that they could, for example, not only see an event but could do so almost as quickly as it happened. Taking its cue from radio, television became a commercial business in 1941. By that time most of the successful radio shows and performers had been introduced to television audiences. Milton Berle's "Texaco Star Theater" not only attracted large nationwide audiences, but also helped to establish the comedy routine as a very important part of television entertainment. Variety shows and soap operas continued to be popular after they were adapted for a visual medium. In 1951 Lucille Ball and Desi Arnaz began working on situation comedies for TV. They became extremely popular for their half-hour hit comedy, "I Love Lucy." The longest-running television show, "Meet the Press," has been broadcast weekly since 1948.

Early television was almost always broadcast live. Live broadcasting can make programs more interesting, but the possibility of something going wrong always exists. Some people remember the time Betty Furness, while doing a live television commercial, found, to her horror, that the refrigerator she was demonstrating would not open when she pulled on the handle. Later, all TV commercials were put on film even if the rest of the broadcast was live.

The invention and increasing use of **videotape** in the mid-1950's permitted television stations to record not only commercials but also entertainment programs on tape for quick rebroadcast. This led to other recording techniques, including instant replay, slow motion, stop action, and split screen. Videocassette cameras and videocassette recorders have become very popular. Almost 20 million homes have at least one videocassette recorder. This number is expected to grow phenomenally in the next few years.

Even with the many technological advances, some talk shows and sporting events are still broadcast live. Newscasts often use a combination of videotape and live broadcasting. The vast majority of television programs today, however, are completely videotaped.

Another important invention, color, first appeared in television in 1954. Now, most of the homes in the United States have at least one color TV set, and almost all programs are produced in color.

The overseas transmission of television through the use of satellites began in 1962. This not only opened up new markets for American broadcasting but also made live television from other countries available to the American public. "What's next?" you may be asking. It is difficult to say exactly what technological changes will be made in television in the future. Most manufacturers promise, at the very least, bigger screens, sharper pictures, and better-quality sound.

Radio Today

Television's quick rise in popularity had a very negative effect on radio, and at one time even threatened to make it obsolete. Radio's survival has depended upon its ability to adapt. By concentrating on its strengths and making necessary programming changes, radio has been able to provide some services that television doesn't.

One advantage radio has is that receivers are often small, lightweight, and inexpensive. Portable radios, run by batteries, have made it possible for people to listen while shopping, sunbathing at the beach, or working outdoors. Most automobiles are equipped with radios. Many people prefer radio because they can listen while they do other things.

Another factor in radio's favor is the fine quality of sound produced. Stereo broadcasts present sound closer to the quality available at live performances than do most television sets. Some people, in fact, have adopted the habit of listening to concerts on their stereos while they watch them on their television screens.

Radio has also made important changes in its programming in recent years. Gone from most radio stations are the soap operas, situation comedies, and variety shows. In their place radio now offers more news, music, and talk shows. In fact, many radio stations attempt to attract listeners by specializing in specific types of programs. People who are interested, for example, in classical music can easily find radio stations that specialize in presenting classical music. Many radio stations have included more live talk shows in their programming. Studies have indicated that these programs attract large numbers of listeners. Experts speak on foreign affairs, or political or environmental issues. Guest speakers give self-help hints and listeners telephone to discuss their opinions on various subjects. President Ronald Reagan speaks to the American public on a popular weekly Saturday radio program.

Television Today

Television, too, has adapted itself to changing times by the technological improvements already discussed and also by the types of television service available. Several different kinds of television have emerged in the last thirty years. Each of these has been designed to fulfill specific audience needs.

Commercial TV The vast majority of available television programs are transmitted by commercial stations. **Commercial television** is paid for by companies who buy air time to advertise their products. The major criticism of this kind of television is that it has become more of a business than a service. Because producing commercial television programs is expensive, large fees are charged for advertising time. Stations and networks must be able to guarantee large audiences for sponsors paying these large fees. Only those types of programs that will attract the greatest number of people remain on the air. The different commercial stations and networks continually compete against each other for a larger share of the audience.

Educational TV The Federal Communications Commission has set aside television channels strictly for educational use. By 1979 over 250 stations were being used for exactly that purpose. Many were run by state education departments and universities. **Educational television** generally broadcasts instructional programs and programs of cultural enrichment, such as concerts, operas, and ballets. Educational TV is funded mainly through government grants.

Public TV **Public television,** which is funded mainly by company grants and donations from viewers, strives to produce a wide variety of television programs, especially those not provided by commercial sta-

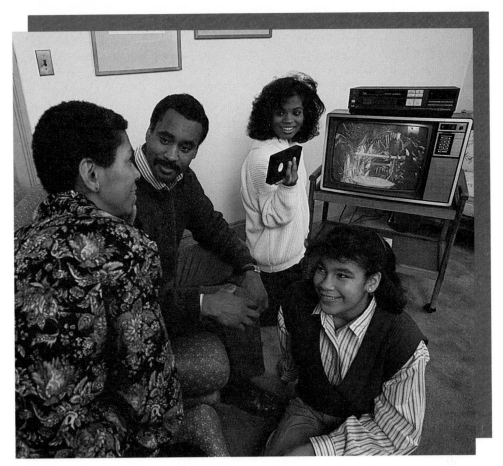

Television today has a new competitor: the videocassette recorder, which lets people "program" their viewing time with videotapes of their choice.

tions. Programs include ones that are entertaining, informative, instructional, and culturally enriching. Public television's audiences are usually smaller than those of commercial television, but very dedicated. Programs produced by local public television stations are made available to other public stations throughout the country. Programs are also purchased from other countries and from independent television production companies. Some of public television's most popular shows are its children's programs including "Sesame Street" and "The Electric Company." Award winners such as "Masterpiece Theater" and the "MacNeil/Lehrer Report" have helped build the number of public television stations to over 300. It is estimated that three out of four Americans watch some public television. Because government funds for public television are limited, and it must depend upon company grants and donations from its viewing audience for support, viewers have more direct control over programming than they have over commercial TV.

Cable TV or CATV **Cable TV** began in the 1950's. It was used originally by people who lived in poor television reception areas, such as the mountains or large cities, to improve the quality of reception. These people would pay a monthly fee to a cable TV company to have their television sets connected by a cable to large antennas. Communities decided which cable TV company would be allowed to provide service in their areas. Cable TV also attracted a large number of people who wished to increase the number of television stations they could receive on their sets. Over 35 million homes have cable television. Some cable systems now produce their own local TV programs and televise local sports events.

Pay TV or Toll TV It has taken a long time for **pay TV** to become popular in the United States. Early experiments with this kind of TV failed miserably. The American public has only fairly recently shown a willingness to pay for television viewing. For the most part, pay TV offers its viewers first-run movies and a wide variety of sporting events not available on other stations. Basically, there are two types of pay TV. Closed-circuit pay TV uses a cable to transmit its programs within a closed system—from a boxing ring in Las Vegas to a movie theater in New York, for example. In this case, the viewers simply go to the theater and pay the price of admission. Broadcast pay TV uses special receivers that can be connected to regular household TV sets. These receivers are designed to decode signals sent through the air. Some of the receivers record the amount of viewing time so the viewers can be properly billed on a per-program basis later. In other cases the company running the service charges a regular monthly fee and subscribers may watch as often as they like.

Radio's And Television's Impact On The Public

Although both radio and television have changed greatly over the years, both have continued to have a strong impact on the public. Perhaps the best example of the potential impact such media can have is found in an account of a Halloween night radio broadcast in 1938. Orson Welles, then a well-known radio broadcaster, gave thousands of people the scare of their lives. In honor of the holiday, Orson Welles broadcast an adaptation of H. G. Wells' *War of the Worlds*—a radio drama made up of fictional news accounts describing a Martian invasion of earth. Many people listening panicked. They besieged police stations with telephone

RADIO ANNOUNCER

Radio announcers entertain and inform their listening audiences. A career in radio broadcasting is best achieved by completing a college degree in liberal arts, broadcasting, journalism, or communications. Regardless of their major, prospective radio announcers should include courses in speech and English composition.

Radio announcers need exceptional verbal and non-verbal communication skills. Announcers also must be able to read script so that it sounds fresh and natural. They must be ready at any time to speak extemporaneously. The ability to sustain a sincere, enthusiastic tone of voice, whether reading from a script or ad-libbing, is a skill an announcer gains from experience.

Radio announcers perform for live audiences, but unlike many performers, they neither hear nor see their listeners. As a result, there is no immediate feedback to help them gauge their effectiveness as communicators during a broadcast. Feedback, when it exists, occurs much later in the form of letters or telephone calls from the listening audience. Because of this lack, announcers must be vigilant about articulating precisely, varying voice volume without speaking too loudly or softly, and altering pitch for emphasis.

Effective radio announcers contribute much more than entertainment to their listeners. Whether broadcasters are speaking informatively about the music they select or alerting listeners to a news update, their facility for expressive communication allows them to improve the quality of life for vast audiences.

Superb communication skills are the radio announcer's most fundamental asset.

calls; some left their houses in search of safety; still others armed themselves and prepared to do battle with the alien invaders. Although this broadcast had a short-term effect on people, it illustrates the potential radio has to influence the behavior of millions.

Another example of radio's power is illustrated by this quotation from S. I. Hayakawa's *Language in Thought and Action:* "It is only a slight exaggeration to say that Hitler conquered Austria by radio."

In the 1930's and early 1940's, President Franklin D. Roosevelt was one of the first American public figures to understand the political potential of electronic mass communication. By using radio to broadcast his "Fireside Chats," Roosevelt was able to sway public opinion in support of his social reforms. Since then, radio and television have greatly affected political campaigns in America. Because candidates are now able to reach millions of people at a time, the public has become more politically aware. This has affected the outcome of many local and national elections.

Some people are very concerned about the long-term effects television has upon the public. TV has raised the hopes of many people for a higher standard of living, but it has also been a source of deep frustration for others who perceive a big difference between the way they have to live and the ideal world that television sometimes seems to portray.

Many parents worry about the effect of TV violence on their children. It is estimated that most American children 14 years old have seen the violent deaths of over ten thousand people on television. Many people believe seeing so much violence is harmful to children.

Television has also affected people's social lives. For the past twenty years television has dominated leisure-time activity in America. In fact, next to sleeping and working, Americans spend the most time watching television.

A recent public survey asked people to name what item in their home was most important to them. Revealingly, 32 percent said, "My TV." Television has long been referred to as the "electronic babysitter." But now many parents are not sure that they approve of the amount of time their children are spending in front of "the tube." Studies show that children (or adults for that matter) who are always "tuned in" to television are often "tuned out" to other equally or more important activities, such as reading, participating in sports, or homework. Some parents have begun to take positive action. They have installed devices that prevent young children from turning on the television set themselves. A number of parents who have used these devices have reported positive changes in the behavior and habits of their children. Other parents try to guide their children toward what they consider the most worthwhile television programs.

"I hate the way these commercials exploit us kids and subtly implant desires in us for nonessential material goods."

THE PURPOSES OF RADIO AND TELEVISION

Radio and television have three major purposes: to entertain you, to inform or educate you, and to sell you something.

For Entertainment

The number of ways radio and television have entertained their audiences in the past sixty years is practically limitless. Comedy has always been one of the most popular forms of radio and television entertainment. Individual comedians like Bob Hope, George Burns, Carol Burnett, and Bill Cosby have become famous for telling jokes and funny stories. The TV comedy series, pioneered by people such as Lucille Ball, Jack Benny, and Red Skelton, have used everything from "one liners" to slapstick in order to make people laugh. Probably the most important development in mass comic entertainment has been the situation comedy. With its beginnings in radio, this type of comedy has come to dominate modern television programming.

Drama is another important form of radio and television entertainment. Westerns, police stories, science fiction, and soap operas are only a few of the kinds of drama that have been used by both radio and television at one time or another. One phenomenally successful type of television drama is the weeknight soap opera. The six- to ten-hour "miniseries" drama is also very popular. This format has made possible the filming of material too long for regular-length drama.

A third form of entertainment that has always been available is music. Whether played or sung, music—rock, jazz, classical, country western, or easy listening—has been an important part of radio's and television's past and present. Music Television (MTV) is a very popular form of cable television. The programming is centered around the dramatization of top pop-rock hits, and is especially popular with high-school and university audiences.

The type of entertainment that has attained the largest single radio and television audiences is the live broadcast of sporting events. Audiences have always enjoyed listening to and viewing events such as the Olympic Games and championship matches between professional sports teams.

For Information

One of radio's and television's most useful functions is to inform and educate the public. The most common way to inform the public has been through frequent news broadcasts. Almost every radio station provides its listeners with some local and world news every hour. And all of the major TV networks schedule several one-half hour and hour-long newscasts every day.

The television **news magazine** is another way people have kept informed. Programs such as "60 Minutes" and "20/20" are news programs that encourage reporting in greater depth.

The **documentary** is another important source of information. Both radio and television present documentary programs. They provide the public with in-depth reports on one important subject.

Finally, educational television and radio also play their part in transmitting important information. Because these special fields of broadcasting tend to deal mostly with academic subjects, the messages they send are more concerned with educational facts than with contemporary up-to-the-minute news.

For Profit

The third major purpose of radio and television broadcasting is to make a profit. Commercial radio and TV stations sell time to advertisers. In this business, time is money. If the stations are able to take in more money from their advertisers than they spend on programming, they make a profit. In turn, individual advertisers make money by using commercials to sell a product or a service. The problem with this system is that the public is caught in the middle. The money that first goes to the advertisers and later to the commercial radio and TV stations comes from the public. Yet, because the public doesn't pay directly for any broadcast time, it has very little control over the quality of programs and commercials.

Someone once said that the trouble with commercials is that they first give you a headache, and then try to sell you something to get rid of it. While this isn't an entirely accurate statement, it does illustrate a common advertising strategy.

But commercials can also fulfill all three major purposes of radio and television by being entertaining, as well as by informing the American public about the existence of new products—thereby enabling people to judge for themselves the comparative advantages and disadvantages of competing ones. Finally, how much would you be willing to pay for television if advertisers were no longer willing to spend the money necessary to get most programs produced?

Application

Exploring the Influence of Radio and Television

Survey the class to determine how many radios and televisions are in each household and how many hours per week family members spend listening and watching. Discuss the effects of the mass media on your interests, attitudes, and behavior. What kinds of shows do you enjoy most? Do shows cater to a variety of tastes? How are you affected by commercials? Do commercials persuade you to buy a certain product? Is this good or bad?

PERFORMING ON RADIO AND TELEVISION

Radio and television performers are people who have learned important and valuable verbal and nonverbal communication skills. In addition, different types of performers have developed special skills in order to be successful at this type of work. This section will look at various types of performers and then at the particular communication skills they must develop.

Types of Radio and TV Performers

Many people immediately connect the word *performer* with the word *actor*. But actors are only one type of performer on radio and television. In fact, on radio today, actors rarely perform.

While actors do perform in television drama, actors and other entertainers often appear not as characters but as personalities on television programs called "specials." One of the most popular types of entertainer is the comedian. Other types of entertainers, including singers, dancers, and musicians, usually communicate by demonstrating a particular talent. These performers spend long hours practicing their skills in preparation for their appearances on television.

Another type of radio and television performer is the talk-show host. This job, common on both radio and TV, is very difficult. Above all else, the talk-show host must be able to communicate with all types of people.

A large number of television and radio performers can be grouped under the category of announcer. One type of announcer is the radio disc jockey whose responsibility is to establish a warm, friendly relationship with the listening audience. Disc jockeys must be good speakers and have the talent to ad-lib between records and commercials.

Another type of announcer is the newscaster. Radio and television newscasters are sometimes responsible for writing and editing news stories as well as for reading them accurately. Newscasters have become very specialized, in recent years. Several newscasters may appear on the same program, each reporting on a particular specialty and handling different news topics, including world news, local news, sports, weather, the arts, and special reports.

Another type of announcer is the news commentator. Most news commentators have had many years of newscasting experience. Now, their job is to analyze the news and give their own informed opinion about important news stories.

The final group of radio and television performers can be called specialists. Some are specialists in the field of children's programming. Fred Rogers of "Mr. Rogers" is a television specialist in children's programs. Another famous specialist performer is Julia Child, who presents cooking lessons on television. There are almost as many different types of specialists as there are interests held by listeners and viewers.

Special Skills Needed for Different Types of Performances

All performers on radio and television must develop their skills as communicators. Special skills are also needed for different types of performers.

If you plan to portray roles in dramatic productions on television as an actor, you must develop your abilities to analyze and develop characters, memorize lines, and relate to audiences. Chapter 17 presents a discussion of these aspects of acting. In addition, television performances require other skills. Viewers of television drama are usually watching and listening alone or in small groups. This makes it necessary for actors to adapt their voices and gestures to a small audience rather than to a larger one. Microphones and cameras are controlled by others, and the timing of performances must be carefully monitored. These aspects of television acting must be considered during rehearsals as well as during performances.

If you are interested in becoming a comedian, you should develop all of the skills required of other radio and television performers. Your words must not only be understood by the audience, but your voice should have a quality that catches and holds people's attention. Remember, it isn't only the joke that makes someone sound funny. It's also the way the joke is told. TV comedians must also have good nonverbal communication skills. Their facial expressions and the way they move communicate something to their audiences. This can be a positive feeling or a negative one, depending on how good the performer is. Comedians must be able to think quickly on their feet, gauge audience reaction, and make slight

TV talk-show host Oprah Winfrey specializes in addressing issues of public concern in a way that is down-to-earth, informative, and entertaining.

adjustments in their performances. If a studio audience is present, these tasks are somewhat easier than they would be if a comedian were trying to judge what effect a performance was having on people in their homes. Timing lines so that audiences have time to laugh, without missing what comes next, is most important. This can be a difficult task for comedians when no studio audience is present. Being a successful comedian takes a great deal of practice and experience.

If you plan to perform as a singer, dancer, or musician on radio or television, concentrate on developing your skill in communicating your particular talent. Be sure to take advantage of every opportunity to perform in public.

A talk-show host on radio or television should have a wide range of interests, be well informed about current events, and be genuinely concerned about people and their problems. Good interviewing techniques (see Chapter 4) and listening skills (see Chapter 3) are essential. You may wish to review Chapter 4 for one-to-one communication skills used by hosts.

If you want to be an announcer, take as many speech classes as you can while you are still in school. Debate, drama, foreign languages, journalism, and English can also be helpful. Announcers must be able to communicate exceptionally well verbally. Their whole line of work centers around what and how they speak.

In studying to be an announcer, you should also develop your ability to read from a script. Make sure you don't rattle it while you read because it will sound to your listeners as if the furniture is being moved. This is because the microphone is designed to pick up the smallest bit of sound and amplify it. Practice using a microphone correctly. Review that section in Chapter 10 that discusses using a microphone. Have someone watch you to see if you have the habit of moving your head back and forth. Moving your head back and forth will do strange things to the volume and pitch of your voice as it is broadcast over the air. If you are interested in television announcing, practice reading from a script or cue cards while looking at an imaginary camera. Develop any special interests you have that could improve your skills in announcing in that field. Scientific subjects, sports, music, and political affairs are only a few of the specialties from which you might wish to choose.

You should be aware that even radio performers are in the public eye. They have a responsibility to be neat, clean, and well dressed when in public or at least to remember that they are creating an image, however unusual or exotic they may choose to be. Radio and television performers must also be dependable people. They always have to show up for work on time. Performers must also be willing to work odd hours of the day and night.

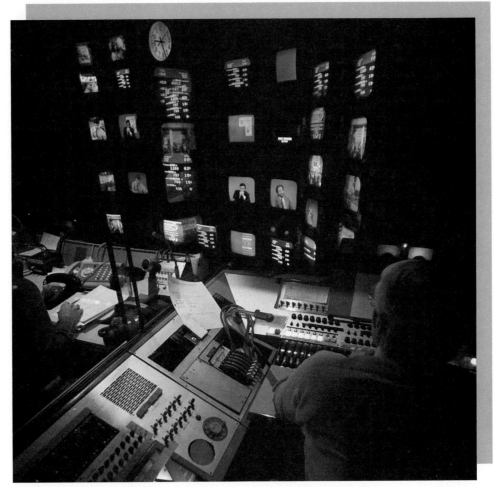

What appears on a television screen is largely the product of efforts that are never seen by the viewing public. Each program is produced by a small army of writers, directors, and designers, along with technicians skilled in camera work, lighting, and sound.

PRODUCING FOR RADIO AND TELEVISION

The production of a redio or television broadcast requires the work of many people you never hear on the air or see on camera. These "behind-the-scenes" people need a wide variety of creative and technical skills to bring radio and television programs to the audience. Many of these skills are similar to those found in producing theatrical events. It should be mentioned that most of the jobs in production today are found in television. Radio programs require small production staffs. In fact,

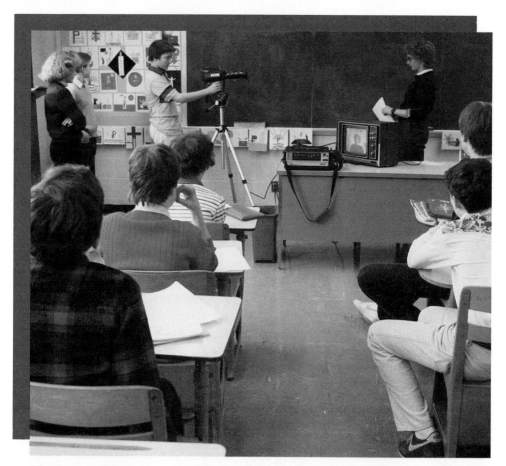

"Ready on camera one. . . ." In this classroom video production, the news commentator, camera operator, director, and producer must work in unison to bring off the finished product, which classmates will later evaluate.

radio performers often do most of the production work themselves. Disc jockeys or newscasters will frequently ad-lib to fill extra seconds between recorded music or commercials. On television, every second of time is carefully planned, and each taped segment of a show or commercial must fit into its time slot exactly. This kind of programming requires professional production people.

Before any production work is started on a television program, a programming committee meets to decide on the kind of program needed. This committee develops what is called a **program concept** and then hires a producer to fulfill this concept. The producer is the executive in charge of all aspects of the production. He or she is responsible for both the budget and the actual activities of the production staff.

A producer's first step in transforming the program concept into a performance is to hire a director and a scriptwriter. The scriptwriter develops a detailed outline and script for the broadcast. Scripts can vary in size from an outline of topics an interviewer will cover with a guest, to a fully developed dramatic dialogue including stage directions. The script is usually revised in rehearsals as the director and performers help to develop their interpretations of it. What finally develops is called the working script.

In cooperation with the director, the producer must then audition and hire any performers needed for the programs. Production specialists, such as a costumer, a set designer, a stage manager, and a composer, must also be hired.

Working very closely with the producer, the director is the one who must imagine the scenes and guide the performers into a unified presentation. A director runs rehearsals. Rehearsals include coordinating all movement on the stage and working with the performers to help them understand the role each one plays in the program. The director may also guide the composer in writing music suitable to the program's theme.

The technical side of directing involves careful planning of camera shots, angles, and special photographic techniques needed for a particular program. Most performances are run with the assistance of many technical specialists under the supervision of a stage manager. Technicians and engineers who have special training and licenses are needed to mix the sounds and to combine background music with the show. Other technicians do the lighting changes, operate the microphones, and run the cameras. Program assistants and stagehands work with a stage manager to help the director. Making copies of the script, distributing them, notifying performers of rehearsal times, taking notes, getting copyright clearance for music, and typing script revisions may be included in a program assistant's tasks. Stagehands move furniture, sets, and props. They also handle cue cards or operate a teleprompter which is used to help the performers remember their lines.

Application

Creating a Newscast

Divide the class into groups of from five to seven members. Each group will decide on the roles of its members and then work together to produce a 15-minute newscast. Rehearse and time your newscast carefully and then stage the show for the class. Record the production on audio tape or videotape. Play each tape in class and evaluate the effectiveness of each newscast. Discuss what each segment of the newscast contributed to the overall production.

15 Chapter Review

■ Summary

Mass communication reaches vast audiences who can "turn off" the message at will. The electronic media of radio and television are available every day to almost every member of this society.

The Nature of Radio and Television   Radio and television reach people over long distances quickly and bring them into immediate contact with the rest of the world and even with outer space. With radio and television, the audience has a great deal of control. If you dislike the message being sent, you can switch to another, turn it off, or leave.

The Development of Electronic Media   Many scientists and inventors working with electricity and magnetism between 1880 and 1920 contributed to the development of radio, which caught on with the American public in the mid-1920's. Advertising helped radio become big business as companies funded comedy, variety, and musical programs between 1930 and 1950. A series of independent discoveries aided the development of television, and in the 1950's television overtook radio in popularity. Most successful radio programs were quickly adapted for television, which was almost always live. Now most television shows are videotaped. To compete with television, radio stations now specialize in music, news, and talk shows. Television programming has also changed. Five basic kinds of television—commercial, educational, public, cable, and pay—offer a variety of programs and services. Radio and television are powerful media whose effects on millions of adults and children have been both praised and condemned.

The Purposes of Radio and Television   The three main purposes of radio and television are to entertain, to inform or educate, and to sell products and services. Educational radio and television often provide information in more depth than do commercial radio and television stations, which make a profit by selling broadcast time to advertisers.

Performing on Radio and Television   The major types of television and radio performers include actors, entertainers (comedians, singers, dancers, musicians), talk-show hosts, announcers (disc jockeys, newscasters, news commentators), and specialists. Each type of performer must develop special skills, as well as those general communication skills necessary for all effective speakers.

Producing for Radio and Television   Radio and television production involves people with a variety of creative and technical skills. The producer is in charge of all aspects of the production. The director helps hire performers and musicians, runs rehearsals, directs the action of the performers, and guides composers in writing suitable music. The scriptwriter develops an outline and later writes a script. Production specialists include technicians, engineers, program assistants, and stagehands, working under the supervision of a stage manager.

 ## Vocabulary

Define each term in a complete sentence.

mass communication	educational television	news magazine
electronic media	public television	documentary
videotape	cable TV	program concept
commercial television	pay TV	

 ## Checklist

Skills for Radio and Television

1. Study the history of radio and television to better understand mass communication.
2. Be aware of the differences between radio and TV.
3. Be aware of the purposes of radio and TV.
4. Be aware of the difference that exists between an actor and a performer.
5. Develop the appropriate acting skills if you wish to act on TV.
6. Take advantage of every opportunity to act, sing, or dance before an audience .
7. Be aware of the importance of speech courses for those who wish to be announcers.
8. Realize the importance of production jobs in radio and TV.

Review Questions

1. Define mass communication.
2. Define electronic media.
3. Explain how the use of satellites has affected television programming.
4. Name several advantages of radio over television.
5. State how radio programming has changed since the development of television.
6. Name several types of television service available today.
7. Name three purposes of radio and television.
8. State what types of performers there are who work in radio and television.
9. Identify some of the special communication skills required for each type of radio and television performer you mentioned in your answer to question 8.
10. Name at least five jobs that must be performed in television production.

Discussion Questions

1. Compare a front-page newspaper story with radio and television coverage of the same story. Discuss the ways in which the treatments differ. What accounts for those differences? How would you present the newspaper story if it were a television or radio account?
2. Hold a class discussion on the question, "Does television newscasting merely report the news, or does it shape public attitudes toward events as well?" Try to reach a class consensus on the proper role of the news media in communicating information to the public.
3. Discuss radio and television commercials and their influence on the behavior of audiences. How large a role does emotional appeal play in commercials? Which commercials do you enjoy and why? Have you ever bought a product because of a commercial?
4. Discuss how public pressure is brought to bear upon the broadcasting networks. Is there any evidence of censorship? What are the dangers of censorship? Can you think of

an instance where censorship might be necessary?

5. Compare the offerings of public television and radio stations with those of commercial networks. Discuss the types of programs that appear on each.

How does the need to produce profits influence programming decisions on commercial networks? How might a lack of adequate funding influence programming at public radio and television stations?

Critical Thinking

1. **Analysis:** Compare news commentary and news reporting. In what ways are they alike? In what ways are they different? Do you think that the public sometimes confuses the two? What effect might this confusion have on public opinion?

2. **Evaluation:** The Federal Communications Commission requires all licensed television and radio stations to devote part of their air time each week to public service programs. What kinds of programs are these and when are they broadcast? How do you think the system could be improved in order to serve the public more effectively?

Activities

In-Class

1. Discuss the impact that pay TV is having on the television industry. Do people judge television differently if they have to pay to watch it? Survey the class to find out which current programs classmates would actually pay to watch. Survey classmates who have pay TV in their homes and determine how satisfied they are with the programming. Make a graph showing the kinds of programs classmates would be willing to pay for.

2. When television first became popular, some people predicted that radio would decline and disappear. Although radio has changed in some ways, it continues to be a popular form of entertainment. In groups of

from five to seven people, develop five programming concepts for radio that might attract a large listening audience. These may be music, news, or talk-show programs, or they may be an altogether different format. As a class, discuss the concepts developed by each group.

3. Imagine that your class has been given the task of programming a television station for one weekday, from 6 A.M. to 12 midnight. Divide the class into six groups, with each group responsible for programming a different three-hour segment. Decide what programs will air. As you make each programming decision, explain why you would offer a particular program at a particular time. When the entire day has been planned, compare each group's programmed segment to a typical day of commercial television. Who might your newly developed programs attract?

Out-of-Class

1. Examine the first few pages of your local newspaper carefully. Determine which stories appear to be most important. In your speech notebook, prepare a script for a ten-minute radio news broadcast. Be sure to include a sports summary and a weather forecast. After you have written and timed your script, make a tape recording of your broadcast to play in class.

2. Prepare a survey form that can be used to judge the listening and viewing habits of people in your community. It should include places for following information and for any other appropriate information.
   (a) age and sex of survey respondents
   (b) hours per week spent watching television
   (c) hours per week spent listening to radio
   (d) best-liked personalities on television
   (e) best-liked personalities on radio
   (f) best-liked programs (by name)
   (g) best-liked types of radio and television programs
   Prepare a rough draft of your survey form in your speech notebook. Then type it, copy it, and distribute it to your selected audience. Be prepared to report on the results of the survey in class.

3. Gather information from your local library about broadcasting laws developed by the Federal Communications Commission. Collect information about

the licensing of stations as well. Write a brief report on your findings in your speech notebook. Be prepared to share your findings with your classmates.

4. Find out as much as you can about the early days of radio. Learn about the most popular programs and personalities. Prepare an oral report on the early days of radio. Try to give your audience a look into the past by playing recordings of news and popular programs during your report.

■

Chapter Project

As a class, develop a topic that would be suitable for a thirty-minute television documentary. Write a script that also includes descriptions of the scenes and situations that would be filmed. Determine how many people would be needed to produce the program and decide when it would be shown. If you have access to a videocamera, it might be possible to tape parts of your documentary.

Performing Arts

467

16 Oral Interpretation

**When you have completed this chapter
you should be able to:**

■ Define oral interpretation.

■ Identify occasions when oral interpretation is appropriate.

■ List different types of literature available for oral interpretation.

■ Analyze a piece of literature for understanding.

■ Practice a selection, using your voice properly to reinforce your meaning.

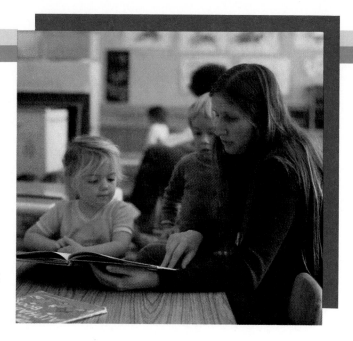

Literature performed aloud has a life and warmth that never cease to enthrall audiences of all ages.

In order for you to hear a piece of music someone must play it. It is a musician's job to transform what is written on a sheet of music into what is played on an instrument. But more than just playing notes, a good musician must interpret the music. What you hear is really a musician's understanding of *how* the music should be played. By interpreting a piece of music a musician is said to *perform* it. People attend concerts not only to hear the music but also to experience a particular musician's performance of that music. *How* the music is played is just as important as *what* music is played.

A good speaker can perform literature just as a good musician performs music. By transforming written words into spoken sounds the speaker can provide a way for you to hear literature. Just as a good musician does not simply play notes, a good speaker does not simply read words. To perform a piece of literature a speaker must interpret it orally. **Oral interpretation** is the process by which a speaker performs literature aloud for an audience.

In this chapter you will study some of the methods used to turn literature into a successful performance. These are the techniques of oral interpretation. First, however, some background information may be in order. How has oral interpretation been used in the past? When is it performed today? What is its value in daily life? What types of literature can be used? With the answers to these questions in mind, you will find it easier to choose selections and prepare to perform.

A BRIEF HISTORY OF ORAL INTERPRETATION

Oral interpretation is one of the oldest of human social activities. Before writing, people communicated primarily by word-of-mouth. Because there were no newspapers, magazines, or books, ideas were handed down orally from one generation to the next. In this way, literature was preserved in memory rather than on paper. Some of the greatest literature survived for hundreds of years in oral form before it was finally written down. Professional storytellers, known as **minstrels** or **bards,** traveled from village to village bringing news and entertaining people with their stories.

As writing became widespread and people learned to read, the oral tradition did not end. Great writers in the nineteenth century not only read their work to audiences, but expected their novels to be interpreted orally by others. In homes where their stories were popular, the best oral interpreter in the family would read aloud a chapter every evening. In the early twentieth century professional oral interpreters traveling through America on reading tours were a common source of entertainment. Young children today are first exposed to literature when their parents orally perform stories and poems for them. Thus the tradition has endured from earliest times to the present.

Occasions for Oral Interpretation

There will probably be many times when you will be able to interpret some type of literature orally. In school you may be called upon to read part of a story or to recite a poem. At home or while babysitting, you may read to younger children. Many professions also call for this ability. Teachers, lawyers, religious leaders, librarians, and broadcasters are only a few of the people whose jobs demand that they read aloud skillfully.

The Value of Oral Interpretation

You may ask: Why study oral interpretation? What value does it have? What are its benefits? In order to answer these questions you must consider two separate points of view—the speaker's and the listener's.

For the speaker, there is often a sense of personal pride associated with reading orally. Aside from the enjoyment of reading something well, it makes people feel good to share their experiences of literature with others. Sometimes people take on the characteristics of the material they orally interpret. It may not be just a joke that is amusing, but also the way it is told. Another person may become more interesting to others when reading an interesting newspaper article aloud.

The traveling bard was a welcome source of news and entertainment.

Oral interpretation also provides a number of other benefits for the speaker. By carefully preparing for a performance, you can develop a better understanding of a piece of literature. The process of developing an oral interpretation encourages you to read carefully and think about the literature to be performed. This extra effort not only helps to improve your study skills, but can also help to clarify meanings and may often lead to new insights. You should see your English grades improve as you develop your skills in analyzing literature.

From the point of view of the listener, oral interpretation is primarily a source of entertainment. When literature is performed, it seems to come alive for the audience. As a listener you not only experience the reader's enthusiasm for the material being performed, but you also benefit from the speaker's understanding of that material. An oral performance may offer you new insights into what you have read before, or it may serve as an introduction to literature you have not previously experienced. Oral interpretation also helps you develop your listening skills. By listening to different interpretations, you become better able to judge a good performance from a bad one. Finally, by giving speakers your full attention, you will not only appreciate others for their skill in communicating literature, but will also discover new ways to improve your own performances.

TYPES OF MATERIAL FOR ORAL INTERPRETATION

One of your responsibilities is to recognize what types of materials are available for interpretation. Just because something is written does not necessarily mean that it is suitable for reading aloud. You would, for example, have difficulty performing a grocery list, a set of directions, or the ingredients listed on the back of a soup can. Essentially, your task is to distinguish literature from other types of writing.

Literature says something of lasting value and says it well. The literature used for oral interpretation in this chapter falls into two very broad categories: prose and poetry.

Prose

Compared to poetry, **prose** is closer to the language of everyday use. When an author writes in prose, he or she generally tries to duplicate the way someone would speak aloud. Although it wasn't a popular literary form until the sixteenth century, prose is now by far the most common form of literature. Every time you read a book or a magazine article you are reading prose. Prose is used by authors to tell or describe something. The two types of prose are fiction and nonfiction.

Fiction **Fiction** is material created in the imagination. The author of fiction has complete freedom to add, subtract, or change any of what is being written. Fiction deals with imaginary characters and events. Novels and short stories are the two most common types of fiction. Do not be misled if an author includes some facts in a work of fiction. In order to make their stories more believable, many authors create their fiction around actual events or real people. These facts, in a sense, serve as a background for the author's imagination. They suggest what did, could, or would happen. For example, a story about the bombing of London during World War II would be based on actual events of history. But by introducing imaginary characters in imaginary situations, the author creates a work of fiction.

Nonfiction **Nonfiction,** on the other hand, is based entirely on truth as the author understands it, on real people, and on actual events. Nonfiction is written to inform the reader and is usually the result of an author's research. A biography, for example, is a work of nonfiction about someone's life. Its very nature demands accuracy and truth. An autobiography is simply a biography written by the person it is about. If you were to do an oral interpretation of an autobiography, you would try to speak and act like the person who wrote it. The quality of your performance would depend upon your ability to show what this person is really like. Another interesting type of nonfiction is the essay. Essays are used to state a position, to analyze, or to interpret something. In writing an essay, an author makes a statement and uses facts to support it.

Poetry

Poetry, the oldest of the literary arts, can trace its roots directly to the very beginnings of the oral tradition. Most of the oldest literature in existence today, which includes such works as *Beowulf, The Odyssey,* and *The Iliad,* is poetry. The bards were really the first poets. Each of their stories had a specific rhythm and rhyme. The rhythm helped them to remember the number of syllables in a line; the rhyme gave them clues as to the actual words. The result was a kind of chanted story-poem.

Poetry can be described as communication of thought and feeling through the careful arrangement of words for their sound and rhythm as well as their meaning. Poetry has not only survived as literature for thousands of years, it is considered by many people to be the most noble form of literature. As an oral performer you will be concerned with two major types of poetry: the narrative poem and the lyric poem.

Narrative Poetry **Narrative poetry** is poetry that tells a story or describes something that has happened. Narrative poetry is not as popular as it used to be. Most modern writers use prose to tell stories.

When you read an essay, story, or poem whose message, imagery, or sound seems to linger in your mind, chances are you've found a good piece of literature to interpret orally.

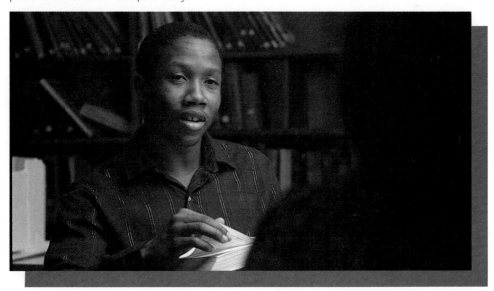

Lyric Poetry While narrative poetry concerns events, **lyric poetry** deals with what happened or is happening inside the poet. Used mainly to express deep thoughts or feelings, lyric poetry frequently takes the form of a sonnet, ode, hymn, or elegy. Lyric poems are usually very musical. In fact, the word *lyric* means "song-like." If you stop to think about it, a song is really just a poem put to music.

Application

Working with Poetry

Choose a poem at the end of this chapter and identify its literary form. Read the selection several times to be certain that you understand the poet's message. Pay particular attention to any figures of speech in the poem, such as metaphor, simile, personification, hyperbole, and allusion. Come to class prepared to explain how an analysis of the poem can help you interpret it effectively.

CHOOSING MATERIAL FOR ORAL INTERPRETATION

The first step in oral interpretation is to choose your material. If you are not assigned to perform a particular piece of literature, then your choices are practically limitless. It is always wise to approach the oral interpretation process with an open mind. You shouldn't be afraid to read something by an unfamiliar author or to consider a type of literature you have not read before. A good library may be your best source since it can provide you with anthologies of poems and prose passages from many different authors and types of literature. Do not hesitate to spend some time carefully examining a poem or a prose passage before making a choice. The range of literature is so wide that it is difficult to suggest specific methods for choosing literature for oral interpretation. However, it is wise to consider some of the basic characteristics of good literature.

Universal Appeal

As you examine a piece of literature keep your audience in mind. Ask yourself: Will this piece be interesting to others? Does it deal with feelings or ideas that are common to all people? Stories and poems that can be appreciated and enjoyed by many people at many different times are said to have **universal appeal.** In other words, they deal with problems or experiences that everyone can easily recognize and identify with. Some of the more popular universal themes include growing up, loneliness, parent-child relationships, and love.

In choosing a selection for oral interpretation, it is usually best to choose a work with universal appeal, a work whose theme is likely to appeal to almost any audience. Consider Emily Dickinson's lyric poem "I'm Nobody! Who Are You?"

> I'm nobody! Who are you?
> Are you nobody, too?
> Then there's a pair of us—don't tell!
> They'd banish us, you know.
>
> How dreary to be somebody!
> How public, like a frog.
> To tell your name the livelong June
> To an admiring bog!

Dickinson's poem can be appreciated by many people because almost everyone has, at one time or another, had the desire to be "somebody." You need not belong to a certain group of people or possess a special kind of knowledge to appreciate the meaning of this poem.

Insight

Good literature also deals with important ideas. It provides a new way of viewing life by drawing your attention to everyday things and helping you to see them in a different light. In this manner, good literature increases your range of experience. As an oral interpreter, you will find it easier to get and maintain the interest of your audience if you choose a poem or a prose passage that offers this kind of experience, that goes beyond the obvious to suggest a new and exciting way of looking at something. Literature with this particular quality is said to offer insight. Having **insight** means that you have a particularly clear understanding of something. In the following prose story from *The Tarot of Cornelius Agrippa* by Frederick Morgan, the author gives the reader insight by having the main character come to a new understanding of something. What did the stonemason think he saw in the mirror? What do you think this experience taught the stonemason about death that he had not realized before? What do you think a reader might gain from this story?

A stone mason who in the course of one winter lost his wife, his son and his best friend, put aside the tools of his trade and went out in search of DEATH, whom he conceived as a tall pale man dressed in black, with a face like a skull. Setting forth from his house, he brought with him only the money he had saved through the years, and his old trusty musket, with which he intended to execute his enemy. "For," he said to himself, "if I find him and kill him, I shall not only have avenged myself—I shall have bestowed the greatest possible blessing on my fellow men and women."—And so he went traveling methodically through the land, searching for his victim in lonely farmsteads, in the streets of great cities, in the homes of rich and poor. But nowhere did he find Death, though he found many who had been marked by him.

Late one night in the tenth year of his quest, when he was staying over at a small inn in a country village, he was awakened suddenly from a dream in which he was being pursued by serpents. Coming slowly to himself, he got down from the bed, stood erect, and opened his eyes. The first faint light of dawn came palely in through the window—and by it he could see a figure that stood at the far side of the room, watching him. The body was that of a skeleton, the head was his own . . . He reached for his musket and was about to fire, when he realized that the person confronting him was his own reflection in a tall standing mirror. As he approached, it became more and more commonplace and recognizable. The sun was rising, he put down his gun.

It was only a mirror—yet he could not escape the conclusion that he had at last come face to face with his enemy. He gave up his search, went back home, and resumed his old ways. But for the remainder of his life he turned his thoughts more and more inward.

Beauty

Another quality to look for in good literature is *beauty*. These lines from Henry Thoreau's *Walden* offer a good example:

> If a man does not keep pace with his companions, perhaps it is because he hears a different drummer. Let him step to the music which he hears, however measured or far away.

In only a few words Thoreau suggests a way of understanding people who do not think and act like the majority. Keep in mind that the best writers are often able to explain difficult ideas in very simple terms. Their skill lends a sense of beauty to literature.

Of course, people disagree about what is, or is not, beautiful. The sounds you find pleasant may not be enjoyed by others. A description may seem well-stated to you but not to your listeners. There are no rules in such cases, but there are guidelines. Look for literature that has noble ideas presented in language that is pleasant to the ear. Avoid poetry that stresses sound too much and has few good ideas. Avoid prose that has many ideas but sentences that are unclear. Literature that achieves a harmony between words and ideas can be truly beautiful.

Application

Technical Quality

The way in which a piece of literature is put together by an author—its **technical quality**—is another thing you should consider when choosing material for oral interpretation. Are the author's ideas expressed clearly? Can they maintain a person's interests?

The way an author introduces an idea to a reader is one aspect of the technical quality of literature. When you read orally, be sure that you choose material that quickly provides your listeners with enough detail to get them involved in the material.

The way an author approaches the high point of a story or poem is also important. Many passages in literature describe events leading up to and passing some critical stage. This is usually called a climax. The point at which the climax occurs is a measure of an author's ability to arrange events properly. Examine passages for climaxes and ask yourself: Does the climax occur in the middle or toward the end of the piece? If it occurs in the middle, does the second half of the material seem less interesting than the first? On the other hand, a selection that drags on and on, finally arriving at a climax that should have occurred earlier, is equally undesirable. Look for prose and poetry selections that will keep the attention of your listeners from beginning to end.

Your Preference and the Occasion

The most important thing to remember when selecting literature for oral interpretation is to choose something you truly like. If you do this, your audience will be more likely to share your enthusiasm for the selection and you will have more fun sharing it with them.

The occasion for a performance, your purpose in performing, and the type of audience are all important considerations in choosing material for oral interpretation. If you were baby-sitting and you wanted to entertain a young child, your choice of material would be vastly different from the choice you would make if you were asked to give an oral interpretation of a literary work at your high school.

Finally, you should be very conscious of the amount of time that you have to interpret a work. Avoid selecting a short story, for example, that you suspect will require more time to perform than you are given. Your oral interpretation will be spoiled if you have to speed up halfway through in order to finish on time. Besides making you nervous, the need to quicken your speaking rate could annoy your audience. If you have a choice between a piece of literature that is too long and one that is too short, choose the shorter one, and do it well. Be aware that you don't always have to perform an entire piece of literature. In fact, most literature is much too long to be read in one performance. It is perfectly acceptable to cut a piece of literature down to a manageable size as long as you make your listeners aware that they are not hearing the whole piece, and as long as you do not change any of the words.

Adapting Material for the Occasion

Many times you must adapt or cut your chosen selection. As you read above, cuts are made if the selection is too long. You will sometimes need to cut because of inappropriate material. You may also need to cut if parts do not read well aloud.

If you must cut or adapt materials, your first consideration should be the preservation of the writer's intent. Just as a pianist would not change the notes of a Chopin polonaise, neither does an oral interpreter have the right to change an author's intent or rewrite creative material. Keeping this restriction in mind you can nevertheless cut prose in some of the following ways:

1. You can cut unnecessary tag lines such as "he said" and "she cried loudly" if you have established the identity of the character by other means, such as vocal changes or physical changes.

2. You can cut explanations of a character's state of mind or manner such as "John's tone was faltering." These indicate to the reader how to read the dialogue.

3. You may condense or eliminate some description.

4. You may omit minor characters.

5. You may omit anything that would offend the taste of your audience. Some language or material may not offend the silent reader but may offend an audience when it is read aloud.

6. You may cut repetitive material if it serves no purpose.

If you need to cut poetry, follow these guidelines:

1. Preserve the rhyme and rhythm of the poem.

2. Cut only to shorten or to eliminate offensive parts.

3. Cut large segments, such as stanzas.

4. Narrative poetry may need more abridgment than other types of poetry.

When you must cut a difficult selection, share the process with your teacher.

INTERPRETING YOUR SELECTION

There are many different ways to interpret orally any piece of literature. Just as two musicians who perform the same musical piece do not sound exactly alike, no two people who perform the same piece of literature interpret it in exactly the same way. A story about "Old Weird Harold" would sound different if Bill Cosby did not perform it. Young children learn that different people interpret the wolf in "Little Red Riding Hood" in different ways.

It is important to remember that there is never a single "correct" oral interpretation of a poem or story. Everyone experiences literature differently. Although a piece of literature can have many "correct"

For a group reading, members must agree on how to interpret the selection.

interpretations, some interpretations are better than others. It is therefore important that you carefully develop the skills necessary for good oral interpretation.

In order to prepare a good oral interpretation you should know all you can about the literature you have chosen to perform. You must understand your selection thoroughly. You must also consider some of the elements within the literature that will affect your performance. These include the person speaking in the selection, the imaginary audience being spoken to, and the setting in which it occurs.

Understand Your Selection

When you choose a selection to perform, be sure you understand the meaning of every word it contains. A dictionary can help you with the meanings of unfamiliar words. Your selection may also contain references to real people or events from history or to imaginary characters from other pieces of literature. Look in encyclopedias, biographical dictionaries, or other reference books to see why these people and events have been mentioned in your selection.

While concentrating on meaning, remember the importance of pronunciation. Don't take a chance on pronouncing words incorrectly during your performance. Check the dictionary, and practice the pronunciation of any words you are unsure of. Feel free to mark accents in your manuscript (as long as you are not using a book).

You may also find it helpful to know something about the author of your selection and why he or she wrote it. Perhaps the piece has some particular meaning based on the time or place in which it was written. Knowing the background of your selection can make your interpretation of it more meaningful for your audience.

Know the Fictional Speaker

You should be aware of who is speaking in any piece of literature you perform. Sometimes the authors themselves speak directly to the reader. Sometimes, however, in order to provide a specific point of view, an author uses a **fictional speaker.** The voice you hear telling the story or poem when you read silently is the voice of the fictional speaker. Quite often, the fictional speaker is a main character in the story or poem.

Consider the speaker in the following passage from Mark Twain's *The Adventures of Huckleberry Finn.*

You don't know about me without you have read a book by the name of *The Adventures of Tom Sawyer,* but that ain't no matter. That book was made by Mr. Mark Twain and he told the truth, mainly. There was things which he stretched, but mainly he told the truth. This is nothing. I never seen anybody but lied one time or another, without it was Aunt Polly or the

In his one-man show *Mark Twain Tonight,* actor Hal Holbrook wove the fictional voices of Huck Finn, Tom Sawyer, and Twain himself into a spellbinding collage of the Mississippian's stories and essays.

widow, or maybe Mary. Aunt Polly—Tom's Aunt Polly, she is—and Mary and the widow Douglas is all told about in that book, which is mostly a true book, with some stretchers as I said before.

The voice you hear in this passage is that of Huck Finn. The story is therefore told from his point of view. In this case, Mark Twain even used the fictional speaker to poke fun at himself. By carefully reading this passage you begin to understand the kind of person Huck Finn is.

If Mark Twain had chosen to make Huck a little older and more educated, *The Adventures of Huckleberry Finn* might have begun something like this:

Unless you have perused the volume entitled *The Adventures of Tom Sawyer,* you can have little knowledge of me, but that is of small consequence . . .

The meaning is the same in both passages, but the characteristics of the fictional speaker have changed. Huck is a different type of person in the made-up version from what he is in the original.

Your experience of literature depends in part upon the author's characterization of the fictional speaker. By paying close attention to this characterization you will be better able to fulfill your role as an oral interpreter. In other words, you are expected to find out as much as you can about the fictional speaker so that you can communicate the story or the poem as if you *were* that speaker.

The text of the literature can help you identify the characteristics of the fictional speaker in two ways: (1) by directly stating facts or details about the speaker; (2) by suggesting details about the speaker.

You will find as you work on your interpretation that in most cases the suggestions far outnumber the facts. Look for a moment at "Stopping by Woods on a Snowy Evening," a poem by Robert Frost.

> Whose woods these are I think I know.
> His house is in the village though;
> He will not see me stopping here
> To watch his woods fill up with snow.
>
> My little horse must think it queer
> To stop without a farmhouse near
> Between the woods and frozen lake
> The darkest evening of the year.
>
> He gives his harness bells a shake
> To ask if there is some mistake.
> The only other sound's the sweep
> Of easy wind and downy flake.
>
> The woods are lovely, dark and deep,
> But I have promises to keep,
> And miles to go before I sleep,
> And miles to go before I sleep.

Notice that while the poem tells us a good deal about what the speaker is looking at, it makes almost no direct statement about the speaker. Perhaps only three facts can be stated as certainties:

1. The speaker is familiar with the scene or at least with the probable owner of the woods.

2. The speaker is dutiful and concerned about the fact that there are "promises to keep."

3. The speaker has made promises of some kind.

When you consider suggestions, you will find that there are more details to work with. The speaker seems to be alone with the horse since no one else is mentioned. The speaker seems to be sensitive to nature since he or she stops to admire the woods, even though there are many things to do. You can also guess from the manner of talking that the speaker is not a child. But, so far, the details still do not give a very clear image of the speaker. In order to bring the speaker into sharper focus you must turn to yet another source.

This source is the interpreter's *imagination* while reading the poem. Whenever you interpret a poem, you combine facts and suggestions found in the poem with other details supplied by your own imagination. Perhaps you have never thought about this process, but you use your imagination every time you see anything. Suppose, for instance, you are out for a walk and you stop to admire a particularly beautiful tree. What you actually see is only half the trunk and half the leaves. To see the other half you would have to walk around to the other side of the tree. Yet, as you stand in one place admiring the tree, you assume without thinking that the other side looks roughly the same, that the leaves on the other side are the same color and size as what you can see on this side. If you walked around the tree and discovered that lightning had sliced it neatly in two and there were no bark, limbs, or leaves on the other side, you would be amazed because you had not found what your imagination had told you to expect.

Look at these two drawings:

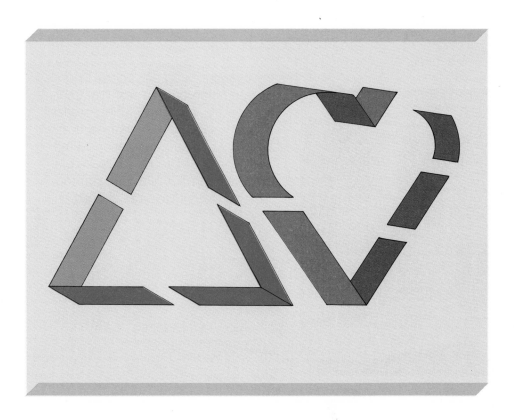

■ CHILDREN'S LIBRARIAN ■

Children's librarians, working in both school and community libraries, use oral interpretation to make stories from folklore and children's literature come alive for their young listeners. A good oral interpreter helps children appreciate good literature, become better listeners, and develop a lifelong interest in reading. Most applicants for librarians' positions have a bachelor's degree and a master's degree in library science.

In selecting literature to be interpreted, librarians consider the age group of their listeners. Because children's librarians have experience working with children and have a knowledge of child development, they understand the interests, needs, and literary tastes of children. Librarians study a story before interpreting it to gain familiarity with the plot, characters, and the language. They also use this time to practice the voices and dialogue that will help them portray the characters.

While they are interpreting a story or poem, oral interpreters use their facial expressions, gestures, and voices to express the different emotions within the story. They vary the pitch and force of their voices and use expressive eye movements to convey levels of excitement.

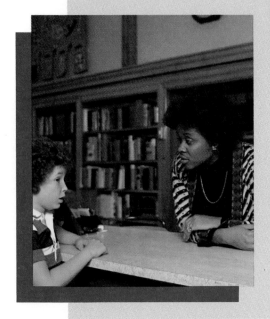

Librarians who are skilled in oral interpretation bring a vast oral tradition to life by transforming stories into rich, vibrant tales that captivate audiences. The preparation, time, and expertise that they devote to oral interpretation are gifts that communicate a love of literature to children.

Literature lives—thanks to oral interpreters like this children's librarian.

You will probably have no difficulty recognizing that one is a triangle and the other a heart. Yet you couldn't do this unless your imagination supplied the missing details.

In interpreting literature, you have to fill in the missing details just as you did with the heart and the triangle. But, note that any information supplied by your imagination must fit in with what you already know from the selection itself. In other words, none of the three kinds of details—facts, suggestions, or details supplied by your imagination—can contradict or disagree with one another. Your job as an interpreter is to put together all the information you can find about a fictional speaker into a clear understanding of that person.

The most vivid interpretations are those in which the performer has carefully thought out all the necessary details about the fictional speaker. Those details include not just the fictional speaker's physical appearance but his or her state of mind and *motives*—the reasons why the fictional speaker behaves and speaks as he or she does.

Know the Imaginary Audience

When a fictional speaker relates a story or a poem, he or she "speaks" to an **imaginary audience.** In "Stopping by Woods on a Snowy Evening" the fictional speaker is alone so you know that the speaker is talking to an audience made up only of himself or herself.

Sometimes the imaginary audience is one or more characters within the story or poem. Consider the audience in the following poem by Edward Field.

At the Coney Island Aquarium:
"An Ode for Ookie, the Older Walrus Child
or The Sibling Rival"

Do not worry, sweet little walrus, about the superior cuteness
Of those two new babies they brought to share your pool.

You keep pushing the twins out of the way
More concerned about keeping them from getting attention
Than having your own scrub-brush nose whiskers rubbed
So that no one gets the chance to give you
The endless hugs and kisses you deserve.
It is impossible of course to be more popular than twins
So finally you sink to the bottom and play dead
Hoping our hearts break—mine does anyway
And the Keeper watches anxiously, so you see it works.
But how long can you sit at the bottom of the water
When lungs cry for air and the heart for love?

No, Ookie, don't seek indiscriminate love from the many
As those two simple-minded children do
Who have not yet met with heartbreak (although they will),
But leap the railing right into my arms
And squirm there fishily always, Ookie, mine alone.

In this poem, the fictional speaker is talking to a young walrus. If you were to do an oral interpretation of this poem, you would have to take into account the fact that a walrus is the imaginary audience. In other words, you would have to perform this poem as if speaking to a fictional or real walrus.

The third type of imaginary audience is the most common. Here, the fictional speaker speaks directly to the reader, as in the following passage from *David Copperfield* by Charles Dickens.

Whether I shall turn out to be the hero of my own life, or whether that station will be held by anybody else, these pages must show. To begin my life with the beginning of my life, I record that I was born (as I have been informed and believe) on a Friday, at twelve o'clock at night. It was remarked that the clock began to strike, and I began to cry, simultaneously.

In consideration of the day and hour of my birth, it was declared by the nurse and by some sage women in the neighborhood who had taken a lively interest in me several months before there was any possibility of our becoming personally acquainted, first that I was destined to be unlucky in life; and secondly, that I was privileged to see ghosts and spirits; both these gifts inevitably attaching, as they believed, to all unlucky infants of either gender born towards the small hours on a Friday night.

Your decision about what kind of imaginary audience is involved in a piece of literature will have a direct effect on how you perform the selection. Your performance should also reflect the kind of relationship you believe exists between this imaginary audience and the fictional speaker. You know from your own experience that the way in which people say things is greatly influenced by their relationship with their listeners. As your become even more attuned to this, look for opportunities to apply it to selections you interpret orally.

Understand the Relationship Between the Fictional Speaker and the Imaginary Audience

The kind of relationship that exists between the fictional speaker and the imaginary audience is important even when the fictional speaker is talking to himself or herself. Notice, for example, the words used when

Lewis Carroll's Alice talks to herself in the following passage from *Alice's Adventures in Wonderland.*

> You ought to be ashamed of yourself . . . a great girl like you . . . to go on crying in this way! Stop this moment, I tell you!

Now compare the way Alice talks to herself with the way the fictional speaker in "Stopping by Woods on a Snowy Evening" talks to himself or herself. Though both fictional speakers are giving themselves advice, Alice advises herself rather sharply. Frost's fictional speaker uses a gentler approach. While Alice speaks to herself as a parent might to a naughty child, Frost's fictional speaker talks as if speaking to another adult. Two important kinds of relationships that can exist between fictional speaker and imaginary audience, then, are one in which the fictional speaker is in some way *superior* to the imaginary audience and one in which the fictional speaker is *equal* to the imaginary audience in some way, such as age, experience, or social status.

A third important relationship is the fictional speaker being in some way *inferior* to the imagined audience. This type of relationship is also found in *Alice's Adventures in Wonderland.* Alice has just fallen down the rabbit hole at the beginning of the story, and as she falls, she talks to herself:

> "I wonder how many miles I've fallen by this time?" she said aloud. "I must be getting somewhere near the centre of the earth. Let me see: that would be four thousand miles down, I think—" (for, you see, Alice had learned several things of this sort in her lessons in the schoolroom, and though this was not a *very* good opportunity for showing off her knowledge, as there was no one to listen to her, still it was good practice to say it over)—"Yes, that's about the right distance—but then I wonder what Latitude or Longitude I've got to?" (Alice had not the slightest idea what Latitude was, or Longitude either, but she thought they were nice grand words to say.)

In the last quotation Alice is showing off her knowledge, trying to impress the listener, much as a child might show off before adults. You could say that the speaker-to-listener relationship is that of a very young child speaking to an adult, or in more general terms, an "inferior" speaking to a "superior."

Following the examples given above, you can capture a major part of the speaker's attitude toward the listener by determining if the speaker's relationship to the listener is superior, equal, or inferior. Keep in mind, however, that relationships can be influenced by many different factors. For example, differences in age and differences in power can greatly influence relationships, sometimes in contradictory ways. Social rank can also have an influence on the relationships between people. The tone of your voice can help make all of these relationships between fictional speaker and imaginary audience clear to your listeners.

Know the Setting

If you wish to communicate all of the important elements of a piece of literature to your audience, you must also deal with the **setting**—the place and the time—in which the fictional speaker and imaginary audience are found.

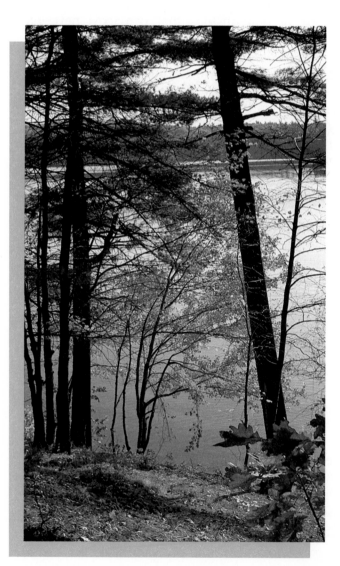

To perform a setting —such as Walden Pond—first capture it in your mind, using all your senses.

Place: the Where of the Setting   To understand how important setting is, return to "Stopping by Woods on a Snowy Evening" on page 482. In the poem most of the details you are given concern the place where the poem occurs. In fact, place seems to be the most important single aspect of the whole situation. Even the title mentions it. In just sixteen lines Frost gives you the following details. The fictional speaker is alone except for the horse, and far from any farmhouses. The speaker is probably in a sleigh, since a harness is mentioned. On one side of the speaker is the woods, further described as "lovely, dark and deep" and on the other side is a frozen lake. You also know that the night is very dark (though there must be enough light to see the woods), that it is snowing, and that the wind is blowing gently. As an oral interpreter, you must capture the feeling of this poem by imagining these specifics *vividly* during the performance.

Time: the When of the Setting   Now focus your attention on the second element of setting—in Frost's poem the time when the scene takes place. Here you will find fewer details and will need to use your imagination to fill in the spaces. You are given some clues to help you however. You know for instance the season (winter) and the time of day (evening). This isn't just any evening, however. It is described as "the darkest evening of the year." Careful readers of this poem have long been fascinated by this little detail. It is a good example of a writer giving readers part of the information and demanding that they fill in the rest with their imagination. Can this detail really be true? Have you ever tried walking on a truly dark night with no starlight or moonlight to guide you? If so, you probably had difficulty even seeing the path at your feet. Frost's fictional speaker can "watch his woods fill up with snow" and can see deep into the woods as well. Perhaps, as some readers have suggested, the fictional speaker intends the detail about the darkest night to describe his or her personal feeling at the time of the poem rather than the real physical setting. You may not agree with this interpretation. But, as an interpreter, what you decide will affect your performance. If you believe that the fictional speaker is going through what another writer has called "the dark night of the soul," the attraction of the speaker for the woods would be far different from the feeling involved if the speaker, in a lighthearted mood, just happens to be attracted by the woods.

Dealing with Time and Place   How do you perform a setting? First, you must see the setting vividly in your imagination and second, you must believe in it throughout the performance. It is one thing to picture in your mind all the necessary elements of the setting and quite another to act as though you really are *in* that setting.

In the Frost poem, for instance, if you are the speaker, where are the woods in relation to you? Where is the frozen lake? From what direction have you come? In what direction are you going? Are you standing or sitting? Are you cold, or warmed by lap rugs in a sleigh? Answering these questions can help you see the setting in your imagination, which is the first step in making it believable to others.

When you first ask questions about the setting of a selection, you are standing outside the selection looking for clues. When you perform the selection you stand inside it. You put yourself in the place of the fictional speaker, inside the setting that you have analyzed. When you read a story or poem silently and read it well, that is, when the literature affects you vividly, you are apt to say that you are "absorbed" by it. What is meant is exactly what you must do in oral interpretation—place yourself within the setting of the story.

If you truly believe in the setting that you have imagined as you perform, those who watch you will believe in the setting too. In performing Frost's poem, if you say "whose woods these are I think I know" and look directly at the audience, you are not *in* the poem. You don't believe in the woods and no one watching you perform does either. Instead, you must look at the woods you are imagining and put yourself in the place of the poem's fictional speaker.

Fill in Missing Details

After you have identified speaker, audience, and setting, there are still likely to be some missing details. Even the most detailed descriptions in literature require a reader to fill in unmentioned details; no description can give a complete picture of the subject described. The reader and the oral interpreter must supply these missing details.

What were the promises mentioned in Frost's poem? They are a missing detail. Why didn't Frost tell the reader what those promises were? Certainly not because they are unimportant. They are the most important motive behind the fictional speaker's decision to move on. One reason for not telling readers what they were could be that Frost wanted each reader to go through what the fictional speaker experienced in this poem. In other words, Frost may have wanted you to identify with the fictional speaker and supply, yourself, the reasons for not staying. What kind of promises would draw *you* away from the beauty and attractiveness of the woods? Your answer is likely to be different from the answer given by anyone else. This is one reason why you and other people would all perform slightly different interpretations of the poem. But it is also the reason why the poem is able to affect almost everyone personally, whether they are reading, performing, or listening.

Application

Analyzing Literature

Choose a piece of literature that you enjoy or find interesting. Analyze your selection by answering the following questions.

1. What is the central idea or theme of the selection?

2. What are the selection's main units of thought and how are they related to each other?

3. Are there any words, phrases, and sentences in the selection that you do not understand?

4. How can you make use of pause, emphasis, pitch, inflection, rate, and volume in interpreting this selection?

If you cannot answer all of these questions, ask your classmates for help as you prepare for an oral interpretation of the selection.

TWO FINAL STEPS: INTRODUCTION AND PRACTICE

Your work is not finished when you have completed your analysis and interpretation of your selection. You must also prepare an introduction and, perhaps most important, you must practice. As you will see, this practice involves many of the same elements found in practicing for a public speech.

Prepare an Introduction for Your Selection

The introduction is an extremely important part of your performance. It provides you with the opportunity to beckon the audience toward the piece you have selected and the interpretation you will bring to it. The four purposes of the introduction are to:

1. Gain the audience's attention.

2. Set the mood for the audience.

3. Give needed information.

4. Establish rapport with the audience.

An audience will not automatically give you its attention just because you are a performer. You must earn this attention. You must *work* to get the audience's interest in the introduction, or you won't *ever* get it.

An audience needs to be prepared for the mood of the material. If the material is funny, don't look serious; smile and look light-hearted. If the material is very serious, your demeanor during the introduction should be serious.

Many times you need to include information in your introduction that will help the audience understand the material. This is particularly true if you are reading only an excerpt from a much longer piece of literature. Remember that the audience only hears *once* what you have probably read dozens of times.

The introduction gives the audience a chance to make some kind of judgment about you as a person. They decide whether they want to listen to you or not. Your appearance, your demeanor, your whole attitude is judged by an audience very quickly. You must appear prepared, enthusiastic about your material, and glad to be there. If you appear nervous, if you lack energy, if you are not dressed appropriately, your audience will not be very interested in listening to your performance.

For a ten-minute performance an introduction should not be longer than thirty to forty-five seconds. The longer the performance, the longer the introduction can be.

Be sure then that your introduction contains:

1. An attention-getting device, such as your relating to the audience the literature's impact on you as a person.

2. Needed information to facilitate audience understanding.

3. Author and title. If possible tell something special about the author to increase audience understanding.

The introduction is so important to your performance that it should be carefully prepared. You may memorize it, but it should appear to be ad-libbed. Your delivery in the introduction should be very conversational. This effort will be worthwhile because your audience will be prepared to listen and will reward you with an enthusiastic response.

Practice Your Selection

Practice is essential to a good oral performance. Thinking about how you will sound when you perform in front of an audience is not the same as actually doing it. The best way to prepare yourself for a performance is to practice aloud again and again. Don't expect every part of your

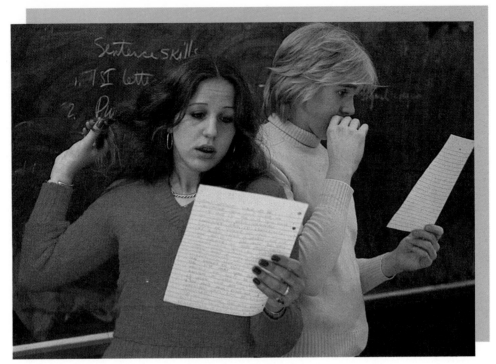

Immersed in their selection, these students practice projecting the story's action and meaning with pauses, emphasis, and intonation.

performance to be perfect the very first time you do it. You must work slowly and carefully on every aspect of your delivery.

Your voice is important in an oral interpretation. Never attempt to vary it artifically. Let the emotion of what you are performing be heard by your audience. If you feel the meaning of what you are saying, your voice will usually take on the characteristics expressed in the words. Your voice should be flexible in pitch, force, and rate so it can respond to various shades of interpretation.

One of the most important aspects of any oral delivery is the use of emphasis. There is no doubt that some words should receive more emphasis than others, but you must be very careful not to disturb the rhythm of the language. This is especially important in poetry. Poets choose their words carefully to create and maintain a particular rhythm. The words that should be emphasized will be stressed naturally. Skillful speakers use pauses as well as stress for emphasis. Did you ever notice that when a good speaker stops speaking for a moment the last few words seem to take on more significance? Use both stress and pauses to emphasize certain words.

Speaking rate is also important in oral interpretation. Speak slowly if the ideas you are expressing are serious or difficult to understand. Light, humorous, or urgent matters can be expressed at more rapid speeds. When dealing with a poem, look closely at its rhythm. Some poems are meant to be read slowly, while others should be spoken quickly. Examples of these different types of rhythm are found in the beginning lines of William Collins' "Ode to Pity" and William Wordsworth's "The Tables Turned."

Ode to Pity

O thou, the friend of man assigned
With balmy hands his wounds to bind,
And charm his frantic woe . . .

The Tables Turned

Up! Up! my Friend, and quit your books;
Or surely you'll grow double:
Up! Up! my Friend, and clear your books;
Why all this toil and trouble?

The two poems quoted above begin in very different ways. The words "Up! Up!" show that the second poem, "The Tables Turned," is to be read at a quick pace. On the other hand, the words "O thou, the friend of man . . ." in the first poem, "Ode to Pity," have a solemn ring to them and suggest a much slower reading.

Good articulation and correct pronunciation are both essential in oral interpretation. Don't be afraid to put your tongue, jaw, and lips to their full use in order to say words clearly and correctly. As in public speaking, your audience must be able to hear your words and understand them. In order to remember how you want to say a particular word or phrase, it is a good idea to mark the manuscript. You can develop your own system, which may or may not include underlining words you want stressed or using accent marks to remind you how to pronounce words you may have trouble with.

Above all, you must establish a rapport with your audience. Your listeners must believe that you are speaking directly to them and not to a piece of paper or to the floor. Although it is not recommended for beginners, some oral performers prefer to memorize what they perform. That way, they do not have to worry about losing their place in the manuscript or losing contact with their audience. If you do choose to memorize, be sure to have a copy of the piece you are performing nearby.

Nervousness in front of an audience can cause you to forget some or all of a selection you thought you knew well. If you do not memorize the entire selection, you should at least know it well enough that you don't have to read every word from the manuscript. This will leave you free to gauge audience feedback.

Your audience will be influenced by what they see as well as by what they hear. It is important that the nonverbal aspects of your interpretation add to the effect of your performance. As a general rule, your gestures and facial expressions should be natural. If you are genuinely concerned with getting your message across, gesture will come naturally as part of the performance. Remember though that body movement is secondary to the spoken words. Exaggerated or nervous movements can distract your listeners from what you are saying. Gestures should be used to clarify, emphasize, or reinforce what you say. The visual aspects of your performance must be appropriate to your audience, the occasion, and the selection you have chosen. Most important, the visual aspects of your performance should be natural to you.

After you have practiced reading your interpretation aloud and feel comfortable with it, try speaking into a tape recorder so that you can get an idea of how you will sound to others. If you have access to a video recorder take advantage of the opportunity to videotape your performance. Videotapes are invaluable rehearsal tools for an interpreter. Then have one or two friends listen and see you perform. In this way you will become used to having an audience in front of you. You will also get a chance to observe and interpret some audience reaction to what you are saying and how you are saying it. By performing first in front of a small audience, you begin to gain the confidence necessary to do the same before a larger group of listeners.

Application

Delivery of an Oral Interpretation

Return to the literary piece you analyzed in the previous Application. If necessary, make cuts so that it will take no longer than eight minutes for you to perform. Write an introduction that will capture your audience's attention and prepare them to listen to your selection. Rehearse your performance several times—at least once before a mirror—until it feels polished enough to share with an audience. Deliver your oral interpretation in class.

16 Chapter Review

Summary

A good speaker can perform literature just as a good musician performs music. Oral interpretation is the process by which a speaker performs literature aloud for an audience.

A Brief History of Oral Interpretation   Stories were preserved orally long before they could be preserved in writing. People still enjoy practicing this tradition, and by preparing for oral interpretation, they better understand a piece of literature. Listeners then share the speaker's enthusiasm and understanding of it.

Types of Material for Oral Interpretation   Literature says something of lasting value and says it well. Prose is closer to everyday language than poetry and includes works of fiction and nonfiction. Poetry communicates thought and feeling through the careful arrangement of words for their sound and rhythm as well as for their meaning.

Choosing Material for Oral Interpretation   Choose literature for oral interpretation that has universal appeal and offers insight, beauty, and technical quality. Choose a piece you enjoy and that fits the occasion, your purpose, your audience, and your time allotment.

Interpreting Your Selection   Know the meaning and pronunciation of every word in any selection you interpret orally and research both its author and the period in which it was written. To find out about the author's fictional speaker, imaginary audience, and setting, consider facts and details in the selection and use your imagination to fill in other details. Your interpretation of these missing details will probably differ from that of anyone else, as will your performance.

Two Final Steps: Introduction and Practice   An introduction for your selection should include the kind of literature it is, its title, information about its author, and its historical background. If you interpret only part of a selection, be sure to include an explanation of the selection in your introduction.

Prepare for a performance by working slowly and carefully on every aspect of your delivery, including vocal flexibility, articulation, pronunciation, gestures, and body movement. Practice your selection until you feel comfortable. Then rehearse again with a tape recorder and several friends. This will help you gain the confidence necessary to perform for a larger group of listeners.

 # Vocabulary

Define each term in a complete sentence.

oral interpretation	nonfiction	technical quality
minstrel	poetry	fictional speaker
bard	narrative poetry	imaginary audience
literature	lyric poetry	setting
prose	universal appeal	
fiction	insight	

 # Checklist

Oral-Interpretation Skills

1. Understand the history of oral interpretation.
2. Choose good and lasting literature for your interpretation.
3. Know the difference between prose and poetry, and use this knowledge when you interpret.
4. Practice pronunciation and learn the meaning of every word in your selection.
5. Research the background of the author of your selection.
6. Know the fictional speaker and imaginary audience.
7. Picture the setting of your selection in your imagination.
8. Be certain that verbal and nonverbal aspects of your interpretation are natural.
9. Prepare an introduction that includes information about your author.
10. Practice before a small group of friends before you perform.

Review Questions

1. Define oral interpretation.
2. Name several occasions when oral interpretation may be needed.
3. Identify the value of oral interpretation for the speaker.
4. Identify the value of oral interpretation for the listener.
5. Name some types of literature that can be used successfully in oral interpretation.
6. Name and explain four characteristics of a literary work to consider when you select a piece for oral interpretation.
7. List personal elements to consider when selecting literature for oral interpretation.
8. Identify the elements within a selection that the speaker must understand in order to perform the work effectively.
9. Name several elements that an introduction to an oral interpretation should include.
10. Identify the steps that a speaker should take when practicing for oral interpretation.

Discussion Questions

1. As a class, choose a piece of literature that everyone agrees is noteworthy. Discuss the techniques used to analyze literature. Go over the chapter and list the specific features that a thorough analysis should contain. Then analyze the piece of literature that the class has chosen.
2. Literature that is best suited for oral interpretation has universal appeal. Discuss what the term *universal appeal* means. What is it that makes literature interesting to people? What does literature really tell us about? What pieces of literature have you read that possess universal appeal?
3. Discuss ways in which nonverbal communication skills support oral interpretation. What are these skills? How do they enhance the effectiveness of an oral interpretation? How do you decide on the appropriate use of these skills?
4. Discuss the importance of determining the author's intent when interpreting a poem or a piece of prose. What can you do to be sure you understand the author's message? If you

did not understand the message, how would you prepare an oral interpretation for it?

5. Discuss the importance of practice in effective oral interpretation. What benefits come to someone who rehearses a selection thoroughly? Why is it important to know your exact speaking rate? How can a tape recorder help during a practice session?

Critical Thinking

1. **Analysis:** What are the steps that you would follow in choosing a piece of literature for oral interpretation? Describe the criteria that you would use in selecting a piece for oral interpretation.

2. **Synthesis:** Imagine that you have been assigned an oral interpretation that will be from five to seven minutes long. Describe the steps you would follow from passage selection to presentation.

Activities

In-Class

1. As a class, select a piece of literature that is suitable for oral interpretation. Discuss the selection, making sure that the author's intent is understood. Then analyze the selection carefully. Make suggestions for words and phrases to be emphasized and decide upon an appropriate reading rate for the selection. After the class has made complete recommendations for interpreting the selection, have several students read sections of it in class. The class will react to the interpretation and offer feedback.

2. Form into groups of from five to seven. Identify and practice vocal exercises for breath control, projection, stress, pitch, inflection, intonation, and articulation. Check one another for progress in voice control. Practice oral interpretation by performing short selections chosen by the group.

3. Working in groups of from five to seven, select three poems with similar themes. Discuss the poems to be sure that you understand the author's intent. Then practice interpreting the poems orally. Choose a member of the group to interpret the poems before the class. The other members of the group will prepare a general introduction explaining how the poems are related and specific introductions for each individual poem. Practice your oral interpretations for a class presentation.

4. Select a short story that you believe is suitable for oral presentation. Edit the selection so that it takes no longer than ten minutes to perform. Mark your script for pause and emphasis. Write an appropriate introduction. Practice your selection until you are confident and then perform the selection in class.

Out-of-Class

1. Select one short story and one poem that you believe possess universal appeal. In your speech notebook, analyze each selection and describe its universal appeal. Then form into small groups of from five to seven. Share your notes with the members of the group. Discuss the appropriateness of the selections for oral interpretation. Interpret your selections orally before the group and ask for reaction and feedback from group members.

2. Locate several fables that have interesting morals. Plan a presentation made up of at least five fables—one that will give listeners an idea of the fable as a literary form. As you practice, pay particular attention to the voices of any animals that appear. Experiment with different voices that help project a distinct personality for each one. Write an introduction to the fables you have chosen and give your oral interpretation in class.

3. Choose a poet whose works you enjoy. Research the poet's life by consulting as many sources as possible. Find four or five poems that seem to reflect stages in the poet's life, or that seem to have been based on actual life experiences. In your speech notebook, write an introduction to an oral presentation for the group of poems you have chosen. Then write individual introductions to each poem. These introductions should link the selections together smoothly. Present your oral interpretation in class.

4. Choose a poem or story and plan an oral interpretation for each of these audiences:
   (a) a small group of children
   (b) your classmates
   (c) a visiting theater company from Europe
   Decide how you would change your presentation to perform for each audience.

────────── ■ ──────────

■ Chapter Project

As a class, discuss the various oral interpretations that have been presented in class. Vote on the best performances. Structure an oral-interpretation program that features the winners. The program could be given at a school assembly or at a joint meeting of several speech and English classes.

Selections to Interpret Orally

TO A PRIZE BIRD

You suit me well, for you can make me laugh,
nor are you blinded by the chaff
    that every wind sends spinning from the rick.

You know to think, and what you think you speak
with much of Samson's pride and bleak
    finality, and none dare bid you stop.

Pride sits you well, so strut, colossal bird.
No barnyard makes you look absurd;
    your brazen claws are staunch against defeat.

Marianne Moore

WINDOW WASHER

And again the screech of the scaffold
High up there where all our thoughts converge:
Lightheaded, hung
By a leather strap,

Twenty stories up
In the chill of November air,
Wiping the grime
Off the pane, the windows

Which have no way of opening—
Those windows with their brooding interiors,
That figure who lets the light in,
One imponderable stroke at a time.

Charles Simic

SEA FEVER

I must go down to the seas again, to the lonely sea and the sky,
And all I ask is a tall ship and a star to steer her by,
And the wheel's kick and the wind's song and the white sail's
    shaking,
And a gray mist on the sea's face and a gray dawn breaking.

I must down to the seas again, for the call of the running tide
Is a wild call and a clear call that may not be denied;
And all I ask is a windy day with the white clouds flying,
And the flung spray and the blown spume, and the seagulls
    crying.

I must down to the seas again to the vagrant gypsy life.
To the gull's way and the whale's way where the wind's like
    a whetted knife:
And all I ask is a merry yarn from a laughing fellow rover,
And quiet sleep and a sweet dream when the long trick's over.

John Masefield

TO JAMES

Do you remember
How you won
That last race . . . ?
How you flung your body
At the start . . .
How your spikes
Ripped the cinders
In the stretch . . .
How you catapulted
Through the tape . . .
Do you remember . . . ?
Don't you think
I lurched with you
Out of those starting holes . . . ?
Don't you think
My sinews tightened
At those first
Few strides . . .
And when you flew into the stretch
Was not all my thrill
Of a thousand races
In your blood . . . ?
At your final drive
Through the finish line
Did not my shout
Tell of the
Triumphant ecstasy
Of victory . . . ?
Live
As I have taught you
To run, Boy—
It's a short dash
Dig your starting holes
Deep and firm
Lurch out of them
Into the straightaway
With all the power
That is in you
Look straight ahead
To the finish line
Think only of the goal
Run straight
Run high
Run hard
Save nothing
And finish
With an ecstatic burst
That carries you
Hurtling
Through the tape
To victory . . .

Frank Horne

I AM INDELIBLE

Some say the path to spiritual and human awareness
goes by way of humbleness and personal sacrifice
and these words are true
yet
if I am to be aware of my self, my possibilities
and my path in this world
I must recognize the uniqueness of my life and all life.
I am indelible.
From the fingerprint message of my genes
to the exact place where the stars stood at my birth.
From the number of seasons I have survived
to the memory and understanding that I keep of those times.
From all the things I have ever thought or said
to all the little pieces and parts of life I have nurtured and encouraged.
From the time my spirit came and moved in my mother's womb
to the coming time of my completion of my life's cycle . . .
and after,
I am indelible.
I am a part of this world,
whether I draw breath as a physical entity
or if I give my spirit form energy.
I am indelible.
I am my mother's child.

earth lodge woman/minnie two shoes

IN HONOR OF
DAVID ANDERSON BROOKS,
MY FATHER

July 30, 1883–November 21, 1959

A dryness is upon the house
My father loved and tended.
Beyond his firm and sculptured door
His light and lease have ended.

He walks the valleys, now—replies
To sun and wind forever.
No more the cramping chamber's chill,
No more the hindering fever.

Now out upon the wide clean air
My father's soul revives,
All innocent of self-interest
And the fear that strikes and strives.

He who was Goodness, Gentleness,
And Dignity is free,
Translates to public Love
Old private charity.

Gwendolyn Brooks

from MACBETH
(Act V, Scene 5)

Tomorrow, and tomorrow, and tomorrow
Creeps in this petty pace from day to day
To the last syllable of recorded time;
And all our yesterdays have lighted fools
The way to dusty death. Out, out, brief candle!

Life's but a walking shadow, a poor player,
That struts and frets his hour upon the stage
And then is heard no more. It is a tale
Told by an idiot, full of sound and fury,
Signifying nothing.

William Shakespeare

17 Drama

**When you have completed this chapter
you should be able to:**

- Explain the elements of drama.
- Develop understanding of a character by doing background research and by analyzing the script.
- Experiment with nonverbal and verbal aspects of character development.
- Describe some of the jobs that are part of organizing a theatrical event.
- Explain the steps necessary in producing a theatrical event.

Both backstage and onstage, there is a special thrill attached to drama that comes from its immediacy—from the fact that live actors are performing before a live audience.

Drama is an art form. Like the art forms of painting, sculpture, music, dance and architecture, drama has been a part of people's lives in all parts of the world throughout history. You are surrounded by these art forms every day.

Drama is special, however, because at one time or another it makes use of all the other art forms. Set and costume designers create with wood, plastic, metal, and fabric, putting materials together in colorful, pleasing designs. Musicians provide sound through which mood and thought are communicated. Choreographers devise movement for interpretation of story and emotion, and architects plan the stage space. All that is needed are playwrights, directors, actors, and audiences.

THE NATURE OF DRAMA

Drama exists to provide people with entertainment, education, and feelings of spiritual uplift and joy. It studies humanity's successes and failures by exploring the relationships of human beings in the past, present, and future.

Drama has four principal elements, all of which are necessary to produce a theatrical event. First, there must be live actors. The major difference between a television show, a film, and the theatrical event of drama is that only in live theater do the actors play and respond to the reactions of a live audience. Second, there must be a plot or story. A stand-up comedy act is not drama because drama presents a story, with a beginning, a middle, and an end. The characters must act and interrelate. Third, there has to be a theatrical area. Drama can occur on a street-corner, in a cafeteria, or in a place specifically designed as a theater; it is essential that some space serve as a stage. Fourth, the presentation must result in a theatrical event. The term **theatrical event** means that there must be both actor and audience. Drama does not truly exist until it is viewed.

A BRIEF HISTORY OF DRAMA

Throughout history, drama has been woven into the social and cultural fabric of human endeavor. Theatrical events have existed because people have felt the need to stand up and act out stories as well as tell them. As you will see, different themes have been favored in different eras, but the four basic elements of drama have always remained.

In ancient Greece, rituals were dedicated to the god Dionysus. In Athens, each March, Dionysian festivals were held, with choral singing, dancing, and plays. The final two or three days of the festival were reserved for play contests, at the end of which the winning playwright, or dramatist, was crowned with a wreath of ivy. Thespis won the first contest in 534 B.C. Since he is also known as one of the first actors, performers are still known as **thespians.** Your own school may have a thespian troupe or club.

Both comedies and tragedies were performed in ancient Greece. Like all good drama, the plays had their basis in human conflict. In **comedy,** the conflict was usually not serious, and the ending was generally happy. In **tragedy,** the conflict was always more serious and generally resulted in the destruction of the hero or heroine.

Greek tragedies were based on ancient myths that were well-known to the audience. The philosopher Aristotle (384-322 B.C.) identified certain rules for tragedy in his book *Poetics:*

1. Plays should inspire the audience to reform their lives through **catharsis,** or by releasing their pent-up emotions.

2. The hero or heroine, who must be of a high social standing, must possess a **tragic flaw,** or weakness of character, that leads to his or her destruction.

3. A change of fortune involving **reversal** (in which the character's actions boomerang) or **discovery** (in which the character's attitudes change from ignorance to knowledge) must be included.

4. Dignified, beautiful poetic writing must be used.

Plays of the Greek period are still performed, and some playwrights today still use the rules of Greek tragedy as a basis for their work.

During the **Middle Ages** (about A.D. 500-A.D. 1450), because many people could not read or write, priests presented dramatic representations of Biblical events and parables to their congregations. During this era drama was also performed on street corners by groups of strolling players. These groups are now thought to have been the first professional acting companies. They performed only for the common people.

From A.D. 1350 to 1650 in Europe, during a period called the **Renaissance** (meaning rebirth), there were new developments in all the arts and literature. Drama changed along with everything else. Wealthy nobles and kings and queens became patrons, or sponsors, of the theater and the arts. In Italy splendid buildings were built for **operas,** a new type of musical drama that provided a social gathering place for the wealthy. At the same time, Italy's **commedia dell'arte** (comedy of art) provided comedy for the common people in productions performed without a script. Commedia actors worked with outlines called **scenarios,** from which they made up speeches, songs, dances, and pantomimes as they went along. This type of presentation is called **improvisation.** Improvisations also remained popular and are still performed today.

The **Elizabethan era** in England was the climax of the Renaissance. It occurred while Elizabeth I was queen of England (1558-1603). William Shakespeare (1564-1616) was the greatest playwright of that age. Shakespeare wrote thirty-eight plays. They include histories, comedies, and tragedies. Many of the phrases Shakespeare wrote for his characters have become common sayings. The chart on page 508 contains a list of popular ones you may have heard and the plays in which they appear.

The Renaissance came late to **French theater,** which developed in the seventeenth century primarily as drama for the court. Theatrical buildings were grand showplaces, like the Italian opera houses. The principal dramatist of this period was Molière (1622-1673). Molière was the first French writer to raise comedy to a point where it could hold its own with tragedy as entertainment for the upper classes. He ridiculed people and ideas. Themes of hypocrisy, medicine and medical fees, and arranged marriages recur many times in his thirty-three plays.

After Molière's death the five theatrical companies existing in Paris merged into one group called the **Comédie Française** (French comedy), the first national theater in the world. Still in existence, this organization is the most important troupe in France today.

In 1660 a new era of drama began in England. Theaters that had been closed during the Commonwealth government led by the Puritans were reopened when Charles II became King. During this period known as the **Restoration,** a new style of writing and acting, called the **comedy of**

Some common sayings from Shakespeare's plays

Hamlet	"brevity is the soul of wit" "neither a borrower nor a lender be"
Othello	"pomp and circumstance" "wear my heart on my sleeve"
Julius Caesar	"it was Greek to me" "masters of their fates"
Macbeth	"the milk of human kindness"
Henry IV, Part 1	"he has eaten me out of house and home"
As You Like It	"too much of a good thing" "all the world's a stage"
The Merry Wives of Windsor	"as luck would have it"
The Merchant of Venice	"it's a wise father that knows his own child"

Some common sayings from Shakespeare's plays

manners, was used to make fun of social customs of the day. Women were allowed for the first time to appear as players, and elaborate stage settings were devised. The free spirit was dampened, however, when the Puritans later regained control of the government. Restrictions then limited the number of theaters to three, making all others illegal. Plays had to pass a censoring committee before they could even be performed.

Thus, the term **legitimate theater** originated. Eighteenth-century English playwrights did, nevertheless, continue to write in the comedy-of-manners style.

During the early nineteenth century, **romanticism** became the most prominent dramatic art style. People tried to escape the problems of reality through imagination and thoughts of adventure and beauty. A reaction to these attitudes took place about mid-century, when a majority of playwrights turned to **realism.** Realism in this period stressed the virtues of directness and truth. **Slice-of-life theater** developed as part of this new movement. Playwrights wrote about everyday, real-life situations, conflicts, and people. Historical works were forgotten for a time. Henrik Ibsen (1828-1906), a Norwegian called "the father of modern drama," August Strindberg in Sweden, and Anton Chekhov in Russia, were important dramatists of realism.

Further changes in theater were brought about in the twentieth century after World War II by the movement that brought the **Theater of the Absurd.** Dramatists in this movement viewed human existence as purposeless, lonely, and out of harmony with its surroundings. They opened the way for the use of very experimental theater techniques. Performances took on a laboratory approach, and experiments were made with attitudes, characters, and ways of using theatrical space.

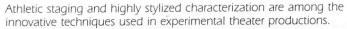

Athletic staging and highly stylized characterization are among the innovative techniques used in experimental theater productions.

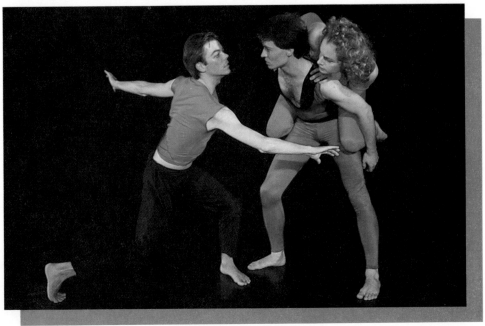

Today, playwrights make use of all ideas and techniques that have been developed throughout the centuries. They create a great variety of theatrical events that entertain, educate, and uplift today's audiences.

DEVELOPING A CHARACTER

One of the main ways a playwright's work is brought to life is through the characters that are developed in the play. An actor must portray a character in ways that fully represent the author's intent. This section will discuss some specific steps an actor can use to develop a theatrical role. Reading the section, you will receive many ideas about how you yourself might interpret a role in a play.

Just as voice and body are used to get messages across in other communication situations, you as an actor must use your voice and body to portray a character. Facial expressions, posture, gestures, speech, and vocal tone combine to provide the audience with a total overview. Your first responsibility then is to interpret and visualize the playwright's words through the character you are portraying. You must also believably expand the character's personality, actions, emotions, and objectives so that the viewer has a clear understanding of what the playwright had in mind when he or she wrote the play.

Secondly, you as an actor must tell the story. This means that you must develop the storyline for the audience by speaking clearly and effectively and providing insight through vocal variety. For example, if you are creating the role of a strong, domineering person, you might want to use a loud, aggressive voice to get the character across. On the other hand, a timid person needs a totally different tone. Each of these roles would also require different postures, gestures, and distinctive clothing to separate them further.

Whether you play a lead role, an animal who speaks no lines, or a chorus part, you must believe in yourself, in the other members of the acting company, and in the project as a whole. You must be secure within yourself before you concentrate on portraying others. Obviously, when you are acting, you must block out all of your own problems before you walk onstage. The audience will not tolerate or believe an actor who bounces in and out of a role. Theater creates an imaginary world and the audience must be able to believe in this illusion of reality. The actors must become the characters while they are performing.

Doing Background Research

To perform a role adequately, you should begin by researching the history of the play, the playwright, the period in which the play takes place, and the type of work it represents (musical, tragedy, comedy, or other). Begin with the play itself. Frequently, scripts contain an introduction to the play and some background about the playwright and his or her ideas. Study the script carefully. It may suggest additional readings. If the play is a modern one and has been previously produced, read any critical reviews you can find. These can provide different interpretations of the play. Recordings are available in libraries of many plays, operas, and musical comedies. Many of the recordings of Shakespeare's works (and other classics) are performances by famous actors such as Laurence Olivier, Edith Evans, Richard Burton, John Gielgud, Paul Scofield, and Orson Welles. Watch newspaper announcements for film presentations of famous theater works. Attend local college and civic theater productions. Especially if you are a newcomer to acting, immerse yourself in different types of theater literature and performances as much as possible. Watching well-directed and well-performed film and television productions can provide a valuable background of acting techniques.

You should next research the era in which the playwright wrote. The social conditions and political environment of the period may be reflected in his or her writing. For example, Oscar Wilde revealed the shallowness and emptiness of much of English society during his lifetime.

In order to portray believable characters of another era, actors first research the play and then bring that knowledge to life onstage.

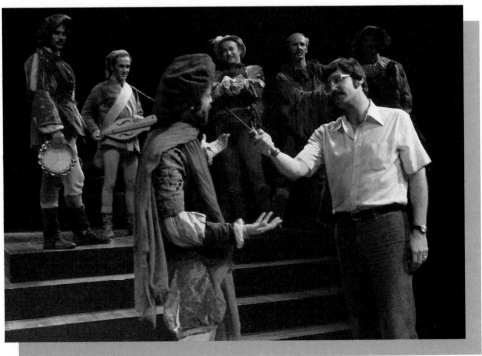

His analysis of hypocrisy and society's willingness to close its eyes to unpleasantness have made his plays among the most beloved of English comedies. A knowledge of Victorian society (1837-1901) will therefore help you understand Wilde's works.

Playwrights sometimes write about a period that is different from their own. Shakespeare's *Julius Caesar* was written in 1599, but takes place in Rome during Caesar's time, 100-44 B.C. In this case thorough research of both Shakespeare's time and Caesar's would help you to understand the meaning of the play.

If you are unfamiliar with the different types of theatrical works, study the style of the play you are reading. Become acquainted with the characteristics of Greek tragedy and compare them with Shakespeare's. Research comedy of ancient Greece, of the Renaissance, the Restoration, and other eras. See if you can find differences in the quality of each type. No matter what the play, the writer intended it to fall within a certain dramatic category. See if you can recognize whether it is a tragedy or comedy or **tragicomedy,** which combines tragic and comic elements.

Analyzing the Script

It may take several careful readings to analyze a play. Try to picture in your mind a production of the play as you read it, and be sure you can answer the following questions:

- What is the theme of the play?
- What is the author trying to say?
- What is the plot?
- Where does each scene and act take place?
- What are the thoughts and problems behind the dialogue?
- What are each character's reactions to other characters?
- What emotional feelings does the play evoke?
- What family or friendship relations are presented?
- What are the social and cultural backgrounds of the characters?

If you have trouble with any of these answers, further research is probably in order.

The **structure** of the play, its form, shape, and development, must also be examined. The presentation of who, what, where, and why is called the **exposition.** The first event to take place, from which the plot develops, is called the **initial incident. Rising action** is the series of the events that develop toward the highest point of interest in the play, the **climax.** This

ACTORS

Actors entertain audiences with their portrayals of characters in plays, films, television and other works. An acting career requires years of study, hard work, and perseverence. While drama schools and college theater programs provide important training, invaluable acting experience is gained from local theater productsions, school plays, and public speaking. Acting students should include the study of speech, voice, and movement to supplement their theater courses.

To prepare for a theatrical role, actors first research the play's and the playwright's background to determine the themes and point of view. Following this scrutiny, they study their part and plan appropriate movements and gestures that will enhance the portrayal of their character.

Actors do much more than say their lines when they play a character. They communicate nonverbally by using a variety of facial expressions and gestures that depict their character's personality. By varying the pitch and volume of their voices, performers can interpret their character's emotions. As they combine these skills with the ability to articulate clearly and project forcefully, they make it possible for the audience to believe in the reality of their character.

When performers convincingly create an imaginary world, they demonstrate the power of effective communication. Their outstanding portrayals inspire audiences to a greater awareness of the influence of communication over the entire human experience. This is perhaps the greatest gift an actor can bestow on an audience—a heightened appreciation and understanding of the tragic and comic dimensions of the human condition.

The actor uses the full power of communication to transform words into worlds.

point reveals whether the major character will succeed or fail to solve her or his problem. Events following the climax tie the loose ends together and are called **falling action.**

Analyzing Character

After you have completed your analysis of the play as a whole, begin to get acquainted with your specific character. Don't waste your time counting the number of lines or entrances you have. It is the quality of your performance—not the quantity—that counts! It may help to begin by underlining your lines or highlighting them with a yellow or pink felt transparent marker. This will help you to distinguish your lines from the others on the page more quickly. Some actors also underline their **cue lines,** the previous speaker's last few words.

Information you will want to know about an individual character include these points:

Physical characteristics and age

Personality traits and emotional stability

Intelligence

Social and personal background

Relationship with other characters

Character, motivation, objectives, and state of mind

Strengths, weaknesses, fears, and hopes

Movement, speech, and type of clothing worn

Remember that these elements may change during the course of the action. If the script does not reveal all the answers, you may want to add interpretations of your own that will fit in with the play. A complete understanding of your character is the basis upon which a creative and memorable performance is built.

After you have become familiar with the attitudes and objectives of the character you will portray, you need to begin to study the lines themselves. Study the **dialogue,** or conversation, for emphasis, phrasing, pronunciation, and meaning. Make sure you know the author's intended purpose for every word, sentence, and paragraph. Determine your objectives or motives in each scene. For each scene you should be able to answer the following:

■ Why am I here?

■ Where did I come from?

- Have I been here before?
- Do I know the other people in the room?
- Why do I leave?

As you begin to memorize your part, try to think, feel, see, move, and speak with your character in mind.

Once in a while actors have to depart from the script because someone fails to make an entrance, forgets a speech, or part of the set breaks. Actors should be ready for these kinds of mix-ups and be imaginative enough to deal with them. The better you know your character, the better you will be able to cope with performance problems. Obviously, if you are on stage and another actor is supposed to enter and does not, you have a problem! Instead of repeating the cue line loudly several times, try to speak some appropriate lines which fit into the action of the play. If your character would do so, pick up a book and recite a poem, look out a window and comment on the landscape, or simply sit down and wait. Whatever happens, do not panic. Backstage, the stage manager will be finding the tardy actor. If you happen to be that actor, do not suddenly rush out on stage. Listen backstage for a moment and find an appropriate time to enter.

Believability is a word which often is mentioned in connection with the theater. Keep believability in mind as you work on your role. Because the first impressions you make on the audience as your character should be believable, you must get into character long before you walk onstage. Many actors feel that the best time to do this is while applying makeup. Some actors rehearse troublesome scenes in the dressing room before a performance. Some directors require company warmup exercises. In any case, you should not wait to get into character until just before making your first entrance. Only when you are properly prepared ahead of time and are eager to share your knowledge, are you ready to go on stage.

Learning the Movements

Your nonverbal communication with your audience is also an important part of the development of your character. Start by becoming aware of how different people move, make gestures, converse, whisper, dress, relax, argue, age, and express themselves. Look around you. Concentrate particularly on facial expressions. Observe the emotions that different parts of the face can convey. Become aware of the ways you can use your own facial expressions by practicing in front of a mirror. See what kinds of expressions you can make using only your mouth. Try to speak holding your mouth in various positions. Then see what feelings you can show using only your eyes and eyebrows.

The face of each actor in this cast of *King Lear* expresses a specific character trait or emotion—stubbornness, despair, bitterness, and cruelty.

You might want to try the following exercise some afternoon when you have a couple of hours to spare. In a park or on a downtown street pick a person out of the crowd who interests you. The first time pick a person just a little older than yourself. Later you can experiment studying people even older. Observe carefully, following your subject as he or she proceeds with normal activities. Do not contact this person in any way. Study his or her manner of walking, arm motions, and posture. Concentrate on details. Watch how your subject carries a purse, a briefcase, a grocery bag, or a baby. After you have observed this person for as long a time as possible, write down a description of what you saw. Begin a diary of observations of different types of people. Refer back to the diary for techniques of movement when preparing for a role.

As you memorize your lines, you should also work on gestures and movements to accompany your dialogue. These details should be written down in the script and memorized along with the words. Some stage movements are naturally required by the plot (Romeo must fight Tybalt, and Juliet must stab herself). Other movements are incidental to the action (Romeo must draw his sword in order to fight). Actions needed to add realism are usually suggested by the plot, stage directions, or dialogue. If a line reads "Please hang up my hat and coat," one of the actors will have to take the items and hang them up. If the scene calls for a family to sit around a table and eat dinner, then there will have to be food, and it will have to be eaten.

Spending time practicing unusual or difficult movements will help prevent awkward movements during a performance. If you are uncomfortable, the audience will notice it. Be sure that you time movements with the dialogue. Wrapping a package, writing a note, eating a sandwich, or putting on a coat all take longer than you think. Even if you cut out some time-consuming details, you can still suggest realistic movements. A package can already be wrapped, and you can simply add a bow. If the wrapping paper roll is placed alongside the work area, it still appears as though the total wrapping job has taken place.

Stage movements can be used to enhance a thin, empty scene. They can also be used to emphasize a dramatic moment. Think, for example, of a scene in which a young man takes out his handkerchief to wipe the tears from a child's face. Activities are often used to fill a momentary gap in the advancement of the plot—during difficult costume changes, for example. Movement also includes necessary movements across stage, the placement of actors, **choreography** (dance patterns), stage fights, love scenes, and gestures. All must be worked out to fit in with the situations and characters of the play.

Once you are familiar with the type of character you will play, experiment with appropriate body movements outside of rehearsal. If the play is an English Restoration comedy, research and study the styles of body movement used at the time. Restoration style includes the use of fans, handkerchiefs, and formal deep bows. Tight breeches, heeled shoes, and formal curled wigs for gentlemen and tight corsets and huge skirts placed over padded hip rolls for ladies determined and restricted movements. Elizabethan hoop skirts do not fit in a small armchair. Find out what kind of clothes are called for in your role and be sure to consider the restrictions of your costume. Make sure that you rehearse in shoes and clothing that are similar to those which will be used in performance. An actor walks and moves differently in jeans and sandals than in high heels and formal clothing.

Application

Experimenting with Movement

Practice the following walking exercises at home or in the classroom. Begin your walk across the room or stage, using your body to communicate one characterization and changing it as you complete your walk. Experiment with movement, posture, and expression.

1. Start walking as a timid person and end as an outgoing one.

2. Start walking with confidence and end with defeat.

3. Start walking as though you did not want to get to your destination and finish as though you did.

4. Start walking as a toddler, taking its first steps; end as an athlete, about to run a marathon.

5. Start walking as though your body were made of steel; finish as though it were made of rubber.

Clear, expressive movements will help to define a character for you and for the audience. When rehearsing a play, write your movements down in the script. As you rehearse, they should become as natural to you as what you say.

Developing Your Character's Voice

As you know, clear, expressive speech is a necessary tool for every part of life. In Chapter 2 you read about the physical aspects of proper speech. You may now want to review some of the technical aspects.

Actors in particular must become very good vocal technicians. As an actor you must learn to:

Stand up straight with good posture so your voice will project better.

Control your breathing.

Change your speaking rate for variation and dramatic emphasis.

Articulate clearly.

Pronounce words correctly.

Project your voice to the last rows of the auditorium.

Have a flexible voice.

Listen to the other characters and respond to them.

Experiment with different voices until you find one that reveals and expresses the character you are portraying.

Begin your character's voice development by listening to as many voices as you can. Tape record interesting speech patterns. Listen to actors on the stage, in films, or television, and on recordings. Listen to your family and friends. Keep a diary of voices you hear the way you did with peoples' movements. Write down what you like and dislike about each voice in your diary. Does the voice make you want to listen more carefully? Can you distinguish personality, nationality, and age? Is it a monotone? Does it project vitality and energy? Is it boring? Can you recognize whether the speaker is sincere in his or her beliefs? Are emotions revealed? Is there variety in pitch, volume, and speaking rate?

As an actor you should become aware of the pitch changes caused by emotional tensions. Low pitch is usually associated with love, sincerity, or sorrow. High pitch is often caused by the emotional stress involved in anger or rage, terror, or excitement.

Three problems related to vocal pitch may arise when you are acting:

1. Your habitual pitch may be too high or too low, limiting the range of pitch changes possible.

2. Lack of variety in pitch may cause uninteresting speech.

3. Your voice may fall into a pitch pattern and thus tend to be repetitive.

An awareness of these potential problems should be very helpful. With practice, you can eventually overcome them.

Another vocal characteristic, volume, is also very important for an actor. Concentration on volume control will allow you to spread a stage whisper across a large auditorium and still maintain the necessary quiet, breathy quality. Ordinarily a director will stand in various parts of the theater during rehearsals to insure that you can be heard at all times.

Like pitch and volume, your rate of speaking can be useful in suggesting changes in emotional states. Anxious or excited characters often speak rapidly. A slower, even sluggish rate might be better for a tragic or awesome passage.

Taking care of your voice, and developing variations in shading, intensity, and mood will be of great help as you begin to develop your character. Look through your diary of voices and pick several types of voices and qualities that might work with your character. Do not be afraid to experiment and overact at first. Use a tape recorder or ask a friend to listen to your ideas. Try the voice out in rehearsal. When you have established a voice that corresponds to your interpretation of the character, return to the script. Note changes of quality, pitch, volume, and speaking rate that should be used for different lines or passages. Continue to rehearse and practice your role until your movements and your voice work well with each other and with the rest of the play.

Exploring Character Relationships

In order to understand your character's relationships with other characters in the play, you must study each of the other characters as well. Don't take the way they relate to each other for granted. Even if the relationship of one character to another character is a family relationship, it may be one that includes deep-rooted feelings of hatred or distrust. Characters who are not blood relatives might relate to each other in the plot through an emotional situation, a business deal, religious circumstances, or simply friendship. Whatever the relationship, you must discover the underlying feelings the characters have for one another.

Understanding the personalities of and relationships between characters helps identify their function within the plot. Each character ordinarily serves several functions, but one is usually most important. The **protagonist,** or principal character, is the one whose story is being told. The **antagonist** is the chief opponent of the principal character. Other characters revolve around these two major characters.

Recognizing the Relationship Between the Actor and the Audience

People go to the theater for a variety of reasons: to be entertained, to lose themselves in the lives of the characters, to be educated, or to see friends perform. Actors have a responsibility to provide a vital, energetic performance. As a beginning actor, you will become aware rather quickly that acting is very demanding work. Plenty of rest, good nutrition, and a full awareness of the play and your role will help fortify you as you prepare to perform.

The spark between actor and audience is what makes for good theater. You respond to the audience, and they respond to you. Many stories have been published about actors who have felt they "lost" the audience during the first scene of the performance and never got them back. Because live theater is an immediate art form, you can correct your relationship with the audience. By changing your volume or rate of speech, or by speaking more personally, you can work for audience approval.

No two performances of an actor are ever alike. Feelings, outside distractions, and energy level influence performance. In turn, differences in the makeup of each audience—age, culture, or social background— contribute to each audience's awareness of and sympathies toward the play's theme.

Application

Developing Character Through Improvisation

Practice developing believable characters by taking part in the following improvisations. Choose a partner and improvise short scenes based on the following characters and situations. Keep your character's motivation clearly in mind as you and your partner work through each conflict to a conclusion.

1. manager - employee *Conflict:* Manager wants employee to work overtime; employee wants to leave early to meet grandmother at airport.

2. doctor - patient *Conflict:* Doctor must convince patient to lose 50 pounds for health reasons; patient believes extra weight is protection against illness.

3. interior decorator - client *Conflict:* Client insists house built in 1680 be decorated in modern, streamlined style; interior decorator's reputation will be ruined if modern furniture is installed in this historic house.

4. astronaut - alien *Conflict:* Alien wants to take astronaut on test drive of intergalactic spaceship; astronaut wants to take alien to NASA laboratory for observation.

ORGANIZING A THEATRICAL EVENT

The **production organization** is the group that works together to choose, finance, cast, direct, design, construct, publicize, and perform a play. Following are some of the roles and functions that are necessary to produce a theatrical event. The Organizational Chart on page 523 shows the relationship between members of such a production organization. As you read the following descriptions of some of these jobs, think of the ones which you would most enjoy doing.

The **producer** heads the organization. This is the person who is responsible for the success or failure of the production and thus the person who has the power to make or overrule all decisions. In the professional theater the producer finances the production or convinces others to do so. Producers make or approve all decisions concerning budget, publicity, hiring, and firing. They often choose the script.

The **director** stages the theatrical production, selecting and controlling everything that happens onstage. After a script is chosen, the director selects the cast and technical designers. The director is also

To help the actors experience and project a sense of place onstage, this director conducts an outdoor rehearsal for *Wuthering Heights.*

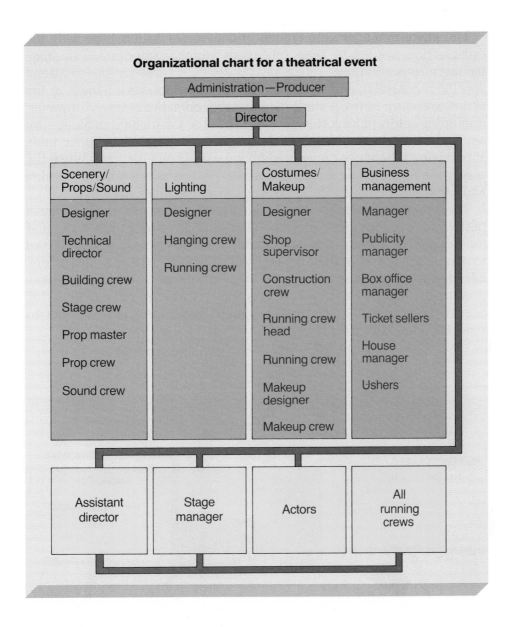

Organizational chart for a theatrical event

Administration—Producer

Director

Scenery/ Props/Sound	Lighting	Costumes/ Makeup	Business management
Designer	Designer	Designer	Manager
Technical director	Hanging crew	Shop supervisor	Publicity manager
Building crew	Running crew	Construction crew	Box office manager
Stage crew		Running crew head	Ticket sellers
Prop master		Running crew	House manager
Prop crew		Makeup designer	Ushers
Sound crew		Makeup crew	

Assistant director	Stage manager	Actors	All running crews

responsible for arranging all movements that take place on stage, teaching dialects (possibly aided by a dialect or vocal coach), developing pace and emphasis, and, perhaps most important of all, establishing an environment of creativity, energy, and trust among all those involved. A director needs to have a thorough knowledge of literature, theatrical periods and styles, as well as scenery, lighting, and costume design. All final technical designs—scenery, costume, lighting, graphics, sound, and properties—are in the director's hands.

The stage manager is in charge of daily organization, especially the organization needed to keep rehearsals running smoothly. The stage manager runs additional rehearsals, posts calls (asks people to attend specific rehearsals), and writes down stage instructions, changes in the script, and actor notes. A stage manager may sometimes act as prompter, reminding actors of forgotten cues or lines. The job includes making sure actors have arrived and are ready to go on stage at the proper time, supervising set-change crews, and taking care of emergencies. When the play goes into technical rehearsals (final rehearsals involving lighting and other technical aspects), the stage manager takes over.

The **scene designer** creates the backgrounds against which a play is performed. Scenery must put the audience in the correct frame of mind for the particular play. The set should, if possible, indicate the type of location, time, and economic and social position of the characters. Effective scenery will suggest a particular emotional atmosphere as well. A comedy might, for example, have scenery that is bright and cheerful. Scenery for a tragedy, on the other hand, might look more somber to reflect the mood of the play.

Floor plan for a scene design, showing walls, furniture, and entrances

The time the play takes place and the director's ideas provide the scene designer with a starting place. The designer must then research the script and time period, consult with the director, and devise a **floor plan** which the director must approve. This plan is a drawing of the position of the walls, entrances, and furniture on the stage. It is drawn from above, giving a bird's eye view of the stage. Next sketches of the set from the audience's point of view must be produced and then drawings must be done to scale. **Scale models** of the set are often built to illustrate spatial requirements. They may include miniature furniture, props, and drapes. Directors use models when planning movements and technicians use them when constructing the set, furniture, and props. The designer must create detailed and scaled working drawings for the builders.

The **lighting designer's** chief function is to light both the actors and the set. In small theaters the same person who designs the lighting often hangs it and sometimes even runs the controls during performances.

Many aspects of lighting design are too technical to be discussed here, but the functions of effective lighting should be mentioned. Lighting design should:

Provide maximum visibility, except where the play requirements suggest otherwise.

Assist in suggesting information such as location, time of day, season, weather, or whether or not an offstage room is occupied.

Create mood and atmosphere.

Contribute to the effectiveness of the entire stage picture.

Distribute emphasis from one stage area to another or from one actor to another.

Provide theme and style indications.

Sources of light (lamps, fireplaces, windows), direction of light, and changes in intensity can be identified by reading the script. Necessary special events (fireworks, Christmas trees, lightning storms) can be found there, too.

The function of the **costume designer** is to help make the characters more believable visually. Costumes should show at a glance a character's occupation, social background, and age. To do this a costume designer must research the script and period and discuss concepts with the director before developing the designs.

Costume designs are done in color, accompanied by fabric swatches and detailed construction drawings. Design decisions are discussed with and approved by the director before the costumes are made.

A basic understanding of some elements of costuming can be of help to a costume designer. **Proportion** relates to the amount of something balanced against the amount of something else. In costume design this principle is seen in the use of color and design elements. A well-proportioned design utilizes one major color, one minor color, and one accent color.

The amount and location of decorations can also make or break a costume design. Remember that the most important part of an actor is his or her face. So instead of just putting trim or a fabric flower anywhere, the designer must position it so that it will guide the viewer's attention toward the head.

Color can affect mood and atmosphere. Light, warm colors (red, orange, yellow) are better for comedy than dark, cool colors (blue, green, violet). Throughout history, specific colors have come to signify certain occupations or stations in life. Royalty is often dressed in purple and burgundy; young women, or **ingenues,** in baby pink or powder blue; devils in black and red; and angels in white or silver.

Fabric choices also can identify people. Shiny or rich fabrics such as taffeta, satin, velveteen, and velvet can be used for wealthy or flashy characters. Plain or open-weave fabrics can be associated with poor, uneducated, or common characters. The **drape,** or hang, of a fabric should also be considered. Heavy or stiff fabrics do not drape well on the body. Softer fabrics such as chiffon, lightweight cottons, and knits hang loosely. A costume designer must look at the fabric from at least ten feet away to see what it will look like from where the audience sits.

After the costumes are designed, about a week before the first dress rehearsal, a **dress parade** is held. This is the first opportunity for the designer and director to see the costumes all together on stage. It also gives the actors the opportunity to find out whether their costumes will withstand stage fights or dance routines. Dress rehearsals allow the actors time to become comfortable in their clothing. An actor who does not work enough in costume will be more likely to look and feel awkward and fidget with stiff collars, lengthy hems, or hooped skirts. The costumer or the crewhead takes care of nightly repairs, washing, and ironing during the run of the show.

Costumes often seem to be last on the list for money. A costume designer must learn to create imaginative and functional costumes with very little money. If you ever work as a costume designer for a school play, you might want to become familiar with the costumes owned by other schools and work out a borrowing arrangement. You might also ask for donations from the PTA and students at your school. Exciting costumes have been made from dyed chenille bedspreads and old curtains, so be creative!

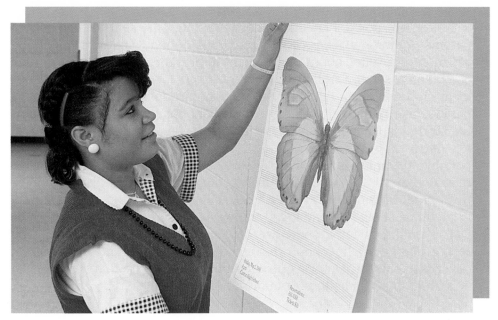

Publicize your production with attractive, informative posters.

A **publicity manager** provides the public with information concerning the production and its participants. Many weeks prior to the first rehearsal, publicity is discussed with and approved by the director and the producer. Poster designs are then created. One good way to find creative graphic designs for a high school production is to hold a poster contest. Contestants should know what the play is about and create their designs so as to include:

name of play (author if necessary)	box office phone
name of organization	permission or royalty information
location	creator's signature
dates	director's name
time	

A well-designed poster catches the eye, can be clearly read, and is interesting and creative. Posters for school performances can be distributed to other schools, area retail stores, churches, and local bulletin boards.

Additional publicity for a school play can take several forms. Advertisements taken out in local newspapers reach a wide range of people. Critical reviews in newspapers are a good way of letting the public know what you are doing. Play announcements might be sent to high school parents or drama teachers at other schools. School window displays can get students excited about the play. Try to present a short scene from the play at an assembly, in the cafeteria, at lunch, for a class, or at a PTA or local club meetings. Publicity stunts are particularly effective. Stage a parade, take costumed players to a local shopping mall, wear buttons or tee-shirts displaying the name of the show, or obtain time on a local television show.

Publicity timing is important. Posters should be distributed no later than two and a half weeks before opening. Newspapers like to receive theater information two to three weeks before publication. Other publicity methods should be employed the week of the opening.

The programs for a show are also part of the publicity manager's responsibility. High school theater departments often sell program advertisements to help offset production costs. Be sure that the program is correct in all its listings of information and names!

Application

The Importance of Organizing

Invite to class people from your area, including students, who have worked on plays as producers, directors, stage managers, designers, and business managers. Ask these guests to explain what their exact duties were and how they fulfilled them in coordination with each group in the production organization. Ask them to explain in detail the decisions that they had to make and how they made them. Ask your guests to participate in a class discussion of the importance of each task to the overall success of the production.

PRODUCING A THEATRICAL EVENT

Now that you have some idea of the many people involved in producing a show, you are ready to consider some of the major steps leading up to and including opening night. The play must be cast. Rehearsals must be held. Numerous problems must be solved to insure a successful opening.

Casting

A play's cast is generally chosen through a process of two or three **auditions,** or tryout sessions. Aspiring actors should, if possible, prepare for tryouts by reading the script. Some directors require **prepared**

readings from the play or another source of the actor's choice, while other auditions are improvisational in nature. After the initial auditions, most directors post **callbacks,** auditions reserved for actors whom the director wishes to hear again. Although the first consideration of casting is the ability of the actor to interpret the role, most directors are also interested in selecting a hardworking group of actors who work well together.

If you are auditioning for a part in a play, you should wear comfortable clothing, have your hair off your face, wear noiseless shoes, speak in a loud, clear voice, and be alert. If you do not get the part you want you should keep auditioning. There are always many reasons for not being chosen. Experience, physical build, vocal qualities, attitude, and script style all must be considered by the director. You should also not be disappointed by a small role. The old saying, "There are no small parts, only small actors," might well be engraved above every stage.

Rehearsals

During the first rehearsal the director discusses his or her **production concept** with the actors, and the cast reads through the script. This concept, the director's interpretation of the play, helps unify the actions

The first rehearsal helps unify the actors' approach to the play.

and thoughts of director, actors, and designers. Throughout the rehearsal period the director holds **production meetings** with the staff to give people a chance to air problems and to make sure that every aspect of the production is running smoothly on schedule. Changes in concept, script cuts, additional technical requirements, and budgets are discussed at production meetings.

A schedule of the entire rehearsal period is handed out to everyone involved in the show. The first rehearsal is a good time for designers to discuss their ideas and present color renderings. It is also a good time for making sure that all participants understand the "rules of the game" and what will be expected of them as members of the production.

When producing a high-school play, five to seven weeks of rehearsal, two to three hours per day, five days a week, is ideal. Weekend rehearsal should be reserved for the final weeks. During the week prior to opening, called **tech week,** rehearsals will generally last longer. Depending upon the play, rehearsals are usually divided into scenes, so that not all of the actors have to attend each rehearsal.

These terms identify different areas of the stage. They are used by directors during rehearsal to block each actor's stage movements.

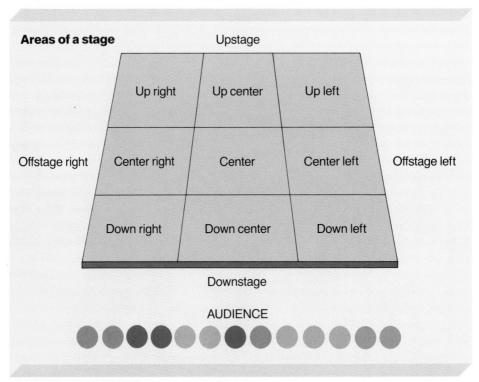

Areas of a stage

Upstage

| Up right | Up center | Up left |

Offstage right | Center right | Center | Center left | Offstage left

| Down right | Down center | Down left |

Downstage

AUDIENCE

During the first few rehearsals, the director gives blocking instructions. **Blocking** is the arrangement of the movements of the actors. It includes how and when actors get onstage and off, as well as how and when they will move about while onstage. Each actor should write blocking instructions down carefully *in pencil,* and then walk through them with the other actors. A normal, full-length play takes about a week to block and set.

The language of stage blocking is not difficult but must be mastered early in the training of all theater people. The diagram on page 530 shows you the terms used for the different areas of a stage. You should also become familiar with the abbreviations used to mark blocking instructions and dialogue interpretation in the script. Some of these symbols are shown in the chart at the bottom of page 531 and in the sample page of marked script on page 532. Careful notation of your blocking instructions helps insure that your position and movements on stage are correct.

The next step for the actors is the memorization of their lines. Both the dialogue and the blocking should be memorized at the same time. Because it is difficult to handle stage movements with a script in hand, actors should memorize as quickly as possible. If you are acting in a play, remember to memorize your lines exactly as written, including the pauses that have been written in by the playwright. If you have difficulty memorizing, have someone help you by reading the scene with you. Be sure to become familiar with your cue lines. You may also find that writing the lines several times helps establish them in your mind. However you memorize, spend considerable time going over and over the material. After three to five weeks of rehearsals, you should be familiar with all the lines of the play. If you try to capture the spirit of every scene in your mind, you will be better able to handle any problems that arise during performance.

Abbreviations for stage directions			
X	Cross	¾	Turn ¾ away from facing center front
X)	Cross on curved line	¼ L	Turn ¼ away from center front toward stage left
XDR	Cross down right	PSR	Stand in profile toward stage right
↑	Voice up	——	Underline words which are to be emphasized
↓	Voice down	✕	Cut

About halfway through the rehearsal period actors are required to be **off book.** This means that they must have all of their dialogue, cues, and blocking memorized. They will then be able to run through a rehearsal without too much prompting. Two weeks before opening, the company should be ready for **run-throughs** during which the play is gone through in its entirety so that the director can concentrate on polishing the fine details of the production.

Sample of script marking

Scene from Act II of BETTER LATE

by Georgina Spelvin

GRADY: (Stunned) Winnie, I never said that. Never. Whoever told you that I said such a thing about you?

WINORA: (Defensive) It doesn't matter who told me—and don't call me Winnie.

GRADY: It matters to me. (Waits for her response; exasperated when he gets none. Turns and walks away; then turns back) Win--ora! What is the problem?

WINORA: (Ready to explode) I'll tell you what the problem is, Grady Bartholomew Sefton. (Turns to him, sees FOOTBALL COACH passing upstage from L to R) Hi, Mr. Wolchek. (Faces down)

GRADY: (Turns and waves to FOOTBALL COACH, then back) What is it? What's going on?

WINORA: (Struggling to find the words) It's just that— well, you seem so far away.

GRADY: What do you mean?

WINORA: (Turns right, close to tears) I always thought I could count on you—as a friend.

532

On with the show! Opening-night jitters and joy—it's the moment everyone has worked for. And afterwards? Celebration, evaluation, and more work—because the show goes on.

Tech Week

The first technical rehearsal is held without actors. Often called **paper tech,** this rehearsal involves the director and technical staff. They run through the entire show, writing down specific cues and deciding set changes. During other technical rehearsals the lighting designer sets and checks lights, while the actors become familiar with the set, their costumes, and the costume changes. Finally, makeup is added, and production photos taken. During all tech rehearsals, the director and designers take thorough notes and discuss them with the cast and staff after each performance.

Opening Night and Evaluation

The director's job is not finished on opening night. He or she should continue to watch each performance and take notes. Before each performance, the director talks to the cast and crews, analyzes the audience's response to the last performance, and encourages a strong, energetic performance. Actors should consider every night "opening night."

When a high-school show closes, the actors and staff generally hold an evaluation session. A discussion of strengths and weaknesses, audience reactions, and the benefits gained by the people involved will provide insights useful in future productions.

17 Chapter Review

◼ Summary

Drama is an art form that utilizes all other art forms, such as painting, sculpture, music, dance, and architecture. It has been a part of people's lives in all parts of the world throughout history.

The Nature of Drama   Drama as a theatrical event exists only when the following are present: live actors, plot, theatrical space, and an audience. Through these elements drama provides entertainment, education, and spiritual uplift and joy. For the participants, drama offers great challenges, insights into history and human existence, and self-esteem.

A Brief History of Drama   From the tragedies and comedies of ancient Greece, theater evolved into a medium of religious education in the Middle Ages and into a source of entertainment for common folk during the Renaissance and the Elizabethan era. During the 1600's in France and England, theater was used for comedic social commentary. In the 1800's it moved from romanticism to realism, and in the mid-1900's it began to portray a vision of human desolation.

Developing a Character   Actors study vocal and body presentations of the past and present, conduct background research, and analyze the scripts and the characters they will play. They then develop the characters' voices, movements, and relationships with other characters.

Organizing a Theatrical Event   The chart on page 521 shows the major jobs involved in organizing a theatrical event. Each artist— producer, director, designer—must understand and coordinate with the work of all the others in order to reach a common goal.

Producing a Theatrical Event   Play production begins with a thorough study of the script. The director establishes a production concept and unifies all theatrical elements, while each actor and technician is responsible for carrying out the director's decisions.

■ Vocabulary

Define at least fifteen of the following terms in a complete sentence.

drama	romanticism	scene designer
theatrical event	realism	floor plan
thespian	slice-of-life theater	scale model
comedy	Theater of the Absurd	lighting designer
tragedy	tragicomedy	costume designer
catharsis	structure	proportion
tragic flaw	exposition	ingenue
reversal	initial incident	drape
discovery	rising action	dress parade
Middle Ages	climax	publicity manager
Renaissance	falling action	audition
opera	cue line	prepared reading
commedia dell'arte	dialogue	callback
scenario	choreography	production concept
improvisation	protagonist	production meeting
Elizabethan era	antagonist	tech week
French theater	production	blocking
Comédie Française	organization	off book
Restoration	producer	run-through
comedy of manners	director	paper tech
legitimate theater	stage manager	

■ Checklist

Drama Skills

1. Keep the purpose of drama in mind, whatever your role is.
2. Know your character so well that you can cope with missed lines and other mix-ups.
3. Keep a diary of observations of different types of people.
4. Use clear, expressive speech in all acting roles.
5. Practice volume control to help project your voice well.
6. Be aware of the organization of a theatrical event.
7. Prepare programs carefully for every theatrical event.
8. Dress properly for auditions.

Review Questions

1. Name the four elements of drama necessary to produce a theatrical event.
2. Define *catharsis*.
3. Name two characteristics of the tragic hero according to Aristotle.
4. Name two playwrights of the Renaissance.
5. Name the playwright who is known as "the father of modern drama."
6. List the steps an actor must take to develop a character.
7. Identify the responsibilities of a director.
8. Name the responsibilities of a stage manager.
9. Describe the elements a costume designer must consider.
10. Name some jobs included on the business staff of a theatrical organization.

Discussion Questions

1. Discuss the benefits of theatrical productions to the individual and society. What qualities make theatre different from other art forms? In what sense are theatrical productions sources or reflections of human knowledge?
2. Discuss the interrelationships among the four elements necessary for a theatrical event to take place. Why does it make sense to say that theatrical drama really can't take place without an audience?
3. Discuss an actor's creative process. What does an actor bring to a role? In what ways is the actor the playwright's accomplice? Is it more accurate to say that the actor is the playwright's assistant? Why or why not? Is the actor responsible for discovering and portraying a role as the playwright intended, or may the actor depart from the playwright's original intention and interpret a role freely?
4. Discuss the Greek concept of catharsis. Why did the Greeks believe that it was a valuable emotional experience? Have you ever experienced catharsis while viewing a theatrical production? Have you ever had such an experience at other times? Do you think catharsis has a valid place in contemporary drama?

■ Critical Thinking

1. **Analysis:** Everyone has witnessed examples of mediocre or poor acting. How do you know when acting is not what it should be? What are the signs that the actor is failing to perform the part adequately?

2. **Evaluation:** Compare and contrast the roles of the playwright, the director, and the actors in a theatrical production. Can they ever operate completely independently of each other? In what sense might the playwright be most distant from the actual theatrical production?

■ Activities

In-Class

1. In each of the following situations, perform the appropriate nonverbal actions. Use no words as you perform each situation. Obtain reactions and feedback from your classmates. (a) You are an older person looking through a photograph album. The photographs are bringing back old memories. React to the various memories that the photographs suggest. (b) You are waiting to see the dentist. The pain of a toothache is compounded by concern about what the dentist is likely to do. As you wait, you hear a scream from the other room. Show your reaction and your final decision. (c) You are waiting at a bus stop with your last quarter in your hand, ready to pay your fare. You drop it accidentally and it rolls into a grate. Reveal how you finally retrieve the coin.

2. With a partner, select a one-person scene or monologue from a play. Decide who will direct and who will perform the monologue. Analyze the character in the scene. Develop a blocking pattern that supports the role and the scene, and rehearse the monologue several times. Present the scene in class.

3. Work in groups of from five to seven. Choose a one-act or a full-length play and imagine that it will be performed three

months in the future. Decide upon the kinds of committees you will need to produce the play. Devise a schedule to be followed in order to meet the date of performance. Make your schedule as complete as possible—from tryouts through dress rehearsal. Be sure to schedule dates for tasks such as costume fittings, publicity photos, and preparation of the manuscript for the program. Compare your schedule with the schedules developed by other groups.

4. As a class, select a play from which two or three scenes can be used for the purpose of auditioning. Discuss how the characters in each scene can be interpreted. Choose a group of five students who will, together, serve as the casting director and evaluate the auditions of the remaining students. The group serving as casting director will then choose the best actor for each part and will explain their choices. The class will discuss the group's decisions.

Out-of-Class

1. At the library, find play reviews by professional theater critics written for newspapers and magazines. Study the reviews carefully. In your speech notebook, summarize the criteria that professional critics use in evaluating plays, actors, and productions. Note the aspects of the plays and productions that these reviewers comment upon most often. Be prepared to share your findings with the class.

2. Attend a theatrical performance in your area. If there is no professional theater company nearby, you should be able to attend a high-school production, or a production presented by a college or community theater group. Evaluate all aspects of the production and write a review in your speech notebook. Be prepared to share your review with the rest of the class.

3. Some people avoid taking part in a theatrical production because they think they have no acting talent. In your speech notebook, write a letter to an imaginary person who holds that belief. Point out the various non-acting skills that are essential for a theatrical production. Suggest activities that a person can participate in without ever facing a live audience on stage. Be prepared to share your letter of encouragement with classmates.

4. Imagine that you have been appointed publicity agent for a theatrical production that opens in one month. Think of ways in which you might publicize the production in your locality. Find out how others have gone about publicizing theatrical events in your community and sketch out a publicity campaign in your speech notebook. Compare your campaign with those of classmates.

▊ Chapter Project

As a class, identify a number of one-act plays that might be suitable for a class production. Read all of the plays suggested and select one that would be possible to stage in class. Select a casting committee and conduct auditions. Name a student director and assign all other students to the various production committees. Rehearse the play and set a date for the performance. You will probably want to invite other classes as your audience.

Appendix of Speeches

INFORMATIVE/COMMEMORATIVE SPEECH

Address on the Anniversary of Lincoln's Birth

Carl Sandburg

On February 12, 1959, the 150th anniversary of Abraham Lincoln's birth, American poet Carl Sandburg delivered the following address to a special Joint Session of Congress. Sandburg, the author of a prize-winning biography of Lincoln, presents in this address a noble and tragic portrait of the beloved President. Note Sandburg's use of quotations and anecdotes to make his subject come alive.

Not often in the story of mankind does a man arrive on earth who is both steel and velvet, who is as hard as rock and soft as drifting fog, who holds in his heart and mind the paradox[1] of terrible storm and peace unspeakable and perfect. Here and there across centuries come reports of men alleged to have these contrasts. And the incomparable Abraham Lincoln, born 150 years ago this day, is an approach if not a perfect realization of this character.

In the time of the April lilacs in the year 1865, on his death, the casket with his body was carried north and west a thousand miles; and the American people wept as never before; bells sobbed, cities wore crepe; people stood in tears and with hats off as the railroad burial car paused in the leading cities of seven states, ending its journey at Springfield, Illinois, the home town.

During the four years he was President he at times, especially in the first three months, took to himself the powers of a dictator; he commanded the most powerful armies till then assembled in modern warfare; he enforced conscription of soldiers for the first time in American history; under imperative necessity he abolished the right of habeas corpus;[2] he directed politically and spiritually the wild, massive, turbulent forces let loose in civil war.

He argued and pleaded for compensated emancipation[3] of the slaves. The slaves were property; they were on the tax books along with horses and cattle, the valuation of each slave next to his name on the tax assessor's books. Failing to get action on compensated emancipation, as a Chief Executive having war

[1]**paradox** (par′ ə däks): contradiction.
[2]**habeas corpus** (hā′ bē əs kôr′ pəs): in law, the right that safeguards persons against illegal detainment or imprisonment.
[3]**compensated emancipation** (kä′ pən sāt′ id i man′ sə pā′ shun): program under which slaves would be freed and slave owners would be compensated for their losses.

powers he issued the paper by which he declared the slaves to be free under "military necessity." In the end nearly $4,000,000 worth of property was taken away from those who were legal owners of it, property confiscated, wiped out as by fire and turned to ashes, at his instigation and executive direction. Chattel property[4] recognized and lawful for 300 years was expropriated, seized without payment.

In the month the war began he told his secretary, John Hay, "My policy is to have no policy." Three years later in a letter to a Kentucky friend made public, he confessed plainly, "I have been controlled by events." His words at Gettysburg were sacred, yet strange with a color of the familiar: "We cannot consecrate —we cannot hallow—this ground. The brave men, living and dead, who struggled here, have consecrated it, far beyond our poor power to add or detract."

He could have said "the brave Union men." Did he have a purpose in omitting the word "Union"? Was he keeping himself and his utterance clear of the passion that would not be good to look at when the time came for peace and reconciliation? Did he mean to leave an implication that there were brave Union men and brave Confederate men, living and dead, who had struggled there? We do not know, of a certainty.

Was he thinking of the Kentucky father whose two sons died in battle, one in Union blue, the other in Confederate gray, the father inscribing on the stone over their double grave, "God knows which was right"? We do not know.

Lincoln's changing policies from time to time aimed at saving the Union. In the end his armies won and his nation became a world power immersed in international politics. In August of 1864 he wrote a memorandum that he expected to lose the next November election; sudden military victory brought the tide his way; the vote was 2,200,000 for him and 1,800,000 against him.

Among his bitter opponents were such figures as Samuel F.B. Morse, inventor of the telegraph, and Cyrus H. McCormick, inventor of the farm reaper. In all its essential propositions the Southern Confederacy had the moral support of powerful, respectable elements throughout the North, probably more than a million voters believing in the justice of the Southern cause.

While the war winds howled he insisted that the Mississippi was one river meant to belong to one country, that railroad connection from coast to coast must be pushed through and the Union Pacific Railroad made a reality. While the luck of war wavered and broke and came again, as generals failed and campaigns were lost, he held enough forces of the North together to raise new armies and supply them, until generals were found who made war as victorious war has always been made, with terror, frightfulness, destruction, and on both sides, North and South, valor and sacrifice past words of man to tell.

In the mixed shame and blame of the immense wrongs of two crashing civilizations, often with nothing to say, he said nothing, slept not at all, and on occasions he was seen to weep in a way that made weeping appropriate, decent, majestic.

As he rode alone on horseback near Soldiers' Home on the edge of Washington one night his hat was shot off; a son he loved died as he watched at

[4]**Chattel property** (chat′′l prä′ ər tē): moveable personal property.

the bed; his wife was accused of betraying information to the enemy, until denials from him were necessary.

An Indiana man at the White House heard him say, "Voorhees,[5] don't it seem strange to you that I, who could never so much as cut off the head of a chicken, should be elected, or selected, into the midst of all this blood?"

He tried to guide Gen. Nathaniel Prentiss Banks, a Democrat, three times Governor of Massachusetts, in the governing of some seventeen of the forty-eight parishes of Louisiana controlled by the Union armies, an area holding a fourth of the slaves of Louisiana. He would like to see the state recognize the Emancipation Proclamation,[6] "and while she is at it, I think it would not be objectionable for her to adopt some practical system by which the two races could gradually live themselves out of their old relation to each other, and both come out better prepared for the new. Education for the young blacks should be included in the plan."

To Gov. Michel Hahn, elected in 1864 by a majority of the 11,000 white male voters who had taken the oath of allegiance to the Union, Lincoln wrote:

"Now you are about to have a convention which, among other things will probably define the elective franchise,[7] I barely suggest for your private consideration, whether some of the colored people may not be let in—as for instance, the very intelligent and especially those who have fought gallantly in our ranks."

Among the million words in the Lincoln utterance record, he interprets himself with a more keen precision than someone else offering to explain him. His simple opening of the House Divided speech in 1858 serves for today:

"If we could first know where we are, and whither we are tending we could better judge what to do, and how to do it."

To his Kentucky friend, Joshua F. Speed, he wrote in 1855:

"Our progress in degeneracy appears to me to be pretty rapid. As a nation we began by declaring that 'All men are created equal, except Negroes.' When the Know-Nothings[8] get control, it will read 'All men are created equal except Negroes and foreigners and Catholics.' When it comes to this, I shall prefer emigrating to some country where they make no pretense of loving liberty."

Infinitely tender was his word from a White House balcony to a crowd on the White House lawn, "I have not willingly planted a thorn in any man's bosom," or to a military governor, "I shall do nothing through malice; what I deal with is too vast for malice."

He wrote for Congress to read on Dec. 1, 1862:

"In times like the present men would utter nothing for which they would not willingly be responsible through time and eternity."

Like an ancient psalmist he warned Congress:

"Fellow citizens, we cannot escape history. We will be remembered in spite of

[5]**Voorhees:** Daniel Wolsey Voorhees, Senator from Indiana.
[6]**Emancipation Proclamation:** proclamation issued by Lincoln in 1862, freeing the slaves in areas of the country still at war with the Union.
[7]**elective franchise** (i lek′ tiv fran′ chīz): the right to vote.
[8]**Know-Nothings:** members of a radical organization dedicated to keeping out of office anyone not a native-born, white, protestant American.

ourselves. No personal significance or insignificance can spare one or another of us. The fiery trial through which we pass will light us down in honor or dishonor to the latest generation."

Wanting Congress to break and forget past tradition his words came keen and flashing. "The dogmas of the quiet past are inadequate for the stormy present. We must think anew, we must act anew, we must disenthrall[9] ourselves." They are the sort of words that actuated[10] the mind and will of the men who created and navigated that marvel of the sea, the Nautilus and her voyage from Pearl Harbor and under the North Pole icecap.

The people of many other countries take Lincoln now for their own. He belongs to them. He stands for decency, honest dealing, plain talk, and funny stories. "Look where he came from—don't he know all us strugglers and wasn't he a kind of tough struggler all his life right up to the finish?"

Something like that you can hear in any near-by neighborhood and across the seas.

[9]**disenthrall** (dis′ in thrôl′): free.
[10]**actuated** (ak′ choo wāt′ id): moved or put into action.

PERSUASIVE SPEECH

Woman's Right to Suffrage   *Susan B. Anthony*

Susan B. Anthony, an activist in the cause of voting rights for women, delivered the following speech after being fined for voting in the Presidential election of 1872. With impeccable logic, Anthony argues that the question of women's suffrage, believed by many to be a question of value or policy, is actually a question of fact. Her argument can be summarized as follows:

The Constitution guarantees the right to vote to all citizens.
Women are citizens.
Therefore, the Constitution guarantees the right to vote to women.

As you read the speech, note how Anthony combines this appeal to reason with appeals to emotion—to justice and fairness. Also note the various kinds of evidence that Anthony uses, including her appeals to the authority of the Constitution and to accepted definitions.

Friends and Fellow Citizens: I stand before you tonight under indictment for the alleged crime of having voted at the last Presidential election, without having a lawful right to vote. It shall be my work this evening to prove to you that, in thus voting, I not only committed no crime, but instead, simply exercised my citizen's rights, guaranteed to me and all United States citizens by the national Constitution, beyond the power of any state to deny.

"We, the people of the United States, in order to form a more perfect union, establish justice, insure domestic tranquillity, provide for the common defense, promote the general welfare, and secure the blessings of liberty to ourselves and our posterity, do ordain and establish this Constitution for the United States of America."

Millions there are who take him as a personal treasure. He had something they would like to see spread everywhere over the world. Democracy? We can't find words to say exactly what it is, but he had it. In his blood and bones he carried it. In the breath of his speeches and writings it is there. Popular government? Republican institution? Government where the people have the say-so, one way or another telling their elected leaders what they want? He had the idea. It's there in the lights and shadows of his personality, a mystery that can be lived but never fully spoken in words.

Our good friend the poet and playwright Mark Van Doren tells us:

"To me, Lincoln seems, in some ways, the most interesting man who ever lived. He was gentle, but his gentleness was combined with a terrific toughness, an iron strength."

How did Lincoln say he would like to be remembered? His beloved friend, Representative Owen Lovejoy of Illinois, had died in May of 1864 and friends wrote to Lincoln and he replied that the pressure of duties kept him from joining them in efforts for a marble monument to Lovejoy, the last sentence of his letter saying, "Let him have the marble monument along with the well-assured and more enduring one in the hearts of those who love liberty, unselfishly, for all men."

So perhaps we may say that the well-assured and most enduring memorial to Lincoln is invisibly there, today, tomorrow, and for a long time yet to come in the hearts of lovers of liberty, men and women who understand that wherever there is freedom there have been those who fought, toiled, and sacrificed for it.

It was we, the people; not we, the white male citizens; nor yet we, the male citizens; but we, the whole people who formed the Union. And we formed it, not to give the blessings of liberty, but to secure them; not to the half of ourselves and the half of our posterity, but to the whole people, women as well as men. And it is a downright mockery to talk to women of their enjoyment of the blessings of liberty while they are denied the use of the only means of securing them provided by this democratic-republican government—the ballot.

For any state to make sex qualification that must ever result in the disfranchisement[1] of one entire half of the people is to pass a bill of attainder, or an *ex post facto*[2] law, and is therefore a violation of the supreme law of the land. By it the blessings of liberty are forever withheld from women and their female posterity. To them this government has no just powers derived from the consent of the governed. To them this government is not a democracy. It is not a republic. It is an odious aristocracy; a hateful oligarchy[3] of sex; the most hateful aristocracy ever established on the face of the globe. An oligarchy of wealth,

[1]**disfranchisement** (dis fran′ chiz mənt): denial of the rights of citizenship, especially of the right to vote.
[2]**ex post facto** (eks pōst fak′tō) Latin: "from after the fact," a term applied to laws having a retroactive effect, especially when these laws deny previously established legal rights. *Ex post facto* laws are expressly prohibited by the United States Constitution.
[3]**oligarchy** (äl′ ə gär′ kē): a type of government in which power rests with a small group of people.

where the rich govern the poor, or an oligarchy of learning, where the educated govern the ignorant, might be endured; but not this oligarchy of sex, which makes father, brothers, husband, sons, the oligarchs over the mother and sisters, the wife and daughters of every household—which ordains all men sovereigns, all women subjects, carries dissension, discord, and rebellion into every home of the nation.

Webster, Worcester, and Bouvier[4] all define a citizen to be a person in the United States, entitled to vote and hold office.

The only question left to be settled now is: Are women persons? And I hardly believe any of our opponents will have the hardihood to say they are not. Being persons, then, women are citizens; and no State has a right to make any law, or to enforce any old law, that shall abridge their privileges or immunities. Hence, every discrimination against women in the constitutions and laws of the several States is today null and void.

[4]**Noah Webster, Joseph Emerson Worcester, and John Bouvier,** lexicographers, or makers of dictionaries. Bouvier's *A Law Dictionary Adapted to the Constitution and Laws of the United States and the Several States of the American Union* was the standard legal dictionary of his day.

PERSUASIVE SPEECH

1984 and 2001: A New Year's Resolution   *Dr. Carl Sagan*

On December 31, 1983, Dr. Carl Sagan—cosmologist, author, Pulitzer Prize winner, and host of the acclaimed public television series Cosmos—*delivered this address at a "Concert for Peace" at the Cathedral of St. John the Divine in New York City. The classical music concert was attended by more than 12,000 people. Dr. Sagan's topic was the danger of nuclear war and the consequences of such a war. In his speech, Sagan compares the present time to the time when human life was new on our planet. He emphasizes the magnitude of our risk of extinction at this period in history.*

There was once a time when humans were newly evolved, when all life on the planet was in a nearly perfect ecological harmony, and when the uranium was still in the rocks. (Doubtless there was music then because all human cultures make music, but it is unlikely that the music then was as lovely as the music we have heard and are about to hear tonight.) If anyone thought about such things then, the future must have seemed bright. There were conflicts perhaps, although they are surprisingly rare among hunter-gatherer societies. Simple weapons were stockpiled, perhaps. Leaders surely were chosen for demonstrated qualities, including a real and tested understanding of the world. In any case, the worst a leader could do was destroy a tribe. There were many tribes. The human species was not then in jeopardy, no matter what the leaders did.

Today it is different. The uranium is no longer entirely in the rocks. Some of it is in nuclear warheads. There are almost eighteen thousand strategic warheads in the arsenals of the United States and the Soviet Union, each of them far more devasting than the weapons that destroyed Hiroshima and Nagasaki. The strategic inventories contain enough destructive power to devastate a million Hiroshimas. But there are only about twenty-five hundred large cities on the planet. We now know that the detonation of even a small fraction of those nuclear stockpiles is sufficient to imperil the human species by triggering a nuclear winter. The clouds of smoke and dust that would be raised would block out the sun, and, according to recent scientific studies, turn all the Northern Hemisphere into a dark, subfreezing radioactive wasteland. Nor would the Southern Hemisphere be spared. By tearing the delicate ecological fabric that sustains life on Earth, it is possible that a nuclear war, even a rather small one, would carry the human species to extinction.

Because we now realize that the steady accumulation of nuclear weapons has placed our species in real jeopardy, it is clear that there must be changes in what passes for conventional wisdom. The Soviet Union has, without doubt, made significant contributions to the nuclear arms race. But, for the moment, consider the United States. In 1945 the U.S. had the most powerful military force on the planet. It was bordered, east and west, by immense oceans, and, north and south, by weak and friendly neighbors. The U.S. had little to fear in 1945. But in an effort to enhance our security, to save lives, we invented things. The U.S. produced the first atomic bomb in 1945. The U.S. was first to use these bombs on civilian populations, again in 1945. The first intercontinental strategic bomber was invented by the U.S. in 1948. The first hydrogen bomb was devised by the U.S. in 1954. The Soviet Union was first to develop the intercontinental ballistic missile in 1957, followed by the first U.S. ICBM one year later. The first submarine-launched ballistic missile was invented by the U.S. in 1960. The first multiple independently targeted reentry vehicle (MIRV) was invented by the U.S. in 1970. The first long-range cruise missile was invented by the U.S. in 1982. Each of these American strategic innovations was evenly matched by the Soviet Union. The total cost to the planet of these nuclear strategic systems has been well in excess of a trillion contemporary dollars.

For what? For the first time in the history of our nation, every American could be killed following the outbreak of a major war. The U.S. is now far less secure than it was in 1945, and so is the Soviet Union. Every step in this mad nuclear arms race had its momentary justification. The mutual recriminations of the U.S. and the Soviet Union are endless. But step back and examine the broad picture. Embrace a planetary perspective. Then you will find that we, the human species, but in particular the U.S. and S.U. [Soviet Union] have done something supremely foolish. The nation states have failed in the most fundamental responsibility of government: to guarantee the well-being, the safety, the future of their citizens. Our governments have wired our lives to a fuse about thirty minutes long. Our survival now depends on the good judgment, the sobriety, the sanity, the mutual sensitivity of the leaders of several nations, and the absolute reliability of machines, all projected into the indefinite future. That is surely taking a very grave risk.

Because the threat of nuclear war engenders a sense of hopelessness, a turning away from the future, it is already claiming its casualties. When our young people find themselves reluctant to work hard to prepare for the future, we are endangering the future, even if there never is a nuclear war. The threat of a nuclear holocaust has already done significant damage to our children and our grandchildren and to the human future.

There are two books, each bearing as title a year. Both are famous in our time. They present two very different visions of the future. In about three hours, 1984 will be upon us. George Orwell's novel *1984* has become a symbol of state suppression of individual growth, of freedom and joy, a code word for a government decoupled from the will and well-being of its people. By contrast, Arthur Clarke's novel *2001* has come to be a symbol of hope for an exploratory future, a future in which humans take a giant stride toward maturity. One pictures a world in which we are robbed of hopeful future, the other in which we are on our way to attaining it. From Orwell's time to our own, the strategic stockpiles have been rising. In the early 1950s, only a few years after *1984* was written, the global nuclear arsenal (almost all of which was then in the United States) reached a kind of threshold beyond which the nuclear winter could be triggered. But no one in either nation had performed the appropriate calculations, and the global confrontation between the two superpowers continued in utter ignorance of the world climatic catastrophe that their actions might unleash.

Conventional wisdom and schoolyard experience teach that stronger is safer, that more weapons mean more security. When, in the early sixties, it became clear that the U.S. and the Soviet Union could each utterly annihilate the other, the idea of saturation or "overkill" arose, the notion that it was pointless to be able to destroy your adversary more than once, the feeling that enough is enough, the suspicion that more nuclear weapons did not buy more security. But this perception was not converted into national policy. The implications of nuclear winter represent a still further departure from the conventional wisdom. It now appears that, beyond a certain point, more nuclear weapons buy dramatically less security, that above a threshold, which is very roughly around a thousand strategic warheads, the world is in significantly greater danger. If the world's strategic arsenals were to be reduced from their present inventory of eighteen thousand weapons to something below one thousand weapons, below the threshold for nuclear winter, the posture of strategic deterrence could still be maintained. But there would be no possibility of destroying the human species. No concatenation[1] of computer malfunction, unauthorized acts, communications failure, miscalculation, or madness in high office could unleash the nuclear winter.

If we begin today, on the threshold of 1984, we can get below this doomsday threshold safely, verifiably,[2] mutually, multilaterally,[3] while preserving the security of all nuclear powers by the year 2001. I am talking about reclaiming our future. In the process there are additional things to do. We can temper childish

---

[1]**concatenation** (kän kat′ 'n ā′ shən): a series of things or events occurring together.
[2]**verifiably** (ver′ ə fī′ ə b'lē): in a manner allowing for verification, or proof. Limiting nuclear or conventional arms depends upon the ability of adversaries to prove that all parties involved are fulfilling the terms of the arms limitations agreements made between them.
[3]**multilaterally** (mul′ ti lat′ ər əl ē): in a manner involving participation by all parties involved.

invective.[4] We can resist the temptation to demonize the adversary. We can reduce the likelihood of strategic confrontations arising from accidents or miscalculations. We can stabilize old and new weapons systems—for example by de-MIRVing missiles. We can abandon nuclear war fighting strategies, and the foolish illusion that it is possible to fight or contain, much less to win, a nuclear war. We can consider, because the nuclear arsenals are so grotesquely bloated, safe unilateral[5] steps, such as the retiring of certain old weapons systems with very high-yield warheads. We can improve communication at all levels, especially between general staffs and between heads of governments. And we can make public declarations of relevant policy changes. I wonder. Does not the nation that invented nuclear weapons, does not the nation that first used nuclear weapons on civilian populations have some special responsibility to reverse the nuclear arms race?

So this is my New Year's resolution, a resolution on the eve of 1984. I invite you to share it with me. We will devote a significant part of 1984 to educating ourselves and our public officials on the apocalyptic implications of nuclear war. We will make certain that every candidate for the House of Representatives, for the Senate, and for the presidency has made a clear public statement, a clear position on the nuclear arms race. And then we will work to elect those who are committed—not to some vague and fence-straddling generalities, but to specific and consistent proposals for major and verifiable reductions mutual in the world inventories of strategic weapons. This does not involve "trusting" the Soviet Union about anything except their commitment to their own survival. Let us convert "1984" from a code word for a government-managed nightmare, to a year in which we start freeing ourselves from the trap that we have carelessly and foolishly set for ourselves. I would like 2001 to dawn on a world that will truly initiate a new millennium,[6] liberated from the danger of nuclear annihilation[7] of the human species.

Let us act this year, so that in 2001 we can look our children and our grandchildren in the eye and say, "Here, we made the world a better place for you. We continued the tradition of the forty thousand generations of humans who came before us. Do the same for your children."

[4]**invective** (in vek′ tiv): violent verbal criticism or abuse.
[5]**unilateral** (yōo′ nə lat′ ər əl): one-sided.
[6]**millennium** (mi len′ ē əm): a period of one thousand years.
[7]**annihilation** (ə nī′ ə lā′ shun): total destruction.

INSPIRATIONAL SPEECH

Address to the Nation: the *Challenger* Tragedy

President Ronald Reagan

In January of 1986, the space shuttle Challenger *exploded, killing the seven crew members aboard, including one civilian passenger, a school teacher from New Hampshire. Following this disaster, President Ronald Reagan delivered this address to the nation. The President refers in the address to the personal grief and loss occasioned by the tragedy. Then he draws an analogy to the death of explorer Francis Drake on the same day, 390 years earlier. He emphasizes that exploration continued after Drake's death as it will continue after the* Challenger *tragedy.*

Ladies and gentlemen, I'd planned to speak to you tonight to report on the State of the Union. But the events of earlier today have led me to change those plans. Today is a day for mourning and remembering.

Nancy and I are pained to the core by the tragedy of the shuttle *Challenger.* We know we share this pain with all of the people of our country. This is truly a national loss.

Nineteen years ago, almost to the day, we lost three astronauts in a terrible accident on the ground. But we've never lost an astronaut in flight; we've never had a tragedy like this. And perhaps we've forgotten the courage it took for the crew of the shuttle. But they, the *Challenger* Seven, were aware of the dangers, but overcame them and did their jobs brilliantly. We mourn seven heroes: Michael Smith, Dick Scobee, Judith Resnik, Ronald McNair, Ellison Onizuka, Gregory Jarvis, and Christa McAuliffe. We mourn their loss as a nation together.

For the families of the seven, we cannot bear, as you do, the full impact of this tragedy. But we feel the loss and we are thinking about you so very much. Your loved ones were daring and brave and they had that special grace, that special spirit that says, "Give me a challenge and I'll meet it with joy." They had a hunger to explore the universe and discover its truths. They wished to serve, and they did. They served all of us.

We have grown used to wonders in this century. It's hard to dazzle us. But for 25 years the United States space program has been doing just that. We've grown used to the idea of space, and perhaps we forget that we've only just begun. We're still pioneers. They, the members of the *Challenger* crew, were pioneers.

And I want to say something to the school children of America who were watching the live coverage of the shuttle's takeoff. I know it is hard to understand, but sometimes painful things like this happen. It's all part of the process of exploration and discovery. It's all part of taking a chance and expanding man's horizons. The future doesn't belong to the faint-hearted. It belongs to the brave. The *Challenger* crew was pulling us into the future, and we'll continue to follow them.

I've always had great faith in and respect for our space program, and what happened today does nothing to diminish it. We don't hide our space program. We don't keep secrets and cover things up. We do it all up front and in public.

That's the way freedom is, and we wouldn't change it for a minute.

We'll continue our quest in space. There will be more shuttle flights and more shuttle crews and, yes, more volunteers, more civilians, more teachers in space. Nothing ends here. Our hopes and our journeys continue.

I want to add that I wish I could talk to every man and woman who works for NASA or who worked on this mission and tell them, "Your dedication and professionalism have moved and impressed us for decades. And we know of your anguish. We share it."

There's a coincidence today. On this day 390 years ago, the great explorer, Sir Francis Drake, died aboard ship off the coast of Panama. In his lifetime, the great frontiers were the oceans and an historian later said, "He lived by the sea, died on it and was buried in it." Well, today, we can say of the *Challenger* crew their dedication was, like Drake's, complete.

The crew of the space shuttle *Challenger* honored us by the manner in which they lived their lives. We will never forget them, nor the last time we saw them, this morning, as they prepared for their journey and waved goodbye and "slipped the surly bonds of Earth" to "touch . . . the face of God."[1]

Thank you.

[1]quotation from a poem by John Gillespie Magee, Jr., an American pilot officer and member of the Royal Canadian Air Force, killed in a plane crash over England in 1941.

SPEECH OF INTRODUCTION

Speech Introducing Indira Gandhi *Alfred Hayes*

In the spring of 1966, Alfred Hayes, president of the Economic Club of New York, gave this speech to introduce to club members Indira Gandhi, then Prime Minister of India. As you read Mr. Hayes's speech, notice that he begins by providing background information about Ms. Gandhi and ends with a brief introductory statement.

Our speaker tonight is the head of government of the world's second most populous nation. She speaks for an ancient country to which we in the West look for much of our heritage of civilization. But more importantly, she speaks for a country which we believe is one of the great hopes of tomorrow's world. Those of us who have visited India have been impressed both by the vastness of its problems and by the importance to the world of their successful solution.

It is no small task to follow in the footsteps of those two brilliant and revered leaders who were in large measure responsible for the emergence of India in this century as a major independent nation. I am speaking, of course, of Mahatma Gandhi and Jawaharlal Nehru, the father of our honored guest. After them, how would India find the leadership needed to sustain it on the path of democracy? Even those who know little about India have the instinctive feeling that the right choice has been made.

It would be presumptuous on my part to try to summarize Mrs. Gandhi's distinguished career, and I know you are impatient to get to the main event of tonight's program. Most of you have read about Mrs. Gandhi's steady rise to political eminence. Certainly she received the best kind of training for her vast responsibilities: as a militant young activist and disciple of Mahatma Gandhi in the noncooperation movement; as a student at Oxford privileged to see the best of Western culture and to view India in perspective; as a member and later as a high official of the Indian National Congress; as a participant in all kinds of social work; as Minister of Information and Broadcasting; and as official hostess and unofficial confidante of her illustrious father. In these and other capacities, she achieved a broad understanding of India's goals and India's problems.

While it would be foolish to overlook her debt to a great father—in natural traits, in an awareness of the importance of service and sacrifice, and in exposure to his wise judgments—the striking fact is that Mrs. Gandhi achieved much of her success through her own merit.

If I have not stressed the fact that India's Prime Minister is a woman, it is because she has won recognition as a statesman in full competition with many able men, and not primarily as a representative of her sex. Nevertheless I am sure she will forgive this virtually all-male audience if we find some special inspiration in the fact that besides all of her other accomplishments, she is a very charming woman as well. It is to India's everlasting credit that Mrs. Gandhi has not been hampered by the prejudices that still handicap her sex in so many parts of the world. Interestingly enough, equal opportunity for women has certainly not been characteristic of India over the centuries; and it has been only through the efforts of leaders such as Mr. Nehru and Mrs. Gandhi herself that India has advanced to the front rank of nations in this respect.

Ladies and Gentlemen, it is with the greatest pleasure that I present to you a person of talent, charm and dignity, a many-faceted human being, Her Excellency Indira Gandhi, Prime Minister of India.

EULOGY

Max Planck in Memorium   *Albert Einstein*

Physicist and philosopher Albert Einstein—twice winner of the Nobel Prize and formulator of the theory of relativity—gave this speech in 1948 at memorial services for fellow physicist Max Planck. Planck, father of the theory of quantum mechanics, which states that energy such as light takes the form of small packets, or "quanta," is considered by many people to be the most important physicist of the twentieth century. Einstein begins his eulogy by praising the work of Planck and explaining the significance of this work. Einstein ends by making a persuasive appeal for free and unhampered research in the sciences.

A man to whom it has been given to bless the world with a great creative idea has no need for the praise of posterity. His very achievement has already conferred a higher boon upon him.

Yet it is good—indeed, it is indispensable—that representatives of all who strive for truth and knowledge should be gathered here today from the four corners of the globe. They are here to bear witness that even in these times of ours, when political passion and brute force hang like swords over the anguished and fearful heads of men, the standard of our ideal search for truth is being held aloft undimmed. This ideal, a bond forever uniting scientists of all times and in all places, was embodied with rare completeness in Max Planck.

Even the Greeks had already conceived the atomistic[1] nature of matter and the concept was raised to a high degree of probability by the scientists of the nineteenth century. But it was Planck's law of radiation that yielded the first exact determination—independent of other assumptions—of the absolute magnitudes[2] of atoms. More than that, he showed convincingly that in addition to the atomistic structure of matter there is a kind of atomistic structure to energy, governed by the universal constant h,[3] which was introduced by Planck.

This discovery became the basis of all twentieth-century research in physics and has almost entirely conditioned its development ever since. Without this discovery it would not have been possible to establish a workable theory of molecules and atoms and the energy processes that govern their transformations. Moreover, it has shattered the whole framework of classical mechanics[4] and electrodynamics[5] and set science a fresh task: that of finding a new conceptual basis for all physics. Despite remarkable partial gains, the problem is still far from a satisfactory solution.

In paying homage[6] to this man, the American National Academy of Sciences expresses its hope that free research, for the sake of pure knowledge, may remain unhampered and unimpaired.

[1]**atomistic** (at′ ə mis′ tik): of or related to atoms, the tiny particles of which the elements constituting the world are made.
[2]**magnitudes** (mag′ nə to͞odz): measurable sizes or quantities.
[3]*h:* an algebraic symbol standing for an invariant quantity of energy, used in physical calculations.
[4]**classical mechanics** (klas′ i k'l mə kan′ iks): in physics, the body of theory concerning motion and force derived from the work of Galileo and Newton.
[5]**electrodynamics** (i lek′ trō dī nam′ iks): the branch of physics that deals with electric and magnetic forces.
[6]**homage** (häm′ ij, äm′ ij): due honor or respect.

KEYNOTE ADDRESS

Address to the Democratic National Convention
Barbara Jordan

In July of 1976, Barbara Jordan delivered this energetic speech at the Democratic National Convention in New York City. Her fresh approach and command of the audience made her the "star" of the convention, according to NBC's David Brinkley.

It was one hundred and forty-four years ago that members of the Democratic party first met in convention to select a presidential candidate. Since that time, Democrats have continued to convene once every four years and draft a party platform and nominate a presidential candidate. And our meeting this week is a continuation of that tradition.

But there is something different about tonight. There is something special about tonight. What is different? What is special? I, Barbara Jordan, am a keynote speaker.

A lot of years passed since 1832, and during that time it would have been most unusual for any national political party to ask a Barbara Jordan to deliver a keynote address[1] . . . but tonight here I am. And I feel that notwithstanding the past that my presence here is one additional bit of evidence that the American Dream need not forever be deferred.

Now that I have this grand distinction what in the world am I supposed to say?

I could easily spend this time praising the accomplishments of this party and attacking the Republicans but I don't choose to do that.

I could list the many problems which Americans have. I could list the problems which cause people to feel cynical, angry, frustrated: problems which include lack of integrity in government; the feeling that the individual no longer counts; the reality of material and spiritual poverty; the feeling that the grand American experiment is failing or has failed. I could recite these problems and then I could sit down and offer no solutions. But I don't choose to do that either.

The citizens of America expect more. They deserve and they want more than a recital of problems.

We are a people in a quandary[2] about the present. We are a people in search of our future. We are a people in search of a national community.

We are a people trying not only to solve the problems of the present: unemployment, inflation . . . but we are attempting on a larger scale to fulfill the promise of America. We are attempting to fulfill our national purpose; to create and sustain a society in which all of us are equal.

Throughout our history, when people have looked for new ways to solve their problems, and to uphold the principles of this nation, many times they have turned to political parties. They have often turned to the Democratic party.

[1]Ms. Jordan is referring to the fact that as a black woman she would have been in the past excluded from public political life.
[2]**quandry** (kwän′ drē): uncertainty.

What is it, what is it about the Democratic party that makes it the instrument the people use when they search for ways to shape their future? Well I believe the answer to that question lies in our concept of governing. Our concept of governing is derived from our view of people. It is a concept deeply rooted in a set of beliefs firmly etched in the national conscience, of all of us.

Now what are these beliefs?

First, we believe in equality for all and privileges for none. This is a belief that each American regardless of background has equal standing in the public forum, all of us. Because we believe this idea so firmly, we are an inclusive rather than an exclusive party. Let everybody come.

I think it no accident that most of those emigrating to America in the nineteenth century identified with the Democratic party. We are a heterogeneous[3] party made up of Americans of diverse backgrounds.

We believe that the people are the source of all governmental power; that the authority of the people is to be extended, not restricted. This can be accomplished only by providing each citizen with every opportunity to participate in the management of the government. They must have that.

We believe that the government which represents the authority of all the people, not just one interest group, but all the people, has an obligation to actively underscore, actively seek to remove those obstacles which would block individual achievement . . . obstacles emanating from race, sex, economic condition. The government must seek to remove them.

We are a party of innovation. We do not reject our traditions, but we are willing to adapt to changing circumstances, when change we must. We are willing to suffer the discomfort of change in order to achieve a better future.

We have a positive vision of the future founded on the belief that the gap between the promise and reality of America can one day be finally closed. We believe that.

This, my friends, is the bedrock of our concept of governing. This is a part of the reason why Americans have turned to the Democratic party. These are the foundations upon which a national community can be built.

Let all understand that these guiding principles cannot be discarded for short-term political gains. They represent what this country is all about. They are indigenous[4] to the American idea. And these are principles which are not negotiable.

In other times, I could stand here and give this kind of exposition on the beliefs of the Democratic party and that would be enough. But today that is not enough. People want more. That is not sufficient reason for the majority of the people of this country to decide to vote Democratic. We have made mistakes. In our haste to do all things for all people, we did not foresee the full consequences of our actions. And when the people raised their voices, we didn't hear. But our deafness was only a temporary condition, and not an irreversible condition.

Even as I stand here and admit that we have made mistakes I still believe that as the people of America sit in judgment on each party, they will recognize that our mistakes were mistakes of the heart. They'll recognize that.

[3]**heterogeneous** (het′ ər ə jē′ nē əs): composed of dissimilar or unlike elements.
[4]**indigenous** (in dij′ ə nəs): native.

Now we must look to the future. Let us heed the voice of the people and recognize their common sense. If we do not, we not only blaspheme our political heritage, we ignore the common ties that bind all Americans.

Many fear the future. Many are distrustful of their leaders, and believe that their voices are never heard. Many seek only to satisfy their private work wants. To satisfy their private interests.

But this is the great danger America faces. That we will cease to be one nation and become instead a collection of interest groups; city against suburb, region against region, individual against individual. Each seeking to satisfy private wants. If that happens, who then will speak for America? Who then will speak for the common good?

This is the question which must be answered in 1976.

Are we to be one people bound together by common spirit sharing in a common endeavor or will we become a divided nation?

For all of its uncertainty, we cannot flee the future. We must not become the new puritans and reject our society. We must address and master the future together. It can be done if we restore the belief that we share a sense of national community, that we share a common national endeavor. It can be done.

There is no executive order; there is no law that can require the American people to form a national community. This we must do as individuals and if we do it as individuals, there is no President of the United States who can veto that decision.

As a first step, we must restore our belief in ourselves. We are a generous people so why can't we be generous with each other? We need to take to heart the words spoken by Thomas Jefferson: "Let us restore to social intercourse that harmony and that affection without which liberty and even life are but dreary things."

A nation is formed by the willingness of each of us to share in the responsibility for upholding the common good.

A government is invigorated when each one of us is willing to participate in shaping the future of this nation.

In this election year we must define the common good and begin again to shape a common future. Let each person do his or her part. If one citizen is unwilling to participate, all of us are going to suffer. For the American idea, though it is shared by all of us, is realized in each one of us.

And now, what are those of us who are elected public officials supposed to do? We call ourselves public servants but I'll tell you this: we as public servants must set an example for the rest of the nation. It is hypocritical for the public official to admonish[5] and exhort[6] the people to uphold the common good if we are derelict[7] in upholding the common good. More is required of public officials than slogans and handshakes and press releases. More is required. We must hold ourselves strictly accountable. We must provide the people with a vision of the future.

If we promise as public officials, we must deliver. If we as public officials

[5]**admonish** (əd män′ ish): to caution, reprove, or urge.
[6]**exhort** (ig zôrt′): to urge.
[7]**derelict** (der′ ə likt′): remiss or negligent.

propose, we must produce. If we say to the American people it is time for you to be sacrificial; sacrifice. If the public official says that, we [public officials] must be the first to give. We must be. And again, if we make mistakes, we must be willing to admit them. We have to do that. What we have to do is strike a balance between the idea that government should do everything and the idea, the belief, that government ought to do nothing. Strike a balance.

Let there be no illusions about the difficulty of forming this kind of a national community. It's tough, difficult, not easy. But a spirit of harmony will survive in America only if each of us remembers that we share a common destiny, if each of us remembers when self-interest and bitterness seem to prevail, that we share a common destiny.

I have confidence that we can form this kind of national community.

I have confidence that the Democratic party can lead the way. I have that confidence. We cannot improve on the system of government handed down to us by the founders of the Republic; there is no way to improve upon that. But what we can do is to find new ways to implement that system and realize our destiny.

Now, I began this speech by commenting to you on the uniqueness of a Barbara Jordan making the keynote address. Well I am going to close my speech by quoting a Republican President and I ask you that as you listen to these words of Abraham Lincoln, relate them to the concept of a national community in which every last one of us participates: "As I would not be a slave, so I would not be a master."

This expresses my idea of Democracy. Whatever differs from this, to the extent of the difference is no democracy.

SPEECH OF DEDICATION

The Gettysburg Address   *President Abraham Lincoln*

In the first three days of July, 1863, a crucial battle of the Civil War took place in the farmland outside the town of Gettysburg, in southeastern Pennsylvania. This battle proved to be a turning point in the war. On November 19 of the same year, a solemn ceremony was held to dedicate a new cemetary for the soldiers who had died in the Battle of Gettysburg. President Lincoln spoke briefly and simply in honor of the dead and in the hope that the Union would endure. In his speech, Lincoln said that "The world will little note, nor long remember what we say here." Ironically, the world has in fact remembered what was said at Gettysburg, for Lincoln's speech is universally acknowledged to be a masterpiece. As you read the speech, notice the simplicity of Lincoln's word choice and the careful phrasing of his sentences. Also notice his use of the rhetorical device known as parallelism—the repetition, with slight changes, of phrases and grammatical structures.

Four score and seven years ago our fathers brought forth on this continent, a new nation, conceived in Liberty, and dedicated to the proposition that all men are created equal.

Now we are engaged in a great civil war, testing whether that nation, or any nation so conceived and so dedicated, can long endure. We are met on a great battle-field of that war. We have come to dedicate a portion of that field, as a final resting place for those who here gave their lives that that nation might live. It is altogether fitting and proper that we should do this.

But, in a larger sense, we can not dedicate—we can not consecrate—we can not hallow—this ground. The brave men, living and dead, who struggled here, have consecrated it, far above our poor power to add or detract. The world will little note, nor long remember what we say here, but it can never forget what they did here. It is for us the living, rather, to be dedicated here to the unfinished work which they who fought here have thus far so nobly advanced. It is rather for us to be here dedicated to the great task remaining before us—that from these honored dead we take increased devotion to that cause for which they gave the last full measure of devotion—that we here highly resolve that these dead shall not have died in vain—that this nation, under God, shall have a new birth of freedom—and that government of the people, by the people, for the people, shall not perish from the earth.

ENTERTAINMENT SPEECH
Society and Nightmares *Eileen Moses*

Effective speakers are sometimes able to present serious messages in lighthearted and amusing ways. As you read the following speech, delivered by Eileen Moses, the president of the Nike Toastmistress Club, ask yourself these questions: What purpose does this amusing speech have other than that of simply entertaining the audience? What kinds of support are used to illustrate the main point that Ms. Moses is making?

Mommie . . . Mommie . . . Mommie . . . I'm afraid . . . I'm so afraid . . . . Sound familiar? A child wakened in the still of the night, terrorized, drenched with perspiration, shaking with fear of the unknown. I'd like a show of hands. How many mothers or sisters or fathers or brothers in the audience have shared this kind of experience? Yes, it has touched most of us and we all usually react by holding the little one very close, reassuring them, trying to calm them, making them as comfortable as possible, just trying to chase away those demons. We tuck them in and feel a sense of pride that we have done everything society expects of us. But . . . do any of us ever question why it happened? Just stop and think about that. Don't the majority of us just completely put it out of our minds? Of course, it couldn't possibly be our fault . . . or could it?

Give me an honest answer. How many in this room have ever said these words to a child that has been very naughty? "Just you wait until your father gets home." Sound familiar? You too, huh? A threat . . . harmless we feel, but is it? Do any of us know how cruel we are to subject a child to this kind of torture? Hours of waiting and wondering just what punishment will be inflicted upon them by the "big bad wolf" better known as good ol' Dad.

And talking about big bad wolves—now that's a great story to be telling our children. You know the one about the poor little defenseless girl going on a mission of mercy to her grandmother's house who gets attacked by a ferocious wolf, who is suspected of devouring her grandma? If that doesn't give them nightmares, nothing will. And how about Hansel and Gretel? There's a great moral to that tale. It actually tells the child that it's perfectly all right to shove someone in the oven and kill them, just as long as it's only a witch. How does that grab you. . . .

But I think the *pièce de résistance* is the Santa syndrome. Heaven forbid that our children shouldn't believe in Santa Claus. Why, it would be positively un-American. Don't you agree? Have you ever watched those poor little tykes being shoved by Mommie or Daddy along a line to see Santa? Crying all the way, most of them are terrified of this giant in a red suit with hair all over his face. It's ludicrous what we inflict on our poor defenseless children. And how about the Easter Bunny—with his gigantic pink ears and those little beady pink eyes and those big buck teeth staring at them? We actually expect these children to fall asleep dreaming that this gigantic white animal will be arriving during the night to leave them eggs. Now that's scary! These kids have to have a nightmare over that one. Let's fact it—how many kids even like eggs?

Yes, threats, nothing but threats, is what our society dictates is the thing to do—even in our songs. How about "You Better Watch Out, You Better Not Cry"? Threats, more threats. If they're not good Santa won't come down the chimney. The Easter Bunny won't come hopping through their doors. If they lie, their noses will grow long like Pinocchio's, and if they're really bad, their ears will grow like Dumbo's. . . .

Wouldn't it be a whole lot better if we could treat our children with a little more respect? They are human beings, you know. Wouldn't it give us a better image of ourselves if we didn't rely on threats to convince them of what is right and what is wrong? Do you think perhaps it might eliminate some of those hidden fears that cause those nightmares? Don't you think it's about time we got wise to ourselves and realized that we are the monster? Well, it's hard to find solutions to the problem. Maybe we could have a workshop on it someday. Oh, my goodness, look at the time. I simply have to run. I'm taking my little grandson to see a movie I know he's really going to love. Maybe you've heard of it? It's called *Dracula!*

Glossary

The glossary provides an alphabetical listing of key words or terms used in this book. The chapter or chapters in which they are treated in depth are shown in parentheses.

abstract words: words that cannot be perceived directly through the senses; opposite of concrete words. (8)

adjourn: a privileged motion to legally conclude a meeting. (14)

affirmative: the side in a debate upholding the proposition being debated; the side in a debate that has the task of attacking the *status quo* and arguing for a specific change. (13)

agenda: a list of the items to be discussed at a meeting. (14)

agreed goal: a purpose or outcome on which both the affirmative and negative sides of a debate agree. (13)

amend: to change a pending motion. (14)

analogy: in public speaking, an extended comparison (8); in debate, a proof of the truth of something by showing its similarity to something else. (13)

anecdote: a short story, often humorous, that is related to a speaker's topic and is used to capture listeners' attention. (10)

antagonist: in a play, the chief opponent of the principal character. (17)

appeal: an incidental motion that allows a member who disagrees with a ruling by the chair to put that ruling to a vote. (14)

appointed leader: a person designated before the discussion begins to perform all the leadership duties. (5)

articulation: the way in which the tongue, teeth, lower jaw, and soft palate are used to produce speech sounds; the process of forming sounds into words. (2, 9)

articulators: the tongue, teeth, lower jaw, and soft palate, which are used to form sounds into recognizable words. (2)

attention device: a technique used to gain or maintain the attention of an audience. (10)

audience analysis: learning everything you can about the background, attitudes, and interests of the people who will listen to you. (7)

audition: a tryout session, as for a play. (17)

author card: a card in a library card catalogue listing a book by the author's name. (7)

bandwagon technique: the logical fallacy that asks people to become part of the supposedly overwhelming group in favor of some person, product, or idea. (3)

bard: a professional storyteller who traveled from village to village with both news and entertaining stories in ancient times. (See *minstrel.*) (16)

begging the question: the logical fallacy of stating that an idea is true without providing proof. (3)

biased: one-sided. (5)

blocking: arranging the movements on stage of actors in a play. (17)

brainstorming: rapidly suggesting ideas without taking time to evaluate each one. (5)

brief: an outline of a debate case, written in complete sentences. (13)

burden of proof: the obligation of the affirmative side in a debate to prove what is asserted by the proposition. (13)

cable TV: a television system that allows people to improve reception and increase the number of channels received by connecting their sets to a large antenna for a fee. (15)

callback: an additional audition for an actor whom the director wishes to see and hear again. (17)

call number: an identification number printed on each library book and on each title, author, or subject card in a library card catalogue. (7)

card catalogue: the alphabetical listing by author, title, or subject of all books located in a library. (7)

card stacking: presenting only evidence that supports the point being made. (3)

cartoon: a visual aid consisting of a funny or satirical drawing used to make a point. (10)

case: in debate, a team's argument on any given proposition. (13)

catharsis: a purifying of the emotions or relieving of emotional tensions, especially through drama. (17)

cause to effect: reasoning from what began something to its result. (13)

central idea: a main point. (3)

chair: a name given to the person presiding over a meeting. (14)

chart: a visual aid that is a drawing showing the relationships among the parts of a whole (often relies on words rather than simply on lines). (10)

choreography: dance patterns; the arrangement of the movements of a dance. (17)

chronological pattern: an organizational arrangement of a speech that proceeds from past to present to future. (7)

cliché: a brief expression of an idea or truth, one that has become almost meaningless through overuse. (8)

climax: in a play, the turning point, which reveals whether the major character will succeed or fail in solving the problem; the point of highest interest. (17)

climax ordering: stating items in a series moving from less significant to more significant and ending with the most important item. (8)

clique: a separate, tightly knit group within a larger group. (5)

closed-group discussion: communication only among group members to solve a common problem, arrive at a decision, or answer a question of mutual interest. (5)

close-minded: refusing to consider ideas that are different from your own. (3)

code: a symbol system. (2)

cohesiveness: a uniting or sticking together; group spirit; morale. (5)

Comédie Française: the first national theater in the world. This organization still exists in France today. (17)

comedy: a drama or narrative with conflict and a happy ending. (17)

comedy of manners: a style of writing and acting, used to make fun of social customs of the day, developed during the reign of Charles II of England. (17)

commedia dell'arte: a type of Italian comedy developed in the 16th century and employing a stereotyped plot, improvised dialogue, and stock characters. (17)

commemorative speech: an inspiring address designed to recall heroic events or people. (12)

commencement speech: an address to honor graduates of a school or university. (12)

commercial television: television broadcasting financed by companies who buy air time to advertise their products. (15)

committee: a small subgroup of a larger organization, one that has been given a specific task or set of tasks to perform. (5)

common ground technique: a means of gaining listener attention by identifying interests or things the speaker has in common with the audience. (10)

communication: the process of sending and receiving messages to achieve understanding. (1)

comparative advantages case: in a debate, an affirmative case that uses the agreed goals → plan → comparative advantages form of argument. (13)

comparison: the presentation of similarities between two dissimilar ideas or situations. (7)

competence: the condition of being well-qualified or capable. (11)

compromise: a settlement in which each member or group of members agrees to give up part of the solution or decision they want, retaining some other part of the solution they favor. (5)

computerized research service: a special library resource that helps locate obscure or specialized information rapidly through the use of a computer. (7)

concrete words: words that enable the listener to perceive the idea by means of the senses. (8)

confidence: belief in one's abilities. (11)

connotation: a meaning attached to a word that goes beyond the dictionary meaning. (2)

consensus: the agreement of all discussion-group members about a solution or decision. (5)

constructive speech: in a debate, a speech used to present and develop the major points of a team's case. (13)

contrast: a language device used to point up differences between similar ideas or situations. (8)

controlled stage fright: the realization that a feeling of tension is natural and can actually sharpen thinking, so that nervousness can be regulated. (6)

conversation: interpersonal communication about matters of common interest to the people involved. (4)

costume designer: the person who plans the clothes worn by actors. (17)

critical listener: one who analyzes and interprets messages carefully. (3)

cross-examination format: in a debate, the format that provides for questioning (cross-examination) by a member of the opposing team following each constructive speech. (13)

cross-examine: to question the opposing side about its arguments. (13)

cue line: in a play, one actor's last few words before the next actor speaks. (17)

cutaway: a visual aid consisting of a model with a section of the outer covering removed to show the interior parts. (10)

databases: collections of information, stored in computer files. (7)

decision-making group: a type of discussion in which members meet with the specific goal of reaching a judgment or conclusion. (5)

decode: to translate incoming information or messages into understandable concepts. (2)

dedication speech: a speech that highlights the meaning of a new creation or endeavor. (12)

deduction: reasoning from general principles to specific cases. (13)

demonstration speech: an informative speech that demonstrates a process or procedure to an audience and that usually makes use of visual aids. (10)

denotation: the basic meaning of a word. (2)

descriptive gestures: hand and arm movements used by a speaker to indicate characteristics of an object such as size or shape. (9)

diagram: a visual aid that relies on lines rather than words to show the relationship of parts to a whole. (10)

dialogue: a conversation; passages of talk in a play. (17)

diaphragm: a thick muscle at the base of the rib cage. (2)

director: the person who stages a theatrical production, selecting and controlling everything that happens onstage. (17)

discovery: in drama, a change in the character's attitudes from ignorance to knowledge. (17)

disinterested audience: an audience that knows about the topic but is unconcerned. (11)

distraction: anything that draws the mind or attention away in another direction. (3)

division of assembly: an incidental motion requesting that a close voice vote be retaken by a show of hands or by having members rise. (14)

division of question: an incidental motion that requests the division of a motion having two or more parts into separate debate and voting. (14)

documentary: an in-depth report on one important subject. (15)

drama: public communication that uses both language and actions to tell a story of human conflict. (1, 17)

dramatic statement: a startling, attention-getting message used during a speech. (10)

drape: in costuming, the hang of a fabric. (17)

dress parade: the first onstage viewing of all costumes by the designer and the director, usually a week before first dress rehearsal. (17)

economy of language: the use of as few words as necessary to state ideas clearly. (8)

educational television: television that is broadcast on stations set aside for instructional and culturally enriching programs. (15)

effect to cause: reasoning from a result back to what started it. (13)

electronic media: technological channels of communication, such as radio and television. (15)

Elizabethan era: the time of the reign of Elizabeth I of England (1558–1603). (17)

emergent leadership: a form of leadership in which one or another of the group members will handle each function of leadership as the need arises. (5)

emphatic gestures: hand and arm movements used during a speech to stress what a speaker is saying. (9)

encode: to put a message into symbols. (2)

enlightenment group: a type of discussion in which members meet to share information. (5)

ethos: the speaker's character in the minds of the audience (including competence, sincerity, and good will). (10, 11)

eulogy: a commemorative speech honoring an individual who has died. (12)

euphemism: a gentle expression for a harsh or unpleasant reality. (8)

evidence: raw material with which you prove or support statements. (11)

example: a specific instance of something being described. (7)

exposition: in a play, the presentation of who, what, where, and why. (17)

extemporaneous method: a type of speech delivery in which speakers prepare ideas for their speeches but do not memorize exact words. (9)

fact: an event or a truth that is known to exist or has been observed. (7)

falling action: the events following the climax of a play that tie the loose ends together. (17)

false consensus: several group members keeping disagreement to themselves, allowing the outcome to be the reverse of what they desire, and leading others to believe all are in agreement. (5)

feedback: the reactions of the receiver to the message of the sender, consisting of words or nonverbal symbols. (2)

fiction: material created in the imagination. (16)

fictional speaker: the voice you hear telling a story or poem when you read literary work silently. (16)

fields of experience: areas of knowledge, interest, or involvement. (2)

figures of speech: phrases and sentences that make a point by stating something in a way that is not to be taken literally. (8)

filibustering: the extension of debate for the sole purpose of delaying or preventing a vote. (14)

floor plan: a drawing showing the position of the walls, entrances, and furniture on the stage. (17)

flow sheet: in debate, a summary outline of how the arguments on each issue are progressing. (13)

formal debate: a type of reasoned argument between parties, which is used in school contests. (13)

forming: the infancy stage of a discussion group in which members become acquainted with one another and leadership roles are established. (5)

French theater: drama in France, which in the seventeenth century included the comedies of Molière presented at the royal court. (17)

germane: logically or directly connected with the subject. (14)

glittering generality: a fine-sounding term, so vague that the exact meaning is unclear. (3)

graph: a visual aid that gives large amounts of information (usually quantitative or numerical) at a single glance. (10)

group discussion: interpersonal communication involving three or more people with a common purpose; the meeting of three or more people to solve a common problem, arrive at a decision, or answer a question of mutual interest. (1, 5)

handout: a visual aid given to each member of an audience. (10)

hasty generalization: a type of faulty reasoning occurring when the speaker does not have adequate evidence to support the broad conclusion drawn. (3)

hearing: the reception of sound. (3)

humor: an attention device utilizing something funny. (10)

hyperbole: a figure of speech that consists of exaggeration used to emphasize a point. (8)

imaginary audience: the audience to whom a fictional speaker relates a story or poem. (16)

impromptu method: a type of speech delivery in which the speaker talks "off the cuff," with little or no prior preparation. (9)

impromptu speech: a short address given with no advance notice and with only a moment or two of preparation. (12)

improvisation: a composing and performing on the spur of the moment, without any preparation. (17)

incidental motion: a type of formal proposal that relates to procedures concerning the conduct of parliamentary business. (14)

induction: reasoning from specific facts or cases to general principles. (13)

informative speech: a public communication in which a speaker imparts new knowledge or more in-depth information on a specific topic to an audience. (10)

ingénue: an innocent, inexperienced, unworldly young woman. (17)

initial incident: in a play, the first event to take place, from which the plot develops. (17)

insight: a clear understanding of the inner nature of some specific thing. (16)

inspirational speech: a speech whose purpose is to exert an enlivening influence on an audience. (11)

interpersonal communication: transmission of messages between two or more people. (1)

interview: a formal kind of interpersonal communication often involving two persons with a particular or definite goal in mind. (4)

interviewee: the person being interviewed. (4)

intrapersonal communication: an inward talking to oneself. (1)

irony: a figure of speech in which the literal meaning expressed is the opposite of the meaning intended. (8)

issue: a major point of disagreement in a debate. (13)

keynote speech: an inspirational address given at the opening of a large meeting or convention. (12)

kinesics: the study of the use of body motions to communicate. (2)

lack of confidence: a feeling of inadequacy often experienced when the symptoms of stage fright are uncontrolled. (6)

larynx: the voice box. (2)

lavalier microphone: an amplification device (microphone) that hangs around the neck. (9)

lectern: a speaker's stand. (9)

legitimate theater: in the Restoration period, the name given to theaters whose plays were passed by a censoring committee before being performed. (17)

lighting designer: a person who designs the lighting for both actors and set and who sometimes runs the controls during performances. (17)

limit or extend debate: a subsidiary motion that either restricts the time to be devoted to discussion on a pending motion or removes any time restrictions in force. (14)

Lincoln-Douglas format: a modification of the cross-examination format in which each side is represented by only one speaker; such debates usually deal with propositions of value rather than of policy. (13)

listening: understanding and interpreting sound in a meaningful way. (3)

literature: prose or poetry considered to have permanent value and excellence of form. (1, 16)

locative gestures: hand and arm movements used by a speaker to direct the listener's attention to a place, object, or person. (9)

logical fallacies: false or faulty methods of reasoning. (3)

logos: the thinking process that allows the listener to arrive at logical conclusions. (11)

lyric poetry: "song-like" poetry expressing emotions. (16)

main heads: the major divisions of an outline. (7)

main motion: a formal proposal that deals directly with an item of business. (14)

maintenance messages: communication designed to create a positive climate by keeping relationships in a group harmonious. (5)

majority vote: a decision agreed to by over half the members of a group. (5)

manuscript method: a type of speech

delivery in which the speech is read to the audience. (9)

map: a visual aid showing information of a geographical nature. (10)

mass communication: one or several senders using printed or electronic media to communicate with a large number of people who are not necessarily present; one or more senders communicating with large groups of people who may be separated from each other and from the sender by great distances. (1, 15)

memorization method: a type of speech delivery in which the manuscript is learned and then delivered word-forword without the use of manuscript. (9)

memory: the brain's storage bin; the power, act, or process of recalling to mind facts previously learned or past experiences. (2)

metaphor: a figure of speech containing a direct comparison that omits the words *like* or *as*. (8)

Middle Ages: the period of European history between ancient and modern times; the period from about A.D. 500 to about A.D. 1450. (17)

minority: fewer than half of the members of a meeting or group. (14)

minstrel: a professional storyteller of ancient times who traveled from village to village bringing news and stories or entertainment. (See *bard*). (16)

model: a visual aid consisting of a scaleddown version of an object. (10)

monotone: speaking successive syllables or words without a change of pitch. (9)

Monroe's Motivated Sequence: a type of speech organization consisting of five steps—attention, need, satisfaction, visualization, and action. (7)

motion: a formal proposal made by a member for consideration and action by a group. (14)

name calling: faulty reasoning that gives a person or idea a bad label without providing evidence to support it. (3)

narrative: supporting material in the form of a story, either real or imaginary. (7)

narrative poetry: poems that tell stories. (16)

nasal cavities: the passages in the nose that act as resonators. (2)

need-plan wedge case: an argument in which the negative does not attack the affirmative's need or plan directly but attacks the logical link between the two. (13)

needs case: a form of affirmative argument based on a need → plan → advantages approach. (13)

negative: in a debate, the side that supports the status quo or denies or attacks the affirmative position. (13)

neutral audience: an audience that is neither for nor against a topic and needs more information in order to form an opinion. (11)

news magazine: a publication or television program that presents informative coverage of several important subjects in some depth. (15)

nominal technique: a form of decision making sometimes substituted for group discussion that involves listing, discussing, voting, and ranking of possible solutions. (5)

nonfiction: material based entirely on truth as the author understands it. (16)

non sequitur: "It does not follow." (Latin) A remark that does not logically follow from what has just been said. (3)

nonverbal: communicating without the use of words. (1)

nonverbal symbols: any means used to encode ideas without words, including gestures, facial expressions, and movements. (2)

norming: the cohesive stage in the formation of a discussion group when members learn to function effectively as a group. (5)

note cards: information cards used by a speaker to remember major points or to read direct quotes or statistics. (9)

notice: an announcement sent to inform members when an organization plans to hold a meeting. (14)

object: a visual aid that is the actual item being referred to. (10)

object to consideration: an incidental motion that allows an assembly to avoid debate and decision on a pending motion. (14)

off book: without a script, having memorized dialogue, cues, and blocking. (17)

one-to-one communication: interpersonal communication between just two persons; speaking with only one other person. (1, 4)

open-minded: willing to listen to all aspects of a question before making a decision. (3)

opera: a musical drama. (17)

opposed audience: an audience that disagrees with the speaker's stand on a topic. (11)

oral interpretation: the process by which a speaker performs literature aloud for an audience. (1, 16)

order of business: the sequence in which various items on the agenda will be taken up during a meeting. (14)

order of precedence: a ranking system that lists the order in which motions may be made and acted upon in parliamentary procedure. (14)

overconfidence: feeling self-assured without adequate reason or preparation. (6)

panel: a group that discusses a topic in front of an audience. (5)

panel-forum: a group discussion that is opened to questions or comments from the audience. (5)

paper tech: the first technical rehearsal, held without actors, involving only the director and technical staff. (17)

paralanguage: the ways in which you say words, including volume, pitch, speaking rate, and voice quality, as well as sounds that are not words. (2)

parallelism: the beginning or ending of several nearby sentences with the same single word or short phrase. (8)

parliamentarian: an expert on rules governing meetings who serves as an advisor to a chair. (14)

parliamentary inquiry: an incidental motion that requests information on the parliamentary procedure dealing with a motion under consideration. (14)

parliamentary procedure: a set of rules used to conduct a meeting in an orderly manner; the established rules of order for conducting group meetings. (14)

pathos: a listener's personal needs, drives, and desires. (11)

pattern of ideas: the flow of the main points of the speech. (7)

pay TV: closed-circuit television broadcasts that people pay an admission fee to

see in a theater, or television broadcasts received in homes with special equipment that is paid for by viewers on a per-program or a monthly-fee basis. (15)

pending motion: a formal proposal that is under consideration. (14)

performing: the final stage in the formation of a discussion group when members bond and work together effectively and harmoniously. (5)

personalizing: bringing human experience into a speech through stories, humor, and specific examples. (10)

personification: a figure of speech that gives human qualities to inanimate objects, ideas, or non-human creatures. (8)

persuasion: a means by which one person can cause another to want to believe, think, or do something. (11)

pharynx: the back part of the throat; the muscular and membranous cavity of the alimentary canal leading from the mouth and nasal passages to the larynx and esophagus. (2)

picture: a visual aid in the form of a drawing, photograph, slide, filmstrip, or film. (10)

pitch: the highness or lowness of sounds. (2)

platform movement: the movement of the entire body while speaking. (6)

poetry: the communication of thought and feeling through the careful arrangement of words for their sound, rhythm, and meaning. (16)

point of order: an incidental motion requesting the attention of the chair and the assembly to an error that has just been made. (14)

positive audience: an audience that already agrees with a speaker's basic persuasive purpose. (11)

poster: a visual aid consisting of print or lettering. (10)

postpone definitely: a subsidiary motion putting off consideration of a motion with the intention of reconsidering the motion at a specific time. (14)

postpone indefinitely: a subsidiary motion to prevent further discussion or voting on a pending main motion. (14)

postpone temporarily: a subsidiary motion to set aside consideration of a pending matter until some time later in the same meeting. (14)

prepared reading: an audition reading that has been read or rehearsed beforehand. (17)

prestige: the power to impress or influence, which comes from one's character or position. (11)

prima facie case: in a debate, the first responsibility of the affirmative side to present a logical argument that would convince a neutral judge who had not heard the response of the other side. (13)

privileged motion: a type of formal proposal of such an urgent nature that it may be considered ahead of any other class of motion; question of privilege, recess, or adjournment. (14)

problem-solution pattern: a type of speech organization in which the first part of the speech describes the problem and the second part develops solutions. (7)

process of association: the connecting of new information with something already known. (3)

producer: the person who heads all organizational components of a play and is responsible for the success or failure of its production. (17)

production concept: the director's interpretation of a play. (17)

production meeting: a group session that is held during a rehearsal period to discuss changes and/or problems in a play production. (17)

production organization: the group that works together to choose, finance, cast, direct, design, construct, publicize, and perform a play. (17)

program concept: an overall plan for a television broadcast. (15)

pronunciation: the production of correct sounds and syllable stresses when speaking. (9)

propaganda: the stating of opinions as though they were proven facts. (3)

proportion: in costume design, the balancing of one thing, such as a certain color, against another. (17)

proposition: in formal debate, a statement to be debated, which can be answered by "yes" and "no" and generally demands that some specific action be taken or not be taken. (13)

prose: the ordinary form of written or spoken language, without rhyme or meter. (16)

protagonist: in a play, the principal character. (17)

proxemics: the study of spatial communication. (2)

public communication: interpersonal communication in which one or more people communicate with an audience. (11)

public discussion: group communication involving members of the group as well as listeners outside the discussion group. (5)

publicity manager: the person who provides the public with information concerning a dramatic production and its participants. (17)

public relations speech: a persuasive speech that promotes and creates a positive image for an organization. (12)

public speaking: communicating ideas verbally to an audience. (1)

public television: television broadcasting financed mainly by company grants and donations by viewers. (15)

purpose sentence: a sentence stating the specific intent of a speech. (7)

question of fact: a discussion question dealing with whether a situation exists, under what circumstances it exists, or how it may be defined. (5, 11)

question of policy: a discussion question directed toward some course of physical or mental action, often including the word *should*. (5, 11)

question of privilege: a privileged motion that requests immediate action on an urgent matter related to the comfort, convenience, rights, or privileges of the assembly or one of its members. (14)

question of value: a discussion question revolving around the worth of an object person, or situation. (5, 11)

quorum: the number of members that must be present before any meeting can be held or any official business conducted. (14)

quotation: the verbatim statement of a person's words or writings. (10)

realism: a dramatic art style that stresses the virtues of directness and truth. (17)

reasoning: the ability to think, form judgments, and draw conclusions; the process of putting evidence together into a logical argument. (3, 11)

rebuttal: in a debate, a speech whose purpose is to refute the opposition's major arguments. (13)

receiver: one who intercepts and decodes a message. (2)

reception: the process of receiving and decoding a message from a sender. (2)

recess: a privileged motion that calls a temporary halt to the meeting in progress. (14)

recognizing: acknowledging the right of a member of an assembly to speak. (14)

refer to committee: a subsidiary motion to submit a matter to a sub-group for further deliberation. (14)

reference section: the area of a library containing works such as encyclopedias, indexes, dictionaries, and other books used to find specific information. (7)

refute: in a debate, to prove an argument or statement to be false or wrong. (13)

Renaissance: the period from about A.D. 1350 to about A.D. 1650 in Europe; a period of "rebirth" in all the arts and literature; a revival of learning. (17)

repetition: the stating of an idea more than once using the same words. (8)

resonators: the pharynx, nasal cavities, and mouth, which act as amplifiers to increase the sound of a voice. (2)

restatement: saying something again in a different way; stating an idea again using different words. (8)

Restoration: the period during the reign of Charles II of England when theaters closed by the Puritans were reopened. (17)

résumé: a typed summary of work experience. (4)

reversal: in drama, a change of fortune in which the character's actions backfire. (17)

rhetorical question: questions that are not meant to be answered aloud. (8, 10)

rising action: the series of events that develop toward the climax of a play. (17)

romanticism: a dramatic art style seeking to escape the problems of the day through imagination and thoughts of adventure and beauty. (17)

round-table discussion: a closed-group session in which information sharing or enlightenment of those taking part is usually the object. (5)

runaway stage fright: feelings of anxiety that are so intense that one loses control; the loss of control of the feelings of anxiety experienced before or during a speech or performance. (6)

running-refutation negative case: in a debate, an argument in which the negative side attacks all parts of the affirmative case. (13)

run-through: a rehearsal, as of a dramatic or musical work, straight through from beginning to end. (17)

scale model: a visual aid consisting of a smaller version of an object; a miniature set design built to illustrate spatial requirements of the stage. (17)

scenario: in drama, an outline or synopsis of a play, opera, or skit, indicating plot, characters, and setting. (17)

scene designer: the person who creates the backgrounds for a play.

second: an indication that one other member of an assembly wishes to see a motion debated and acted upon. (14)

sender: one who transmits a message. (2)

setting: the time, place, environment, and surrounding circumstances of an event, story, or play. (16)

shock technique: an attention device used to demand instantaneous attention from the audience by using a hard-to-believe or upsetting statement. (10)

simile: a figure of speech that presents a brief comparison of two basically unlike things using the words *like* or *as*. (8)

simple majority: at least one more than half the people who voted. (14)

sincerity: truthfulness; genuineness; straightforwardness; honesty. (11)

slang: informal language, outside of conventional or standard usage, which often comes in and goes out of style very rapidly. (8)

slice-of-life theater: a realistic, dramatic art style in which playwrights write about everyday, real-life situations, conflicts, and people. (17)

slogan: a catchy phrase that encapsulates a main idea, often restated at the end of a speech. (10)

spatial pattern: in a speech, the organization of ideas by order in space. (7)

speaking rate: the speed at which one talks. (2)

specific purpose: the intention of a speaker; that which the speaker wants the listeners to know, think, believe, or do as a result of hearing a speech. (7)

specific words: words that refer to a limited class of objects. (8)

speech communication: the transmission of information or ideas by means of vocalized words. (1)

speech of acceptance: a short speech of thanks given by the recipient of a gift or award. (12)

speech of introduction: a short speech used to build enthusiasm and interest for a guest speaker. (12)

speech of presentation: a speech honoring the recipient of a gift or award. (12)

speech to entertain: a humorous speech designed primarily to relax and amuse an audience. (12)

stage fright: the nervousness felt when appearing as a speaker or performer before an audience. (6)

stage manager: in play production, the person who is in charge of the day-to-day organization needed to keep rehearsals running smoothly. (17)

standard format: the debate format in which each of the speakers gives both a constructive speech and a rebuttal. (13)

statistic: a fact stated in numerical terms. (7)

status quo: "the state in which" (Latin); the existing state of affairs at a particular time. (13)

stereotyping: assigning qualities to people or objects, because they are part of a general group, without considering individual differences. (8)

storming: the adolescent stage of a discussion group in which members challenge goals and approaches in an effort to express individuality. (5)

stress: the amount of emphasis placed on different syllables in a word or on different words in a sentence. (2)

string-of-beads pattern: a type of speech organization consisting of a series of items strung together like beads on a string and tied loosely to a central theme, used mainly for entertaining. (7)

structure: in drama, the form, shape, and development of a play. (17)

subheads: the subdivisions of the main heads in an outline. (7)

subject card: a card in a library card catalogue that lists a book by its specific topic. (7)

subsidiary motion: a type of motion that allows members to change the nature of a main motion or to alter the way in which it is debated or voted upon. (14)

summary: the main part of a speech conclusion in which the basic message is briefly restated. (10)

support: evidence (facts, statistics, testimony, narrative, examples, and comparisons) used in speeches to prove the accuracy of statements. (7)

suspend the rules: an incidental motion that allows members to set aside some procedural rule so that members can do something not ordinarily allowed by that rule. (14)

suspense: an attention device developed by temporarily withholding specific information from the audience. (10)

symbol: anything that stands for an idea and is used for communication. (2)

symposium: a series of short, uninterrupted public speeches, often involving a panel of experts. (5)

symposium-forum: a symposium that is opened to questions or comments from the audience. (5)

syntality: the personality of a group as a whole. (5)

task messages: communication designed primarily to help a group achieve goals or complete tasks. (5)

technical language: terms used during a speech that can be easily understood only by listeners who are very knowledgeable about a specific field of thought or endeavor. (10)

technical quality: the way a piece of literature is put together. (16)

tech week: the week prior to the opening of a play in which technical problems are resolved. (17)

tension: mental or nervous strain; apprehension. (6)

testimonial: the not-always-expert opinion of a well-known person on a particular issue. (3)

testimonial speech: an address of praise or celebration honoring living persons at occasions such as weddings, retirement dinners, or roasts. (12)

testimony: the quoting or restating of opinions of others to support a point. (7)

Theater of the Absurd: a drama movement in which dramatists viewed human beings as purposeless, lonely, and out of harmony with their surroundings. (17)

theatrical event: live actors performing a plot or story before a live audience in a space serving as a stage. (17)

theme: the main purpose or message, often restated vividly at the end of a speech. (10)

thespian: an actor. (17)

thinking: the ability of humans to understand, conceive, and manipulate ideas. (2)

title card: a card listing a book by title in a library card catalogue. (7)

topical pattern: a type of speech organization in which the subject is broken down into its natural parts. (7)

trachea: the windpipe. (2)

tragedy: a play that presents serious conflict dealing with the problems of a central character and that has an unhappy or disastrous ending. (17)

tragic flaw: a weakness of character that leads to a major character's destruction. (17)

tragicomedy: a dramatic category that combines both tragic and comic elements. (17)

transition: a word, phrase, sentence, or group of sentences that relates a preceding topic to a succeeding one. (10)

transitional gestures: hand and arm movements used by a speaker to show movement from one part of a speech to another. (9)

understatement: a figure of speech highlighting the significant by treating it as insignificant. (8)

universal appeal: common, recognizable experiences or problems with which everyone can identify. (16)

unsupported assertion: a statement made without giving any supporting evidence. (13)

verbal: of or by means of words. (1)

verbal symbols: spoken or written language symbols or words. (2)

videotape: a magnetic tape on which the electronic impulses of the picture and sound portions of a television program can be recorded for later broadcast. (15)

vocal cords: two folds of membrane, located in the larynx, which vibrate to produce sound. (2)

vocalized pause: the habit of filling in time between words or sentences with "uh," "er," "like," "you-know" or similar sounds. (4, 9)

voice quality: the uniqueness of vocal sound that enables people to recognize others by their voices alone. (2)

volume: the loudness or quietness of sound. (2)

vote immediately: a subsidiary motion to cut off debate on a pending motion and bring it to a vote at once. (14)

warrant: justification or reasonable grounds for some act, statement, or belief. (5)

withdraw a motion: an incidental motion by a member who has made a motion to remove it from consideration before a vote is taken. (14)

Index

Commercial TV, 446
Committee, 113, 422
Common ground technique, 280, 339
Communication, 25, 45 (*See also* Mass Communication, Nonverbal communication, Speech communication)
feedback, 44–45
group discussion, 6, 111–139
interpersonal and intrapersonal, 6
mass (*See* Mass communication)
memory and, 28–29
need for, 29–31
nonverbal (*See* Nonverbal communication)
one-to-one, 6, 83–103
reasoning and, 29
reception, 41, 43
speech (*See* Speech communication)
symbols for, 31–37
verbal (*See* Speech communication)
Comparative advantages case, 391, 394
Comparisons, 184, 339
Competence, 331–333
Composer, 459
Compromise, 137
Conciseness, 126
Conclusion of speech, 253
Concrete words, 217
Confidence, 331–332 (*See also* Stage fright)
building, 149–163
lack of, 153
Connotation, 32, 231
Consensus, 137
Constructive speech, 394
Contrast, 222
Conversation, 6, 87–103
accuracy in, 84–85
courtesy in, 85
defined, 83
enjoyment of, 86–87
feedback in, 84
interrupting, 85
interview, 96–103
nonverbal aspects of, 87–94

open-minded, 85
telephone, 94–96
topics for, 86
Cooperation, 111
Cosby, Bill, 451, 479
Costume, 525–526
designer, 459, 525–526
Critical listening, 67, 164–165
Cross-examination, 382, 404–405
format, 394, 396
Cue lines, 514
Cutaways, 309

D

David Copperfield, 486
Daydreaming, 58
Debate, 379–394
analysis of proposition in, 382, 384
clash of ideas in, 380
cross-examination in 382, 404–405
evidence in, 387–388
flow sheet for, 400–403
formats, 383, 394, 396–398
notes in, 388, 400–401
opposition in, 381–382, 398–401
partner in, 385, 387
preparation for, 382–390
propositions in, 380
reasoning in, 388–390
Decision-making, 94, 112
Dedication, 363–364, 556
Deduction, 388–389
Delivery of speech
appearance and, 252
combining methods for 244–265
comparing methods for, 242–243
conclusion to, 253
distractions from, 57, 262–263
extemporaneous method, 241–245
impromptu method, 241–245
interruptions to, 57, 262–263
lectern for, 260–261

manuscript method, 241–245
memorization method, 241–245
microphone use, 261–262
nonverbal aspects of, 246–255
notes and, 251
pauses and, 258–259
special problems in, 260–263
voice used in, 253–259
Demosthenes, 204
Denotation, 32, 231
Diagrams, 305
Dialogue, 514
Diaphragm, 38
Dickens, Charles, 486
Dickinson, Emily, 475
Dionysian festivals, 506
Director, 458–459
Disc jockey, 454
Discovery, 506
Discussion (*See* Group discussion)
Disinterested audience, 327, 329
Distractions, 57, 262–263
Division of Assembly, 429
Division of question, 428
Documentary, 452
Douglas, Stephen, 396
Drama, 452, 505–531
casting, 528
character development, 510–521
comedy, 451, 506
commedia dell'arte, 507
defined, 505–506
Elizabethan, 507
French, 507
Greek, 506
history of, 506–509
medieval, 507
movements in, 515–517
organizing, 522–528
producing, 528–531
rehearsing, 529–530
Renaissance, 507
Restoration, 507–508
slice-of-life, 509
Theater of the Absurd, 509
tragedy, 506
Drape, 526

Text Acknowledgments

Unit four: 429, adapted from Alice Sturgis, *Sturgis Standard Code of Parliamentary Procedure, 2nd ed.,* Copyright © 1966 by Alice Sturgis. Reprinted by permission of McGraw-Hill Book Company. 358, 361, 365, 371 Stephen E. Lucas, *The Art of Public Speaking.* Copyright © 1986 by Random House, Inc. Reprinted by permission of the publisher. 358, Gregory Peck, introducing Danny Kaye of the 1982 Academy Awards. Reprinted by permission of Academy of Motion Picture Arts & Sciences. 361, Danny Kaye's acceptance speech for the Jean Hersholt Humanitarian Award at the 1982 Academy Awards. Reprinted by permission of Academy of Motion Picture Arts & Sciences.

Unit five: 475, "I'm Nobody! Who Are You?" by Emily Dickinson. Reprinted by permission of the publishers and the Trustees of Amherst College from *The Poems of Emily Dickinson,* edited by Thomas H. Johnson, Cambridge, Mass.: The Belkap Press of Harvard University Press, Copyright 1951, © 1955, 1979, 1983 by The President and Fellows of Harvard College. 482, "Stopping by Woods on a Snowy Evening" from *The Poetry of Robert Frost* edited by Edward Connery Lathem. Copyright 1923, © 1969 by Holt, Rinehart and Winston, Inc. Copyright 1951 by Robert Frost. Reprinted by permission of Henry Holt and Company. 485–486, "An Ode for Ookie, the Older Walrus Child" in *Stand Up, Friend, With Me,* by Edward Field. Reprinted by permission of the author. 486, Charles Dickens, *David Copperfield,* New York: Macmillan Publishing Company, Inc., 1962. 487–488, Lewis Carroll, *Alice's Adventures in Wonderland,* New York: Macmillan Publishing Company, Inc., 1966. 494, William Wordsworth, "The Tables Turned" in *Complete Poetical Works.* Boston: Houghton Mifflin Company, 1932. 502, "To a Prize Bird" from *Observations* by Marianne Moore. Copyright 1924 by The Dial Press, Inc. Reprinted by permission of Doubleday & Company, Inc. 502, Charles Simic, "Window-Washer" in THE VIRGINIA QUARTERLY REVIEW, Fall 1977. Reprinted by permission of THE VIRGINIA QUARTERLY REVIEW. 502, Reprinted with permission of Macmillan Publishing Company from *Poems,* "Sea Fever" by John Masefield. 502, Frank Horne, "To James" in *Literature III,* Albert R. Kitzhaber, Gen. ed., Stoddard Malarkey and Donald MacRae, copyright © 1969 by Holt, Rinehart & Winston, Inc. Reprinted by permission of Henry Holt and Company. 503, Gwendolyn Brooks, "In Honor of My Father, David Anderson Brooks" in *Selected Poems,* published by Harper & Row, Publishers, Inc. Copyright © 1963 by Gwendolyn Brooks Blakely. Reprinted by permission of the author. 522, Reprinted by permission from *Public Speaking* by Linda Huen & Dick Huen; Copyright © 1986 by West Publishing Company. All rights reserved.

Appendix of speeches: 553–556, Barbara Jordan, "A New Beginning: A New Dedication" delivered at the Democratic National Convention in New York City, July 12, 1976. reprinted by permission of the author. 551–552, The Philosophical Library for speech entitled "Max Planck in Memoriam" from *Out of My Later Years.* Copyright © 1950 by The Philosophical Library. Reprinted by permission of the publisher. 545–548, Carl Sagan, "1984 and 2001: A New Year's Resolution." This speech, written with Ann Druyan, was delivered as a New Year's sermon before 15,000 people at New York's Cathedral of St. John the Divine on Dec. 31, 1983. Reprinted by permission of the author and the author's agents, Scott Meredith Literary Agency, In. 845 Third Avenue, New York, New York 10022. 550–551, Economic Club of New York for introductory speech by Alfred Hayes delivered Spring 1966 in New York, entitled, "Alfred Hayes Presents Indira Gandhi." Reprinted by permission of Economic Club of New York.

Art and Photo Acknowledgments

Technical art program: **Martucci Studio**
Original 4-color cartoons: **Martin Riskin**
B & W cartoon p. 451: **Sidney Harris**

Cover photo: **Lou Jones**
Interior photos:
The Bettmann Archive: 152, 225, 258, 291, 324, 443, 471, 481
Black Star: Brack 175, 438–39; Dratch 387; Friedman 160, 378, 399; Howard 529; Kokojan 157; Meyer 42; Morris 422; Pickerell 99, 173, 185
Elizabeth Crews: 7, 281, 469
Culver Pictures: 255
Michal Heron: 215, 293, 320, 355, 428, 449
Harrison Jones: 455
Lou Jones: 359
Ken Karp: 25, 228, 246
Susan Lapides: 84, 362
Magnum: Erwitt 88, 457; Hartmann 89; Manos 53, 384; Richards 333; Stock 150
McConnell, McNamara & Company: i, ii (left), iii, x–1, 2, 3, 24, 52, 80–81, 110, 138, 146–47, 149, 172, 212, 218, 240, 241, 244, 250, 260, 270–71, 272, 279, 301, 323, 348, 349, 376–77, 412, 413, 447, 473, 527
Monkmeyer: Conklin 395; Forsyth 231, 416; Rogers ii (right), 440

Omniphoto Communications: Griffiths 191, 203, 379, 401, 519, Lei 17, 311, 468, 479
Photo Researchers: Foote 114; Gilbert 511; Green 275; Hutchings 493; McIntyre 15, 58, 334, 441; Ursillo 95
The Picture Cube: Herwig 54, 148, 329, 516; Kaminsky 289; MacDonald 337; McQueen 365; Putnam 117, 321; Roth 285; Rowin 488; Schaefer 504; Siteman 102; Sloan 64; Walker 221; Walsh 505; Wood 11, 273
Shostal Associates: Carle 466–67
Stock, Boston: Abramson 351; Brown 82; Crews 43, 484; Dietz 14; Franken 243; Gupton 155; Lei 213; Mancuso 127; Menzel 61, 70, 188; Morrow 26; Myers 91; Pasley 72; Siteman 111; Snitzer 509, 513; Wolinsky 33, 522
Arthur Swoger: 178
Martha Swope: 533
Taurus Photos: Cloyd 286; Hahn 68; Hasegawa 112; Weber 83
Uniphoto: Domke 226; Feingersh 426; Gupton 100; Kezar 458; Pick 182
United Nations: 257
Wide World Photos: 366, 397